RELIGIOUS MOVEMENTS:

Genesis, Exodus, and Numbers

Edited by RODNEY STARK

A New ERA Book

Paragon House Publishers

New York

Published in the United States by Paragon House Publishers
2 Hammarskjold Plaza New York, New York 10017

A New Ecumenical Research Association Book.

Library of Congress Cataloging in Publication Data
Main entry under title:

Religious Movements.

   "A New ERA book."
   "Essays . . . were originally prepared for an inter-
national conference held in May 1982 on Orcas Island,
Washington"—Editor's introd.
   Bibliography: p.
   Includes index.
   1. Sects—Congresses.   2. Cults—Congresses.
3. Religion—History—20th century—Congresses.
4. Sociology and religion—Congresses.   I. Stark,
Rodney.   II. New Ecumenical Research Association

(Unification Theological Seminary)
BL85.R378   1985   291.9   85-9539
ISBN 0-913757-43-8 (hardbound)
ISBN 0-913757-44-6 (softbound)

Text and Jacket designed by Paul Chevannes

Contents

Introduction

Rodney Stark

TRENDINESS is the curse of social scientists. When we rush to take up a topic simply because it has attracted media attention we not only surrender control of our intellectual agenda to public whim, but we usually make fools of ourselves as well—trendy sociology is rarely more than "slow journalism."

Recently this curse has struck hard in the sociology of religious movements. The mass media have discovered the opportunities for sensationalism presented by many religious movements. In pursuit of lurid exposés about "the cults," the media receive a great deal of encouragement: from angry parents who refuse to believe their children willingly took up a new faith; from liberal clergy who despise intense religious commitment of all varieties; from conservative Christians who oppose "the cults" as false religions; from cynical liberal politicians who seek to discredit their opponents by provoking fears that resurgent evangelical Protestantism is but disguised facism; and from a variety of humanists looking for a *safe* way to condemn religion as superstition. The net result is an implicit

1

media message that "if the Moonies don't get you, Jerry Falwell will."

Fear and controversy always surround religious movements, for these movements propose changes in things held sacred. The Unification Church proposes a revision of Christian theology. Jerry Falwell proposes to rescind the theological revisions enacted by liberal Protestants. And many other new faiths, such as the Hare Krishnas, propose to supplant Christianity entirely.

It is natural that each of these proposals will be perceived by many as a threat, thus arousing some degree of public anger and anxiety. But, it is not natural that so many social scientists now interested in religious movements should be indistinguishable from journalists or alarmists. Granted that science cannot be value-free. Granted too that not every scientist must personally collect empirical data. But, science does require respect for evidence and the willingness to revise one's beliefs when they do not square with the relevant data.

Many current "studies" of cults have been written by putative social scientists with no detectable competence in the subject and who do not even acknowledge the existence of a substantial research literature that makes shambles of their conclusions. Worse yet, many persons with apparently valid professional credentials give scientific merit to the most outlandish and absurd "revelations" about religious movements. Some of them have become minor media stars, regular circuit riders going from city to city to appear on local talk shows and to lecture on the threat of the cults. Their primary assertion is, of course, the brainwashing or mind control thesis—that religious movements use diabolical mental techniques to snare converts. I remain dumbfounded that even talk show hosts don't wonder how it is that just about any little group of cultists can so easily achieve what *no social scientists can do*. That is, those who charge mind control cannot control minds—else they would be world famous and some of them would be busy "treating" our prisons-full of people in great need of some brain-washing. But, apparently, even with a couch and thousands of hours of therapeutic time, modern psychiatrists with years of training cannot do (not even with drugs), what any young Moonie can do in an hour or two of contact. Perhaps I'm narrow-minded, but I just can't bring myself to believe that.

While it is not surprising to find absurd claims about cultist mind control in sensationalist tabloids (next to stories about vampires in

South Dakota and Martians in Dallas), it is astonishing to find them certified by expert social scientists—or at least by people with advanced degrees whom the media present as experts. It also seems odd that the media, usually so eager to reveal dirty secrets, fail to discover that some of their experts on religious movements are poorly regarded by others in the field, while most are held in no regard at all, since they have never participated in the field.

Contributors to this volume are, in every sense of the word, experts. They are scholars who made substantial contributions to the study of religious movements—long before the media knew the topic existed—when only a few specialists were delving into the subject. Each contributor is widely respected in the field, and each attempts to break new ground.

Essays included here were originally prepared for an international conference held in May 1982 on Orcas Island, Washington, located in Puget Sound. There, more than a dozen scholars from the United States, Canada, Australia, England, and Northern Ireland spent three days sharing their most recent work. We arrived on the island after a five-hour cruise from Seattle aboard the "Viking Star," a chartered yacht. We returned in a squadron of single-engine float planes that picked us up on the beach and then landed on Lake Union in downtown Seattle.

The unusual transportation was in keeping with the character of the conference. Many of the participants chose this opportunity to pursue unorthodox and risky themes. William Sims Bainbridge described his own paper as "crazy." It is not, of course, but it is unconventional and original. Moreover, it is a paper that demonstrates a very important principle: If we are to come to grips with truly difficult issues (that is, important ones), we must be ready to try out novel ideas. Indeed, Roy Wallis's important tracing of currents within the human potential movement is the perfect introduction to Bain- bridge's paper because together they clearly locate a new frontier, one which encompasses far more than the study of religious move- ments.

Before saying more about the substance of the conference and the structure of this volume, it is necessary to discuss who paid for our conference, why, and whether that matters. The conference was funded by New ERA, an organization backed by the Unification Church, popularly known as the "Moonies." Some, including colleagues who engage in social scientific research, are bound to wonder about the

propriety of scholars meeting to discuss religious movements under the
auspices of a religious movement—especially one that has achieved such
notoriety.

There are two relevant issues here: First, did the sponsorship of the
conference have any bearing on its contents. Or, to put it bluntly, did
the Moonies tempt, coerce, or otherwise shape what people chose to
write about or what they chose to say? Second, by their participation in
a Moonie-sponsored conference, did these scholars somehow endorse
the religious validity of the Unification Church?

When I was invited to the first of these conferences I was not
especially concerned about its sponsorship. I have been to conferences sponsored by a great variety of religious groups and organizations, and nothing was ever made of that fact. Therefore, my main
concern was with whether I would learn anything. I decided to
go because of the chance to meet some of the people whose work
I had admired but had never met. It was not until I had accepted
the invitation that someone suggested that there was something
special about the Moonies that might compromise the conference.
They were partly right. There is something special about the
Moonies, and it makes them unusually good sponsors of scholarly
conferences.

The Unification Church has a remarkable, if little noted, record of
cooperation with independent researchers. The Moonies are easier to
study than are most mainstream denominations. This was true more
than twenty years ago when they allowed John Lofland and me to study
them and did not complain about what we wrote, even though it surely
was not a sympathetic account (Lofland and Stark 1965; Lofland
1966). Later they cooperated again when David Bromley and
Anson Shupe (1979) studied them. More recently they have gone
to unusual lengths to permit Eileen Barker to conduct her detailed
and long-term research on the Unification Church—continuing
to encourage her despite the fact that she often has reported on
sensitive matters of the sort that even powerful and secure religious
organizations prefer not to have aired. All of this forces the conclusion that the Unification Church leaders are genuinely interested
in what social scientists can tell them about their movement—
which is among their primary motives in sponsoring these conferences.

Having attended the first conference, I could not find any fault with
the way the Unification people there conducted themselves. Those who

attended our sessions listened attentively, even when discussions grew technical, and they did not flinch when we freely discussed such sensitive matters as their failed prophesy of the millennium in 1967. Moreover, they made useful, objective, and candid contributions to the discussions.

In his preface to the first volume in this series, Bryan Wilson made it clear that, as sponsors, the Unification people did not commit the slightest lapse in the ethics of academic and intellectual freedom. Indeed, he correctly noted that the Unification Church had done us a great service by providing us with the opportunity to meet and talk—something we otherwise could not have done. Whether the sponsors learned anything useful from our sessions, only they can say. But, clearly, the social scientific study of religious movements was enhanced: Speaking for most of us who have attended these meetings I feel that the quality of our subsequent work has improved as a result of the exchange of ideas. As a case in point, I offer my own essay in this volume.

I could not have begun it had I not met Eileen Barker at our first conference in Berkeley. It was through our subsequent correspondence that I learned of an obscure book listing headquarters of many cult movements in London. Although it was out-of-print, Eileen was able to make a copy of it for me. This gave me just enough of a start to attempt to assemble a list of cult movements active in Great Britain. From these beginnings I then discovered other means for assessing the success of new religions in Europe more generally—a crucial case for my revisionist thesis about secularization. Moreover, I still might not have undertaken this particular piece had I not also become friends with David Martin at these conferences. David more-or-less dared me to back up my assertions that northern Europe must be awash with novel religions.

It is this sort of thing that conferences are supposed to produce. The New ERA conferences on religious movements have done so.

A question persists, however. What is the Unification Church getting out of this association? Part of the answer to this question is so obvious that many will not find it satisfying. The Unification people know that the truth about them is at extreme variance with their public image. As I have already mentioned, the media uncritically accept magical notions of mind control. And they have made the Moonies the primary target of these charges. But, the Moonies know perfectly well that they can't perform these mental feats (and, like any conversionist group, they probably regret their inability). They also know that all competent social scientists who actually have studied the conversion process know that the brainwashing thesis is unsubstantiated. Thus, it is in the interests of the Moonies to get the truth out to the public. Indeed, this vindicates their willingness to submit to research. Think of the impact on public opinion if Eileen Barker's essay in this volume becomes widely known. In more than five years of quantitative research done in London on Moonie conversion, Barker found that of all who actually attended an initial session of instruction into Unification Church doctrines (and who therefore had been fully exposed to mind control during prior contacts with Moonie missionaries), less than 5 percent ended up joining the church. And, of those who did, at least half quit within a year or so. That's got to be the most ineffective brainwashing around! And it also bears on the point that once the Moonies have you, it takes deprogrammers to get you out. If half the Moonie converts do indeed quit, it must not be very hard to do.

Given the irresponsible nonsense circulated about them, the Moonies know that if they let competent, objective scholars study them close up, they can only benefit. For this they don't need "tame" social scientists, nor do they need flattering reports. The simple truth, including all the dirty laundry, will suffice.

A second aspect of the Unification Church's interest in sponsoring these conferences is that they believe we actually know something. Contrary to popular opinion, new religious movements greatly over-recruit the more, rather than less educated. If I had to criticize the Moonies I know, it would be for excessive intellectualism. I think they put too much faith in ideas. This aside, what the Unification people who attended our conferences wanted from us was knowledge. They took profound interest when, for example, Bryan Wilson discussed generic problems that arise for all religious movements. In short, our sponsors wanted to learn how the sociology of religious movements squared with their perceptions of their own movement and what we could tell them about how to cure defects in the Unification Church. They paid particular attention to understanding ways to equalize sex roles and to increase the involvement of the rank and file in decision-making. And, they were understandably interested to learn what they could about the impact of a second generation of socialized (rather than converted) members on religious movements like theirs. Should the Moonies be allowed access to such knowledge? So long as conventional social science is a public activity, rather than classified research, I can find no justification for denying it to *any* group. And if some of my colleagues fear the Moonies will learn things from me that will help them, I would be ashamed if they could not.

Since the subject matter of the conference and of this book is "religious movements," it seems useful here to explain that collective noun, and to trace how the names of our conferences shifted while we searched for the correct label. Our first conference, held in the spring of 1980, was devoted to "new religious movements." But, some of us objected, many of the groups we study, and *ought* to study, are not *new*. For example, the spate of religions from India active in the United States today are only new here. So, when Gordon Melton organized our second conference in Chicago in the spring of 1981, he called it a conference on "alternative religions." But, what does that term mean? It would seem to imply that Spiritualism or the Hare Krishnas are "alternatives" while the more conventional faiths are not. This seems to be but a polite way of naming a conference on "deviant" religions. As an antidote to media treatment of "crazy" religions, the term alternative is admirable. But many of us were uncomfortable with its illogic. Seeking a better word forced us to more adequately recognize our fundamental subject.

It is impossible to understand *any* religious movement in isolation from its surrounding religious economy. None is the complete master of its fate, each will succeed or fail in part because of what other religious groups around them do. New religions succeed only to the extent that the older, more conventional faiths have weakened and are failing to serve the market. As I emphasize in my essay in this volume, if we want to know why and where new religious movements prosper we must examine the overall condition of religious economies, looking for major market opportunities for new faiths. Furthermore, most of the time the significant religious movements are not *new religions*, but merely *new organizations* of an old religion. That is, sects and revival movements arise to restore or maintain the vigor of conventional religions. To the extent that revival movements or sect movements flourish in a society, new religions will languish. Thus, even those devoted to the study of new religions must study old ones as well.

The proper topic for a group such as ours is simply, and most generally, *religious movements*. The term includes revival movements within major religious organizations (for example, the Catholic Charismatic Movement, and to some extent the Moral Majority Movement). It includes sects: new organizations that have split off from more secularized religious bodies (for example, the current crop of new evangelical Protestant groups). It also includes religious movements imported from other societies such as Hinduism. And, it applies to movements embodying a new faith of which the Mormons are a prime example. Since the interplay among all these movements is vital to understanding any of them, religious movements are what we actually study.

This provides the key to understanding the logic behind the apparent diversity of the conference and of this volume. What could essays on the Moral Majority in Canada (Simpson and MacLeod) and on the revival of astrology in nineteenth-century America (Melton) have in common? Or, what does a scholar interested in the commitment structure of ISKCON have in common with another interested in the dynamics of evangelical Protestant theology? A lot! For one thing, many essential matters are the same whatever the group. Each must recruit, retain its members, socialize the young, resist schism, and so on. Thus all cases are the relevant universe for explanatory propositions on these topics. Moreover, as mentioned above, it is useless to focus entirely on one group because of the great interdependence among religious groups. For example, no one studying new religious movements in Europe and North America can ignore the very great overrecruitment of Jews by these groups. But this fact cannot be explained as long as one concentrates only on these movements; instead one must also examine the current state of Judaism. Similarly, it is impossible to understand the present growth of evangelical Protestantism without understanding the organizational weaknesses of liberal Protestantism.

Diversity *is* the unifying feature of this volume. That is, religious movements in any society function within an organized and diverse market system—a religious economy. And these underlying market relations unite students of all kinds of religious movements into a common pursuit.

Editors of conference volumes are often tempted to argue that the papers they have before them form a highly integrated work. Perhaps sometimes they do, but I have yet to attend such a conference or read such a book. So, I shall not attempt to claim this book in other than a collection of very significant essays on religious movements. In fact, I didn't choose participants with an eye towards a highly integrated volume. Frankly, I invited people who I thought would write papers I would find interesting.

As the chapters will show, this was a terrific conference. Everyone came with a serious contribution. And we learned a great deal from one another, both at the conference table and on the beach. Unfortunately, several colleagues were unable to attend—Bryan Wilson and David Martin were especially missed.

Having admitted that there is no unifying structure among the essays, let me point out that there are many recurrent themes. Both Robert Balch and Eileen Barker deal with defection, albeit in rather different degrees and from rather different sorts of movements. Together they greatly enhance our understanding of this overlooked topic which is, of course, the vital "flip side" of conversion. Larry Shinn's paper is likely to become a classic statement and illustration of the inherent organizational weaknesses of the guru system of authority. It also goes well with Arvind Sharma's case study of the movement built by the West Coast's most famous guru, Bhagwan Shree Rajneesh. The Rajneesh movement in turn is a nice introduction to the papers of Roy Wallis and of William Sims Bainbridge on the human potential movement as a great spawning ground for new religious culture and new religious movements. For, the Rajneesh movement is, in effect, human potential Hinduism and grows directly out of the human potential movement of the West.

The connections between Stephen Warner's study of evangelicalism and Simpson and MacLeod's analysis of the failure of the Moral Majority to thrive in Canada are apparent. And major themes found in both essays arise in David Taylor's study of Ian Paisley's militant Protestant movement in Northern Ireland.

Gordon Melton's essay explores the interplay between movements and their sociocultural environment. He pursues the somewhat ironic thesis that advances in scientific astronomy directly stimulated the vigorous rebirth of astrology in the United States.

Finally, I have tried to explicate the way in which religious movements interact and to show that, for this reason, new religious movements are currently more successful in the highly secularized nations of Northern and Western Europe than they are in North America.

To conclude this introduction I should like to thank Mr. David Kim,

President of the Unification Theological Seminary, and Mr. John Maniatis, director of New ERA, for being such generous and graceful sponsors of our meeting and for publishing this volume. I also thank John Craigen for arranging our cruise to Orcas Island and our scenic return flights. The staff at Rosario Resort made our weekend extremely pleasant.

Rodney Stark
Seattle, Washington

1

"When the Light Goes Out, Darkness Comes": A Study of Defection from a Totalistic Cult

Robert W. Balch

LTHOUGH religious cults have been a matter of popular and scholarly concern for over a decade, the subject of defection has been largely ignored by social scientists. The oversight is unfortunate because most new religions have high membership turnover (Bird and Reimer 1982). Although reliable figures are lacking, apostasy is probably the most common outcome of membership careers in new religious movements. Consequently it is vitally important to understand how and why defection occurs.

Among the few studies of defection from new religions, Norman Skonovd's research (1979, 1981) is the most comprehensive.[1] Skonovd interviewed sixty defectors from several totalistic cults and sects, including thirty former members of the Unification Church. The rest had belonged to various Eastern religions, Scientology, the Peoples Temple, and an assortment of Christian fundamentalist groups. By "totalistic" he means groups that (1) recognize only one source of knowledge, truth, and authority, (2) demand a high level of commitment, and (3) require renunciation of one's previous identity.

According to Skonovd, the defection process was initiated by one or more events that weakened the network of relationships that constituted the member's "religious support structure." Sometimes the support system was undermined by factors outside the cult's control, for example, deprogramming or a death in a member's family. On other occasions the process was triggered by internal factors such as being sent on a mission to a remote outpost of the faith or taking part in a fund-raising venture which thrust members into threatening encounters with the public.

In the context of a weakened support system, members experienced a crisis of belief in the form of steadily increasing cognitive dissonance. The sources of dissonance varied widely, but included antinomian practices, new information which challenged fundamental beliefs, and personal conflicts that alienated believers from fellow members. In the crisis stage members began to view the cult with a measure of detachment, suggesting that a subtle "gestalt switch" was under way.

Skonovd found that most doubters tried to shore up their sagging faith by repressing their impulse to question, avoiding anxiety-provoking situations, or explaining away their dissonance in terms of the cult's conceptualization of reality—for example, by defining doubt as the work of Satan. Those who could not dismiss their concerns so easily often tried to reform the organization or escape to an enclave within the cult where they were less apt to feel threatened. The most extreme response was physical withdrawal from the group, although at this point members had no intention of leaving permanently. In each case they spent increasing amounts of time pondering the faith, reviewing the history of their involvement, and seeking ways to resolve their dissonance.

When their efforts failed, members found themselves trapped between two symbolic worlds. Though seriously disillusioned, they still were strongly attached to the cult's familiar environment and were afraid of what awaited them outside its protective confines. In this painfully anomic period potential defectors continued to play the role of member while trying to decide on a course of action. No longer supported by conviction, their continued role performance constituted a kind of side-bet (Becker 1960) in case they eventually decided not to defect.

Once the stage had been set, the act of leaving could be triggered by any number of minor events. However, Skonovd found that precipitating events were not necessary to push disaffected members over the brink. Some defectors made an explicit decision to leave after rationally assessing the situation, and they often developed elaborate plans to slip away unnoticed in order to avoid unpleasant confrontations.

Even when members had made a carefully reasoned decision to defect, the transition back to "civilian" life was almost always a painful process. The initial burst of exhilaration that often followed defection quickly gave way to disorientation, indecisiveness, and depression. Life outside the cult seemed shallow and materialistic, and defectors often had trouble coping with the simplest responsibilities. Some feared retribution by either human or supernatural means, and many were plagued by guilt for abandoning their ideals. It was common for defectors to feel a profound sense of inadequacy, and a few even attempted suicide.

Like Singer (1979), who has conducted therapy with many defectors from totalistic cults, Skonovd found that the transition period generally lasted from six to eighteen months. Defectors who worked through the adjustment process on their own tended to take more time than those who had been deprogrammed or who had sought professional counselling. The end of the period was marked by the development of a personally believable justification for having devoted so much time and energy to an endeavor that now appeared to have been a mistake. One common reaction, especially among those who had come in contact with the anti-cult movement (Shupe and Bromley 1980), was anger. These defectors accused the cult of brainwashing and deception, and sometimes they became militant crusaders against the new religions as if converts to yet another cult. Another common response, which often followed the period of hostility, was to emphasize the positive aspects of the cult experience. The perceived benefits included the discovery of new philosophical truths, the resolution of an adolescent identity crisis, the development of inner strength, or the realization that authoritarian religion is not the answer to one's problems. Skonovd calls the final stage of the defection process "cognitive reorganization" because it marked the conclusion of the transition from one symbolic universe to another (Berger and Luckmann 1967).

While Skonovd's study is the best available description of defection from the new religions, it has one important limitation: Skonovd's research is based entirely on retrospective accounts that are subject to gloss, memory error, and retrospective reinterpretation.[2] Consequently there is good reason to suspect that crucial aspects of the defection process may have been obscured or overlooked altogether.

As Berger and Luckmann (1967; Berger 1963) have pointed out in their work on the sociology of knowledge, people have a natural tendency to reinterpret their past in light of present identities and circumstances. The trouble with interviewing defectors is that the research usually begins long after the past has been successfully reinterpreted, so it is difficult for social scientists to verify the "facts" reported by their informants.

With respect to the study of conversion, Taylor (1976) has argued that the problem of retrospective reinterpretation is so serious that sociologists should not even bother with the factual content of accounts, but instead should study conversion stories as a form of reality construction. While I think that Taylor's critique of the conversion research is overly nihilistic, I agree that researchers need to study the way that accounts are generated. The problem is that reconceptualizing accounts as reconstructions of the past will not necessarily tell us anything about the *process* of reinterpreting one's biography. If we are to understand how accounts are created, we must have information collected at various points in time before the reconstruction process is complete.

The following study is an attempt to overcome the limitations imposed by exclusive reliance on interviews with former members. By incorporating participant-observer data on disillusioned believers, as well as accounts obtained after defection, it reveals how retrospective reinterpretation occurred, especially in the course of ordinary conversations between members. The paper has a dual focus: Consistent with Berger and Luckmann's (1967) interest in the relationship between consciousness and social structure, it emphasizes both the subjective experiences of defectors and the structural context of those experiences. Because so little is known about defection from totalistic cults, my purpose is primarily descriptive, and the paper will mainly interest other students of new religions. However, the study's implications transcend the esoteric field of religious cults. By stressing the process of reality construction as it is revealed in everyday behavior, this paper is essentially an excursion into what Taylor (1976) calls the micro-sociology of religious knowledge.

The Study

In 1975 David Taylor[3] and I began an ethnographic study of a totalistic UFO cult. Our intent was to develop a complete description of the group's history, organization, beliefs, and membership careers from recruitment through defection.[4] During the first phase of the study we joined the group as covert participant-observers in order to record everyday activities normally hidden from outsiders, while in the second phase we interviewed defectors to gather additional data about their personal experiences. By supplementing retrospective accounts with direct observations of members while they were becoming disillusioned, we were able to develop a relatively complete picture of the defection process which both supports and refines Skonovd's conclusions.

The UFO cult originated in 1975 when a former music professor, Herff Applewhite, and a registered nurse, Bonnie Nettles, recruited two dozen followers in Los Angeles, California. Applewhite and Nettles called themselves Bo and Peep, but to most of their followers they were simply "the Two." The name refers to the two witnesses who are prophesied in Revelation 2. Bo and Peep claimed they would fulfill the prophecy by being assassinated and returning to life three and one-half days later. After their resurrection they expected to be lifted up to a UFO that would return them to "the Father's kingdom" in outer space. Bo and Peep referred to this event as "the demonstration" because their deaths and resurrections would demonstrate the truth of their mission to a disbelieving world.

In order to accompany the Two on their journey to the heavens, their followers had to overcome all attachments to the human level. This entailed leaving behind friends, family, loved ones, jobs, and all but a few material possessions needed to survive during their last days on the planet. Although Bo and Peep refused to set a date, and often hinted that the overcoming process could take several years, they generally led their followers to believe that the demonstration would occur within a few months.

After leaving Los Angeles members of the cult traveled around the country holding public meetings to recruit new believers. Some of these meetings attracted audiences of several hundred people, and when many of those who attended began to disappear mysteriously, the cult suddenly, if briefly, became a media sensation. However, despite the publicity, the cult probably never included more than 200 believers at any one time.[5]

The UFO cult was one of the most totalistic of the new religions. Bo and Peep claimed that members who followed their "guidelines" sincerely and diligently would ultimately become immortal, androgynous beings complete with physical bodies that would be free of all human limitations. They compared the transformation to the experience of the lowly caterpillar who emerges from his cocoon as a beautiful butterfly. Their guidelines were explicitly designed to create an encapsulated environment where members could devote all their energy to overcoming their "caterpillar ways." The transformation was called Human Individual Metamorphosis, although members usually referred to it as "the Process."[6]

During the period covered by our observations members of the cult led a nomadic existence. They travelled constantly, camping in secluded locations, and they went to great lengths to conceal their identities from other campers when complete isolation proved impossible. According to Bo and Peep, the outside world was pervaded by spirits that would attack their followers in the form of doubts, questions, and second thoughts about leaving home, and they took precautions to protect members from these influences. Internally they discouraged idle socializing, especially any discussion of the past, and externally they either eliminated contact with outsiders or structured it in order to preserve the group's psychological insulation. Members were not supposed to communicate with friends and relatives, listen to the radio, pick up hitchhikers, or read anything except the Bible and the mimeographed statements that described the fundamentals of Bo and Peep's message.

Contact with the public was generally limited to two occasions: The first was called "testing." Since money, food, and gasoline were always in short supply, members survived by "testing the churches." That is, they relied on preachers for hand-outs while traveling from town to town. In practice the concept of testing was applied to any establishment where members might find help, including restaurants, gas stations, and grocery stores. During these encounters members rarely engaged outsiders in lengthy conversations and almost never revealed that they were followers of the Two. The other reason for regular contact with the public was to present the message to interested seekers. During public meetings interaction with the audience was limited to a formal presentation followed by a question-and-answer period and then a follow-up meeting a day or two later. Between the first and second meetings members usually concealed the location of their campground to prevent the intrusion of spirits (often in the form of reporters), and afterwards new recruits were taken to a "buffer camp" where they were introduced to the Process by some of the more committed members.

At the buffer camp every new member was assigned a partner. According to the Two, the trials of living in close quarters with another person for months at a time would bring out the human qualities that still had to be overcome. These ranged from minor but irritating habits to the most basic human emotions. Even love and affection, at least in the human comprehension of those terms, had to be eliminated, and sex was prohibited on the grounds that it would burn up energy required for the metamorphic process. Sexual attraction proved to be a difficult test for many because Bo and Peep usually paired men with women and expected them to be together twenty-four hours a day. Much of this time was spent in relative isolation from other members because each partnership was intended to function as a self-contained unit, ideally with its own car, tent, and cooking equipment. Yet, in spite of the close contact, sexual relations between partners rarely occurred because nearly all members were eager to conform to Bo and Peep's guidelines.

An essential part of the Process was communication with "members of the next level." Everyone on the Process was encouraged to "strain for a connection" with the highly evolved beings known as "the Fathers" who were "in close range" in their spaceships to help with the "harvest." Messages from the next level were usually experienced in the form of fleeting thoughts, feelings, hunches, and intuitive flashes of insight. Bo and Peep compared this communication to radio waves, and they used the expression "tuning in" to describe the process of making contact. At first new recruits would be able to pick up only intermittent bits of information, but if they kept their "receivers" clear by avoiding mind-altering substances such as drugs and alcohol, they could reduce the static, and eventually their communication with the next level would become clear and consistent. Although most members had trouble explaining what it meant to be in tune, they usually described the experience in terms of feeling sure of themselves and supremely confident about the validity of Bo and Peep's message. Some compared it to the clarity of vision experienced on an LSD trip.

In the UFO cult the concept of metamorphosis was the dominant metaphor for framing everyday experience. In any belief system understanding is essentially a process of grasping relationships between seemingly unrelated phenomena, and the imagery of caterpillars into butterflies served this purpose for Bo and Peep's followers. Headaches were a sign of expanding consciousness. Menstrual irregularities meant that women were becoming androgynous. Craving sweets indicated that the brain required more energy for its "changeover." Physical "rushes" and ringing in the ears suggested that members of the next level were close by. In each case the metaphor rendered these experiences meaningful by locating them within an over-arching metaphysical framework. As members learned to apply Bo and Peep's interpretive scheme, even the most mundane events took on cosmic significance, and every aspect of their lives was imbued with purpose. The popular expression, "seeing the light," is therefore a fitting description of the conversion process as it was experienced by new recruits. As one of them remarked shortly after coming on the Process, "I think I'm finally going sane—I've been crazy all my life."

The UFO cult attracted a wide variety of members, but most were spiritual seekers in their early twenties. Almost all of them had some first-hand experience with other, unconventional spiritual paths before they heard about Bo and Peep. While a few left behind large families and expensive homes when they joined, the vast majority had relatively few material possessions or social commitments to prevent them from coming on the Process. Most were single, separated, or divorced, and they tended to be highly mobile, moving frequently in search of new experiences. On the whole they felt profoundly alienated from the materialism of American society, and many were already committed to overcoming their dependency on material attachments even before they joined the UFO trip. The cult included a large proportion who had been hippies, musicians, craftspeople, college students, and antiwar protestors during their "human lives." Overall the UFO cult is best classified as a "post movement" group which appealed primarily to disillusioned members of the counterculture whose idealism was fading rapidly during the early 1970s (Foss and Larkin 1976).

The following description of the defection process is based on loosely structured interviews with forty-three former members as well as our own observations conducted during a two-month period late in 1975. In a manner consistent with the group's high membership turnover, all but ten informants defected within six months after joining. The interviews ranged in length from forty-five minutes to over nine hours. In each case informants were asked to provide a detailed chronological account of the significant events in their lives from the time they joined until they were contacted for an interview, on the average about seven months after they defected. All informants left the Process of their own volition, and none had been deprogrammed.[7]

In order to supplement these accounts I have drawn on the field notes we compiled as participant-observers. We were fortunate to have joined the group at a time when disillusionment was becoming widespread, so we had an opportunity to observe members during the early stages of the defection process. Although Bo and Peep discouraged socializing, members often confessed their doubts to each other when it became apparent that others shared their concerns. We were present during many rambling discussions around campfires and picnic tables when members first began to discuss their disillusionment, and on occasion it was possible to question them in depth about their feelings in one-to-one situations.

The inclusion of data collected before, during, and after defection makes the study truly longitudinal. Not only did we observe members during periods of strong conviction and extreme disillusionment, but we were able to interview twenty-two of the same people after they defected. The rest of the interview sample includes defectors we had never met before or whom we had not known well during our field work. Because we actually observed many of the situations later described by our informants, we also were able to check on the validity of at least some of the retrospective accounts, and generally they proved to be accurate, if sometimes incomplete.

Becoming a Defector

In this study defection is defined as physically separating from the group and resolving not to go back. The definition does not include the element of belief because to this day, several years after defecting, some former members continue to believe much of what the Two had to say.

I have divided the defection process into nine stages. While most informants passed through every stage, the line separating one step from the next is often more analytic than empirical. Unlike the process of becoming a member, which in many cults is marked by a carefully orchestrated sequence of socialization experiences, defection has no socially defined milestones or rites of passage to punctuate the transition from one stage to the next. It is a fluid process that resists the urge to divide it into discrete categories. Even granting the overall validity of the model, one must bear in mind that the following description does not fit all defectors equally well. Some individuals experienced two or more stages simultaneously or passed through them so quickly that it is impossible to determine where one left off and the other began. In addition, the defection process was often marked by idiosyncratic events that prevented members from going through every stage. For example, one member was arrested for hitchhiking after his car broke down. When the police discovered that he was only fifteen, they notified his parents and sent him home, thus sparing him many of the agonizing decisions that other defectors had to make. Consequently the following model must be viewed as a general characterization of the defection process which obscures individual differences and imposes a somewhat unrealistic degree of order on the data.

The crack in consensual validation: Like Skonovd's informants, almost everyone we interviewed defected during a period when the group's reality-defining power had been seriously weakened. Bo and Peep had deliberately created a social cocoon to help their followers overcome earthly spirits, and defection usually began when that structure was not functioning the way the Two intended. In twenty-nine cases the defection process was precipitated by the unexpected disappearance of the Two. Late in 1975, when the UFO cult was making headlines throughout the country, Bo and Peep decided that the demonstration would happen very shortly. After calling their followers together in Oklahoma, they announced that they were going to withdraw into the "wilderness" to prepare for the event. Before leaving they divided the cult into small groups, appointed spokesmen for each, and sent them in different directions to continue spreading the message. However, the cult was ill-prepared to cope with the absence of its leaders, and within two weeks it was already showing signs of social disorganization. As one informant described the situation, "The trip lost its focus and the energy was starting to dissipate."

One reason was that the cult lacked a well-established authority structure. Although group spokesmen generally had superior leadership skills, their authority was undercut by the belief that no one on the Process was more spiritually advanced than anyone else. A few spokesmen, by virtue of their grasp on the message and their personal charisma, were able to keep their groups together, but most were unable or unwilling to exert much control. The group we joined, for instance, made all its decisions democratically and appointed new spokesmen every time it held a public meeting.

Another reason for the increasing disorganization was a strong thread of epistemological individualism running through the message (Wallis 1974, 1975). While the Two explicitly stated that the Process was the only way to achieve membership in the next level, they also claimed that it would be a unique experience for every individual. Because members required different tests to complete their metamorphosis, Bo and Peep said they would be guided individually through the final stages of the transition by direct communication from the next level. As a result, when disputes arose, each individual could justify his or her opinions by claiming to have received guidance directly from a member of the next kingdom.

The dispersion of groups all over the country also contributed to disorganization. Each group went wherever its members felt led to go, and they rarely had contact with each other while they traveled. On those occasions when two or more groups were reunited, members were often surprised and chagrined to discover how far others had departed from what they considered to be the true path.

A few weeks after the Two disappeared, the group began to split into liberal and conservative factions. The liberals tried to water down the message by claiming that Bo and Peep's guidelines were intended only to get people started on the Process. Once the metamorphosis was underway, the rules could be relaxed. This line of reasoning was used to justify a wide variety of actions that had been discouraged by the Two. These included socializing with other members, seeking out old friends who were also on the Process, smoking marijuana, and on a few occasions, going to movies. The breakdown of the rule against socializing was especially important because it allowed members to discover just how widespread demoralization had become. The conservatives tried to counter this trend by insisting on a strict interpretation of the message, and they often antagonized other members by demanding strict adherence to the rules even though they lacked the authority to do so. Social relationships became increasingly strained and arguments flared over trivial situations.

Still another sign of disorganization was the cult's loss of control over its boundaries. As members began to disregard the rules governing contact with outsiders, they were increasingly confronted with challenges to their faith. Visiting friends outside the group, picking up hitchhikers, reading metaphysical literature, and discussing the message with strangers all became common. One member, for example, had his faith badly shaken when he and his partner spent the night with a metaphysician in San Francisco who was known as the "destroyer of trips" because of his extreme distaste for any form of spiritual dogma.

During the four months that elapsed before Bo and Peep reappeared, the UFO cult was characterized by the steady disintegration of consensual validation. Members were aware that the group was losing its focus, and in moments of candor they expressed deep concern about the situation. As one of the older members put it: "When we would all get together for a common purpose, there was a great deal of energy, and there was validity in my mind, providing everybody was focused.

But when the energy started dissipating into factions—some of us going this way and some going that way—then it considerably weakened the idea." (interview)

Of the remaining thirteen informants, five left the Process before the chaotic period I have just described, and eight defected afterwards. The loss of consensual validation played a role in most of these cases as well. One of the five who defected before the Two disappeared was Bo and Peep's first follower. She spent three months on the Process in 1974. Then the Two were arrested for failing to return a rented car, and without their support she immediately returned to her family. The other four belonged to the group of two dozen believers who were recruited at a meeting in Los Angeles several months later. This event marked the real beginning of the UFO cult. Only a month after they joined, Bo and Peep sent them out on the road "to be tested by the Fathers," and they spent most of the next three months traveling, working at odd jobs, and trying to recruit new members in one-to-one encounters. Not only did they have limited contact with the Two, but at this time there was almost no structure for preventing internal conflicts or protecting members from outside influences. As one informant explained, Bo and Peep were surprisingly lax in those days: "The first meeting that I attended around the campfire we were told that there were no rules, that this was an individual trip, and we could do whatever we wanted to do." (interview) The result was confusion, disillusionment, and ultimately defection. Almost half of this group dropped out within five months.

It was not until 1976 that Bo and Peep were able to significantly reduce the group's drop-out rate. One of their first steps was to stop recruitment. As they explained, all the ripe fruit had been picked so final preparations for the harvest could begin. The move not only reduced contact with outsiders, but it also bolstered the group's self-conception as the elect. Boundary maintenance was a dominant theme during this period. Shortly after the group quit holding meetings, they withdrew into an isolated hideaway in the Wyoming Rockies. To prepare members for life in outerspace, Bo and Peep divided the group, which then numbered eighty-eight, into four camps representing spaceships. In each camp the tents were arranged in a uniform circular pattern, and the camp itself was set off by a perimeter of logs layed end to end. Sentries roamed the hills to keep an eye out for other campers who might stumble across one of the "ships." Bo and Peep had their own camp a short distance away.

During the day members took part in various activities designed to teach them to think and act like members of the next level. In an exercise called the "smooth whirlwind" the Two rotated each person through every other camp in the space of a few days. The purpose was to improve social relationships by requiring everyone to adopt the roles of host and guest in rapid succession. Each new activity was intended to teach a lesson or test one's determination to continue. Some of the tests, such as enforced silence or wearing hooded uniforms for extended periods, proved extremely difficult, and Bo and Peep frequently encouraged the weaker members to leave.

The Two also clarified several aspects of the Process in a way that enhanced their authority. The most significant change concerned the nature of communication with the next level. Whereas members once believed they would enjoy direct contact with the Fathers, Bo and Peep now revealed that information from the next kingdom always came down to their followers through them. From then on only the Two were called the Fathers in everyday conversation. By defining themselves as indispensable interpreters and guides, they made it very difficult for anyone to question their wisdom.[8]

By all accounts the overall level of conviction increased considerably during this period, and the defection rate dropped sharply. Assuming 200 members in October, 1975, 56% had left the group by June 1976, just eight months later. Not all of them can be classified as defectors because some members who had lost track of the group may have remained committed believers well past the summer of 1976. However, I am aware of only one person who falls into this category—a young woman who continued to hold meetings by herself for over a year after the rest of her companions defected. Even granting the possibility of similar cases, the dropout rate probably approached 50%. In contrast the reports of recent defectors suggest that less than 10% left the group during the three years between the middle of 1977 and the same time in 1980.

Only eight of our informants defected after the new phase began in Wyoming. For two of them the loss of consensual validation was a major factor in their decision to leave. Late in 1976, after the cult moved from Wyoming to Utah, Bo and Peep separated nineteen of the weaker members from the rest of the group and sent them to Arizona with instructions to get jobs and support themselves. Although the Two kep in touch with the Arizona group by mail, most of the nineteen quickly defected. Our informants indicated that the group experienced the same kind of fragmentation that beset the cult after the Two disappeared in 1975:

> . . . there was no focal point to say this is the "most right" thing to do [a common expression]. Everything was up to us and everybody had a different idea of what should be done. And it got so hostile! One of the things that we were told was that you had to follow your own feelings. But if one person is saying "no" and the rest of the group is saying "yes," who's right? Nobody would accept anyone else's being the authority. (interview)

The remaining six informants do not fit the general pattern because they defected when the cult was highly cohesive and most members were strongly committed. Only one of them questioned the validity of the Process when he left. The others continued to believe, but lacked the will to continue Bo and Peep's demanding routine until the ships arrived. Unfortunately my sample of recent defectors is too small to draw any conclusions about the impact of the cult's reorganization on the nature of the defection process.

Demoralizing experiences: In any cult members will occasionally confront situations that contradict their expectations and challenge their faith, but dissonant events usually can be explained away by interpreting them in terms of the group's symbolic construction of reality (Berger and Luckmann 1966). As Lofland (1966, 195) remarked in his study of an early group of Moonies, ". . . one finds a structure that is logically impossible to confront with disconfirming or negative evidence, at least in the short run."

The UFO trip was no different. Hardships were accepted as tests and good times as rewards from the next level. If members felt clear and acted decisively, they were in tune, while confusion meant they were not straining hard enough for a connection with the next level. Doubt was merely the work of spirits. In a typical account one informant explained how he reacted to a rumor that Bo had once been a mental patient: "I fingered through a dozen thoughts in my mind then suddenly remembered how the Two spoke of negative statements being made against them. How could I be so stupid as to forget that? I thought. [*sic*] This is supposed to happen. It's part of the set-up for the demonstration." (from an autobiographical account written by a defector)

Bo and Peep's message is an example of what Snow and Machalek (1982) call a self-validating belief system. In self-validating systems any empirical outcome, no matter how damaging it might appear to outsiders, can be interpreted as support for one's faith. Because such systems are virtually immune to disconfirmation, Snow and Machalek have argued that cults do not require systematic organizational strategies to protect their members from dissonant information. However, they may have overstated their case. Strictly speaking, a belief system does not validate itself. Instead it is validated by individual believers who are often persuaded more by their own ineffable, intuitive sense of truth than by the system's internal consistency or its resistance to disconfirmation. Bo and Peep's message may have been immune to disconfirming evidence, but in practice the intuitively grounded faith of its adherents proved to be a very fragile commodity. In the context of social disorganization believers waged a continual struggle to sustain their convictions. Minor events that once might have passed without a second thought came to be seen as troublesome discrepancies, and members increasingly paused to reflect on their significance.

In the broadest sense a demoralizing experience was any cognition that challenged one's faith in Bo and Peep or one's determination to see the Process through to its conclusion. Our informants reported four major types of demoralizing situations. The first was the discovery of *information that appeared to undermine the validity of the message*. The fact that the demonstration did not occur was very discouraging for some. At one time members of the UFO cult thought they would be "beamed up' almost any day, and a sense of urgency pervaded every aspect of their lives. While we were in the field, a young woman told us, "Every time I go to buy toothpaste, I buy a small tube, thinking I'm going to be here just a little longer. But," she added wistfully, "I always end up buying another tube." (field notes) However, the Two never set themselves up for failure by predicting a date for the demonstration. Members could always rationalize its failure to occur by insisting that they were not ready to leave the planet because they needed more time to complete the overcoming process.

Equally disheartening for some was the lack of discernible changes in their bodies. At first new recruits noticed all sorts of physical changes which suggested that a physical metamorphosis was actually taking place. These included headaches, changes in eye color, and for many women, drastic reductions in their menstrual flow. Some women lost their periods altogether, and they took this as a sign that they were becoming androgynous. Eventually, however, their periods resumed. When this happened in the context of the group's frequent social disarray, it was interpreted as a sign that they were no longer making progress, and it raised questions about their ability to continue the Process.

The second commonly mentioned source of demoralization was *information that challenged the credibility of the Two*. Despite the fact that charismatic leaders are relatively free to fashion whatever reality they please, they still have to live up to their followers' expectations. In the UFO cult members often experienced moments of disillusionment when the Two behaved in ways that were considered "too human" or when they failed to provide the leadership that believers expected. Some of their lapses seem trivial to outsiders. For instance, one informant told us that he began to question the authenticity of the Two during an argument with his partner about the best way to choose a campground:

> He says, "Why don't we do it like the Two do it?" And I go, "I'm sorry Paul, I assumed we *were* doing it like they told us—that they vibed [i.e., tuned in] to the Fathers, and the Fathers told them where to go." And he goes, "Well, they do, but Bo gets out the International Campers Guide and he looks up all the services and nightly fees, and *then* he vibes: Oh, that one feels good!" I go, "You're kidding!" That's when I really started having some heavy second thoughts. (interview)

Other discrepancies were more serious: a rumor that Peep had been seen playing the slot machines in a Las Vegas casino; the fact that the Two began charging admission to meetings that had always been free; a story that Bo and Peep had rented motel rooms under assumed names and then left without paying their bills; and squabbles between the Two that reminded their followers of ordinary marital spats. One of the most upsetting contradictions was Bo and Peep's prolonged absence in 1975. Many members could not imagine that the Two could allow such chaos to continue if they were really who they claimed to be. As one recruit, who lasted only three days on the Process, explained, "I just thought it was pretty untogether." (interview)

It is worth noting that members did not necessarily question the message when they became disillusioned with the Two. At one point in our observations our group received word that Bo and Peep had changed their minds about the demonstration. According to the rumor they were now saying that their deaths and resurrections, once thought to be imminent, might be cancelled by the next level. Some members were badly shaken by the news, and one man openly challenged the legitimacy of the Two: "It says in Revelation that the demonstration will occur, and Biblical prophecies are never wrong. They have always been proven correct . . . If the Two say the demonstration isn't going to take place, then they're phonies!" (field notes) In the ensuing discussion, however, no one questioned the validity of the Process. As another disillusioned man explained, "I don't care if the Two dress up in tuxedos and move to France and live there forever—I'm still going to continue the Process." (field notes)

A more important source of demoralization was *interpersonal conflict*. Friction between partners, normally considered a necessary part of the Process, became increasingly troublesome whenever members were separated from the Two for a prolonged period of time. For example, a member who was troubled by "music spirits" described how his partner deliberately antagonized him:

> We'd be driving down the road and he'd pull out his harmonica and start playing, and I'd say, "I wish you wouldn't do that because it's putting me in a bad space, an old one, that I don't want to be in." And he'd look over with the most devilish grin and just go right back playing his harmonica. At one point, I tried to grab it away from him and throw it out the window. Things were getting that way. I was thinking, "You aren't on this trip for anything but to get me off of it." (interview)

Other sources of conflict that believers found demoralizing were factionalism and the growing prevalence of rule violations. After the Two disappeared in 1975, the more conservative members became discouraged at the way the group was crumbling around them, and the liberals resented their efforts to enforce conformity. During part of our field work, when we belonged to one of the cult's more liberal groups, the conservative members tried to isolate our group by excluding us from meetings and keeping new recruits away from us on the grounds that we were bringing negative spirits into the camp. In turn members of our group reacted with disgust, alienation, and increased determination to go their own way.[9] During the period of extreme disorganization in 1975, the level of interpersonal conflict became so severe that one defector described his group as a "pit of snakes."

The most important source of disillusionment was the widespread feeling among members that they were *no longer growing*. The initial sense of excitement and challenge that members felt when they came on the Process began to fade as their experiences on the road became routine and predictable: "I told my partner that I was getting bored. You know, I'd tested, I'd had my experiences in the cold, sleeping in tents and camping out, meeting all kinds of people, and I said, 'I'm tired of that. I think I've grown from it, but I need a change. This isn't going anywhere.'" (interview) In every case our informants interpreted their boredom as spiritual stagnation: "I just felt that nothing was happening anymore. I wasn't doing any growing. I reached a plateau, and I was getting tired of doing this floating around the country and begging from churches. I wasn't feeling that I was accomplishing anything." (interview)

For many informants boredom was the most difficult test they had to endure. Yet the demoralization it caused did not necessarily raise doubts about the validity of the Process or the authenticity of the Two. This was especially true for those who defected during the highly cohesive period which began after the Two stopped recruiting in 1976: "I never had any doubts about the message. The only doubts I had were about my own strength, about whether I could stay with it much longer." (interview)

Vacillation: Skonovd argued that disillusioning experiences create a "crisis of belief." However, our field observations suggest that the term crisis is too strong. In the UFO cult disaffection usually set in gradually with no clear beginning. Whatever the source of demoralization, the clarity of vision that members once experienced became increasingly cloudy, and the "highs" more intermittent. Early in the defection process members vacillated between periods of doubt and conviction, or, as one member put it, between spells of "murkiness and light." Rather than a steady downhill slide, the early phase of disaffection was marked by a series of highs and lows:

> There were times when I felt growth, and then I would tell myself when I was down that I was probably kidding myself. I would feel really bad because I wasn't growing, but then I would recall things that I'd read saying the greatest growth occurs when you can't tell that things are happening. It was very up and down. (interview)

Members usually interpreted the flickering light of conviction as losing their connection with the next level. Staying in tune became a nagging problem. "When I try to tune in," one woman confessed, "all I do is think about tuning in. I tune in and think about tuning in, and think about thinking about tuning in, but nothing ever happens. . . . I don't feel like I'm getting through." (field notes) Without the guidance of the Fathers, members felt confused and unsure of themselves. During a particularly poignant meeting that we observed, a member of our group expressed the confusion that many were feeling but, until then, none had been willing to admit. "Four or five weeks ago I felt very close to the Father," he said, "but now his voice seems to be getting weaker and weaker." (field notes)

In this phase of the defection process, the highs experienced by members became increasingly tied to specific situations. After an inspiring meeting, for example, my exuberant partner told me that Bo and Peep's message was so clear that she could not understand why everyone was not on the Process. "You know," she said, "there's so much love here. You can feel the power when we're all gathered together. It's what I've been looking for all my life." But the next day, after calling an old friend who told her that the message sounded "far-fetched," she was totally demoralized. "It does sound so weird," she admitted, referring to the role of UFOs as heavenly taxis. "Somehow it just doesn't fit." (field notes)

Members often had trouble verbalizing their questions and doubts. Instead they were more likely to experience an uneasy, inchoate sense that something was not quite right: "It wasn't even really all that conscious. It was more like a bug way down deep that was going, 'Wrong! Beep, beep, beep! Something's wrong here!'" (interview) When specific questions did arise, they were usually limited to particular events. Members might think it odd that Peep would want to play the slot machines, or they might wonder why the Two found it necessary to steal a car, but at this point issues like these were generally treated as isolated incongruities. Rarely did they suggest, at least not for more than a fleeting moment, that the message might not be true.

During the vacillation stage members usually kept their questions to themselves. In public or the company of other believers, they continued to play the role of member: "The whole time, even though I was doubting, I was still rapping it with people [i.e., proselytizing] and handing out statements." (interview) One reason why members did not discuss their questions was that they still did not know how to express them clearly: "I didn't know how to bring out the doubts verbally. They were there, but I never expressed any of them." (interview) Another reason was that even members of the same group had been effectively isolated from one another by the restrictions on interpersonal communication. Doubt was a test to be borne alone by each individual to accelerate one's personal growth. Bo and Peep claimed that members who sought support from others not only deprived themselves of growth experiences, but hindered the progress of their companions by becoming a drain on their energy.

When doubts were finally revealed, partners were usually the first to hear, but even within partnerships open communication could be difficult: "Nobody was to talk about the past. Nobody was to talk about anything. If you had an especially heavy partner like mine, you wouldn't talk about nothing." (interview)

The result was widespread ignorance about the extent of disillusionment, especially in the first three weeks after the Two disappeared in 1975. Though a "gestalt shift" was beginning, members continued to go through the motions of being on the Process:

> Everything was more or less business as usual. People didn't talk about the doubts they were having. Like me, I didn't talk to anybody about what was happening to me. Except once or twice I said something like, "Something's got to give." Very shapeless statement that could be construed many different ways. The feeling behind it was kind of depressed. Every now and then people would say, "I'm going to lay down for a while—I'm getting really bombarded [by spirits]." But it was still business as usual. (interview)

In the context of "business as usual" members were forced to rely on the *behavior* of others to assess the level of conviction in the group. When others appeared highly committed, the doubters often blamed themselves for failing to understand or make progress. Feeling alone in their doubt, they not only kept their questions to themselves, but redoubled their efforts to make the Process work: "I had occasional flashes of doubt when I arrived at the [buffer] camp, and then I kind of overcame them and got more and more into it. There was always the seed of doubt in everyone, but you have to have the determination to keep surging ahead." (interview)

Disaffection: In spite of their efforts, however, the questions lingered, and loss of contact with the next level became a chronic problem. As members became less and less able to explain away the contradictions, they began to disengage from the Process, at first psychologically and later behaviorally. In retrospect most reported reaching a turning point consisting of one or more events that changed their relationship to the Process.

The precipitating events varied widely: getting a new partner, being reunited with a former lover, assuming the position of group spokes-man, encountering an old friend outside the cult, or attending a poorly presented public meeting:

> It was beginning to happen after the Eugene meeting. . . . It was at the Eugene library, and they [members of the audience] were asking questions. They wanted to know what the deal was. But all I could hear coming from the stage was, "That's irrelevant, that's not important, that doesn't matter." And wow! If I had gone to a meeting like that, I sure wouldn't have gone [on the Process]. (interview)

We attended a meeting in Arizona where the two men who were presenting the message actually got into an argument with each other. Nearly every member in the room was embarrassed by the incident, and those who were already starting to doubt left the meeting even more demoralized than they had been when they arrived.

Of particular importance was the sudden loss of social support. Because of the cult's nomadic existence and disdain for planning ahead, accidental separations were a common occurrence. Without social support, even the most committed believers had trouble sustaining their convictions:

> My partner took off with my sleeping bag and all my money. . . . So I traveled around for the first month really broke, going to campgrounds just looking for somebody in the group. I really needed the security of being close to somebody who was doing the same trip. You know, that was my reality at the time, and the only thing there was to support that reality was me and my car, and at that point I needed somebody else to substantiate my reality. . . . It was pretty heavy. You know, where has the trip gone now? What happened to the group? I was all by myself. I had to sustain that reality alone, which at the time was really hard. (interview)

Whatever the trigger, the disaffection stage was marked by cognitive restructuring. Not only did questioning intensify, but doubts began to coalesce, raising fundamental questions about the validity of at least parts of the message as well as one's determination to continue. Dissonant information, which had once been explained away or dismissed as unimportant, became a matter of serious concern: "In Arizona I started looking back on everything. You know, how things fell into place and what I'd actually done, and I really noticed that feeling of being wrong. I thought, 'Hey, wait a minute, there's something wrong here,' and that feeling was right." (interview)

For the first time members began to see the UFO trip in a new light, often quite objectively:

> That McGrath [a campground on the California coast] was the funniest place I'd ever been. I never spent the night there but I enjoyed coming in for a few hours and watching. One day Dave and Jan and a few other people were all sitting around and the group was getting together, and Dave says, "I have to go tune in." And he turned away, then stopped and realized what he'd said. He looked back at me and I was laughing. The whole thing was getting to be absurd. (interview)

It was during this stage that members first considered leaving the group even though they typically continued to accept major parts of the message.

Some members set personal deadlines by resolving to leave if something significant, usually the demonstration, did not happen by a certain date. Date setting was especially common during the long absence of the Two. One partnership in our group decided that something would have to happen by the winter solstice which was then about a month away:

> I don't know what it was that we expected. I think what I expected to happen was a kind of gathering, a strengthening of forces, a regrouping, possibly by the Two, because I felt the situation was getting out of hand. There were too many loose ends, and it seemed logical to me that at this point the Two would call some kind of meeting, not necessarily a big meeting, but a *regrouping* meeting. Let's all get together and see where we are, and who's doing what, how we are doing, you know. And I am sure that had this happened I would have probably stayed with it. Well, nothing happened and [my partner] definitely made up her mind first that she was going to go. (interview)

While members continued to act like committed believers, their performance was hollow and they felt detached from their actions. As one informant explained, disillusioned members, including himself, were "just going through the motions and using the right vocabulary, which concealed the fact that inside they were very mixed up." (interview)

Disaffection was characterized by an intense approach-avoidance conflict which Skonovd likened to being trapped between two symbolic worlds. Members may have had good reasons for wanting to defect, but there were also powerful psychological forces that kept them from leaving, not the least of which was the fact that life at the human level was distinctly unappealing. Another reason for remaining in the group was fear of "missing the boat." A young man who was thinking of defecting described how he felt when another member reminded him of this possibility: "Sonny told us, 'You guys are going to miss out on the resurrection. You're going to miss out. I wouldn't miss this for anything.' And that was the heavy part." (interview) Still another reason for hanging on in the face of disaffection was the fact that members had committed themselves by cutting all ties with the past (Gerlach and Hine 1970). A fifty-eight year old member of our group who had left his home and family to come on the Process summed up the predicament: "It's a put-up or shut-up situation. All of us have burned our bridges behind us. It's either true or it isn't. If not, then it's a horrible waste." (field notes)

Many informants told us they had been reluctant to leave because of profound psychic and spiritual experiences on the Process which they still considered to be genuine: "Sometimes I would wonder why nothing was happening, but then at the same time there would be these incredible buzzes at three or four in the morning [when members of the next level were supposed to be in close range], incredible rushes, and then I would be going, 'Yes, this is happening, this is real.'" (interview) As another member explained: "That's what keeps you hanging in there. 'Cause there's all these other phenomenal unexplained things that I couldn't explain to myself with any degree of satisfaction, so it kept me hanging in there." (interview)[10]

Not surprisingly, considering the intensity of the approach-avoidance dilemma, many disaffected members were unable to make even the simplest decisions. For example, during a period of extreme disillusionment when our group was camped in Arizona, a couple who had planned to join a buffer camp in California drove in and out of the campground several times in the course of a day because they could not decide if the next level really wanted them to go. Almost every night members engaged in long, inconclusive discussions about their next destination, how best to present the message, or whether to present it at all. One of the spokesmen for our group, once considered one of the most "tuned in" believers, confessed to feeling lost. "I never used to have any doubts about where to go," he said, "but this is the first time I haven't had any clear direction at all." (field notes) Some, like this member, admitted their discouragement openly, but others simply projected an air of fatalism. "Anything I can't understand, I just chalk up as part of the great mystery," one of them told us. "I mean, how much faith do I really have?" (field notes)

Indecisiveness was generally interpreted as loss of contact with the next kingdom:

> I was saying, "Wow! What am I supposed to be doing?" At the beginning of the Process I always knew what to do. It felt right when I made a decision. You could feel a vibration inside, but later, then I didn't know what to do, where to go. Should we hold another meeting or not? I was stagnating. I stopped growing and I was wondering where to turn to start growing again. (interview)

Another informant recalled seeing a poster whose message haunted him for weeks. "When the light goes out," it read, "darkness comes." (interview)

Members had always been attuned to unusual coincidences which suggested messages from the next level, but now they intensified their search for revealing signs. Still clinging to the hope that the demonstration would happen soon, they debated the significance of fires, floods, earthquakes, and volcanic eruptions in other parts of the world, and they scoured the Bible for prophetic passages which might provide clues about the future or suggest some course of action.

In spite of their disillusionment, most members continued to tune in, but now instead of asking for tests, they pleaded with the next level to reveal the truth. At the close of an evening meeting in Arizona where the authenticity of the Two had been challenged for the first time, a young man urged the group to "go to the Fathers" for answers: "We should walk out the door of our lives again, and leave behind all our thoughts and ideas up to this point, and ask the Father to show us the truth. We should ask if the statements are true, and where we should go from here. And if we're all in tune, we'll all get the same answer" [to which there were some "amens"]. (field notes) Members in other groups reported that they too had begun asking the next level for the truth. The following comment is typical:

> I'd been vibing for a week [but] instead of going [to the Fathers] and asking over and over for the strength to complete the Process, I started saying, "I just want to know the truth, man. That's all I want to know. I don't care if I leave the planet, I don't care what happens. I just want to know the truth. I want to know what's going on. (interview)

A young woman in our group jotted down a revealing list of questions that she planned to "take to the Father." Her list, reproduced in part here, captured the concerns of almost everyone in camp:

Am I trying 100%? How do I know when I am?

Big fear—I'm not going to make it. I'm going to miss the bus.

Am I doing right? Should I continue with the Process? Should I go off by myself?

I'm asking for it, Father. Truth to the MAX, Dad.

Should we stay here? Should we move? Where?

Is there to be a demonstration?

This testing business. I don't understand why it's called that. Why should they give us this stuff? What are we testing?

What's this tuning in jazz? How do I do it? How do I pull answers out of the ether?

I will NOT give up, Lord. This is for me. I will overcome these things. With your guidance. Guide me, Father. Answer these questions.

Why am I so slow in getting this? Father, please help me!

I can't function any more with all these half-answered questions. I need *more clarity*, Father. More light. More knowledge. Put it in place, focus the frame, Father!

Have I overcome anything? What does it mean to overcome?

Sex feelings. How do I overcome them? Motherly feelings?

Lost and tired. My feet are cold. (field notes)

Behavioral disengagement: Once members began to raise fundamental questions about the validity of the message or their own
determination to continue the Process, it was not long before their
disaffection became noticeable to others. Little by little disaffected
members stopped conforming to Bo and Peep's rigid guidelines for
"doing the Process." The very fact that members had begun to discuss
their doubts during group meetings was a serious violation of the rules.
    At first the changes were subtle. The early signs of behavioral
disengagements are best described by Goffman's (1961) term "role
distance." Members continued to give the appearance of being on the
Process, but their role performance was half-hearted at best and often

calculated to minimize their involvement in the trip. My partner, for example, let me do all the talking when we tested churches because, as she explained, testing made her feel "like a criminal." Disaffected members also relied on their partners to answer questions at public meetings so they would not be forced to defend beliefs which they now feared might be indefensible. When in doubt silence was the safest strategy: "I wouldn't do it, I never said a word. I just couldn't talk to anybody because I didn't believe what they were saying. I mean, I'd hear them up on the platform and I'd say, 'Oh, no, who'd believe that?'" (interview)

In extreme cases disaffected members divorced themselves from the scene so completely that anyone who noticed them would have assumed they were part of the audience. At some meetings they could be seen sitting apart from the group or standing alone at the back of the room watching impassively while the message was being presented. Usually disaffected members preferred to avoid meetings altogether. "At that point I wouldn't have given another meeting. I wouldn't have gone out in front of anybody and said to them what I believed. I really didn't believe anything at that point—pro or con. I was just on a camping trip with a bunch of friends." (interview)

The usual justification for not holding meetings was that members needed time out to reestablish their connection with the next level. Sometimes entire groups stopped presenting the message so members could "recharge their batteries." Our group, for instance, decided to retreat to a remote hot spring in southern California. However, rather than getting closer to the Father, the defection process accelerated. Deviant behavior became widespread. Members socialized with other campers in the hot pools, and when offered a beer or a hit on a passing joint, about half of them accepted. From the perspective of the few members of our group who were still relatively committed to the trip, the most serious problem was that partners were splitting up. As they reminded the group, the Two had said that it was absolutely essential to have a partner in order to be on the Process.

Behavioral disengagement was a gradual process that proceeded unevenly. At first members usually violated the rules privately or inconspicuously while maintaining a facade of conviction. For example, the members of one partnership in our group were secretly smoking marijuana and shooting heroin even though almost everyone else assumed they were still highly committed. New believers often had no idea how widespread disaffection was because the "older" members deliberately concealed their disillusionment whenever new recruits were around. At a buffer camp in Arizona one of the group spokes-women confessed to us that she had serious reservations about the authenticity of the Two, but she still felt a strong responsibility to explain the message to new members exactly as it had been presented to her.

Outsiders were usually the last to realize that members were highly disillusioned. In one meeting I observed, two disaffected members carefully explained that the Process required overcoming one's attachment to all mind-altering substances, including everything from hard drugs to alcohol and cigarettes. As soon as the last member of the audience had departed, one of the speakers turned to her partner and asked, "Where's that butt? I could really use a smoke."

A dramatic example of the unevenness of the disengagement process occurred at the hot springs shortly after ten members of our group decided to leave the trip. While they were preparing to leave, word suddenly arrived that several groups from other parts of the country were converging on southern California. There was talk about a big meeting in Los Angeles and speculation that Bo and Peep might be there. Within an hour after we got the news, all but two of the ten who had planned to leave were trying to reestablish their partnerships, and they were beginning to talk like committed believers again.

The ultimate form of behavioral disengagement was deliberate separation from the group. Separation should not be confused with defection. At most it could be considered a "trial defection," an experiment in psychological survival without group support. Separation was usually justified on the grounds that the group's "low vibrations" were hindering one's growth. Members who broke away from the group on a trial basis always left with their partners and usually came back after a few days. During their absence they often visited old friends or investigated other spiritual trips. Usually these encounters only added to their confusion, and in some cases they triggered outright defection. We observed several partnerships who made two or three such trial runs before they finally decided not to return. These members wrestled with an impossible dilemma: Although they wanted to escape the demoralizing effects of social disengagement, they were not strong enough to sustain their faith alone. A member of our group who had just returned from a trial separation explained his predicament:

> I want the strength to do it alone. Whenever I'm on the bandwagon I don't have any trouble, but as soon as I get off by myself, it all seems

absurd. Now that I'm back with the people and I can hear the rap again,
I'm back on the bandwagon and everything is OK. But I can't seem to do
it without the group. (field notes)

One of the most important signs of behavioral disengagement was
the change that occurred in the way members talked about the Process
among themselves. Early in the trip new recruits learned how to talk
like members. They adopted Bo and Peep's stereotyped jargon and
mimicked their idiosyncrasies and pet expressions. Bo, for example, had
a tendency to use the word "that" to underscore references to the next
level—as in "becoming a member of *that* next kingdom"—and his
followers quickly picked up the habit. When explaining the message to
outsiders or clarifying points for each other, members borrowed heavily
from the statements, as if following a script. Not until disaffection set in
did members become aware of the script-like character of their everyday
talk. For instance, a disillusioned member at the Arizona buffer camp
complained that every time he asked another member a question he got
a "tape recorded message" in reply.

Disaffected members typically began to alter the script shortly before
they dropped out of the cult. The change in their talk helped ease the
transition back to the outside world by reasserting their previously held
identity as "seekers along the path."

Before joining the UFO cult, most of Bo and Peep's followers had
organized their lives around the pursuit of spiritual meaning. For some
this had been a relatively recent development spurred by the onset of
serious personal problems. But for others, perhaps the majority, the
search for enlightenment had been a long-term pursuit. In either case,
they defined themselves as spiritual seekers and organized their lives
around the quest for truth. My partner is a good example. She ran away
from home at fifteen "to find the truth," and for the next six years she
explored psychedelic drugs, the Jesus movement, witchcraft, and the
Human Potential Movement before she finally heard about Bo and
Peep. Shortly after leaving the UFO cult, she became a Moonie.
"Before I started talking to you," she said, "I never realized how much
shit I'd been into." (field notes) Another member characterized his
perennial search for truth as a "bumper car ride through a maze of
spiritual trips." (field notes)

For members of the UFO cult, being a seeker was a positively valued
social identity. Whatever their real motivation for dabbling in such a
wide array of unconventional religions, they justified their search by

appealing to beliefs that are widely shared in the cultural underground known as the cultic milieu (Balch and Taylor 1977; Campbell 1972).

Of particular importance in understanding the seeker's outlook on life are two fundamental beliefs. The first is the principle of monism (Ellwood 1973; Judah 1967). God is conceptualized as an impersonal life force that pervades every aspect of the universe. In the cultic milieu this principle translates into an eclectic, antidogmatic philosophy: Because divine light is reflected in all facets of Creation, there is a measure of truth in every religion.

The second belief follows directly from the first. If all religions contain an element of truth, then there may be many equally valid means of achieving enlightenment. This viewpoint is called epistemological individualism because it makes the individual the final arbiter of truth. In the cultic milieu one often hears the remark that "there are many paths to the top of the mountain." The expression reflects a pragmatic conception of truth: What works best for one individual may be a waste of time for someone else, and as soon as one stops growing spiritually, it is time to move on to another path. The philosophy of epistemological individualism justifies the seeker's characteristic pattern of sampling widely from the spiritual smorgasbord without making firm commitments to any particular trip. The irony of recruitment in the UFO cult is that seekers who prided themselves on the individualistic pursuit of truth could be attracted to an authoritarian belief system such as the Process.

Bo and Peep understood the seeker's conception of the Search because they had been seekers themselves (Balch 1982a). Although they stated flatly and without qualification that the Process was the only way seekers could enter the next kingdom, they softened the epistemologically authoritarian tone of their message by casting it in language that appealed to the seeker's tolerance of diverse paths. In one of their mimeographed flyers, for example, they told seekers that all the paths they had tried in their spiritual quest were worthwhile because they had enabled them to reach the top of the mountain. The Process, however, was the only way *off* that mountain. All our informants had been seeking some sort of personal transformation before they had ever heard of the Two, and they found the metaphor of caterpillers into butterflies especially appealing.

The Two did not try to destroy the seeker's old identity, but to reshape it. Rather than rejecting the seeker's past history of spiritual exploration as evil or meaningless, they defined it as a necessary progression of growth experiences which enabled their followers to achieve a state of awareness where they, and they alone, could grasp the truth of the message. The Process was simply "the next logical step" in their growth.

Once seekers had taken that step, however, Bo and Peep proceeded to eliminate the symbols of their previous spiritual involvements. Like other attachments to the human level, they too had to be overcome. The "stripping" process began as soon as new recruits reached the buffer camp. Members who had used drugs to achieve spiritual insight were told that mind-altering substances would break their connection with the next level. Those who had been in the habit of daily meditation learned that the practice would open the psyche to spiritual bombardment. Macrobiotic vegetarians were informed that the next level would test them by giving them only junk food to eat. Bo and Peep once claimed that metaphysical works like OASPE and the Urantia Book were only good for starting fires. Even talking about other spiritual trips was considered a serious impediment to growth because it pulled members back into the human level.

Thus Bo and Peep facilitated the transition from seeker to follower by linking the message with the seeker's quest for truth, and then subtly destroying the symbols of that connection. When members became disaffected, however, they reversed the process by reestablishing the connection in their talk.

One sign that members were beginning to reassert their identities as seekers was the selective elimination of jargon from their speech. Two types of talk were most likely to be eliminated. The first consisted of references to the unique features of the UFO trip that distinguished the Process from other spiritual paths. This included talk about UFOs, the demonstration, the physical nature of the next level, and the biological transformation that Bo and Peep claimed would accompany the overcoming process. The second category was made up of terms and expressions that fostered conformity to Bo and Peep's guidelines, especially tests and spirits. The concept of the test had enabled members to endure physical hardships and periods of despair, while wariness of spirits prevented them from socializing, smoking marijuana, telephoning friends, and indulging in any number of other unacceptable actions.

The disappearance of these topics from their conversation was accompanied by increasing emphasis on those aspects of the message that were most consistent with the seeker's philosophy of epistemological individualism. Members continued to talk about growth experiences and overcoming attachments, but with a new twist. They no longer described the Process as the only way off the mountain or even as a unique philosophy:

> I think the Process is different for everyone. You have to be true to yourself before you can make a connection with God. The most important thing is the Process of becoming—don't get hung up on the future. Just let it be. It doesn't matter what you call it—the Process is the path, the Way, the Tao. All the great teachers were saying the same thing—Jesus, Lao Tse, Buddha, the Two. The Two are possibly the greatest teachers of all time, certainly the greatest in this age. The Process is whatever you want it to be as long as you're free of attachments. (field notes)

In our group this reconceptualization of the Process first appeared at the hot springs in southern California, and within a few days it had been adopted by ten of the fourteen members who were camped near the springs. The same ideas appeared independently in other groups. For example, a member whose group had been travelling in New England explained that "somehow Bo and Peep and their teachings didn't seem to be 'the way off the top of the mountain,' but just another path accessible to the seeker." (from an autobiographical account written by a defector)

The new way of talking about the Process constituted an emergent "vocabulary of motives" (Mills 1940) that was used to justify deviant behavior. When I asked a disaffected member at the hot springs how he could justify smoking marijuana, he replied: "Smoking dope is an individual thing. If you can handle it and it doesn't affect your contact with the Father, then go ahead . . . The thing is not to lose contact with the Father. If you can smoke dope and keep that contact, then far out." (field notes) He added that Bo and Peep never intended the Process to become a rigid collection of rules:

> There are no "shoulds" any more. The rules were just guidelines in the beginning. They became hard and fast rules when they were interpreted and applied by others. The Two never meant them to be applied rigidly. For example, they never told us not to read. They just said it's a good idea not if it's going to call up spirits. (field notes)

Some disaffected members in our group insisted that members who mechanically followed the rules were not really on the Process: "Now there are lots of traditionalists [true believers] who would really come down on me for this, but to me sitting in a tent and reading the Bible is not the Process. The Process is a way of becoming—you have to experience life to become this way. I know lots of people who follow all the rules, but they aren't on the Process." (field notes)

Having come this far in their reconceptualization of the Process, it was easy for disaffected members to justify leaving the group. As my partner explained, "We also have to break our attachments to the Two and their teachings. We have to move beyond them." (field notes) However, moving beyond the Two did not mean leaving the Process. When members defected they usually insisted they were only leaving the group, not the Process. It was fascinating to hear the ways that members used the trip's jargon to justify defection, which of course was the ultimate form of behavioral disengagement. They capitalized on the individual nature of Human Individual Metamorphosis by reminding the more conservative members that each individual required different experiences to complete his or her growth at the human level. If anyone disputed their reinterpretation of the Process, they usually claimed that they were merely acting on directions received from the next level. Because Bo and Peep had told them that each member would have direct communication with the next kingdom, no one could dispute the claim.

Once members began to adopt the new vocabulary of motives, it was usually only a short time before they left the group. Social scientific descriptions of religious conversion frequently emphasize the importance of bridge-burning acts in breaking ties with the past (e.g. Gerlach and Hine 1970). In defection we see a bridge-*building* process at work. Members attempted to bridge the gap between the reality of the cult and the reality of the seeker by constructing a new version of their experience: In pursuit of truth they had closed the door to their past and overcome their attachments to the human level. They had grown from the experience, but now it was time to move on to new endeavors, new tests, and growth in new directions. If the UFOs came, perhaps they would be picked up, but if not, then, as one member told us, "at least I will have grown." (field notes)

Departure: Even when members were able to construct a plausible justification for leaving, they did not necessarily find it entirely convincing. Instead they usually continued to vacillate indecisively until one or more events forced them to make a decision. Skonovd found that defection was often a planned event that took place in the absence of clear-cut precipitating incidents. However, most of our informants could recall specific situations that caused them to leave. The actual events varied widely: a heated argument around the campfire; the shock of discovering that one's partner had secretly defected in the middle of the night; the passing of a personal deadline for the demonstration; a night in jail for driving with an expired license; and so on. In the context of deepening disaffection, these events convinced members that they had to make a decision. As a woman who had been on the Process for five years put it, "I realized that I had gone as far as I could go." (interview)

The precipitating event was usually a minor incident that marked the culmination of a long series of demoralizing situations. Consider the example of a man who belonged to our group for several weeks. Although severely disillusioned by the cult's increasingly acrimonious atmosphere, he and his partner helped run a buffer camp in southern California. When the camp broke up, everyone except the two of them decided to go east. In the weeks that followed he sank into a deep depression as they searched unsuccessfully for another group of believers. His partner was still strongly committed, and she constantly berated him for being so weak. Finally, after an unusually bitter argument, she drove off in their car, leaving him alone in a remote, empty campground. He hitched a ride to a nearby city, tested for a place to stay, and eventually found a room in a house owned by a left-wing commune. The ensuing events triggered his defection:

> I had time to kill, and there was another girl crashing there, so I talked to her about the Process. She was a street-person type, pretty, nice, free. She asked me a couple questions about the Process that somehow did a number on my head. Suddenly all the frameworks shifted. The questions were like, "Are you happy? Are you benefiting from what you are doing now? Do you feel that you're undergoing change? How does it compare with the community where you lived before?" It made me look at the Process from a different perspective. (interview)

Although the precipitating incident in this case involved contact with an outsider, the account also illustrates the role played by the sudden loss of social support. Both factors were mentioned frequently as the immediate causes of defection. For other informants public meetings marked the turning point. Inept attempts to present the message had always been demoralizing, and once disaffection set in, a particularly poor meeting was often enough to push members over the brink: "The final point was when I went to the Santa Monica meeting. To me it was the epitome of being a robot. I mean, I was not digging the vibes. . . . It had become a rigid dogma." (interview)

Whatever the immediate cause, the decision to leave was almost always marked by ambivalence:

> . . . These realizations came into my mind, and suddenly I said, "Maybe I'll leave the Process." And suddenly this incredible feeling of expansion of power, of limitless possibilities, came in, like a magical sense. Almost a drug-induced state, of power and possibility. At the same time, though, there was guilt. I felt like a failure. It wasn't denial of the Process. I just couldn't do it any more. (interview)

A few members dealt with the ambivalence by engaging in deliberate acts to commit themselves to their decision: "I realized that as soon as I called home, that was it. If I called home and said something, where I was, then that was as good as leaving the Process. Because that would be a point of no return." (interview) Another defector immediately bought a pint of Southern Comfort and a pack of Camels, knowing that if he drank and smoked himself into oblivion, he could never go back to the Process. Such steps may have made it more difficult to turn back, but they did not make the psychological ordeal any less traumatic. As the man who burned his bridges by getting drunk explained, "It was heavy duty trauma time—I mean *heavy duty!*" (interview)

Most defectors tried to justify their decision by telling themselves (and others, if there were others to be told) that they were only leaving the group, not the Process. The rationalization may have made the decision easier, but it did not provide defectors with the clarity of mind they so desperately wanted. Whereas members often reported feeling directed by higher powers when they joined the cult, they rarely felt that way when they defected:

> We just prayed a lot. Tried to be as straight with God as we could. We never did get a vivid answer that we were supposed to leave. We just ended up leaving on our own and not going back to the campground. We didn't know what we were doing. We just felt kind of lost, you know. We just drove on down the road. (interview)

Floating: The term "floating" was first used to describe the detached, ambivalent state which usually follows deprogramming (Patrick 1976). Deprogrammed cult members often appear listless and preoccupied, and without strong social support, they may attempt to return to the cult. Although none of our informants had been deprogrammed, most of them could be described as floating during the period immediately following defection.

An informant from Oregon explained the defector's predicament by drawing an example from the writings of Carlos Castaneda: "When Don Juan took Carlos' reality away from him, he replaced it with his sorcerer's explanation. Because if you take someone's reality away from him and don't replace it with anything, you end up in a big void unless you are really strong." (interview) Subjectively, then, floating refers to the experience of being trapped between two symbolic worlds. Defectors had cut themselves off from the cult, often with no chance of returning, but they usually looked on the outside world with a mixture of ambivalence and dread: "I was looking out at the world and I saw nothing but a bunch of garbage. I saw things that I didn't like, and that I didn't understand, and that I didn't want to get caught back up in. I was scared and I didn't know how to deal with it." (interview)

Very few informants claimed to have returned home immediately without a trace of guilt or remorse. The vast majority continued to vacillate, sometimes spending weeks or months on the road before deciding to go home. The man who compared himself to Castaneda travelled back and forth across the country three times, putting 25,000 miles on his car while he tried to "get his head straight." Once he came within a few miles of his hometown and suddenly turned around again. As he explained: "I still wasn't clear on if I really did want to come back to Newport because, you know, I don't see how anybody could be the same person as when they left, which I wasn't. I didn't know if I should come back and try to be somebody I'm not." (interview)

Reentry: I have borrowed the term "reentry" from one of our informants because, in his words, going home was "like coming back to earth." Reentry meant taking decisive steps to reestablish a lifestyle compatible with the demands of life at the human level. That could mean applying for food stamps, renting an apartment, taking a job, moving in with one's parents, or readopting the transient style of the street person. Most defectors eventually returned to their hometowns, but facing family members and old friends was an unpleasant prospect, and some put off the ordeal for several months.

Although very few defectors sought psychiatric help, virtually all had trouble readjusting to what they perceived as the banality of human existence. Defectors typically remained aloof from their surroundings. To their friends and relatives they seemed distant and preoccupied. Most avoided group activities such as parties and family gatherings, and when they were forced to participate, they often reported feeling as though they were standing beside themselves watching dispassionately, sometimes with a measure of disgust, as each new scene unfolded:

> I was just in a different place. I was in one dimension and they were in another dimension. As long as I was in that different plane, I couldn't relate to them and their trips. I mean, they seemed totally silly to me. What a waste! Look at all these silly people running around being so fucking emotional, just blowing off that important energy! I couldn't relate to it. I couldn't relate to people any more. (interview)

In a situation reminiscent of the hollow conformity that characterized the disaffection stage, defectors again found themselves playing a role without fully embracing it. Because they were only "going through the motions," they were acutely conscious of every move.

In the encapsulated environment of the UFO cult, life had been basic and members fully believed that the Fathers provided for their every need. Now they had to confront the realities of survival in the secular world. A few defectors believed the Process had enhanced their ability to deal with the human level, but they were exceptional. Most were extremely apprehensive about reestablishing themselves:

> When I got off the trip and came back, it jarred me. I had to start dealing with this conscious-type stuff—a job, thinking about money, gas, this, that. *I* had to take over. It was no longer the Father in Heaven running the show. So it was rather traumatic in the beginning. . . . Sometimes I even wanted to go back on the trip, you know. It would have been so much nicer to go back on the trip so I wouldn't have to be bogged down with these things. (interview)

As this remark suggests, the pull of the cult was still a force to be reckoned with. The Process remained a powerful idea, and initially few defectors were willing to dismiss the Two as frauds, yet the reality of the cult was fading rapidly. "I can see, for myself," said a man who had been off the trip for seven months, "that the influence of the Process, or the clarity of it, is gradually dimming as each day goes by." (interview) The result was a feeling of disorientation:

> It was a period of distress for me. I was feeling a senselessness to the whole thing, a pointlessness. If God really directed me to go [on the trip], then why is this happening now? If I really got a message to go with Bo and Peep, then why did they leave me behind? What kind of destiny is this? I felt thrown off the path of destiny. And that's a very

lonely, odd place to be. I had hundreds of things going through my head, a squirrel cage. (interview)

For a few the confusion lingered for years:

I was just drowning in questions about my own ability to discriminate. Was I just totally indiscriminate and brought all this pain on myself for no reason, except that I didn't have the ability to determine that they [the Two] were not true to start with? Or were they really true and was it the right thing? I spent nearly two years of diving within myself for those answers. (interview)

In rare cases defectors were gripped by periods of fear. For example, a woman who had gone to the press accusing the Two of mind control asked the Father to surround her with "white light" to protect her from psychic attack. Other defectors reported episodes of acute paranoia:

I felt quite sure I was being attacked by spiritual demons or influences that just wanted me to lay it all down. They were ready to take over my body. It wasn't a dream state. I was awake and I was scared. I could feel the presence of something going on around me. I was afraid to go to sleep for a while because I felt something might happen. (interview)

In most cases defectors had to cope with their confusion and anxiety without much social support. The situation they encountered in their hometowns was not unlike that of patients returning from a mental hospital. In their network of friends, and relatives they occupied an ambiguous position that made interaction with them awkward and uncomfortable. This was generally true even when defectors had friends who shared their interest in metaphysics. As one explained, "people are reticent to prod you in a tender space." (interview) Another informant was more specific:

I had lost all my credibility. There was no credibility left because you're considered either weird, or off-beat, or crazy by everybody you've ever met. They have to totally avoid you or just never bring up the subject. Nobody had the guts to really question me. They couldn't relate to what I had experienced. (interview)

Although our informants had been "off the trip" for an average of seven months when we interviewed them, a surprising number claimed that they had not discussed the Process with anyone until we arrived because they feared no one would understand.

The trauma of reentry was compounded when defectors were unaware that others had left the trip. The simple discovery that they were not alone often made the ordeal easier to bear: "The first week I was here I was very withdrawn. I had no idea anyone had left the Process besides me. I had the feeling that everyone else was still on the Process. But, see, once I found out that John was off, that lessened the trauma." (interview)

For a while in late 1975 and early 1976, a small group of defectors operated an informal halfway house in Los Angeles to help former members "get their heads together." Located in a secluded canyon near the city, it provided defectors with a place where they could "lower their vibration levels to the point where they could relate again." Almost every informant who visited the halfway house believed the experience had been beneficial. Although I have no reliable way of comparing rates of readjustment, it appears that defectors who were able to share their feelings with each other were able to adapt more rapidly than those who were forced to cope by themselves.

Even with social support, defectors usually spent weeks just getting to the point where they could deal with the simple burdens of everyday life. Their behavior could best be described as "hanging out"—aimless and indecisive. In the first issue of a short-lived newsletter for "ex-ultimate trippers," a defector captured the feelings of everyone who had recently returned to the human level:

> Dear Friends along the Path:
>   The other day, three inactive UFOers stopped by to see us at Mountain Grove. We met like old friends and with some joy, although we'd never been particularly close. It was a reunion.
>   It seemed we shared some thoughts in common. This was not the end of the process for any of us. Most thought that the first stage was over and that we were "on hold," waiting for word of what to do next. All agreed that returning to the everyday life we left behind was not it.

Only in rare cases were defectors able to avoid the "hanging out" phase. For example, a fifty-six year old metaphysician started a tarot class immediately after he returned to Los Angeles. He had managed to work out his problems during the floating stage. After leaving the group, he spent a month meditating in the Los Angeles hills before he was prepared to cope with the city.

Cognitive reorganization: The defection process was not complete until former members evolved a new symbolic framework that reconciled the confusing events in their recent past. Skonovd used the term "cognitive reorganization" to describe this stage, and for the sake of consistency, so will I.

Conway and Siegelman (1978) report that many defectors suddenly "snap" back to reality as if awakening from a dream. However, only one of our informants reported a similar experience:

> I was really confused and tripped out, still thinking I might get off the planet. I started getting freaked out because I couldn't relate to people, so I went up to John's house and smoked a bunch of good dope. Something in my head just went *pop!* and I went, "Where has my head been at? Oh, shit, what have I been doing? This is ridiculous." I started taking a whole new look at things. I started putting pieces together, things that didn't feel right, that didn't fit. . . .(interview)

Even in this case the notion of snapping back to reality is a gross oversimplification. "Snapping" out of the mental set created by the trip was not accompanied by the sudden embracing of a new interpretive framework. As Singer (1979) and Skonovd (1981) discovered in their work with defectors from other new religions, cognitive reorganization is a gradual process. They estimated that readjustment generally takes anywhere from six to eighteen months, and our data corroborate their findings.

It is difficult, if not impossible, to determine when cognitive reorganization was finally achieved because, as Berger and Luckmann (1967) point out, the reinterpretation of one's biography is an on-going process that continues throughout life. In addition, some informants were not as far along in the readjustment process as were others at the time of our interviews. For example, a man who had been one of the nineteen who were separated from the main body of the cult in 1976 was still very confused when I interviewed him over two years later. He had not had a steady job in all that time, and he was drinking heavily to escape his sense of personal failure. Another defector remained thoroughly confused five years after defecting because he had never been able to account for a puzzling series of synchronistic events that had prompted him to join the cult in the first place. In a recent letter he wrote: ". . . perhaps I am a victim of *superstitious ignorance*. But I *SAW* a U.F.O. and I had IDEAS that WERE Bo and Peep's *BEFORE* I met them . . . I don't know where to draw the line between fantasy and reality." (emphasis in the original)

Most defectors, however, eventually developed a personally believable account that reconciled the contradictions in their past.

One of the first signs of cognitive reorganization was hostility toward the Two. Many defectors, especially those associated with the halfway house, accused Bo and Peep of fraud and mind control. One defector compared his experience in the UFO cult with his tour of duty in the Marines, claiming that he had been brainwashed on both occasions. Another defector threatened to kill Bo and Peep if he ever saw them again, and a few others went to the press to level charges against the Two.

According to Borhek and Curtis (1975), defectors from totalistic belief systems tend to be "noisy apostates," and that picture is reinforced by the media attention given to angry defectors who have aligned themselves with the anti-cult movement. Even the Two reorganized this phenomenon, as Bo pointed out at a public meeting in 1975:

> Anyone who pursues this endeavor and does not endure it, or loses sight of it, and chooses to go back to the level of existence that they had, would *have* to choose to condemn it to justify their going back. It is the same thing that Jesus said: "You are for me or you are against me." There are no two ways about it. (from a tape recording of their public address)

However, we should not exaggerate either the prevalence or the degree of hostility. Almost all the newspaper stories which alluded to the cult's alleged mind control techniques originated with a single person in Los Angeles. Because of the disproportionate amount of attention she received in syndicated stories, the public was presented with a misleading image of the typical defector. Not only was extreme bitterness relatively rare, but it usually faded rather quickly.

The consistency in our accounts was surprising. All our informants, including the Los Angeles defector who received so much press coverage, accepted full responsibility for their decisions to go on the Process. Most of them vehemently rejected the claim that they had been brainwashed. The following comment is typical:

> They never talked me into doing anything. I made up my own mind . . . The basic law of the universe is free will, and if your will is so weak that somebody could brainwash you, that's still your own fault. No matter what happens, it gets down to the fact that you are responsible for your actions and your life. No matter how it comes across. It really disgusts me to hear people say, "You *made* me do this." That's a falsehood. Nobody makes you do anything. (interview)[12]

Everyone we interviewed claimed that the trip had been a valuable learning experience, and all but one strongly emphasized the positive aspects of the trip. For example: "I don't know whether to label it as a mistake or what. All I know is that I've looked at everything as being a learning experience, so I did make a wrong choice, I still look on the positive side." (interview) Several even told us that they were still on the Process, although they were often vague about what that meant: "I still agree with a lot of the philosophy. I'm not really *off* the Process— I'm still living on *some* type of process." (interview) Even those who claim to have left the Process entirely usually continued to accept parts of the message. For example, several told us that they still believed the ships were coming. "It would not surprise me at all," said one, "if you wisk off in a UFO tomorrow!" (interview)

Although defectors sometimes wondered about the real nature of Bo and Peep's mission, and occasionally questioned their sanity, they generally believed that the Two had been tuned in to some higher force: "I've been off the trip six months and I still don't know if they are who they say they are or whether they're nuts. If they are nuts, then they are in tune with some pretty high information. As far as I'm concerned, that's a fact, because I learned a lot from them." (interview)

To outsiders statements like these might appear to the transparent rationalization for what, in retrospect, seemed like a bad mistake. Yet they are significant because of what they tell us about the nature of the cognitive reorganization process. Nearly all our informants attempted to reinterpret their experience by linking it with the seeker's unending quest for spiritual growth. When we asked them what the Process meant to them, they described it in terms that were compatible with both the central tenets of Bo and Peep's message and the epistemologically individualistic values of the cultic milieu. The Process meant growing spiritually, seeking new experiences, freeing oneself from attachments, and placing total trust in God. In retrospect, most defectors defined the UFO trip as a catalyst for experiences that they required at a particular stage in their spiritual growth. One defector reminded us of the old saying that the master appears when the student is ready. Having learned her lessons, however, this informant said it was time for her to move on to new endeavors. By the end of the defection process, then, the symbolic bridge between the authoritarian belief system of the UFO cult and the individualistic world of the seeker was finally complete, and our informants were able to make the transition back to the reality they had left behind when they decided to come on the Process.

There is no question in my mind that the UFO trip was a valuable learning experience for most of our informants. By stressing the value of relentless self-examination, as well as thrusting members into unfamiliar situations where they had to rely on their inner resources, the Process compelled individuals to reflect on their needs, desires, hopes, fears, and personal inadequacies in a way that few had ever done before.

Although some defectors were vague about the lessons they had learned, most were able to cite specific ways they had grown. Some lessons were highly personal. For example, a young man who had always taken a passive role in his relationships with others believed the partnership arrangement had forced him to become more assertive:

> The partnership was great. I mean, I learned a lot. I was put into relationships that I would normally avoid. I didn't pick my partners—I wouldn't have picked a battle of wills. I would have gracefully said, "Okay, bye, bye." It's not my way to fight it out, and yet I was forced to fight it out. So, I learned a lot from that. (interview)

Ironically, a few others told us that the experience of trying to overcome their attachment to love and friendship had taught them the value of loving and serving others in a human way.

Most of the lessons, however, were expressed in language that reflected the seeker's orientation to life. Learning to trust in God was a commonly mentioned lesson:

> I arrived back into the world literally without a cent to my name, driving a borrowed car, but with an inner security and confidence I never before knew existed. Anything I needed day by day just appears before me, job, money, contacts, which I see as the result of Tuning In. [sic] What was it the Man [Jesus] said? Something like, Your Heavenly Father knows what you need before you ask it, and it is His good pleasure to provide it. (from an autobiographical account written by a defector)

A related theme was the importance of overcoming attachments. For example, a defector who, before joining the UFO cult used to pride himself on his nonmaterialistic life style, told us that the Process "taught me that I do have a lot more material attachments than I realized—I mean, when I gave up my truck, it was heavy!" (interview) Another defector, who had hoarded $500 under the back seat of his car, reported that his most valuable growth occurred when he finally turned the money over to the group:

The main thing is that I was able to actually get rid of human props that I had been hanging on to. That was the big thing because I was very heavy on relying on physical objects and things of this world for my security. Even knowing in my head it was wrong, I still couldn't break it off. And that "breaking off" in the trip was worth fifty million dollars to me. (interview)

The most common lesson cited by our informants was the importance of overcoming the need for gurus and spiritual trips. An Oregon defector quoted a Sufi parable to explain why he could not imagine joining another cult: "There's a Sufi saying that there are three steps to heaven: Quit this world, quit the next world, and quit quitting. And in a sense, to do it again would be to still have an addiction to quitting. You got to quit quitting." (interview) Some defectors characterized the UFO trip as an archetypal symbol of man's eternal search for meaning. They argued that seekers will continue to fall under the spell of prophets, gurus, and messiahs until they overcome their need for a spiritual crutch:

In the Process that Bo and Peep outlined, I think the final overcoming has to be Bo-Peep. And I think that Bo-Peep would even admit to that at this point. You have to overcome any attachment to a leader, to a father figure. . . . Why did we need an Adolph Hitler? We created him. The human culture spit him out. He was just a manifestation of what humans had to go through. Finally he arose. Bo-Peeps will continue to arise 'til people quit looking up to a father to tell them what to do. (interview)

These comments should not be misconstrued to mean that our informants had given up their search. Nearly all of them still considered themselves seekers, but most claimed to have rediscovered the age-old truth that wisdom and peace of mind lie within the soul of each individual:[13]

The UFO trip was a mystical journey, a rite of passage. You have to go inside yourself on an interior trip to get further along the path . . . I'm still looking around, and I'm still trying to find the way, but I'm in a different flow. So I'm still seeking, if you want to use the word. But as far as expecting to meet a master, expecting to meet a Don Juan, I wouldn't trust anybody but myself. I wouldn't trust Don Juan. (interview)

The following statement by a woman who helped organize the half-way house captures the general tenor of these reflections. Significantly, she borrowed one of Bo and Peep's favorite analogies to express her renewed allegiance to the seeker's individualistic orientation to Truth: "Until man, the human, acknowledges his Christ within, he will be bound by the cocoon of his human nature. Only when he overcomes all the paths and all the teachers will he be able to fly free as the beautiful butterfly envisioned by Bo and Peep in their philosophy." (Culpepper et al., unpublished)[14]

Conclusion

In this paper I have outlined a model of defection from a totalistic cult. The model is remarkably consistent with Skonovd's description of the defection process in other new religious movements. The striking similarity in our findings suggests that the organizational characteristic of totalism has a much greater impact on the nature of defection than does the content of any particular belief system. The two studies complement each other. By surveying defectors from a variety of groups, Skonovd demonstrated the generality of the process reported by my informants. In turn the present study, though limited to one group, provides additional insights by including direct observations of members at various points in the defection process.

The most important discovery may be the way Bo and Peep's followers bridged the gap between the Process and the outside world. Bridge-building played a major role in the reconstruction of reality and occurred during defection. Berger and Luckmann (1967) contend that social constructions of reality are maintained through normal conversation, and my observations of everyday life in the UFO cult support their argument. The role of ordinary conversation in sustaining reality became apparent during disaffection when disillusioned members began to change the way they talked about the Process. In effect, defectors constructed a new vocabulary of motives that justified their departure from the cult. Bo and Peep's metaphor of caterpillars into butterflies was subtly replaced by the familiar imagery of seekers on the path. Because both metaphors reflect the value of personal transformation, the shift enabled defectors to maintain, however tenuously, a sense of self while loosening the grip of Bo and Peep's authoritarian belief system.

Anthony et al. (1977) discovered a similar pattern in their study of the Meher Baba movement. Members often had considerable experience with psychotherapy prior to their conversions, and they found Eastern spirituality appealing because, like secular forms of therapy, it provided a means of achieving self-insight and self-improvement. But when former patients became devotees, they rejected conventional therapy as superfluous. According to Anthony et al. (1977, 870), "spiritual involvement superceded psychotherapy because it offered an *integrated* cosmological and moral framework which psychotherapy had not." (emphasis in the original) After a period of years, however, the goal of mystical enlightenment receded into the distant future and members once again turned their attention to coping with the mundane problems of human existence. At this point psychotherapy reemerged as a valuable aid to self-understanding, but in a manner consistent with the tenets of the movement:

> Meher Baba is now perceived as a metapsychologist, rather than as embodying an incompatible alternative to psychotherapy. For Baba-lovers who return to therapy, Baba is now seen to *work through the formal therapy situation*. Meher Baba's thought and discourses with regard to spiritual awakening, dissolution of the ego, Karma, and *Maya* are now seen not as an incompatible alternative to psychology, but as an overarching *metapsychology* within which particular psychological concepts can be located. (Anthony et al. 1977, 876; emphasis in the original)

Although the Baba-lovers in this study were not disaffected like the UFO people, they engaged in a similar process of symbolic bridge-building to ease the transition back to a practice they had once abandoned. In both examples members constructed a new account of their experiences which provided a sense of meaningful continuity in their lives.

There is no reason to suppose that bridge-building is a necessary part of defection, but the process was so important in the UFO cult that social scientists would be remiss if they ignored it in subsequent studies of apostasy. Future research may reveal that rates of defection from totalistic cults, as well as the character of retrospective accounts, are closely related to the opportunities for bridge-building talk during everyday conversations between members. Even if the bridge-building process observed in the UFO cult proves to be an isolated occurrence, the data reported in this paper underscores the need for greater attention to the sociolinguistic features of defections.

Notes

1. For related studies of defection see Beckford 1978; Brinkerhoff and Burke 1980; Mauss 1969; Richardson 1975; Singer 1979; and Wright 1981.
2. See Kitsuse 1962; Snow and Phillips 1980; and Taylor 1976, for further information on the problem of retrospective reinterpretation.
3. David Taylor was then a graduate student at the University of Montana. He recently completed his doctorate in Sociology at the Queen's University in Belfast, Northern Ireland.
4. For related papers on the UFO cult see Balch 1979, 1980, 1982a, and 1982b; Balch and Taylor 1976a, 1976b, 1977a, 1977b, 1978; and Lewinson and Balch 1980.
5. Estimating the size of the UFO cult is difficult because there was no membership list and believers were scattered in small groups all over the United States. When a reporter asked Bo and Peep about the number of followers early in 1976, they estimated the membership at 200, but by then even that figure was probably an overestimate.
6. Most members probably would not capitalize the term "Process." I

have done so in order to avoid confusion with other terms used in this paper, such as the "defection process" or the "readjustment process."

7. The absence of deprogrammed respondents is not surprising because the UFO cult was virtually immune to deprogrammers. I am aware of only one member who was successfully deprogrammed. The lack of deprogramming cannot be attributed to the persuasiveness of the group's indoctrination, however, because the UFO cult, by virtue of its extreme secrecy and constant mobility, never had to contend with the problem.

8. At this writing the UFO cult still exists, although the extreme secrecy surrounding the group has made it difficult to obtain reliable information about recent developments. At last word Bo and Peep and their followers were living in two houses somewhere in Texas, and each house, like their previous encampments was treated as if it were a spacecraft.

9. Brinkeroff and Burke's (1980) speculation about the role of labelling in apostasy provides a good description of the predicament faced by the liberals, as well as other deviants in the group. For example, one left in disgust after concluding that no matter what he did, he would always be dismissed as the "screw-up" by the others.

10. Skonovd found that many of his informants lingered in their respective groups because of friendships they had formed with other members. This factor, however, was never mentioned by any of our respondents because the structure of social relationships within the UFO cult discouraged the formation of close interpersonal ties.

11. The importance of ordinary conversation in the bridge-building process raises an interesting question: How would defection have differed if members had not been able to discuss their feelings with each other?

Bo and Peep had always discouraged socializing, and beginning in 1976 they took steps to eliminate it completely. They developed an intricate system of synchronized schedules that enabled members to carry out all their daily activities with a minimum of talk, and occasionally none at all. Another innovation was a uniform designed to eliminate the last vestiges of the human personality. It consisted of baggy pants, a loose-fitting long-sleeve blouse, slippers, gloves, and a hood with wire-mesh eyes. One effect of the uniform, especially the hood, was a drastic reduction in the amount of nonverbal communication. All nonessential talk was prohibited, and members designated as "eyes" recorded rule infractions and reported them to the Two.

If bridge-building proceeds mainly through conversation rather than through the internal dialogue of solitary thought, then it should have been short-circuited by the inability to communicate. Two possible results come to mind. First, recent drop outs might have more difficulty readjusting to life in the outside world. Second, they might be more likely to remain committed to their belief in the Two after leaving the cult.

Unfortunately I do not have the data necessary to test either hypothesis because my sample of recent defectors is too small. Only three of my informants defected after the end of 1977. However, unverified reports strongly suggest that the second hypothesis may be correct. Most of my information comes from a California woman who has organized an informal network of parents whose children belong to the UFO cult. She reports that most recent drop outs still profess complete faith in the Two. Unlike most of the defectors described in this paper, they appear to have departed as "deployable agents" (Lofland 1966) who are able to sustain their convictions without social support. They still believe the ships are coming, and they hang on to the belief that they will be picked up, if not in this harvest, then certainly the next. Their reasons for leaving the group generally revolve around their own inability to see the Process through till the end. This is an intriguing change that I hope to pursue in future interviews.

12. The willingness of our informants to take responsibility for their actions stands in sharp contrast to the common view that cult members are systematically deprived of their free will. Conway and Siegeman's (1978) study, though cast in the language of information theory, is a good example of the popular viewpoint. I suspect that the difference between their findings and my own is a function of our respective sampling methods.

While Taylor and I used a "snowball" technique to locate a representative sample of defectors, Conway and Siegelman relied heavily on the accounts of deprogrammed cult members. They claim to have discovered "very few people who got out of the Unification Church or any other cult on their own" (1978, 36). In view of the high dropout rate in most cults, and our own inability to locate former Bo-Peepers who had been deprogrammed, there is good reason to suspect that Conway and Spiegelman based their conclusions on a very biased sample.

Deprogrammers typically portray cults as manipulative, deceptive, and fraudulent (Patrick 1976; Shupe and Bromley 1980), and cult members who have been successfully deprogrammed often adopt this point of view. Consequently it is not surprising that Conway and Siegelman concluded that their informants had been victimized by powerful mind control techniques.

13. Unfortunately, I have lost track of most of our informants because of their frequent mobility. It would be interesting to see how many of them have become reinvolved in religious cults since they were interviewed.

14. This passage comes from an unpublished manuscript entitled *In Search of a Spaceship,* written by Joan Culpepper, a Los Angeles psychic, and several other former members of the UFO cult. My thanks to her for allowing me to quote from the manuscript.

References

Anthony, Dick, et al. 1977. Patients and pilgrims: Changing attitudes toward psychotherapy of converts to eastern mysticism. *American Behavioral Scientist* 20:861–86.

Balch, Robert W. 1982a. Bo and Peep: A case study of the origins of messianic leadership. *Charisma and the Millennium,* edited by Roy Wallis. Belfast: The Queen's University Press.

———. 1982b. Conversion and charisma in the cultic milieu: The origins of a new religion. Presented at the annual meeting of the Association for the Sociology of Religion, Providence, R.I.

———. 1980. Looking behind the scenes in a religious cult: Implications for the study of conversion. *Sociological Analysis* 41:137–43.

———. 1979. Two models of conversion and commitment in a UFO cult. Presented at the annual meeting of the Pacific Sociological Association, Anaheim, Calif.

Balch, Robert W. and David Taylor. 1978. On getting in tune: Some reflections on the process of making supernatural contact. Presented at the annual meeting of the Pacific Sociological Association, Spokane, Wash.

———. 1977a. Seekers and saucers: The role of the cultic milieu in joining a UFO cult. *American Behavioral Scientist* 20:839–60.

———. 1977b. The metamorphosis of a UFO cult: A study of organizational change. Presented at the annual meeting of the Pacific Sociological Association, Sacramento, Calif.

———. 1976a. Salvation in a UFO. *Psychology Today* (October): 58–66, 106.

———. 1976b. Walking out the door of your life: becoming a member of a contemporary UFO cult. Presented at the annual meeting of the Pacific Sociological Association, San Diego, Calif.

Becker, Howard S. 1960. Notes on the concept of commitment. *American Journal of Sociology* 66:32–40.

Becker, James A. 1978. Through the looking-glass and out the other side: Withdrawal from Reverend Moon's Unification Church. *Archives de Sciences Sociales dess Religious* 45:95–116.

Berger, Peter L. 1965. *Invitation to Sociology*. Garden City, N.Y. Doubleday Anchor.

Berger, Peter L. and Thomas Luckmann. 1967. *The Social Construction of Reality: A Treatise in the Sociology of Knowledge*. Garden City, N.Y.: Doubleday Anchor.

Bird, Frederick and Bill Reimer. 1982. Participation rates in new religious and para-religious movements. *Journal for the Scientific Study of Religion* 21:1–14.

Borhek, James T. and Richard F. Curtis. 1975. *A Sociology of Belief.* New York: John Wiley and Sons.

Brinkerhoff, Merlin B. and Kathryn L. Burke. 1980. Disaffiliation: Some notes on falling from the faith. *Sociological Analysis* 41:41–54.

Campbell, Colin. 1972. The cult, the cultic milieu and secularization. In *A Sociological Yearbook of Religion in Britain,* vol. 5, edited by Michael Hill, 119–136. London: SCM Press.

Conway, Flo and Jim Siegelman. 1978. *Snapping: America's Epidemic of Sudden Personality Change.* Philadelphia: J.B. Lippincott.

Culpepper, Joan, et al. n.d. *In Search of a Spaceship.* Unpublished manuscript.

Ellwood, Robert S., Jr. 1973. *Religious and Spiritual Groups in Modern America.* Englewood Cliffs, N.J.: Prentice-Hall.

Foss, Daniel A. and Ralph W. Larkin. 1976. From 'the gates of Eden' to 'day of the locust': An analysis of the dissident youth movement of the 1960s and its heirs of the early 1970s—the postmovement groups. *Theory and Society* 3:1–44.

Gerlach, Luther P. and Virginia H. Hine. 1970. *People, Power, Change: Movements of Social Transformation.* Indianapolis: Bobbs-Merrill.

Goffman, Erving. 1961. *Encounters: Two Studies in the Sociology of Interaction.* Indianapolis: Bobbs-Merrill.

Judah, J. Stillson. 1967. *The History and Philosophy of the Metaphysical Movements in America.* Philadelphia: Westminster Press.

Kituse, John I. 1962. Societal reaction to deviant behavior. *Social Problems* 9:247–56.

Lewison, Thea S. and Robert W. Balch. 1980. Bo and Peep: The tale of a modern religious odyssey. *Zeitschrift für Menschenkunde* 44:369–92.

Lofland, John. 1966. *Doomsday Cult.* Englewood Cliffs, N.J.: Prentice-Hall.

Mauss, Armand L. 1969. Dimensions of religious defection. *Review of Religious Research* 10:128–35.

Mills, C. Wright. 1940. Situated actions and vocabularies of motive. *American Sociological Review* 5:904–13.

Patrick, Ted. 1976. *Let Our Children Go!* New York: Ballantine.

Richardson, James T. 1975. New forms of deviancy in a fundamentalist church: A case study. *Review of Religious Research* 16:134–42.

Shupe, Anson D., Jr. and David G. Bromley. 1980. *The New Vigilantes: Deprogrammers, Anti-Cultists, and the New Religions.* Beverly Hills, Calif.: Sage.

Singer, Margaret Thaler. 1979. Coming out of the cults. *Psychology Today* (January): 72–82.

Skonovd, Norman. 1980. *Apostasy: The Process of Defection from Religious Totalism.* Ann Arbor, Mich.: University Microfilms.

———. 1979. Becoming apostate: A model of religious defection. Presented at the annual meeting of the Pacific Sociological Association, Anaheim, Calif.

Snow, David A. and Richard Machalek. 1982. On the presumed fragility of unconventional beliefs. *Journal for the Scientific Study of Religion* 21:15–26.

Snow, David A. and Cynthia L. Phillips. 1980. The Lofland-Stark conversion model: A critical reassessment. *Social Problems* 27:430–47.

Taylor, Bryan. 1976. Conversion and cognition: An area for empirical study in the microsociology of religious knowledge. *Social Compass* 23:5–22.

Wallis, Roy. 1975. Scientology: Therapeutic cult to religious sect. *Sociology* 9:89–100.

————. 1974. Ideology, authority, and the development of cultic movements. *Social Research* 41:299–327.

Wright, Stuart A. 1981. Deconversion and reality-transformation: A model of defection from new religious movements. Presented at the annual meeting of the Society for the Scientific Study of Religion, Baltimore, Md.

2
People Who Attend Unification Workshops and Do Not Become Moonies

Eileen Barker

I T is frequently asserted that conversion to the Unification Church is the result of brainwashing—that those who become Moonies do so because they have been subjected to some kind of irresistible mind control while attending a Unification workshop. Such assertions do not, however, offer any explanation as to why over 90% of those who attend the two-day introductory workshops in Britain (and most other centers in the West) do *not* end up as Moonies. The existence of this large, unconverted majority suggests that there must be a powerful differential susceptibility to the "lure of the cult" and that independent factors (that is, factors brought to the workshop by the guests) must be at least as crucial as the workshop in determining the final outcome.

This paper attempts an analysis of such factors by supplementing the more familiar question, "What are the values, hopes, and past experiences that predispose a person towards becoming a Moonie?" with the further, complementary question, "What are the factors which protect the vast majority of those who attend Unification workshops from falling victim to the alleged brainwashing techniques?" Through a comparison of the joiners and non-joiners in which we are able to hold as a constant the *objective* reality of the workshop situation, we shall be concerned with the *subjective* experience of the situation as our primary variable. Each individual will be seeing the workshop and the proffered vision of the Unification Church in the light of his predispositions and past experiences. The Moonies, like most evangelizers, will be trying as hard as they can to present the beliefs and practices of the movement in their most attractive and appealing light. For some of the guests they will succeed in creating a new *gestalt,* a new pair of glasses with which to see the world, a new vision of reality, a new meaning for existence, a new hope, or a new direction for the future. Life in the Unification Church will seem to offer a new security, a new family, a new kind of loving, or a new sense of identity. But for others all that the Moonies will be seen to be doing is (to borrow the phraseology of one vociferously eloquent informant) spewing out a load of boring old cod's wallop.

Participant Observation and Questionnaire Responses[1]

During the course of my five-year study of the Unification Church I attended numerous workshops. On these occasions one of my first self-appointed tasks was to try to predict which of the "guests" were likely to become Moonies, or at least to continue to a further workshop. I would make notes categorizing them as "probable," "possible," or "no-way." At first I failed rather miserably. I found, for example, that the argumentative young man who kept slipping outside for a quick smoke and whom I had classified as "no-way" would continue to the next stage, while the quiet, neatly-dressed girl whom I had thought looked rather like a Moonie (as I then perceived Moonies to be) would not continue. After some time, however, I developed a remarkably high rate of predictive accuracy. My trouble was the prediction rested (and to some extent still does) on a subjective feeling or recognition which I found difficult to verbalize, even to myself. I did eventually decide, however, that the intensity of interest or curiosity shown by the guest was one of the most important variables—irrespective of whether this took a positive or a negative form. The most effective "protection" undoubtedly seemed to be apathy, lack of interest, or boredom.

The next question then became why, when we were all listening to the same lecture, were some sitting on the edge of their chairs, listening with fascination, excitement, disgust, or disbelief to every word, while others were lost in a daydream, gazing out of the window, or glancing at their watches every five minutes? What were the different personalities, the different interests, the different experiences that were responsible for these different reactions?

Obviously, the people who turned up at a workshop were not representative of the population as a whole, nor, presumably, as not all of them became Moonies, were they likely to share all the characteristics of the Moonies. It seemed rational to assume that some sort of initial "natural selection" procedure would already have taken place. Workshop attenders seemed, for example, to share with the Moonies some easily recognizable characteristics with respect to such variables as age and social background. I had already compared Moonies with a control group of people who were not Moonies but whom I had "matched" for age and social background. Perhaps, I hypothesized, those who came to the workshop would form a group which occupied an *intermediate* position. As, for example, the Moonies were disproportionately male and from Catholic homes, might the workshop group contain more males and Catholics than the general population, but less males and Catholics than the Unification Church? If, for example, one were to find that two-thirds of the Moonies had considered a particular goal or value to be of great importance while only one-third of the control group had done so, might we expect roughly half of the workshop group to consider the goal or value to be of great importance?

Neither informal chats nor participant observation would supply the data necessary to test such hypotheses. Larger numbers and a more systematic comparability were needed. From application forms for workshop attendance in the London area during 1979, I was able to code for computer analysis the sex, occupation, date of birth, religious background, and nationality for 1,017 two-day workshop applicants. In addition to this information, by checking through various other lists and membership application forms, I was able to trace the "Unification careers" of these thousand or so persons. The careers were short-lived for the majority—there were more who left before the end of the initial two-day course than there were eventual converts. Roughly a third of the applicants went on to a seven-day workshop, about a fifth to a twenty-one-day course, and just over half of these then declared that they would join, although in fact they did not all do so. Out of the original 1,000, a *maximum* of 50 (19 of whom were British) were full-time members of the Church by the beginning of 1981. This number had dropped to a maximum of 36 by March 1982. This is probably an overstatement as it includes several people who had returned to their own countries saying they would join the church, but about whom no record of their continuing membership was available. The maximum number of affiliated members was 66 persons (48 by March 1982)—this figure including 9 (6 by 1982) Home Church members (who live in their own homes and follow an independent occupation but profess to accepting the teaching of the church) and 7 (6 by 1982) CARP members (students who are continuing their studies at a university or other place of further education and usually living with other CARP members in a center—CARP standing for Collegiate Association for the Research into Principles).

In other words by the end of 1980, of all those who had been sufficiently interested in the Unification Church to start a two-day workshop in the London area during the previous year, no more than 5% were full-time Moonies and no more than 7% were still affiliated with the movement. By March 1982 the percentage of survivors was a maximum of 3.6% for full-time Moonies and 4.8% for all affiliated persons.

In order to obtain further information about the workshop applicants, I persuaded the Moonies to allow me to use the addresses on the forms to send out a six-page questionnaire to the two-day applicants. This elicited a response of 136 questionnaires (only 131 of which were worth coding) 8 letters, and 6 telephone calls and an inquiry addressed to a colleague checking whether I was really a Moonie who had got hold of University of London note paper.

In an attempt to gauge how representative the respondents were of all the workshop attenders, the information on the application forms of those who filled in questionnaires was compared with the information on the forms of the entire applicant population. These data were then subjected to a chi-square significance test. Except in the case of nationality, those who had filled in the questionnaire did not differ significantly from the applicants as a whole. In other words, in much the same way as the vast majority of randomly selected samples would faithfully reflect the total population, questionnaire respondents reflected the total population of the two-day workshop applicants with respect to such variables as sex, age, religion and occupation. There was, however, some bias in favor of British and Irish respondents when the nationalities of the two groups were compared. This could be accounted for largely by the fact that questionnaires were not sent to the majority of overseas addresses, and that people from overseas tend to be a fairly transitory population while in Britain—two-thirds of the hundred or so envelopes which were returned unopened were addressed to people with non-British sounding names. This suggests that what bias there was could be explained by factors which were external to the person concerned rather than by his subjective response to the Unification Church. It is also true, however, that it would be more difficult for those whose native language is not English to fill in the questionnaire (two of those questionnaires which were uncodable were so because of obvious misunderstandings of the questions due to language difficulties).

However encouraging it is to learn that there is little significant bias in characteristics which are known, it is, of course, a bias in the characteristics which are *not* known which will always be of concern to those who have to work from samples. It must be admitted that this could well exist. It was reassuring, however, that the sample did contain a wide spread of reactions and "types" of respondents which seemed to reflect the range of reactions and types with which I had become familiar through talking to individuals at workshops. Neither the anti- nor the pro-Moonie, neither the caring nor the indifferent, were necessarily put off responding. Furthermore, the fact that the ratio of the non-joining to the "joining-and-still-some-sort-of-a-Moonie" re- spondents (100:7) reflected the ratio for the workshop applicants as a whole pretty accurately was another reassuring sign.

Because of this last fact, however, there were not enough Moonie respondents to provide a sufficiently large basis for a statistically significant comparison with the non-joiners. Accordingly, further questionnaires were sent to all those Moonies in Britain who had joined during 1979 or 1980. The final total of 217 usable questionnaires came from 64 people who were currently full-time Moonies, 11 Home Church members, 13 CARP members, 25 persons who joined and then left the movement, and 104 who never joined.

First Contact with Unification Church

For the majority of those who go to a workshop, the first contact they have with the Unification Church will be a meeting in the street or other public place. However, a quarter will be introduced to the movement by a friend or a relative and the rest will usually have been contacted in their homes by a Moonie knocking on the door. Those who became Home Church members were most likely to have been contacted in their own homes or by a relative (usually a son or daughter), but generally speaking, those who were introduced to the movement by a friend or relative were the least likely to end up joining, and they were also the people who, when persuaded to try out a seven-

or twenty-one-day workshop, were most likely to drop out before the end of the course. One also found the highest rate of antagonism expressed towards the movement by those introduced to it by friends, the most positive feelings being expressed by those who had first made contact in the street or a public place. This would seem to suggest that a "friendship network" explanation as to why people join a new movement is not particularly cogent in the case of the Unification Church in Britain. While a friendship with a Moonie may temporarily overcome the preliminary "natural selection" process which filters out the vast majority of non-joiners at the point of first contact (so that they do not even agree to attend a workshop), the persuasive powers of the workshop are not as effective on those selected by friends as they are on those who have agreed to attend because of other factors which, presumably, have a greater "resonance" with *their* (rather than a friend's) predispositions.

The myth that Moonies track their prey with attractive members of the opposite sex is not borne out by the British data. All the 1,017 application forms gave information about the person who had first contacted the applicant and analysis of these showed that opposite sex contacts were almost exactly balanced by same-sex contacts.

In answer to a question as to why they agreed to go to a workshop, a third of the respondents who were to join (and almost a half of those who were to join then leave) said they were actively seeking the truth and hoping to find it. Only a fifth of the non-joiners gave such a reason. While the joiners (and leavers) were slightly more likely to say that they thought the lectures might be interesting than were the non-joiners, the latter group was more likely to say they were curious about the members or had nothing better to do. Around one in ten of leavers and non-joiners said that it was the insistence of the members which made it hard to refuse to go to the workshop.

Over half of the respondents said that they had known that it was Reverend Moon's Unification Church before agreeing to go to the workshop (the percentage was higher among joiners, including leavers); but several of those who said that they had not known added a rider to the effect that they had not realized that it was Reverend Moon's movement although they had been told it was the Unification Church. Half of the respondents said that they had not heard about either the Unification Church or Moonies before they first went to a church center. Only 3% reported having heard anything good about the movement (and I suspect that this had been from Moonies). Almost everyone else who had heard anything had heard negative evaluations.

Very few factual details were known (this pattern of only having picked up a negative evaluation with little or no factual information mirrored the responses which had been given by my control group), but it may seem rather surprising that half of those who had heard anything, had heard that Moonies brainwash people—the interesting fact being not that they had heard this but that they had been prepared to attend a workshop with this information.

As might be expected, those who were to join the movement tended to declare that their experience did not substantiate what they had heard, but a third of the non-joiners also said that they had found what they had heard to be untrue, a further one-third saying they had found it only partly true and the final third saying it was either true, or mostly true.

Sex, Age and Class

In an earlier article[2] I demonstrated how, by controlling for age, sex, and social class, one could increase the statistical density of Moonies from 0.001% to 0.04% of the British population. In other words within the category of middle-middle and upper-middle class males aged between 21 and 26 the chance of finding a Moonie is roughly forty times greater than it is in the general population. We would, of course, still be a long way from selecting which one was the Moonie (and we would be leaving 80% of the British Moonies out of the search), but we would have been able to narrow the field down enough to make it pertinent to ask how far the composition of workshop attenders reflected a selection in the direction of the Moonie population with respect to these variables.

When we look at the sex distribution we see that the selection of roughly two males to every female has already occurred by the time people come to a two-day workshop. Men are more likely to leave immediately, women being more prepared to at least wait until the end of the course. It might also be noted that although fewer women than men join, those women who do join are more likely either to leave immediately or else to stay longer than the men. (Nearly all those who become student CARP members are male.)

As with sex, the main selection for age seems to have been carried out before the guests arrived for the workshop. Like the Moonies, workshop attenders tend to be in their early twenties, but they are not so tightly concentrated as the Moonies. It looks as though those who are to become Moonies are particularly "ripe" around the age of 22 or 23.

While it is sometimes argued that these people are particularly impres-
sionable because of their youth, so are therefore most likely to fall
victim to any mind control techniques, a histogram clearly shows that
the non-joiners are not only those who are older than the joiners—they
are also those who are younger. The short-term leavers do, however,
tend to be slightly older than the Moonies who stay in the movement
for a longer period. There are several possible reasons for this. It may be
that being older they find it easier to assert themselves and so leave once
they have to face the reality of Unification Church life; it may be that
they are the ones who are the "professional joiners and leavers" and
have grown old trying out all sorts of lifestyles without success; it may
be that Moonies who are still in the movement will in fact leave when
they, too, reach that age.

Again it looks as though initial selection procedures seem to have
been at work on the social class of the potential Moonie before he or
she reaches the workshop, the majority coming from the middle-class.
There is, however, an interesting further selection that is to take place
after this initial stage. This is observable if one does not make the
distinction according to a crude manual/non-manual division, but
according to degrees of responsibility and the kinds of values that are
associated with the father's occupation. A higher proportion of joiners
than non-joiners come from the upper working class which contains
skilled workers, often in positions of considerable responsibility. Over
twice as many non-joiners as joiners have fathers in the more routine
non-manual (lower middle-class) occupations; but non-joiners are also
twice as likely to have come from the *upper* middle class. Leavers are the
only group which had (just) a majority of fathers in manual occupations, 48% coming from the middle or lower middle classes. Non-
joiners' fathers are more likely than joiners' fathers to be involved in
occupations which are concerned with making money (such as the
stock exchange).

Protections and Propensities

In several ways it would seem that the non-joining group contains *both*
a sub-group which is "protected" from joining because it does *not*
contain certain characteristics embodied in the Moonie population, *and*
a sub-group which contains these characteristics to a *greater* degree
than the Moonies. It is as though, while the workshop does gather in
those who are more predisposed towards Unification Church beliefs
and practices than the general population, if the characteristics go

beyond a particular stage, strength, or level then they acquire what the economists would call a negative marginal utility. We have already seen, for example, that while youth is an important predisposing factor, the youngest cohorts are less rather than more likely to join.

This negative marginal utility factor is even more obvious among those who join and leave within a short time than it is among the non-joiners. It is as if those who are the candidates most likely to be susceptible to the Moonies' techniques, according to proponents of the brainwashing/mind control thesis, are indeed the ones selected at the initial stages from the general population, but they are also the ones who are subsequently rejected by, or will themselves reject, the Moonie environment. This is, for example, apparent in the degree to which the workshop guests could be classified as religious "seekers" (30% of the non-joiners, 50% of the leavers, 45% of the continuing members).

It is probable that the greatest protection against conversion for a guest in a *European* Unification workshop is atheism. (This is less clearly the case in California where the lectures given by the "Oakland Family" have not been so obviously based on the theological tenets of Unification thought.) Among the questionnaire respondents none of the full-time joiners (8% of the non-joiners) said that they definitely did not believe in God at the time they went to the workshop and only 6% (8% of the leavers and 18% of non-joiners) coded "not really." Two-thirds of joiners and one-half of non-joiners had "definitely believed in God." The leavers as a group held the strongest belief.

Although denominational differences between joiners and non-joiners do occur, the most important factor seemed to be that the Christian tradition—perhaps accepting the Bible as a source of revelation—while not exactly a necessary condition, is at least conducive to joining in England. The small number of Jews and Muslims who come to the workshops tend to leave before they finish. Hindus are slightly less inclined to do so, their comments suggesting that they see many ways to God and for some the *Divine Principle* might be described as "acceptable" rather than the truth. The overweighting of Catholics in relation to the wider society which is found in the Unification Church is reflected among the workshop attenders but this is not an over-weighting if one takes church membership, rather than nominal affiliation, as a reference group, and takes into account the nationality of the workshop attenders (and, more especially, that of their fathers). In other words, it is coming from a Catholic country and being actively involved with religion which would seem to be more pertinent "selectors" than Catholicism *per se,* the apparent "protection" offered, relatively speaking, by Church of England membership being more traceable to the loose use made of that label than to any particular characteristics of Anglican dogma or practices.

The non-joining group contained more people who never went to church during childhood or (less markedly) during the period before attending the workshop than either Moonies or the control group which, it will be remembered, consisted of persons "matched" with Moonies on such characteristics as age and social background but who had had no personal contact with the movement. But there were a few more non-joining workshop attenders than control group who attended frequently in early childhood. Respondents from *all* the groups in the study expressed disillusionment with established religious institutions, but this did not mean that they might not still have been trying to find something in a church as a considerably larger proportion (of Moonies in particular) were attending a place of worship more frequently than the general population.

Of the workshop questionnaire respondents, Moonies were the least likely, and leavers the most likely, to have "shopped around" in different organizations or movements before joining the workshop. Non-joiners had the greatest percentage of respondents trying out secular movements, especially political ones (in which Moonies tended not to have been particularly interested).

All the respondents were asked to assess the extent to which they thought important, and were actively seeking a set of nine different values. Few people put a "high standard of living" high on their list of priorities, the leavers valuing it least of all. "Success in their careers" was most important for the non-joiners but it was also very important for the majority of the control group; neither leavers (in particular) nor Moonies valued their careers so highly—though a few had valued them very highly indeed.

"Better relations" were important to all groups but least by the leavers and the non-joiners and most by the control group; and "ideal marriage" was sought after less by non-joiners than by joiners, leavers, or the control group. Moonies, and especially leavers, claim to have been more actively seeking and to have considered "improving the world" more important than either non-joiners or the control group. For all groups "control over one's own life" was the most important of the values. This was particularly so for leavers (58%), slightly less so for the control group and Moonies (49%), and least so for non-joiners (33%). Both "spiritual fulfillment" and "understanding God" were, quite markedly, most important first for the leavers, then for the

Moonies, then for the non-joiners, and least important for the control group.

The greatest discrepancy between the groups showed up when they were asked to rate the importance of "something but don't know what." The majority of Moonies claimed to have considered this very important and to have been actively seeking it at the time of attending the workshop—a considerable, but smaller, proportion of the leavers made a similar claim. Although a third of the non-joiners said it was important and they were seeking it, more of them said that they did not think about it at all (and probably thought the question rather daft). This might suggest the hypothesis that some of those who were to become Moonies go to a workshop with an already existing gap waiting to be filled—in other words society has already done some "brainwashing" but has not offered anything with which to fill the vacuum it has created. It may be that while not just anything can be "poured into" the void, those who are to leave have a slightly clearer idea of what it was they were seeking than had some of the Moonies.

Next to atheism, it is possible that the most effective "protection" against the lure of the Unification Church is having a stable or permanent relationship with another person. The majority of people in all the groups were most likely to spend their leisure time with a few close friends (rather than by themselves or in a large group). While Moonies were slightly more likely than members of the control group to have spent their time by themselves, the non-joiners and especially the leavers were even *more* likely than the Moonies to have been isolated in the period six months before the workshop. In their subjective (retrospective) assessments of happiness during that period, Moonies as a group were less likely to have been very happy than were the members of the control group at the time of filling in the questionnaires. Non-joiners also tended to have been happier than the Moonies (Home Church members in particular said they had been unhappy). Leavers were the least happy of all the groups during their childhood and adolescence.

Considering the youth of the respondents it was hardly surprising that over 80% of all groups said that they enjoyed either excellent or good physical health. Full-time Moonies were most inclined to claim that their health was now excellent, although slightly more of them had suffered some sort of illness in the past. Leavers had the poorest health.

The numbers of those who reported any kind of psychiatric problem was small in all groups, by far the highest percentage (22%) being in the group of immediate leavers. Next were the non-joiners (16%), then the Home Church members (12%), then full-time Moonies (5%). None of the CARP members reported having had any such problems. Most of the cases were of a mild depression; only ten respondents to the workshop questionnaire said their illness had been severe enough to seek medical help, seven of these were non-joiners, two immediate leavers and one became a full-time member. In the earlier comparison I had made between a far larger number of "established" Moonies and the control group, 14% of the Moonies and 12% of the control group had reported some history of psychiatric problems; this had been severe in the case of 6% of the Moonies and 7% of the control group.

On another, albeit highly subjective level the research assistant who coded the questionnaires was asked to give an overall impression of each respondent. Four-fifths of the Moonies, and half of the non-joiners and the leavers were placed in the "nice, ordinary boy/girl next door" category; 5% of the Moonies, 15% of the non-joiners and 8% of the leavers were typecast as "mildly peculiar" and 4% of the non-joiners and 8% of the leavers were coded "psychopathologically peculiar"; 5% of the Moonies, 4% of the non-joiners, and 16% of the leavers were seen as "rather sad and pathetic."

The respondents were far more educated than the general population, over half of all the groups having been educated up to or beyond the age of 20. Leavers tended to have been educated for either less or for more time than the Moonies or the non-joiners, but they were less likely to have had further education at a university. As a group, Moonies got better grades than the non-joiners or leavers, but the non-joiners could be sub-divided into those who did slightly better than the average Moonie and those who did considerably worse. The leavers tended to have the poorest grades and to be the most individually erratic in their results.

Over half the Moonies (59%) and non-joiners (53%) and 64% of the leavers were qualified for some sort of job. Most frequently the qualifications for all groups, but particularly for leavers, were of a lower professional type (such as school teacher or nurse), but within other categories non-joiners were more likely to have clerical-type or semi-skilled manual qualifications while the joiners (Moonies and leavers) were more likely to have "lower technical" or responsible manual skills. Exactly a third of the non-joiners, slightly fewer Moonies and slightly more leavers were not either students or in paid employment at the time of attending the workshop. The non-joiners (41%) and the leavers (40%) were more likely than those who were to become full-time Moonies (23%) to have been students at the time of the workshop, but of course nearly all those who were to become CARP members were already students. At the time of the workshop, the Moonies had been the least and the leavers the most settled retrospectively, but prospectively short-term leavers were the least and Moonies the most settled— that is, leavers were likely to have had settled jobs in the past but to have been uncertain about their future, while Moonies were slightly more likely to have had definite career prospects ahead of them.

Thus far I have attempted to indicate some of the already existing differences between those who, as a result of attending a workshop were to become Moonies, those who were to join then leave, and those who were not to join at all. Some of these differences were described in comparison either to characteristics of a control group of similar age and background or to characteristics of the British population as a whole. Further quantitative findings have been reported elsewhere.[3]

In the next section an attempt will be made to indicate the range of subjective experiences of the workshop participants by quoting some of their comments, most of which were written in response to "open questions" in the questionnaire.

The Workshop Experience

The number of guests at a workshop will range from one to thirty or possibly even more at a "peak" period such as the summer or Easter vacations. Most frequently there are between eight and twelve guests and then, on the Unification Church side, there will be a lecturer and his assistant and perhaps two other members of the staff and two more Moonies who will be in charge of domestic arrangements, including the kitchen. The guests may be accompanied by the person who first introduced them to the movement, but this is by no means always the case. A brief schedule for the two-day workshop is given in Appendix 1.

The intention in this section being to inject a qualitatively subjective flavor into the paper in order to illustrate the diversity of the workshop experiences. No attempt will be made to assess the quotations for objective accuracy—indeed to do so would be to miss the whole point of the present exercise. But, bearing in mind the methodological dangers of selecting examples for descriptive purposes, an indication of the relative frequencies of the different kinds of assessments made in response to some pre-coded questions is to be found in the tables in appendix 2.

From these tables it will be noticed that while the lectures were an important and appreciated factor for the joiners (including those who were to leave), there was less enthusiasm from the non-joiners. Among the non-joiners who employed the "other" category for what they liked best, 4% said they liked nothing, 5% said they liked everything, and indeed most of the remaining "other" answers reflected the diversity of subjective experiences by frequently having their counterpart in the "other" response given by someone else to the question asking what they liked *least* about the workshop. Thus for quite a few people the food seemed to be the high point of their stay, while for others it was the major source of complaint; while one non-joiner could write that he had particularly liked the "eccentric modes of behavior e.g., running across the common at 6:45 before breakfast and listening to Beethoven over lunch," another would write:

> The childish games went on and nobody could refuse to do things whether they were asked to sing or dance and were all made to feel like children. But my character will not allow me to do these things and I became unpopular (the members would say I was typical English and that (I) did not know how to enjoye [sic] myself but I could see everyone making fools of themselfs [sic].

It was pretty clear from responses to the open questions that the primary assessment of the workshops rested upon the respondents' evaluation of the truth of the Divine Principle. There were a few non-joiners who said that they thought that Unification theology was the truth but that they did not feel they were prepared to join. There was, for example, one respondent who wrote that she had had quite a frightening shock when what she had come to perceive as the truth was revealed to her:

> I feel that people condemn the UC because they will not admit that what the members say makes sense, probably fear is in most people's minds. The members have answers to all questions, answers that are so real that one does tend to get a little fearful. Most people like to pop along on a Sunday evening and say a few prayers and sing a few hymns and they think they have done their duty. I am the worst culprit, I don't even do that! Most people are not dedicated enough to join this church. Some won't even listen, they are too busy trying to persecute them. . . . I am aware (acutely) of God's presence, in my life. I know what I ought to do but I do not do it. It is too much for me to comprehend I feel. The Unification Church DO know the answers, there is NO doubt in my mind on that, and there are very few things that I can say I am not doubtful about.
> P.S. They have not brainwashed me by the way!

Another respondent, admitting that it was for selfish reasons he had not joined (he had put "not being able to smoke inside" as the thing he had liked least about the workshop), wrote: "I thoroughly believe in the UC and that the other churches are both ignorant and arrogant toward the UC. The UC has God in their hearts and not just in their mouths."

Many of the respondents felt that they could accept a great deal of the theology but had some doubts about certain aspects of it—particularly the idea that Sun Myung Moon could be the messiah. One respondent who had agreed to join and then decided not to (partly because of parental pressure) wrote:

> I still think a great deal of them. Although all contact with them is over. They really are lovely people from all accounts trying to make a better world. But the question of Rev. Moon comes into it and I cannot accept him; and of course if you can't accept him that destroys the whole argument. Unfortunately with the Moonies it's all or nothing. Which is a shame, as they are wonderful people.

Another respondent agreed to join as a Home Church member but then changed her mind:

> There were parts of the teachings that I felt some doubt about, and felt that to be a UC member I needed to give 100% of myself but I was not willing to do so—my career etc. I think more people should look at UC because some of their ways and ideas are good. When I decided not to join full time I was not pressurised to stay but allowed to do what I wanted to do.

At the other end of the spectrum there were those people who were violently opposed to the movement. There was, for example, the man who had converted to Christianity at the age of fifteen. It had, he said, meant something for a little while, "but cooled off as I faced new temptations of sex and drugs and rock and roll which seemed to offer greater excitements and fulfillment." About the Unification Church he wrote:

> The UC is evil. I hate everything about it. I don't blame the members—they are victims of some dark satanic force. I'm glad I was challenged, and was able to resist. People shouldn't be subjected to this sort of thing. We should be free to walk down a street without being emotionally assaulted by these Moon-worshippers.

A Jamaican woman who was lonely and thought that the Unification Church was a debating society where she could have interesting discussions and make new friends dismissed the experience with the words, "I thought it was a load of intellectual clap trap. I couldn't accept the written philosophy. It seemed pseudo-intellectual."

The majority of people, however, were more inclined to show some kind of respect for the status of the teachings, even when they did not accept them. Often the respondents would compare them with other beliefs. One fairly typical response came from a Malaysian who said that he did not continue to the seven-day course because he "couldn't find the time. Besides can't live for seven days with so much holiness." He wrote:

> I find the UC's belief is much more logical than others and has better solutions to some problems. Like others they believe in love and peace. But they certainly try and have a good way of achieving it. Of course I do find some of their "theories" "unbelievable". If you get to *understand* more religions, you'll find it hard to tell which is the truth!!

Another respondent said that he had not continued to the seven-day workshop because it was "too expensive (£15) also tedious to listen to things one could not accept when they would not argue constructively." He commented:

> My impression is divided between my own experiences and the media's "version". My experience has not been wide enough to see the dubious financial base or Moon's politics or the changed character of the estranged children of concerned parents. The Moonies did not seem to have lost their rationality except that they fervently accepted Moon's doctrine. To me an Anglican vicar appears equally irrational except his arguments are based on more serious scholarship and study of the bible. Apart from this I envy the UC members for not being part of our society like other communes.

A further fairly typical response came from a highly educated Indian:

> UC's beliefs as far as I can judge are nothing new: they contain the good points which are basic to all major religions, however, what they are trying to achieve is to involve people, irrespective of their religious backgrounds, nationality or ethnic grouping, which is definitely needed in our modern day world. I believe in good humanitarian aims in general and in overall harmony, but can't accept anything or any principle blindly. Its members are good, sincere and devoted workers.

Several of the evaluations of the theology gave clues as to the kinds of "protection" with which the respondents might have come to the workshop. There was, for example, the tolerant indifference of the British lapsed Catholic who wrote, "Nothing wrong with it, if you like that type of thing. I was bored." And there were those who were already confirmed in their beliefs—beliefs which could take various forms. There was, for example, a Marxist community worker: "A capitalist venture camouflaged in a kind of religious revelation. Mr. Moon thinks of himself as a second Christ which is rubbish. Waste of time." And there was the French atheist:

> They are not stupid. I find the ideal of brotherhood fine. But it is difficult to approve such beliefs when you don't believe in any deity. On the whole (the members are) sensible people, agreeable, nice, open to other people's ideas etc. But I wouldn't like to share their way of life. I want to achieve my spiritual fulfilment myself.

And there was the seventy-seven year old inveterate searcher: "So far Theosophy is the nearest to satisfy me. But I search and keep an open mind on other teachings." And there was the "True Believer":

> Boring, very claustrophobic and I found no truth at all. The truth was not there. In one month they could turn your mind into a cabbage. The members have *no* longer minds of their [sic] own. Their beliefs are of the mind but not of the hard [sic]. The church and its practices is *just* for money . . . My faith is in God and *Christ said blessed is he who hears my word and keeps it,* and he who keeps the commandments shall have eternal life.

As will already be apparent, many of the respondents found themselves liking or admiring the members, sometimes feeling rather sorry for them, perhaps, but generally acknowledging their commitment and dedication. A few respondents talked of individual Moonies whom they had not liked, and one or two dismissed all Moonies as brainwashed zombies, but the most frequent criticisms levelled against the Moonies were that they were *too* nice and *too* dedicated. One fairly typical comment came from a young woman who had a Moonie relative: "Well the members are nice people and most of them, like X, are truly believers in the beliefs, but who knows what there is behind the organisation? . . . Why are they so kind? . . . too kind . . ." Another respondent was put off by the general lack of realism he found:

I think that its beliefs are too "positive" to have any significance on the
everyday life of today. Their values and practices cannot possibly be
relevant to present day society. The members seem to me to be on cloud
9 trying to escape reality on the whole! To me they are too "nice" and
"good" and "obliging" for me to be able to relate to them as real people."

And there was the African who had only been in the country for three
months and said he had not really fitted into the society and (despite the
fact that he had heard that the Unification Church "were a sect not
unlike the Rev. Jim Jones's catastrophe in Guyana") had agreed to go
on the seven-day course because he "got bored staying at home and it
was a chance to see places outside London and live on a farm." He got
as far as starting the twenty-one-day course but did not finish it
because:

It was too much time to waste on a thing the essence of which I don't
agree with and I got bored with the lectures. I don't agree with their
teachings or the methods employed; they stress too much on making
people feel guilty and since they dogmatically believe in their principle
the people themselves become boring to talk to.
The members themselves are nice and fraternal people but rather
boring and uninteresting to talk to because they are enthusiastic about
one subject only—their Divine Principle.

Some respondents reported feeling rather hurt or disappointed that
they seemed to be unable to continue a friendship with a Moonie once
they had said that they were not going to join, but many others
reported that they still kept in touch with one or two, often claiming to
maintain a deep, spiritual relationship with their Moonie friends. One
fairly extreme case was that of the Briton who confessed:

I must be honest that I fell in love with one of the members and had
decided that I had met the perfect match. Even though I am extremely
anti-Unification Church I still keep in touch with her in her own country.
It is my conclusion that she being involved in the church has moved away
from her family and therefore comes more to rely on the Church. After a
recent programme on the Church I got in touch with her, trying to tell
her the truth, but to no avail.

A more commonly cited experience was:

Within two weeks of my becoming acquainted with one of its members I
realized that my hope of making friends on a social basis was quite
unrealistic. Since this was the reason I had agreed to go to the workshop,

I decided fairly quickly that I could not benefit from its superficial overflow of joy for mankind. Most of its members were so happy on the surface that people like me were forced to adopt a cynical attitude if only because it was impossible to reconcile what we had heard from the press with our present experiences. In spite of this initial turn off I was still very impressed by the dedication of many of its members. I still receive regular letters from the person who introduced me to the church—all the way from (Africa). Instead of sending stereotype forms asking you to contact them they send very personal messages about their hopes, fears, and spiritual desires. This very positive attitude towards thinking about themselves—and the fact that many of them travel world-wide to spread their news—really does deserve my admiration (even if I do not agree with everything they say).

And a fairly typical comment from a woman who had joined and then left was:

In a nutshell, the UC members are basically good and sound people being totally led up the garden path. If the spiritual energy expounded by these people was channelled into a Christian movement (instead of "fake Christian" movement) the world would truly benefit from their work.

The longer term effects of the workshop experience are examined in the next section, but some examples might be given here to illustrate the range of more immediate emotional responses elicited by the Unification Church. The most disturbing account of a respondent's reaction was not as the result of a workshop experience but came from a woman who had joined and then left:

When I went to London to work about two years ago, I became very interested in spiritualism. I had always felt there was more to life. Spiritualism answered a lot of questions for me, e.g. was God really a condemning God, the true meaning of Heaven and Hell. Man's free will and karma. I also had a deep feeling for Jesus Christ. Who was he really—was he meant to die. In the [Unification] Church I studied the mission of Christ. The results of the deep study upset me very much. Everything became acutely out of proportion. I felt that man was so evil, that I was better off taking my life than living in this world.

For another woman who became a Home Church member the opportunity to talk about the spirit world and life after death brought her feelings of immense relief; "For the first time in my life I have met people who did not think I was strange to talk about such things."

Among the non-joiners the reactions reported as a result of the workshop ranged from: "I was stunned by being thrown into the outside world again after the workshop. My entire concentration had been in the artificial environment at Greenwich: no papers, television, etc.," to: "[the workshop] was one of my best spent weekends." As had already been mentioned, several of the non-joiners found the experience boring, but several others found it highly stimulating. Some people felt irritated and/or frustrated: "They only wanted to tell me what they wanted me to know. I wanted them to tell me what I wanted to know." Others felt gratitude and interest:

> I learned a lot from the two-day workshop. I did not go with the intention of changing my religion [RC] but to help me understand it more. It helped me a lot.
>   As for "brainwashing" I don't believe it. I was not forced to do anything I did not wish to do.

Several people made a point of saying that accusations of brainwashing were obviously rubbish, but some did say they had felt watched or pressured—for non-joiners this tended either to take the form of irritation at the Moonies' controlling the environment in ways such as saying what to do when, or not allowing people to ask questions when they wanted to, or else it took the form of concern for guests other than the respondent himself: "I was terrified by the very young age of many of the people who were being brought to the workshops, youngsters who were easily influenced." It is from the ranks of those who joined and then left that one is most likely to find those with a deeper fear of having themselves been influenced: "I wonder sometimes whether my thoughts are my own or whether they are there because they have been put there."

In this section none of the quotations has been made by respondents who were full-time members of the Unification Church at the time of filling in the questionnaire. This is partly because the paper is not about conversion experiences but is more concerned with the subjective experiences of the non-joiners. It might however be helpful for comparative purposes to finish with a couple of brief examples from those who became committed Moonies. First there was the medical student who wrote:

> Right from the start I felt it was the truth. For a long time I asked questions which no one but the UC answer. I believe that anyone who

hears this new truth from God and does nothing about it knowing how much we need help in this messy world needs a good wollup.

And, finally, there was the English woman who had been a nun for two-and-a-half years and who said she agreed to go on to a seven-day workshop because: "After a month from two-day w/s I, was almost convinced it was the truth—after a theological and prayerful struggle with myself. And so I wanted to find out more (so I could decide on further information)." She agreed to go on a twenty-one-day workshop because, she claims: "After seven-day w/s I knew it was the truth." She then agreed to join "Because it is the Way, the Truth and the Light!" Talking about difficulties in relating to many people, she mentioned that she had developed a problem of speaking much too quickly: "Sometimes I still retain these problems, but already I feel far more free to be myself and to be understood and accepted without barriers."

The Non-Conversion Experience

Thus far the only consequence for non-joiners which we have considered was that they *were* non-joiners. It would, however, be a mistake to assume that the workshop is nothing more than a passing non-event (although one inveterate seeker did write a letter claiming that he had been to so many of these sorts of things that he was not really sure that he could remember which had been the Unification Church).

Unintended consequences can be as interesting as intended purposes. Non-joiners may not have become converted, but it does not follow that they were unaffected by the workshop. Indeed, when they were asked whether they felt that they had changed in any way as a result of attending the workshops, a third of the non-joiners said that they felt they had and a further quarter answered "perhaps." (Not surprisingly, those who had joined and those who had joined and then left were even more likely to claim that they had changed as a result of the experience.)

Well over half the non-joiners who admitted to a possible change said that they had become more convinced of the truth of some religious belief other than that of the Unification Church (e.g., "I have become stronger in my Catholic religion"); 26% saying that this was as a *negative* reaction to Unification teachings: "It has made me more aware of false christs as prophesised in 'Revelations' (New Testament) . . . and has made me look at the Bible more closely . . . it has been a marvellous education and confirmation of the one and only true Bible;"

and 20% saying that hearing the *Principle* had been a *positive* help in their understanding of their religious beliefs; and 25% claiming to have actually discovered God or to have been given a renewed experience of God as a result of attending the workshop: "Now I have a very firm belief in God"; "I now can talk deeper about God and know more things about him"; "My faith in God has grown stronger"; "More stable in my religious belief." Disbelief also could be reinforced: "[I now] hate everything to do with religion and my past values and beliefs were greatly strengthened."

Concentrating on more secular changes, 15% of the non-joiners said that they were happier or more contented in some way: "I came out of my depression and no longer take tablets. I am bright and alert as never in my life before"; "More optimistic." On the other hand 11% said that they had become unsettled or unhappy: "Bad tempered sometimes, unsure of life in general, edgy"; and a further 11% intimated that they had learned to be more careful in the future: "Less naive—more cautious about this sort of thing"; "I used to be very friendly and trusting. Now I am more suspicious."

Several people felt that they had improved, having learned how to become better people as a result of the workshop: "I seem to look at things differently. I still pray. I had morals anyway, but they have been upheld even more strongly"; "I feel I can discipline myself much more—and care for more people unselfishly—plus many personal changes."

Many felt that they had become more open-minded or recognized the need for open-mindedness: "Now appreciate more other people's beliefs"; "I think a lot more and question most things"; "Opened my mind to religion, but not blinded my view. For I can see both sides of the coin, unlike some who only see one"; "Opened my eyes to unexplored avenues"; "The workshop did not change me to the extent of making me want to join but made me more aware of the need for a greater understanding and a greater fellowship between churches."

One or two said that while they themselves had remained immune, they were worried about those who had not had their strength: "I have not changed. But I have realized how easy it is to influence people with certain ideas." One person was rather unsure as to whether he might or might not have been affected: ". . . what I was told in the lectures subconsciously affecting the way I think perhaps."

So much for the comments of those who did not join. It is hardly surprising that some of those who had joined and then left were forcefully resentful of the effect that the Unification Church had wrought in their lives: "At the time I joined I felt I had something worth living and working for . . . After I left the workshop, I saw everything from a completely different viewpoint . . . Everything seemed very evil . . ." She continued in a letter:

> I would also like to say that I left the movement about five months ago. At first I really didn't think that I was going to survive. The Unification Church strips you completely of your ego. You become very frightened of life. I left with X. He has suffered the same reactions. Since then we both feel more able to cope, although there are of course occasions when we both revert back to this childlike fear and acute depression. Our faith in God and the Spirit world have not been completely destroyed.

Another leaver wrote:

> As an ex-Moonie I am not bitter towards the members but astonished, rather, at my own gullibility. I think if I had not left when I did it may possibly have been too late. After making the decision that I had to get out or sink because I could no longer swim with the movement, I truly found myself doubting my sanity—even now, after having left six months, I find myself wondering what they will do next!

Perhaps it was more surprising to find that the majority of those who had joined then left still saw the experience in positive terms:

> I [now, because of the UC] believe in God, the Bible, Jesus, spiritualism and the probability that Rev. Moon is what the UC claims him to be. I have a guide line by which to set my life morally and feel more capable of responsibilities of life.

Another person who left wrote, "I feel I think more deeply—to a degree I feel my morals are higher." Another wrote that ". . . my views on relationships between people has altered. I find I am trying not to be so self-centered. Perhaps I am still searching to find the truth." Another leaver wrote, "I understand better why I should love other people and the need for helping others less well off than me." Finally, another leaver wrote, "I became more sensitive generally about life and more open-minded."

Whether or not the respondents have indeed changed in the sorts of ways they claim to have changed and to what extent, if they have so changed such changes are indeed attributable to the Unification Church is not something that the present data can tell us. The responses do, however, indicate that the social context of the workshop might well result in a not inconsiderable variety of influences which affect the subjective experiences (at least) of the participant in ways other than that of ensuring his life-long membership in the movement—one ironic twist of fate being the possibility that more persons are convinced of non-Unification beliefs than are brought to Unification beliefs through the offices of the Unification workshop. It is not inconceivable that the Unification Church's techniques of persuasion are, numerically speaking, less effective in swelling the ranks of Moonies than they are in swelling the ranks of other religions.

Summary

The focus of this paper arises from the fact that more than nine out of ten of those who attend a Unification two-day workshop do not join the movement and that this suggests that factors *brought to* the workshop by the guests are likely to be the most important determinants of the final outcome.

It was suggested that while a selective process had already been brought into play at the point of initial contact, certain other selective factors came into operation during the workshop experience. In the case of the British workshop the greatest "protection" would seem to stem from a boredom with the lectures and a lack of interest in the alternative views and way of life offered by the movement. This in turn would seem to be strongest among those who are uninterested or uncommitted to religious, or, more specifically, biblically based answers to personal and social problems. An already strongly held set of beliefs if unambiguously held can also offer some, though not as much, protection. Those who already have an established, strong personal relationship with another person are also likely to be less attracted to the church. But while certain factors which are frequently presumed to be associated with suggestibility or need (like youthfulness, seekership, isolation, history of psychiatric problems, or boredom) might select people for attending a workshop, these were not necessarily precipitating factors for joining. Indeed, such factors might have a negative marginal utility in that they selected people *out* rather than *into* the movement. The variety of subjective experiences of the workshop situation further reinforces the probability that the guests' values or social background, their predispositions, and their presuppositions about society were operating actively in this selection/protection process.

The argument underlying this essay has been addressed to those who wish to insist that conversion to the Unification Church is due solely, or even predominantly, to the irresistibly manipulative techniques employed at the workshops. The data challenge such people to answer the question: How is it that these techniques are so successfully resisted by the ones who got away?

Appendix 1

Timetable for typical weekend workshop, UK

Arrive Friday afternoon or evening. No formal arrangements.

Saturday

7:45	Rise
8:15	Excercise or walk in park
9:00	Breakfast
10:15	Lecture I
11:30	Coffee break
11:45	Lecture II
1:00	Break
1:15	Lunch

Afternoon playing games or taking a walk

5:00	Lecture II
6:30	Break
7:00	Dinner
8:00	Singing, entertainment, band, etc.
10:00	Break
11:30	Bed

Sunday

As Saturday morning but often with service rather than first lecture

1:00	Lunch

Afternoon short walk

3:00	Final Lecture (V)
4:30	Discussion and break up for people to go home

Appendix 2

Reactions to 2-day Workshop

(Figures are given in percentage, but do not add up to 100% in (1) as some respondents coded more than one option. In (1) and (2) "everything" and "nothing" were not precoded options but were in sufficient responses to create a separate category for coding.)

	Non-joiners N = 104	Leavers N = 25	Full-time joiners N = 64
(1) What did you like most about the 2-day workshop?			
The lectures	24	57	52
The people	31	11	31
The general atmosphere	34	35	35
Everything	5	4	6
Nothing	5	–	–
Other	9	–	2
(2) What did you like least about the 2-day workshop?			
The lectures	43	32	16
The people	15	5	5
The general atmosphere	14	5	5
Nothing	8	26	46
Other	20	31	20

(3) How would you rate your reaction to the
following during the 2-day workshop?

(a) *the lectures*:

You thought they were the truth	9	44	63
Quite a lot of truth, but you couldn't accept it all	40	44	30
Interesting, but you did not accept their truth	43	8	8
Boring and uninteresting	4	–	–
Nothing but a load of rubbish	5	4	–

(b) *the members*:

Really nice people whom you liked a lot	53	60	84
One or two you liked, others not so much	27	36	13
You found them rather strange and peculiar	18	4	3
You did not like them at all	2	–	–

(c) *the general atmosphere*:

Friendly and homey	52	68	61
Stimulating and exciting	8	12	31
Quite pleasant, but not really your cup of tea	29	20	8
Oppressive, claustrophobic, frightening	12	–	–

Notes

1. The research upon which this paper is based has been carried out with funds from the Social Science Research Council of Great Britain, to whom I wish to express my gratitude. Further details of the methods employed in this study (participant observation, in-depth interviews, and questionnaires) can be found in Eileen Barker, *The Making of a Moonie: Brainwashing or Choice* (Oxford: Blackwell, 1984); "Confessions of a Methodological Schizophrenic: Problems Encountered in the Study of Rev. Sun Myung Moon's Unification Church," *Institute for the Study of Worship and Religious Architecture Research Bulletin* (University of Birmingham, 1978); or "The Professional Stranger: Some Methodological Problems Encountered in a Study of the Reverend Sun Myung Moon's Unification Church," Open University Course Media Notes for D207: *An Introduction to Sociology*, O.U., 1980; or "Der professionelle Fremde: Erklärung des Unerklärichen beim Studium einer abweichenden religionsen Gruppe," *Das Entstehen einer neuen Religion: Das Beispiel der Vereinigungskirche*, edited by Gunter Kehrer (Munich: Kosel-Verlag, 1981).

2. "Who'd Be a Moonie? A Comparative Study of those who join the

92

Unification Church in Britain," in *The Social Impact of New Religious Movements,* edited by Bryan Wilson (Barrytown, N.Y.: Unification Theological Seminary, 1981). Other papers resulting from the study include "Living the Divine Principle: Inside the Reverend Sun Myung Moon's Unification Church in Britain," *Archives de Sciences Sociales des Religions* 45 (1): 75–93, (1978); "Whose Service is Perfect Freedom: The Concept of Spiritual Well-Being in Relation to the Reverend Sun Myung Moon's Unification Church in Britain," *Spiritual Well-Being,* edited by David O. Moberg (Washington, D.C.: University Press of America, 1979), 153–71; "Free to Choose? Some Thoughts on the Unification Church and Other New Religious Movements," pt. 1, *Clergy Review* (October 1980):365–68, pt. 2 (November 1980):392–98; "Who Draws the Lines Where?" *Intermedia* 9 (2):12–14: (March 1981); "With Enemies Like that . . . : Some Functions of Deprogramming as an Aid to Sectarian Membership," in *The Brainwashing-Deprogramming Controversy: Sociological, Psychological, Legal and Historical Perspectives,* edited by David G. Bromley and James T. Richardson (Lewiston, N.Y.: Edwin Mellen Press, 1984).
3. See especially "Who'd Be a Moonie" and *The Making of a Moonie: Brainwashing or Choice.*

3
Conflicting Networks: Guru and Friend in ISKCON

Larry D. Shinn

N their essay, "Networks of Faith . . . " (1980), Rodney
Stark and William Bainbridge argue that older sociological models of deprivation theories which focus on the
ideological appeal of so-called "cults" or New Religious Movements
(NRM) must be supplemented by theories which place more emphasis
on interpersonal relationships and contacts to explain the joining
process. Calling this latter approach the "network model," Stark and
Bainbridge say: "It argues that faith constitutes conformity to the
religious outlook of one's intimates—that membership spreads through
social networks" (1980, 1377). In broadening their claim even further,
they say: " . . . not merely cult and sect recruitment, but commitment
to conventional faiths as well, is supported by social networks" (1376).

Building upon the 1965 study of the Moonies by Stark and Lofland
(1965), Stark and Bainbridge argue that the social network theory can
demonstrate:

1. that interpersonal bonds between cult members and potential
    recruits are essential to new member recruitment;

95

2. that a recruitment process must include making new friendship networks if it does not or cannot work through existing social contacts;

3. and that what had been shown through qualitative studies can now be demonstrated quantitatively as well, namely, that "final conversion was coming to accept the opinions of one's friends" (1379).

The authors provide quantitative evidence of the critical importance of social and kinship networks in spreading religious faith by turning to Jane Hardyck and Marcia Braden's 1962 data on a doomsday group, Ted Nordquist's 1978 study of the Ananda Community, and their own statistical survey of Mormonism (1980).

In an analysis of Mormon missionary strategy, Stark and Bainbridge show how Mormons consciously attempt to develop personal relationships first before preaching to potential converts. Specifically, only by step five of a thirteen step proselytizing process does religion enter the picture (1980, 1387). Finally, they note that Kevin Welch's study of conventional faiths not only supports the notion of recruitment through interpersonal bonds, but also points to that same process in *sustaining commitment* to mainstream religious traditions (1389–1390). They further conclude that deprivation will be a more important variable the more a group is in contention with the surrounding culture or the more an individual is isolated from that culture (1382). Yet regardless of the importance of the deprivation variable, Stark and Bainbridge conclude: "Interpersonal bonds appear to be a crucial situational element for any theory of recruitment" (1393).

To a great extent my research among the Hare Krishna devotees in America supports the general conclusions of the Stark and Bainbridge social network theory (Shinn 1982). First nearly all of the devotees I interviewed reported a significant "godbrother" or friend who nurtured them through the early decision to join and then to stay after doubts arose. Second, as members of a highly deviant NRM by traditional American religious values and beliefs, in their dress, diet, theology, etc., ISKCON devotees also fit the high deprivation end of Stark and Bainbridge's variable continuum (1381–1382). And third, since its appeal is so limited ideologically (as a "foreign" religion and deity), and in terms of its intense monastic and missionary lifestyle, ISKCON's recruitment does depend upon attracting "social isolates" and is growing slowly if at all in finite numbers of adherents.

How does ISKCON make necessary social contacts with potential recruits? A variety of avenues exist according to my interviews. One avenue is through book distribution (now called Sankīrtana) in airports and other public places. Another avenue is through street singing and dancing (*nāma*-Sankiīrtana) where the curious or mildly interested are engaged in conversation and urged to come to a Sunday Feast. Yet another avenue is through one friend introducing another to ISKCON's books, ideas, and rituals (usually ending with a trip to the temple during a Sunday Feast). Still another avenue, though one only infrequently mentioned in my interviews, is the direct initiative of the potential recruit based on reading books or viewing devotional activities from afar. But regardless of the type of initial encounter, the Sunday Feast has been the friendship-building arena. Every ISKCON temple provides such a free Sunday meal, complete with deity worship and a lecture, as the prime contact with the general public.

The vast majority of the devotees I interviewed described being singled out at a Sunday Feast by a devotee who would pay special attention to the same person on each visit. Friendships with new recruits appear to be nurtured through a combination of preaching, eating the Sunday specialty meals together, and sharing the devotional singing and dancing. Thus in the process of building friendships with potential recruits who often felt isolated from the society and peers around them, new "mazeways" also were formed (Wallace 1979, 423). And throughout this process of recruitment to new ideas and the fully-committed lifestyle, constant appeals to the "good associations" with Krishna devotees versus the "bad associations" with "karmis" (outsiders under the weight of *karma* or evil affects of past actions) were made. By the time I had finished several hundred hours of interviews over the span of eighteen months, I became sensitized to certain code words or insiders' terms, and "good associations" was one of them.

It is clear that from the beginning ISKCON has tried to build temple communities marked by what Victor Turner calls "communitas." More than just fellowship, he explains:

> Communitas breaks in through the interstices of structure in liminality; at the edges of structure, in marginality; and from beneath structure, in inferiority. It is almost everywhere held to be sacred or "holy," possibly because it transgresses or dissolves the norms that govern structured and institutionalized relationships and is accompanied by experiences of unprecedented potency. The processes of "leveling" and "stripping" . . . often appear to flood their subjects with affect (Turner 1969, 128).

As in the case of many other religious utopian communities, ISKCON represents an "ideological communitas," that is, an intentionally and permanently marginal community built on religious ideals (Turner, 132–34). While hierarchical roles and statuses have developed as ISKCON has evolved from its movement to its institutional stage of development, it is clear that societal roles and statuses have been levelled and homogeneity and comradship are apparent *especially* during the collective rituals each day. With scriptural support for the notion that all persons are equal before Krishna (God), devotional activities ideally should be periods of social levelling and egalitarian comradship which support the larger social bonding of the community (Bhagavad Gita, 5:18). But in my observation and research, I have found a counter-thrust to community and social network-building in the individualism and personal isolation that even the communal acts of worship promote. While most devotees dance and sing together during the morning and evening periods of deity worship *(ārati),* the stress on individual sincerity and obligation in one's dancing and singing before God leads to atomization of attention and behavior for most devotees. This isolation of individuals before God is encouraged by the daily one-and-a-half to two hours of chanting done privately or individually each day.

To add to the weakening of social network bonds, especially during the first ten years of the movement in America, devotees have moved frequently between temples with little regard to personal friendships (though a few friendship groups do exist). Only as ISKCON temples have developed more formal institutional structures and farm communities have had time to normalize their memberships, have more settled patterns emerged. Nonetheless, as I pondered the failure of ISKCON to develop cohesive fellowships of devotees *built on social bonds,* or even to attempt to do so, I realized that such a fellowship of spiritual and social equals—what I will call "horizontal communitas"—has never been their goal. While recruitment may in fact be assisted by building social networks of friendship between devotees and potential recruits, it would appear that commitment in ISKCON is not supported as directly by social bonding (Turner's communitas) as I had expected to find.

Consequently, the social network process Stark and Bainbridge describe is important in understanding the recruitment of members to ISKCON, but appears to take a subordinate place in the commitment process which follows soon upon the heels of the Sunday Feast and the friends made there. I would argue that it is submission to the spiritual master, the guru, and the personal and spiritual roles that relationship implies that is the key to understanding the commitment process. Thus recruitment and commitment are not so easily connected as the network model suggests, as applied to ISKCON. Therefore, in the following discussion of the guru/disciple relationship, I offer a modification and extension of the Stark-Bainbridge network model and Turner's notion of communitas as the evidence from my Krishna research seems to require. While the following conclusions are only suggestive musings, they do seem to point to a need to reassess sociological models built upon data from Western religious traditions alone. For it is not the Krishna tradition from Asia alone which requires taking into account religious commitment models that are not congregational or group oriented in their basic faith-nurturing structures. Much of what is said below of the guru/disciple relationship is also true of other Asian religious relationships.

Guru-Disciple in Ideology and Ritual

In the Gauḍīya Vaishnava religion, the Bengali tradition which worships Krishna as the supreme god and from which Bhaktivedanta, the founder-guru of ISKCON descends, the guru is God's direct channel (along with scriptures) to ordinary human beings. The *Bhāgavata Purāna*, tenth-century scripture, reports Krishna as saying: "One should know the *ācārya* (guru) as myself, and never disrespect him in any way. One should not envy him, thinking of him as an ordinary man, for he is a representative of all the demi-gods" (Śubhānanda 1978, 1). In the notion of *paramparā* (literally, "uninterrupted series"), or "disciplic succession," ISKCON draws on the traditional claim of most Hindu theistic sects that their gurus stand in a connected chain of disciples leading back to primordial teachers and, finally, God himself. Bhaktivedanta himself made such a claim based upon his ordination by Bhaktisiddhanta Saraswati who stood in the Gaudiya Vaishnava line of *ācāryas* ("spiritual teachers") linking him by tradition to Caitanya (sixteenth-century reformer), Vyāsadeva (the narrator and compiler of the Krishna scriptures), the creator god Brahma, and finally Krishna himself. The guru (usually referred to as the "spiritual master" in ISKCON) is more than simply an initiated, institutionalized representative of God; he is an externalized manifestation of Krishna himself. Bhaktivedanta turns again to the *Bhāgavata Purāna* for scriptural support for this assertion: "A disciple has to accept the spiritual master not only as spiritual master, but also as the representative of the

Supreme Personality of Godhead and the Supersoul. In other words, the disciple should accept the spiritual master as God because he is the external manifestation of Krsna" (Bhaktivedanta 1970, 59).

In addition to being a disciplic heir of a spiritual tradition and a physical representative of God, the spiritual master has "seen" the truths the scriptures convey and has lived those truths as a "pure devotee." Thus the guru can impart precise instructions to each disciple according to his or her ability or condition. The *Bhagavad Gītā* (second-century B.C. Krishna text) agrees: "Just try to learn the truth by approaching a spiritual master. Inquire from him submissively and render service unto him. The self-realized soul can impart knowledge unto you because he has seen the truth" (4:34). The implication of this theological line of argument is that each person needs a spiritual master who can discern his or her spiritual condition, recommend learning and behavior appropriate to that condition, and thereby lead the person "back to Godhead." To surrender to a guru is, in effect, to place your whole life under his care as if he were God himself. A medieval Vaishnava text makes such submission an obligation, not just a preference: "It is the duty of every human being to surrender to a bona fide spiritual master. Giving him everything—body, mind, and intelligence —one must take a Vaiṣnava initiation from him" (Śubhānanda 1978, 4).

The disciple, the *śiṣya,* is clearly the subordinate partner in this hierarchical relationship. The similies used to depict the guru/disciple relationship include father/son, father/daughter, king/subject, and god/ human pairs. Satsvarūpa dāsa Goswāmi, one of the eleven initiating gurus Bhaktivedanta appointed to succeed him, makes clear in the many letters he has sent to his new disciples the proper position and attitude required of the disciple in the guru/*śiṣya* relationship. In a letter published in a newsletter distributed to all of his disciples, Satsvarūpa says:

> I am sure that before too long the temple authorities there will recommend you for initiation, and I will be glad to accept you as my disciple. Please consider the matter very seriously in the meantime. It is not a matter of simply being in the temple a certain amount of time; it is a matter of realization. You have to agree to become thoroughly submissive to the orders of the spiritual master, which are especially fixed up in faith and practice of chanting Hare Krṣṇa and following the regulative principles. Whatever personal instructions he gives has to be taken as coming from Krṣṇa. So before one agrees to such a relationship, he should be certain [Letter dated 27 April 1979] (Satsvarūpa 1982, 10).

The language of submission, surrender, and complete devotional service is ubiquitous in the teachings of ISKCON *and* the traditional scriptural teachings which support it. Just as one must abandon all self-centeredness in one's devotional stance before God, so too must one adopt the same stance before God's messenger, the guru.

The logic of the subordinate position of the disciple to another human being has often been misunderstood, especially when the words used to describe the disciple include metaphors which can be twisted to demonstrate the charge of "mind control" rather than to reflect the relative spiritual positions of guru and disciple and the consequent need for pliability and surrender on the disciple's part. In much of the ancient and modern Vaishnava scripture and literature, the disciple is called a "fool" or an "idiot" who is ignorant of his or her true self or nature. Likewise, the disciple is likened to a "dog" whom the master must feed and train and who in return is to be loyal and is to obey the master. And still yet another image used is that of the disciple as a "puppet" who is fully dependent upon the puppetmaster for all thoughts and actions. Satsvarūpa makes clear spiritual and practical implications of this image:

> You have asked that as your spiritual master I engage you like a puppet to dance. Repeatedly we hear this—the devotee is asking to be the puppet of the spiritual master or of Kṛṣṇa. So what should the spiritual master do when the disciple asks, "Please make me dance." I think in this case my responsibility is simply to command you, "Then dance! Distribute books, chant Hare Kṛṣṇa, dance, dance, dance!"
>
> If one doesn't say that merely as a poetic expression, asking to be the puppet and to dance, then when the spiritual master commands, we must jump and dance [Letter dated 1 February 1979] (Satsvarūpa 1981c, 7).

The logic of the guru/disciple model and relationship is that one normally does not approach Krishna directly. Rather, Krishna has arranged a controlled channel through which his grace and salvation is imparted and through which he receives the devoted love *(bhakti)* of his spiritual children. This two-way channel of divine grace and human love is the *gurū-paramparā* or disciplic succession of spiritual masters. Satsvarūpa's letters to his disciples reflects this traditional Vaishnava view:

> In your letter you mention my love for you. This love is as amazing to me as it is to you, because it is simply going through me out of the causeless love of Śrīla Prabhupāda and is ultimately coming from Kṛṣṇa. Kṛṣṇa's

love is there for everyone, but this arrangement of *guru-paramparā* and
guru-disciple is the best method to churn the actual love which everyone
is looking for. Everyone really wants love of Kṛṣṇa. But unless we
approach a bona fide representative of Kṛṣṇa and take to all the practices
of austerity and chanting, that love is not available. So we are all very
fortunate that we are under the shelter of this *guru-paramparā* by which
Kṛṣṇa is giving us His love through the spiritual master [Letter dated 16
June 1978] (1981b, 13).

Although it may appear to the outsider that any given guru is an
authoritarian master with no controls or checks on his power, each
guru in the Krishna tradition represented by ISKCON has had his own
guru before whom he was a "fool," "puppet," or obedient "dog." Thus
each guru has experienced both the inferior and superior positions of
the guru/*śiṣya* relationship. For example, the founding-guru of
ISKCON, Bhaktivedanta, wrote on his guru's birthday in 1936 the
following disciplic adoration:

1. Adore adore ye all
    The happy day
Blessed than heaven,
    Sweeter than May.
When he appeared at Puri
    The holy place,
My Lord and Master
    His Divine Grace.

2. Oh! my Master
    The evangelic angel
Give us thy light,
    Light up thy candle.
Struggle for existence
    A human race.
The only hope
    His Divine Grace.

3. Misled we are
    All going astray,
Save us Lord
    Our fervent pray.
Wonder thy ways

> To turn our face
> Adore thy feet
> Your Divine Grace
> —(*Śrī Vyāsa Pūjā* 1976, 19).

And in 1961, long after his guru's death, Bhaktivedanta wrote of that event: "On that day, O my master, I made a cry of grief, I was not able to tolerate the absence of you my guru. On this auspicious day [fifteenth anniversary of his guru's death] I have come with this offering just to worship you, remembering your lotus feet" *Srī Vyāsa Pūjā* 1978, 20). In a like fashion, Bhaktivedanta's disciples have produced each year on his birthday ("appearance day") a volume of prayers, praises, and testimonies directed to him for all that he has done as a spiritual master.

While the books written by anti-cultists (e.g., Ted Patrick or Rabbi Rudin) stress the authoritarian control and attitudes of all gurus in ISKCON, the ideal model requires that each guru remain at the same time both a master and a pupil, a leader and one who is led. Consequently, one of Bhaktivedanta's disciples, Hrdayānanda, wrote in 1976 of his low position: "O beloved Gurudeva, let our relationship never be broken! I am your eternal servant, and you are my eternal master, my only shelter! Let the full implications of this master-servant relationship unfold! You are *kṛṣṇa-preṣṭha* and I am hellish and fallen. Now I am begging that you fix me and fasten me as an atom at your lotus feet. Your eternal servant. Hrdayānanda dāsa Gosvāmī GBC—South America" *(Śrī Vyāsa Pūjā* 1976, 32). And that same disciple after serving for more than one year as one of the new gurus of ISKCON still wrote on Bhaktivedanta's birthday:

> Now ISKCON is a great worldwide institution. Everywhere preaching is going on, book distribution is going on, *prasāda* distribution is going on. Personally I am a very insignificant, poorhearted beggar at the lotus feet of my spiritual master, Om Viṣṇupāda Paramahamsa Parivrājakācārya Aṣtottara-śata Srī Śrīmad Bhaktivedanta Gosvāmī Mahārāja Prabhupāda, and at his lotus feet I am simply begging, pleading, "Please give me a drop of your mercy; please allow me to help Śrī Caitanya Mahāprabhu in His mission, please allow me to participate in your ISKCON movement, please give me the power to always satisfy you. Although you are self-satisfied, still if I cannot satisfy you then life is finished."
> In this mood I call upon all my Godbrothers and Godsisters as well as the new disciples who are now entering the house of *bhakti* to please work together cooperatively for the pleasure of Śrīla Prabhupāda *(Śrī Vyāsa Pūjā* 1978, 85).

The tradition of guru/śiṣya, or master/disciple, not only has built into the ideology a corrective to overweaning pride in the guru—namely, the honoring by every devotee of his/her guru *even* when one achieves that status and role himself—but in the Krishna tradition, the sacred scriptures *and* other *sādhus* (respected masters in the tradition) stand as corrective standards to anything one's guru might say. Thus, if a guru preaches any teaching contrary to the Krishna scriptures or to the interpretations of those scriptures by accepted saints *(ācāryas)* who have stood in disciplic line, that teaching is to be judged inauthentic or misguided. On the other hand, only godbrothers of the guru can make this determination finally, since the disciple's scrutiny ends when he takes initiation. Satsvarūpa confirms this interpretation:

> Your understanding of the relationship of the disciple and the spiritual
> master is correct. The check and balance system of guru, *śāstra* and *sādhu*
> is used to find out who is a bona fide guru. But once we find out a bona
> fide guru and take initiation from him, it is understood that we are not in
> the position to make any more check on him. It is not that whatever the
> bona fide guru says, you go to the *śāstras* to see if it is right or ask some
> other *sādhu*. It is a method to find out who is a bona fide spiritual master
> (1981a, 9).

The guru is the perfect teacher, said Bhaktivedanta, not because he is perfect, but because his teachings are perfectly in accord with the revealed scripture and tradition. Just like a mailman can deliver a money order for $1,000 without being wealthy himself, so can a guru deliver perfect teachings without being perfect, said Bhaktivedanta. Therefore he concluded: " . . . our quality is that we are not perfect, we are full of imperfections, but we don't go beyond the teachings of Krishna. That is our process" (Bhaktivedanta 19, 13–14).

Whatever else we may conclude about the ideology of the guru/ disciple relationship, it is apparent, on the one hand, that the guru ideally (1) stands in a disciplic line (the *paramparā*) that reaches back to God himself, which means (2) he acts as the *only* vehicle for God's salvation and grace and the devotee's love and devotion, and, therefore, (3) the guru's teachings are "perfect" and are to be honored as God's own word. And yet the guru is not to be confused with God nor forget his humble place before his own guru. On the other hand, the disciple should surrender to the guru as a spiritually ignorant, fully subservient, and completely devoted dependent of the guru. (Yet such a disciple may himself become a spiritual master of others even before the goal of perfection is actually reached.) This symbiotic relationship of guru and devotee in ISKCON quickly replaces, as the relationship of highest priority, any peer relationships or social network which might have facilitated a devotee's joining a Krishna temple. Because from the very beginning of one's life in the temple, each ritual occasion includes a bonding ceremony to one's guru, and commitment to this new faith soon becomes commitment to one's guru. Nonetheless, peer relationships do continue to exert influence on all devotees, if to varying degrees.

Given the above understanding of the guru/disciple relationship, it is not surprising that the Gaudīya Vaishnava tradition in India, and now in ISKCON worldwide, provides ritual expression and repetition of this special bonding. The initiation ritual (both for first and second initiations) confirms the role of "spiritual father" the guru is to play for the new devotee. But it is the *guru pūjā* or services of "honoring the guru" which are appended to the four prescribed deity *pūjās* or *āratīs* each day in ISKCON temples which provide repeated reinforcement of the guru/disciple relationship. During the *gūrū pūjā,* the very same ritual gestures, prayers, and songs of submission are offered to one's spiritual master (in person or before a pictoral of image likeness) as one offered to the images of Krishna and the other deities. And as the disciple lies prostrate before the image of person of their spiritual master, he or she may say: "I am not a priest, nor a warrior, nor a merchant, nor a slave . . . but I am simply the servant of the servant of . . . Sri Kṛṣṇa" (Adhikārī 1978, 49). And another prayer which explains one's relationship to the guru says: "The spiritual master is to be honored as much as the Supreme Lord because he is the most confidential servitor of the Lord. This is acknowledged in all revealed scriptures and followed by all authorities. Therefore I offer my respectful obeisances unto the lotus feet of such a spiritual master, who is a bona fide representative of Sri Hari (Kṛṣṇa)" (Adhikārī 1978; 52). The ideology explains that because any guru who has been initiated into the *paramparā* or disciplic line can trace his spiritual lineage back to Vyāsa, the divine sage who compiled all Krishna scripture, such a person sits in "the seat of Vyāsa" or the *Vyāsāsan.* While preaching or interpreting scripture from that seat, the guru speaks *ex-cathedra* in his inherited role as a bestower of Krishna's teachings and grace. As the disciple prostrates himself or herself before the Vyāsāsan, the following prayer is repeated: "The spiritual master is receiving benediction from the ocean of mercy. Just as a cloud pours water on a forest fire to extinguish it, so the spiritual master delivers the materially afflicted world by extinguishing the blazing fire of material existence. I offer my respectful obeisances unto the lotus feet of such a spiritual master, who is an ocean of auspicious qualities" (Adhikārī 1978, 50).

In the final analysis, the guru deserves such an honored ritual place because he is a *perfect* devotee who not only is the mediator between God and his disciples through the chain of previous gurus, but also manifests in his devotional acts the submission and unselfish love required of *all* devotees in all ages. Thus a prayer often recited during *gūrū pūjā* ceremonies reveres the guru as one who embodies the devotion it is his duty to teach and transmit to his disciples:

> Chanting the holy name, dancing in ecstasy, singing, and playing musical instruments, the spiritual master is always gladdened by the *saṅkīrtana* movement of Lord Caitanya Mahāprabhu. Because he is relishing the mellows of pure devotion within his mind sometimes his hair stands on end, he feels quivering in his body, and tears flow from his eyes like waves. I offer my respectful obeisances unto the lotus feet of such a spiritual master (Adhikārī 1978, 50).

My point in describing the nature of the guru/śiṣya relationship in such detail is to underline its centrality theologically (ideologically), ritually, and socially for ISKCON. For it is my contention that the guru/disciple relationship becomes the *primary* "social network" for most ISKCON devotees. And further, that this relationship, though one of unequals, is invested with both the emotional and rational elements conducive to the commitment process. Unlike the "horizontal communitas" of most religious communities that build commitment through peer support and social network structures, the guru/disciple bonding reflects a "vertical communitas" which links the devotee to a transcendent divinity through an ascending succession of saints of whom his guru is the most immediate. To be sure, peer support and community does exist to greater and lesser degrees in the various temples and farms in which I lived. However, fragmentation, isolation, and separation are all part of the experience of every devotee the extent to which his or her religious quest is viewed as a solitary quest with the guru as the primary guide. The farm communities I visited were often more "communal" in nature than city temples partly because of the "householder" status of the families there and partly because of the required cooperation it takes to run dairy farms. But even on those farms, the resident gurus were clearly the focal point of the community and its common activities. I observed much more social atomization in the city temples where persons could be quite alone in the midst of other devoted seekers.

If my assessment about the primacy of the guru/disciple bonding is correct, then we should expect a devotee's relationship to his or her spiritual master to be a greater priority and of greater value than that to one's spouse, friend, or even ISKCON as an institutionalization of one's faith in guru and Krishna. Following upon such a proposition is the related one that says if one's relationship with one's guru becomes the primary social and commitment relationship, then the absence or death of the guru should be expected to cause difficulties for the continuation of the devotee's faith. It would appear that my data support both hypotheses.

Guru/disciple Relationship in Practice

One obvious place to turn to confirm or refute the hypothesis proposed above is to the founding-guru's death and the effects it had on the faith of his disciples. It appears that Bhaktivedanta's death did have a dramatic impact on the faith of many ISKCON devotees since as many as 20 to 25% of his American devotees abandoned their commitment when their spiritual master died. The difficulty with this data is that the records of ISKCON defections are not readily accessible to confirm the percentage "guesses" of my interviewees, and more importantly, the variables for what was a large exodus of devotees by everyone's estimate may have been more numerous than can be easily measured. For some defectors the increased anxiety caused by the immediate organizational vacuum which followed immediately upon the death of a founder may have been a strong contributing factor. For others it may have been the occasion to abandon a faith held only partially or marginally. For still others, it may have been the feeling that the "pressure" of the spiritual master was the only remaining attachment to ISKCON and once that was removed there was no reason to stay. Yet the fact that a significant percentage of short and long term devotees left when their spiritual master, Bhaktivedanta, died can't be ignored, for to some extent the guru/disciple bonding underlies all of the variables just mentioned. Nonetheless, it is the case that such a personal bonding of disciple and guru as I have claimed above will likely be demonstrated better in the ideosyncratic example than in general statistics; and it is to two such examples I now turn.

While the death of Bhaktivedanta provides only scanty evidence of the strong personal and social bond which develops between guru and devotee, a recent schism in ISKCON provides more direct evidence to support my hypothesis. The initiating guru for the Northern European and London Zone is a man I will call Mahadeva. He became a disciple of Bhaktivedanta in the early years of ISKCON and was noted for his emotional displays in chanting, enthusiastic preaching, and in good business management in those early and difficult years of the movement. When Bhaktivedanta died in 1977, Mahadeva became one of the eleven young men chosen to succeed his master in the disciplic line *(paramparā)*. Throughout his tenure as one of the gurus of ISKCON, Mahedeva was noted for his emotional sermons, ecstatic chanting, and success at attracting new devotees to ISKCON. After the death of his master, Mahadeva took *sannyāsa* (i.e., became a renounced ascetic), but later briefly rejoined his former wife (a highly irregular action given the vows of chastity and renunciation taken earlier). During the past couple of years, Mahadeva's godbrothers became increasingly concerned with the reports of nearly debilitating public displays of ecstatic ferver Mahadeva exhibited during chanting and preaching from his guru's seat (the *Vyāsāsan*). Accusations that Mahadeva had been resorting to hallucinogenic drugs to increase his devotional experience came from his zone and worried his godbrothers. In addition, other charges of improprieties in Mahadeva's behavior finally erupted in a confrontation (more complex than can be presented here) with the Governing Body Commission (GBC), the organizational council of last resort in ISKCON.

In April 1982, the confrontation between Mahadeva and the GBC came to a climax when the GBC issued a stern warning at its annual meeting in India that Mahadeva had to restore his behavior to that of a guru or face removal from his position in Europe. Mahadeva's response was to seek advice from one of Bhaktivedanta's godbrothers who was himself known for his ecstatic devotion. Mahadeva was so overwhelmed by the advice and encouragement of this old Krishna ascetic that he asked for initiation from him (a truly unorthodox practice by Indian religious standards). My first question upon learning of this strange turn of events was, What did his disciples do?

In spite of Mahadeva's increasingly bizarre behavior (both in near-catatonic ecstacies and immoral behavior) over the past couple of years, his disciples had increased in number and commitment to Mahadeva. Many of them have since argued that while the guru may not be perfect, *his message is*. Would this kind of loyalty and commitment to one's guru be undermined by his defection to another guru outside ISKCON as an institution (though still within the Krishna faith)? The answer for nearly half of his disciples was a resounding, "No!" According to two different accounts by godbrother's of Mahadeva, more than three dozen disciples of Mahadeva boarded themselves inside the London temple (Mahadeva's home temple) to keep ISKCON's official representatives away until the disciples could fly to India to rejoin their master. In a short time after the defection of their own master, nearly forty ISKCON disciples defected with him. ISKCON's first major schism had occurred.

If it is true that in ISKCON the primary spiritual and social bond is with one's guru, is it so surprising that when his master died Mahadeva's social and spiritual bonds to ISKCON were weakened? For if it is the master/devotee relationship which is supreme in ISKCON, there must be a very high level of commitment to the ideology of the spiritual connection which can transcend even death for a disciple to overcome the physical separation from his or her spiritual master. It would seem that the theological arguments for the devotee's need to surrender to a guru fail to recognize the extent of *social* bonding such a relationship entails as well as the great social role adjustment that must take place when one who has learned only to submit to another now must lead others. In the case of Mahadeva, is it shocking that when his guru died and he became a guru himself that this young man found himself in a position for which he was not well prepared? Is it surprising that under threat of losing that position he would simply escape the problem (if only temporarily) by adopting the position of submission and subordination to another spiritual master? What seems an inescapable conclusion regarding the behavior of Mahadeva's own disciples is that, like their master, their bond to their guru was more important than that either to ISKCON as an institution or to the larger fellowship of disciples in ISKCON. Another example of a person related to Mahadeva makes the same point in quite another way.

Mahadeva's wife is a woman I will call Mahema. Though Mahema's biography is an interesting one, I will reveal only enough of her personal religious past to make clear her level of commitment to her guru, Bhaktivedanta (Shinn 1980). She was born in Chicago, reared a devout Catholic, and lived a rather traditional life up to her college years (she was a good student, cheerleader, Homecoming Queen, etc.), but Mahema broke with her rather protected past during her college years. After only two years at Loyola University in Chicago, Mahema set off for the liberating experience of commune life in a variety of farm communes in the Midwest and West Coast. While living on such communes, she came into contact with Eastern philosophy and religious practices like chanting mantras (potent prayers), doing yoga, and becoming a vegetarian. It was on one such commune that Mahema learned the Hare Krishna mantra as just one of many used by commune members.

While visiting friends in San Francisco, Mahema met ISKCON devotees for the first time. She was intrigued by their dress and lifestyle and especially by their commitment to the Hare Krishna mantra. The devotees asked Mahema to stay in the San Francisco temple and she did for a few months, about which she said, "I liked the association of the devotees." But when it became clear to Mahema that it was submission to the spiritual master which provided the true focus of temple life and the Krishna faith, she remembers feeling, "I needed a teacher . . . but I didn't know if I could surrender that much." After several periods of leaving the temple and living with her friends on the communal farm, Mahema finally decided to join ISKCON. The day before she joined, Mahema went to a nearby Catholic church and asked for the permission of Jesus for her to join ISKCON, and she got it. "I'm not going to turn my back on you Jesus," she said in her prayers. And she reported that the feeling that Jesus supported her decision led her to feel that submission to a guru "was a path that could lead me even further than I had experienced in Catholicism." So after two months of living in the Los Angeles temple, Mahema was initiated. She described her decision to surrender to Bahktivedanta this way: "I really took my vows to heart. I couldn't leave my spiritual master now. It's my promise to him that I'm going to follow these four regulative principles [no meat eating, no unlawful sex, no gambling, and no intoxicants], and that I'm going to chant my three rounds [of the Hare Krishna mantra] every day. So then, once I was initiated, there was no question of me, in my heart, quitting. . . . " (Shinn 1980). Mahema remarked concerning her relationship with her spiritual master, Bhaktivedanta (whom she calls by the more affectionate title, Prabhupāda):

I didn't fully understand. As time goes on, you understand more. But at that time I really felt like I could learn something from Prabhupāda, and I really felt that he was my teacher. And I once prayed that if he wasn't my teacher that he would send me one (Laugh) because I didn't want to get on the wrong path! And then I really knew, like when I was at the church, . . . and I developed really close friendships here as well. . . . Though I didn't have such a close relationship with Srila Prabhupāda, I saw him as my teacher. And when he gave me my name Mahema, he said it was a Gopi name. And the Gopis are cowherd girls, you know. And they are always serving Krishna. And that's all I wanted to do—serve. . . . Coming to the temple was service to Krishna through my spiritual master. So I actually felt that it was satisfying to be of service. And then—as now—I just kept real busy cooking, sewing, making garlands, and doing preaching as well (Shinn 1980).

Both by her own admission and by that of several devotees whom I interviewed, Mahema became known over the years (she joined more than a decade ago) for her depth of faith, especially in her spiritual master, Bhaktivedanta. Physically and geographically distant from her guru, except for a short stint as his cook, Mahema lived in various temples on both the East and West coasts, and finally in London where she met and later married Mahadeva. Though she was personally attracted to Mahadeva and bore him a son in 1978, she had already been "widowed" by Mahadeva's decision to renounce the world when I interviewed Mahema in 1980. She accepted her fate of being a widow to a living guru because her husband had reported that his decision was based upon a dream he had in which Bhaktivedanta, his guru, had told him to become a *sannyāsa* or ascetic preacher.

Then in the summer of 1981, the bottom fell out of this spiritually occasioned separation. Both Mahema and Mahadeva wanted to be rejoined due to their attachment to each other and their rejoining caused a stir throughout ISKCON. I lost track of Mahema who was off in London until I heard of the recent defection of her husband, Mahadeva. I was really interested to know if her professed loyalty to Bhaktivedanta, even after his death, would be stronger than her affection for Mahadeva. "Did Mahema defect with Mahadeva?" I asked my informants. "Oh, she couldn't leave Prabhupāda," said one informant. And what became clear in the subsequent conversation about Mahema's second separation from her much loved husband was that regardless of other contributing factors, Mahema's decision to remain in ISKCON was one based mainly on the guru/disciple bond. And even further, what became clear was that this bond could operate beyond the guru's life, and serve as an ideological or theological bonding of a different order from the bond of a husband and wife. Thus in the recent schism within ISKCON it is the "vertical communitas" of devotion to guru and Krishna which explains the behavior of most of those participants rather than an explanation based primarily or only upon the social network theory (understood as "horizontal communitas").

The social network model of Stark and Bainbridge seems to have a built-in Western bias toward the "horizontal communitas" explanations of religious faith formation which does work quite well in assessing the congregational faiths of Christianity and Judaism (and their many offshoots). What the commitment process described above as ISKCON's guru/disciple model requires is a recognition of a vertical bonding of a more individual kind than the network model suggests. It would appear that while social networks *are* significant vehicles for recruitment in ISKCON, they recede in importance as the commitment process (certainly an extension of the decision to join) continues. For in ISKCON, both the ideological and ritual traditions support the more socially fragmenting process of guru-disciple bonding as the dominant relationship socially and religiously defined.

It is true that the guru/disciple model of community building does pose special problems for developing social cohesiveness, cooperation, and comradeship in ISKCON. This is even more true when eleven successors instead of one are appointed to succeed the founding guru. But what is also clear is that a very high level of commitment can be achieved from such an individualized bonding structure. And what is also apparent is that the social network theory needs to be modified to allow for the vertical as well as the horizontal type of community building the guru/disciple relationship represents.

References

Adhikāṛ, Jayathīrtha dāsa, editor. 1978. *The Process of Worship (Arcana Paddhati)*. Los Angeles: Bhaktivedanta Book Trust.

Bhagavad-Gītā: As It Is. 1972. Translated with Purports by A. C. Bhaktivedanta Swami. Los Angeles: Bhaktivedanta Book Trust.

Bhaktivedanta, A. C. Swami Prabhupada. 1970. *The Nectar of Devotion*. Los Angeles: Bhaktivedanta Book Trust.

———. 1980. *Consciousness: The Missing Link*. Los Angeles: Bhaktivedanta Book Trust.

Hardyck, Jane Allyn and Marcia Braden. 1962. Prophecy fails again: A report of a failure to replicate. *Journal of Abnormal and Social Psychology* 65:136–41.

Lofland, John and Rodney Stark. 1965. Becoming a world-saver: A theory of conversion to a deviant perspective. *American Sociological Review* 30:862–75.

Nordquist, Ted A. 1978. *Ananda Cooperative Village*. Uppsala: Borgstroms.

Satsvarūpa dāsa Goswāmī. 1981a. After initiation, the disciple must accept the spiritual master as absolute. *Sadhu-bhusanam* [sic]. Port Royal, Pa.: Gita-nagari Press 9.

113

————. 1981b. Kṛṣṇa gives his love through the spiritual master. *Sādhu-bhusanam.* Port Royal, Pa.: Gita-nagari Press. (April–May): 13.

————. 1981c. Sit down, roll over, dance! *Sadhu-bhuṣaṇam* [sic]. Port Royal, Pa.: Gita-nagari Press. (Oct.–Nov.): 7.

————. 1982. Initiation means to become submissive. *Sādhu-bhuṣaṇam.* Port Royal, Pa.: Gita-nagari Press. (Jan.–Feb.): 10.

Shinn, Larry D. 1980. Interview with "Mahema." Los Angeles ISKCON Temple, July.

————. 1982. The many faces of Krishna. In *Alternatives to American Mainline Churches,* edited by Joseph H. Fichter, 113–135. Barrytown, New York: Unification Theological Seminary.

Śrī Vyāsa Pūjā: August 19, 1976. 1976. Los Angeles: Bhaktivedanta Book Trust.

Śrī Vyāsa Pūjā: August 27, 1978. 1978. Los Angeles: Bhaktivedanta Book Trust.

Stark, Rodney and William Sims Bainbridge. 1980. Networks of faith: interpersonal bonds and recruitment to cults and sects. *American Journal of Sociology* 85:1376–95.

Śubhānanda dasa brahmacārī, editor. 1978. *The Spiritual Master and the Disciple.* Los Angeles: Bhaktivedanta Book Trust.

Turner, Victor W. 1969. *The Ritual Process.* Chicago: University of Chicago Press.

Wallace, Anthony. 1979. Revitalization movements. In *Reader in Comparative Religions,* edited by William Lessa and Evon Z. Vogt, 4th ed., 421–30. New York: Harper and Row.

4
The Rajneesh Movement

Arvind Sharma

THE founder of the movement I am going to talk about is referred to as Bhagwan Shree Rajneesh by his followers.[1] The word *bhagvān* is essentially an honorific[2] but is also the word in common use in northern India for God.[3] Its use by the founder of the movement or his followers may or may not be an attempt to exploit this ambiguity. The word *śrī* is also an honorific[4] and although also used with divine beings in ancient times has become the equivalent of the English "mister" in many modern Indian languages, especially as *śrīmān*.[5] The word *Rajnīśa* represents the proper name of the founder who was originally known as Rajneesh Chandra Mohan. It may be of some interest to point out that the honorifics attached to his name show a certain progression, perhaps even geometric in nature. He was originally known as Professor, but after giving up academia he came to be known as *ācārya,* a title reserved within the tradition for its classical exponents, for the Indian equivalent of, for example, a Thomas Aquinas. Finally, he became known as *bhagvān* after becoming a cultic guru, an honorific of far greater encomiastic potency than *ācārya*. One more point must be made before his life is reviewed—he is, strictly speaking, not a Hindu but a Jain.[6] The Indic religious tradition comprises four major traditions: Hindu, Buddhist, Jain and Sikh, although the last two are not as well known as the first two. The purpose in identifying his Jain background is twofold: First, to indicate that Rajneesh has moved beyond the confines of his Jaina tradition, and second that Jainism is not regarded as a missionary religion. Even if some missionary activity on its part within India is conceded, it does not seem to possess any record of carrying on such activity outside India until very recent times. What Rajneesh has done is, therefore, not typical of Jainism, rather the contrary.[7]

The life of Rajneesh can be seen as consisting of six distinct phases:[8]

The pre-Enlightenment phase: Rajneesh was born on 11 December 1931 in a village in Central India. A somewhat hagiographic account of his life emphasizes his spiritual precocity.[9] It is, however, claimed by him and of him that on 21 March 1953, when he was twenty-one, *it* happened—he became Enlightened.[10]

The 1953–1957 phase: His Enlightenment did not lead to an interruption of his academic career. He took his M.A. in 1957.

The 1957–1967 phase: During this period he taught at the Raipur Sanskrit College and at the University of Jabalpur.[11] This phase marks the transition from the Professor to the *Ācārya*. "In the summer of 1964 he conducted his first ten-day meditation camp in the hills of Rajasthan, his approach becoming less and less theoretical, more pragmatic and experiential."[12]

The 1967–1974 phase: He resigned his academic position to dedicate his life to the "spiritual regeneration of humanity."[13] He travelled for three years, and then in 1969 he settled in an apartment in Bombay[13] with a "nucleus of disciples" around him. Around this time "he created his 'Neo-Sannyas' and accepted his first Western disciples. This form of initiation involves donning the ochre robe, taking a new name, wearing a *mala* with the traditional 108 beads and Bhagawan's picture, and meditating in some way an hour a day, but it does not require the renunciation of the world or a uniformly imposed discipline. It is described as a *sannyas* of relationship, a life of love and awareness, 'living life in its totality, moment to moment—and then, if you can allow this much, life allows you a transcendence.' By 1972 about fifty Westerners had taken *sannyas* along with a much larger number of Indians."[14] In 1974 Rajneesh moved to Poona, where the Shree Rajneesh Ashram was established.

The 1974–1981 phase: During this period the ashram flourished in Poona. According to a colleague who visited the ashram in April 1977 it then had about 150 inmates, 50% of whom were foreigners. When I visited it in January 1979 it had about 200 resident inmates, 80% of whom were foreigners. The Ashram seemed to be doing well and Rajneesh was certainly publishing and not perishing. I am not surprised that he has now 336 titles to his credit based on his discourses, which have also yielded the crop of 4,000 hours of listening time on audiocassettes. And 154 discourses have been recorded on videocassettes.

The post–1981 phase: On 11 April 1981 Rajneesh announced that he would be "entering a new and ultimate stage of his work." From May 1 he would speak only through silence.[15] During this period he moved from India to the United States. It was reported that the warehouse of his ashram in Poona was torched, and an incendiary device exploded in the health facilities.[16] This may or may not be true but there was certainly hostility in the air when I was there.

Unlike some of the other Swamis, Rajneesh had not been outside India until he moved to the United States, and he was, in fact, reluctant to make the move. It became necessary as a result of pressure and persecution. Efforts to secure other sites for the ashram in India had consistently failed. The one at Poona was deemed too small and in a hostile environment. Rajneesh was not on good terms with the government which replaced Mrs. Gandhi, and he openly sided with her when she was out of power. Her return to power, however, did not restore Rajneesh to favor. Some inmates of the ashram suggested that Rajneesh's reluctance to leave India may have been due in part to the inhibiting example of Gurdjieff who became a wanderer once he was out of his native Russia. Whatever the reluctance, it was obviously overcome.[17]

Once in the United States Rajneesh spent some time in New Jersey having medical treatment for a slipped disc,[18] after which he settled in central Oregon with around 280 of his followers. They are involved in transforming the 64,229 acre Big Muddy Ranch[19] into Rajneeshpuram or The City of Rajneesh.[20]

Rajneesh entered the United States on a tourist visa which was due to expire in June 1982.[21] In the meantime, he married the daughter of a Greek millionaire who holds a United States passport,[22] which should assure him continued residence in the country.

Of particular note is the movement's involvement in local politics. As Rajneesh's disciples descended on Antelope, the local residents felt threatened and moved to disincorporate. The move against disincorporation was defeated by 55 to 42, with 68 voters registering within the last 30 days of voting.[23] There had been speculation that some followers of Rajneesh would run for political office,[24] but it now appears that the commune has decided to incorporate a new city.[25]

Before any attempt can be made to summarize the basic teachings of Rajneesh, one must make mention of some of the obstacles involved in such a task. Of all the recent Swamis from India, he is perhaps the most eclectic. He ranges freely over all the major religious traditions of mankind—especially in their mystical dimension. This makes it difficult to assess his teachings in relation to the various traditions, just as the voluminousness of his writings makes it hard to summarize his teachings.[26] It does appear though, that the keynote of his teachings is "egolessness."[27] At least four spheres of the application of this central theme can be distinguished:

The metaphysical dimension: The ultimate reality in the metaphysics of Rajneesh is closely associated with Emptiness or Void whether it is understood as the Hindu *nirguna brahman* or the Buddhist *śūnyatā*. It is the Beyond, and whether this Void is emphasized to jolt one into a realization of its utter Otherness from our normal range of experience or is inherently constitutive of it—if anything can be—is not quite clear, nor perhaps can it be.

The psychological dimension: This aspect is far more important than the metaphysical one. While speaking of the psychological dimension, one must bear in mind that in traditional Eastern thought, psychology is not sharply distinguished from philosophy. One of the basic questions on which the seeker is asked to reflect is "Who am I?" In the so-called "intensives" at the Rajneesh Ashram, the initiates are subjected to similar questioning.

At this point distinction between Hindu and Buddhist thought must be drawn, for it has significance for the rest of the discussion. In Hinduism the fundamental metaphysical assumption is that one is ultimately the *Ātman,* which may be roughly defined as soul. In Buddhism the fundamental metaphysical assumption is that one has no *Ātman,* no soul; in fact, one is ultimately void. What is being suggested is that constant intensive reflection on "Who am I?"[28] is ultimately going to cause some degree of identity anxiety. In such a situation the Hindu view leaves one with some metaphysical anchor. While this is not to suggest that one becomes a cosmic waif with the Buddhist view, which is the basis of Rajneesh's thought, but one *is* probably left more psychologically vulnerable to cultic influence.

The socio-economic dimension: The achievement of egolessness can be speeded up by abandoning those *things* with which it is bound up (and perhaps even one's ideas!). One's possessions, for instance, are an extension of one's person (or ego). Thus by divesting oneself of things and handing them over to the ashram, one comes closer to becoming egoless. (Ironically, in Jainism, the tradition into which Rajneesh was born, this argument cuts the other way—because a person's possessions constitute a part of his personhood; depriving him of them is regarded as a form of violence.) Thus, in practice, egolessness doctrinally supports the socio-economic institution of the commune into which Rajneesh's followers are organized.

The interpersonal dimension: Rajneesh teaches that modern man is repressed and that this repression, the major expression of which is sexual repression, only makes him more obsessed with his ego. Uninhibitedness then is a move in the right direction because it leads to the achievement of egolessness. And, the extent to which one genuinely loves and cares for someone else, the less "egocentered" one is and therefore is on the way to egolessness. It is this constellation of ideas which accounts for Rajneesh's views on "free love" which have, on the one hand, given his movement a somewhat dubious reputation, but on the other, may have attracted many to it.

The actual form his teachings take when reduced to practice represent a whole array of techniques. One of them is called Dynamic Meditation. The idea of catharsis is central of the technique, as pointed out by Robert Gussner, who also offers the following description of the process by which egolessness is achieved.[29]

What does one do in Dynamic Meditation? It is usually done blindfolded in an open air hall holding several hundred people to the accompaniment of music. It lasts an hour, usually six to seven in the morning. The instructions with minor variations or wording, are as follows:

First Stage: Ten Minutes: Breathe chaotically through the nose, concentrating always on the exhalation. The body will take care of the inhalation. Do this as fast and as hard as you possibly can—and then a little harder, until you become the breathing. Use your natural bodily movements as an aid to build up your energy for exhaling. Feel it build up during the first stage, but don't let go.

Second Stage: Ten Minutes: Explode! Let go of everything that needs to be thrown out. Go totally mad, scream, shout, cry, jump, move, shake, dance, sing, laugh, throw yourself around. Hold nothing back, keep your whole body moving. A little acting often helps to get it started. Never allow your mind to interfere with what is happening. Whatever you feel to do, do it. Be total, and just be a witness to whatever is happening within you.

Stage Three: Ten Minutes: With arms raised, jump up and down shouting the mantra, HOO, HOO, HOO! as deeply as possible. Each time you land on the flats of your feet, let the sound hammer deep into the sex center. Give it all you have, exhaust yourself totally.

Fourth Stage: Fifteen Minutes: Stop! Freeze where you are in whatsoever position you find yourself. Don't arrange the body in any way. A cough, a movement, anything will dissipate the energy flow and the effort will be lost. Be a witness to everything that is happening to you. Be incapable of movement as if dead inside the body.[30]

It is difficult to assess any movement in progress and more so the Rajneesh movement while it is undergoing a continental shift from Asia to North America. Nevertheless, an assessment may help in understanding the movement and what becomes of it, even if some of the assessments may turn out to be preliminary in nature. One may assess the movement as (1) a student of meditation; (2) as a psychologist; (3) as a Hindu missionary; and (4) as a comparative religionist.

As a Student of Meditation

We referred earlier to Dynamic Meditation as a meditative technique and to the centrality of catharsis in this context. Before we proceed to assess the effectiveness of Dynamic Meditation it might be helpful to examine what meditation is. Our normal consciousness consists of an awareness of individuals and things and our relationship to them which we will call the contents of consciousness. The fundamental claim of meditation is that if we empty our consciousness of these contents, then a new dimension of existence is disclosed.

This aim of meditation, sometimes called the state of no-mind inasmuch as the mental contents have been emptied, is common to both

Dynamic and what may be called traditional meditation. Dynamic Meditation differs from traditional meditation in two ways: In Dynamic Meditation the contents of consciousness are seen to be not merely what we might call normal or empirical but also sub-empirical. In other words, the contents of the subconscious mind have to be emptied along with those of the conscious mind. Traditional meditation does not emphasize, even if it may occasionally recognize, this aspect. Second, Dynamic Meditation differs from traditional meditation not only by emphasizing what is to be emptied, but also in indicating how this emptying is to be brought about, namely, through a much more physically vigorous procedure than the one recognized by traditional meditation. The term catharsis seems to refer to both of these differences.

At this point we can distinguish between two fundamental approaches to meditation, which I describe as the "hovercraft" and the "immersion" techniques of meditation. The metaphor of crossing a body of water obviously underlies these terms. A hovercraft goes from one shore to another without touching the surface of the water. In this mode of meditation, one takes hold of the mind, makes it focus on a single element which raises it above empirical and sub-empirical concerns, and merges it into the object of meditation—the usual yogic procedure (*Yogasūtra* 1.17). The immersion technique also makes the crossing, but by going through or under the water rather than over it. This approach has a link with the Tantrika tradition in Hinduism. In this approach the mind goes *through* rather than *above* the ordinary flow of thoughts in order to get beyond them. Dynamic Meditation adopts the immersion approach rather than the hovercraft one.

The question then arises as to whether it is really necessary to make the repressed elements surface. Rajneesh speaks of an "anarchy"—"suppressed from centuries of past birth"—and it is argued that without its cathartic elimination, sound meditation is not possible. In the *Yogasūtras,* however, the memory of past births is not associated with the *attainment* of yogic meditation but is discussed in dealing with the *results* thereof (*Yogasūtra* 2.39). In other words one might say that according to orthodox yoga, the kind of catharsis which is described above is taken to be the *result* of successful meditation and is not the source of success in meditation. This point remains: Is it really necessary to stir up the deep waters in order to cross over them?

However, now let it be conceded that both the *conscious* as well as *subconscious* psychic latencies must be exhausted before the experience promised by meditation can be realized. And Dynamic Meditation does well, in that case, to emphasize the role of the *subconscious*. Having said that, we must consider the following questions:

(1) If the "unknown anarchy" of the psyche "is suppressed from centuries of past births," then how do we know that after it has been made to surface, it will not sink down to the bottom again? The fact that the water has been made muddier deliberately does not necessarily mean, when it becomes still again, that the muck has been removed—it has only been raised up and may settle down back at the bottom again. On the other hand, a cleansing operation *will* have the effect of making the water muddier too—but how do we decide which of the two cases is represented by Dynamic Meditation? By the results, perhaps. One of our students researched the so-called Orange People in Sydney and her feeling was, based admittedly on personal interaction with them, that they were more egocentric than members of the other religious groups she had met. The observation of the student may have a personal bias or may be based on a partial sample, but it does raise the issue whether raising the muck amounts to removing it. On the other hand we must take into account the positive experiences with Dynamic Meditation of people like Professor Robert Gussner.

(2) Could not the elements buried in the subconscious be made to surface in a more relaxed manner? If you will allow me to mix cultural metaphors, why sit on a bed of nails when you can recline on a psychoanalyst's couch?

(3) Although it is said that in modern times there is "more repression" and hence the need for catharsis, is not modern culture more free and open in so many ways by contrast with ancient cultures, and could it be that modern man is at least in some ways *less* repressed? If we set up three human types *modern man, traditional man,* and *primitive man,* then maybe modern man is more repressed than the primitive, but is he more repressed than the traditional?

(4) Even if it is conceded that elements in the subconscious must be made to surface through *activity,* must it be respiratory and physical activity? Could the same results be achieved by acute introspective activity? Weren't the extensive Tantrika visualizations devised to achieve precisely this result?

(5) Hindu meditational techniques entering the West tend to be treated as things physiological and psychological rather than spiritual. The literature on Transcendental Meditation (TM) seems to have become increasingly psycho-physiological in its orientation; is a similar development represented by Dynamic Meditation, wherein there is

more talk of the psyche than of the soul? Does Dynamic Meditation involve such despiritualization?

As a Psychologist

It is reported that practitioners of Dynamic Meditation achieve a "high" after practicing it. But, physiologically, the euphoria which follows vigorous exercise is the result of biochemical changes brought about by the exercise. It is apparent that oxygenation results from shallow breathing involved in Dynamic Meditation which generates a sense of freshness. One is thus tempted to ask: Are the results experienced by Dynamic Meditation really physiological, albeit dressed in spiritual garb? How does one determine the authenticity of meditative experience? There are two dangers here—one of imputing spiritual quality to a non-spiritual experience, the other of reducing spiritual experiences to its non-spiritual concomitants. True, the fact that we can see microbes only through a microscope should not lead us to claim that the microbes are *produced* by the microscope. On the other hand, the fact that we feel high does not necessarily mean that it is a spiritually induced high, and may merely represent physical exhilaration. I do not know how precisely we can avoid the Scylla of superimpositionism and the Charybdis of reductionism—but at least one should be alert to the danger.

As a Hindu Missionary

The first major Hindu movement to succeed in the west was the *Rāmakrsna* mission. Those movements which followed were similar inasmuch as they emphasized *meditational practices,* an area relatively neglected by Protestant Christianity. Meditation thus may be seen as compensating for what one Christian student in Sydney described as the "spiritual emptiness of the Protestant Ethic." The success of these movements, therefore, is not surprising. They were meeting a religious need not met by the spiritual resources then available to the people. The success of TM can also be understood in these terms. But the success of a movement such as the Hare Krishna poses a puzzle, for it is fundamentally devotional in nature as is Christianity. Obviously, then, conversion to Hinduism is no longer "religious" but rather "cultural"— or "counter-cultural." Members of groups like the Hare Krisha, are rejecting Western *culture* (rather than just Western *religion*) by joining it—and rejecting religion as a part of their culture. The problem with the Rajneesh movement is: Where does it fit into this scheme? Though it does emphasize meditation, it extensively incorporates Western psychological techniques. Whether this blend of Western psychology and Hindu spirituality is going to be sterile or fertile it is too early to say, though there is no reason to doubt that the optimists may be proved right.

As a Comparative Religionist

It has been said that when Christianity began to spread through the Roman Empire, the great danger was of Christianity becoming pagan instead of the Roman Empire becoming Christian. Now when the Indic religious tradition is making some impact on the West, I sense a similar danger in movements such as the one associated with Rajneesh: Indic religious tradition will become Westernized rather than the West becoming Indianized. The TM movement has virtually detached yogic meditation from its metaphysical anchorage by presenting it as a technique for improving one's physical, psychological, and even material well-being, and now the Rajneesh movement seems to be dissociating yogic meditation from the specific techniques associated with it in the Hindu milieu. I do not know whether in doing so these movements are distilling a more potent form of "Hinduism" or diluting its strength.[31]

In conclusion it might be useful to draw attention to the controversial component of Rajneesh's teachings. But controversial from whose point of view is the next logical question: Indian or Western?

The Indians in general seem to resent the implication of sexual laxity in Rajneesh's teachings and the lifestyle of his Western followers in India. The wearing of the ochre robe, reserved for those who lead a life devoted to the ascetic life by "mostly young, unmarried couples obviously not celibate"[30] is resented as are his attacks on Mahatma Gandhi and Vinoba Bhave—both known for their puritan ethic. Briefly, "his defense of sex as a legitimate path of spiritual practice" is viewed as unacceptable. At another level the question has been asked:

> . . . what happens to "the tradition" in this instance when it is in the presence of a fifteen day Primal Scream therapy group and the group is in the presence of an enlightened master, who is not present in the group, but whose discourses they hear daily and whose *darshan* they take at the beginning of the group and at its end? What does it mean to approach the spiritual life through Gestalt therapy, Psychodrama, Bioenergetics, Rolfing, Encounter groups, Hypnotherapy, the Alexander method, Polarity Massage, Psychosynthesis, Marathon groups, and Psychomotor

therapy? And why do it? Is this simply an opportunistic bid for followers and money? Has the movement taken note of what draws seekers in the West and installed it in India, hoping it will 'play in Poona' as well? Does this acceptance of the American Human Potential Movement as a context for the spiritual life imply a sort of subordination of the ages to the fads of the sixties? Or do we have merely an inorganic juxtapositioning of two ill fitting things—a development bizarre, undigested, uncoordinated? Or, finally, is this development part of something new and powerful that is happening in several groups as Asian *gurus* learn how better to approach Western students?[32]

In the midst of all this controversy, however, it may be helpful to be reminded of the sage words of Jacob Needleman that "the passage of a genuine teaching from one culture to another is an event nearly as extraordinary and rare as the original appearance of the teaching itself,"[33] even if one had reservations about its genuineness and even if one feels somewhat disoriented regarding the exact direction of the movement.

Notes

1. The name, according to now standard academic usage should be transcribed in the Roman script as: *Bhagvān Śrī Rajnīśa*.
2. S. Radhakrishnan, ed., *The Principal Upaniṣads* (London: George Allen & Unwin, 1953), 196.
3. Ved Mehta, *Portrait of India* (New York: Farrar, Straus & Giroux, 1970), 114.
4. Monier Monier-Williams, *A Sanskrit-English Dictionary* (Oxford: Clarendon Press, 1970), 1098.
5. C. Bulcke, *Angrezi-Hindi Kośa* (Ranchi: Catholic Press, 1968), 406.
6. Padmanabh S. Jaini, *The Jaina Path of Purification* (Berkeley: University of California Press, 1979), 293, n. 30.
7. It may be a fact of some linguistic interest that the name of the founder means the "moon" so that his followers could be called "moonies!"
8. These differ from those presented on the back of the leaflet entitled: *Books, Films, Audio and Videocasettes of Bhagwan Shree Rajneesh* (Antelope, Oregon: Chidvilas Rajneesh Meditation Center, September 1981), 26.

9. "The Master: A Short Biography," 4–17. It will henceforth be cited as *The Master*.

10. *The Master*, 10–11. For Rajneesh's own account hear the audiocassette "The Discipline of Transcendence" 1, no. 21 (9.10.76). It is "described in great detail in an October 1976 newsletter of the Rajneesh Foundation, and in his book, *Dimensions Beyond the Known* (1975), the nearest thing to an autobiographical effort by Rajneesh," Robert Gussner, "The Rajneesh Ashram: The Indian Tradition in an Esalen Context?" (Paper presented at the annual meeting of the American Academy of Religion, San Francisco, 29 December 1977), 5–6.

11. *The Master*, 11.

12. Ibid., 12.

13. Vishal Mangalwadi, *The World of the Gurus* (New Delhi: Vikas Publishing House, 1977), 126. For an account of a meeting with him in this phase of his life see Peter Brent, *Godmen of India*. (London: Allen Lane The Penguin Press, 1972) 150–57.

14. Gussner, 6.

15. *Books, Films,* 26.

16. *Life* 4(11): 73 (November 1981).

17. Rajneesh's departure from India has a mysterious twist to it. Mr. Johar, a prominent figure in Indian film circles, filed a report with the Inspector General of Police alleging that the original Rajneesh may have been murdered and replaced by a double see *Overseas Hindustan Times* 17 September 1981, 14). Nothing more has been heard on this "whodunit" aspect of his departure.

18. Information provided by Swami Ananda Christopher. Rajneesh is also allergic to strong odors so that one is given a sniff test (usually by two women) before one is allowed in his presence.

19. *The Times of India* 17 March 1982, 13.

20. See *Rajneeshpuram: A Blueprint for Man's Future* (Antelope, Oreg.: Rajneesh Neo-Sannyas International Commune, 1982).

21. *Life* 4(11): 78 (Nov. 1981).

22. *Hindustan Times Overseas* 3 Sept. 1981; 7 Jan. 1982.

23. *The New York Times* 16 April 1982, 7.

24. *The Philadelphia Inquirer* 17 April 1981.

25. Ibid. 20 May 1982, 3–A.

26. For an attempt to do so in 1978 see B.D. Tripathi, *Sadhus of India: A Sociological View* (Bombay: Popular Prakashan, 1978), 231: "Acharya Rajneesh was formally associated with the Department

of Philosophy, Jabalpur University. He is essentially a thinker and philosopher.

"Acharya has written many books. The common theme of his books is that man should look within to know his real self or nature.

"Acharya extends this theory to collectivities as well. If a community or society develops the habit of looking within, it raises its confidence which is a pre-condition of growth and progress."

27. Mangalwadi, 142–43.
28. See Rāmacandra Prasāda, *Acārya Rajnīśa* (in Hindi) (Delhi: Motilal Banarsidass, 1969), pt. 1, chaps. 5, 9.
29. Robert Gussner, "Through Insanity to Silence: The Transformational Strategy of Dynamic Meditation of the Rajneesh Movement in the 1970s" (Paper presented at the meeting of the American Academy of Religion, San Francisco, December 1981).
30. I was able to videotape a session of Dynamic Meditation during the trip to Poona. While doing so I realized why the movement is heavily associated with sex. On the notice board I found an outline of the technique of Dynamic Meditation. There was nothing surprising in this, but to my amazement I found another notice next to it which read: "How to know whether you have V.D." In other words, whatever the spiritual effects of arousing sexual energy may be, its pathological effects were fairly obvious. In saying this, of course, I am only betraying my neo-Hindu bias against Tantrika practices.
31. It should be noted that Rajneesh does "seem to accept some of the basic Hindu concepts such as transmigration and *karma*" (Mangalwadi, 132).
32. Robert Gussner, "The Rajneesh Ashram," 2–3.
33. Gussner, 4. For an account of the life and teachings of Rajneesh according to the movement itself see *The Sound of Running Water*.

5

The Dynamics of Change in the Human Potential Movement[1]

Roy Wallis

Introduction

IN this paper I propose to describe some of the main features of the Human Potential, or Growth, movement which has developed over the past thirty years. In the course of time the movement has undergone various changes. I shall take issue—in a preliminary way—with relevant aspects of a "theory of religion" presented in a range of recent papers by Rodney Stark and William S. Bainbridge, which purports to throw light on one of these changes, namely increased spirituality, and seek to show that this, along with other changes, must be understood as the consequence of the movement's diffuse belief system and its individualism.

The Human Potential, or Growth movement is not readily defined. The very vagueness and elasticity of its boundaries, the shifting character of its constituent elements, are, I shall argue, among its most significant features, but they clearly hinder the task of easy definition. These labels are generally taken by those involved to refer to a broad range of activities concerned with enabling people to realize a greater amount of the potential that they possess by way of ability, awareness, creativity, insight, empathy, emotional expression, capacity for experience and exploration, etc. It is generally felt that the pristine human being possesses these characteristics, but loses or represses them as a result of the impact of society and its constraining structures. They atrophy in a social context which ignores them and tries to suppress them especially in adults. Oscar Ichazo's assessment of this phenomenon could be duplicated from numerous other sources:

> A person retains the purity of essence for a short time. It is lost between four and six years of age when the child begins to imitate his parents, tell lies, and pretend. A contradiction develops between the inner feelings of the child and the social reality to which he must conform. Ego consciousness is the limited mode of awareness that develops as a result of the fall into society. (In an interview, see Keen, 1973).

Michael Barnett, an early innovator and leader in the Growth movement in Britain, and later to become a prominent sannyasin in the movement of Bhagwan Shree Rajneesh, made a similar point: "The Human Potential Movement sees that we have sacrificed ourselves unknowingly, as children, in the name of society, or of our parents" (Barnett 1973, 69). Jerome Liss argues along similar lines, when he says that: "A child's development warps when his parents restrict attention to what pleases them . . . A child will program himself to fit in because of the urgent need for attention. Only many years later might he realize the deception he's participated in; his grief is to have lost real self-awareness for a false social self" (1974, 27).

At the core of the Growth movement is the field of *humanistic psychology* which John Rowan has identified in the following terms:

> Humanistic psychology is not just a new brand of psychology, to set side by side on the shelves with all the old brands. It is a wholly different way of looking at psychological science. It is a way of doing science which includes love, involvement and spontaneity, instead of systematically excluding them. And the object of this science is not the prediction and control of people's behaviour, but the liberation of people from the bonds of neurotic control, whether this comes from outside (in the structures of our society) or from inside (Rowan 1976, 3).

Humanistic psychology finds its roots in developments of psychoanalytic therapy through group therapy and the work of Wilhelm Reich, Otto Rank, and other psychoanalytic "heretics"; group dynamics and T-groups developed by Kurt Lewin; Abraham Maslow's ideas about self-actualization; Carl Rogers's development of non-directive and client-centered groups; Moreno's methods of psychodrama; and Gestalt psychology, particularly as presented in the work of Perls and Schutz (Rowan 1976; Kovel 1978).

These ideas, often having their roots in earlier decades of the century, were in some instances stimulated by an interest in the sources of authoritarianism in and after World War II, and in methods for promoting democratic participation. In other cases they represented developments in the search for more effective modes of therapy, less time-consuming than psychoanalysis and less alienating than behavioral therapeutic practices or psychopharmacological techniques as they in turn developed in the 1960s.

The boundaries of humanistic psychology, however, are as unclear as those of the Growth movement. Misiak and Sexton point out: "Although there are common elements, the protagonists of humanistic psychology differ widely among themselves. They are far from unanimous. In 1967 Bugental, an enthusiastic leader of the movement, was still able to say, 'humanistic psychology is as much distinguished by what it is not or by what it opposes as by what it affirms'" (Misiak and Sexton 1973, 116).

Rowan, quoted above, refers to humanistic psychology as a "science," yet the advent of what are known as "Transpersonal psychologies" has blurred this category somewhat, taking as their focus the evocation and therapeutic use of mystical and spiritual states and experiences. However, if humanistic psychology has been largely naturalistic in orientation, it has also been distinctive in its commitment to the priority of individual experience. Traditional therapies have sought to impose one person's experience on others through some particular intellectual formulation and authoritative practice. Humanistic psychology has taken the contrary view that, since each individual possesses resources to attain his full human potential, he is also ultimately the best judge of what he needs. John Rowan refers to this as the one theme which all the early strands of humanistic psychology had in common: "people are all right as they are. There is nothing extra which they need in order to be whole . . ." (Rowan 1976, 7). The movement thus tended to reject the notion of an authoritative guide to what an individual needs, and therefore to reject the idea of the expert and the professional as someone radically distinct from the client. All were viewed—at least in the movement's early years—as *participants,* engaged in an exploratory enterprise in which some already have experience and can, for that reason, facilitate that experience for others.

Experience was given priority over intellectualization, and the qualification for leading groups was the greater extent of that experience rather
than any academic or other formal training.

But, whatever the boundaries of humanistic psychology, they spill
over into the broader domain of the Human Potential movement which
comprises a wider variety of techniques, activities, and ideas devoted to
enabling people to realize their potential. These include meditation,
dance, forms of martial art, and movement such as T'ai Chi, yoga,
massage, etc. At the boundaries of the movement, overlapping it within
a broader cultural and social milieu, are a number of movements
possessing a much more authoritarian vision of what constitutes human
potentiality and its attainment. An example would be Scientology
(Wallis 1976), which possesses many comparable goals and methods,
but which is generally not viewed as part of the Growth movement
because of its efforts to exert a substantial degree of control over its
followers, and because of its authoritarianism.

More ambiguous in this respect are movements such as Synanon
(once a model for the Growth movement but now drifted beyond the
pale because of its growing authoritarianism, control over members,
and willingness to employ violence); est, which employs authoritarian
and control methods in the training situation but does not thereafter
seek to exercise constraint and authority over its graduates; the
following of Bhagwan Shree Rajneesh, Janov's Primal Institute, Arica,
and Re-Evaluation Counseling, which contain elements of submission
to authority and of control combined with elements of personal
autonomy.

Indeed, the Human Potential movement inevitably overlaps not only
with these more authoritarian forms of human development, but with
other disciplines and activities claiming insight into human growth and
how it can be attained. These other overlapping movements can be
categorized as follows:

Physical: Bates eye method, Alexander technique, vegetarianism and
other dietary practices, natural child birth.

Meditative practices: TM, yoga, martial arts.

Occultism: Astrology, Eckankar, Benjamin Creme, Theosophy,
Gurdjieff's Work.

Social change: Ecologism, Feminism, Gay Lib, "Participatory Politics."

"Traditional" therapy and counseling: Psychoanalysis, Jungian analysis, marriage guidance, other counseling.

Evidence of the extensive overlap of interest and following between the Growth movement and related areas of health and spirituality can be found in such publications as *Common Ground,* a periodical published in the San Francisco Bay Area, which lists and provides information on available therapy and human potential activity, spiritual practices, martial arts, healing practices, dietary supplies, feminist and gay groups, astrological services, and alternative employment. A related resource in Britain is the annual Festival for Mind and Body (or more recently, interestingly, Mind, Body and Spirit) which has been run since 1977. These festivals display exhibits and demonstrations by occult and spiritual groups, vegetarians, dancers, yoga and T'ai Chi enthusiasts, human potential practitioners, environmentalists, communitarians, and space ship contactees.

Some idea of the overlaps involved can be gained from figure 1, although the two-dimensional format does not permit these to be shown in all their detail or with great precision. Another way to show some of the major connections is, as in figure 2, by way of a more genealogical representation of the links between some principal ideas and practices of the Growth movement and their sources both within and beyond humanistic psychology.

The Growth movement, then seems to bear the characteristics of what Herbert Blumer has called a *general* rather than a *specific* social movement. It consists of a congeries of independent groups, leaders, communication media, etc., which display no common structure of authority or membership, with divergences of purpose and practice, yet recognizing that they share in common a commitment to the attainment of personal growth by self-directed means. The ideology of such a movement is, therefore, inevitably a *diffuse* one (Budd 1967), setting few limits to what may be believed or undertaken by those who construe themselves as members.

The component elements of such a movement tend to possess few resources for controlling members and clients should they wish to do so, nor may they demand extensive commitment from them. There are always alternative suppliers of a relatively similar commodity, and few of those recognized as being part of the movement claim to have discovered a generally and uniquely efficacious means of securing all those ends sought by the movement's clientele. Some display a very high level of mutual tolerance in this respect. *The Movement,* a periodical published by the Church of the Movement for Inner Spiritual Awareness with which is associated a human potential training (akin to est) called Insight, carries articles describing other spiritual leaders and guides in the warmest terms, as well as a wide range of

Figure 1   The Milieu within which the Human Potential movement is located

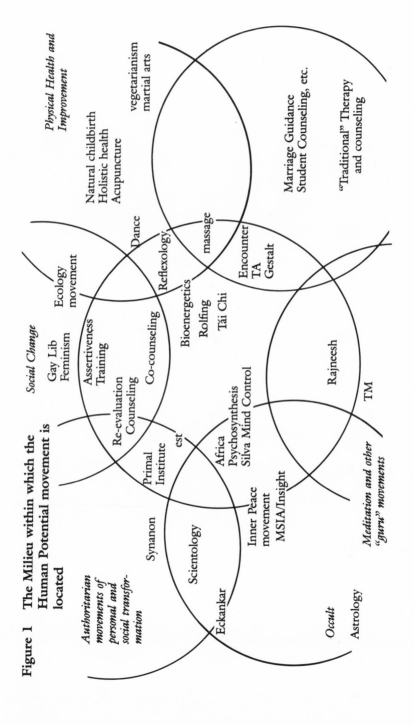

Physical Health and Improvement

vegetarianism
martial arts

Natural childbirth
Holistic health
Acupuncture

Marriage Guidance
Student Counseling, etc.

"Traditional" Therapy
and counseling

Social Change

Gay Lib
Feminism

Ecology
movement

Dance

Reflexology

massage

Encounter
TA
Gestalt

Assertiveness
Training

Bioenergetics
Rolfing
Tai Chi

Re-evaluation
Counseling

Co-counseling

Rajneesh

TM

Primal
Institute

est

Africa
Psychosynthesis
Silva Mind Control

Authoritarian movements of personal and social transformation

Synanon

Scientology

Inner Peace
movement

MSIA/Insight

Eckankar

Meditation and other "guru" movements

Occult

Astrology

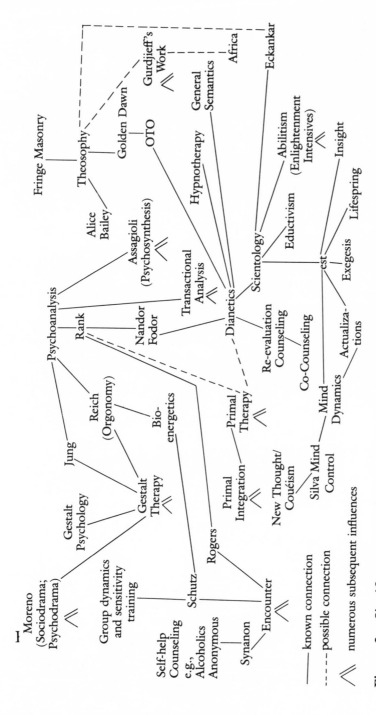

Figure 2   Significant connections between some major elements of the Growth movement and their sources.[2]

advertising for Growth facilities. An editorial presents the newspaper's purpose as follows:

> *The Movement* is a vehicle for the energy of love, cooperation, spirit—whatever you call it—to present itself. This can take many different forms and points of view, as we acknowledge that different people connect with different expressions of the truth. We hope to offer a wide range of approaches so that anyone who reads *The Movement* can find one that will tune him or her in to that alive place within (*The Movement* January 1981, 1).

Yogeshwar Muni (formerly, Charles Berner), founder of the Enlightenment Intensive, similarly carried favorable references to other spiritual teachers in his publication *Vishvamitra*, as well as devoting considerable time in earlier years, to bringing such teachers together, thereby recognizing the similarity in their enterprises and at least the possible validity of their alternative methods.

Don Stone observes that:

> Participation in human-potential groups is not mutually exclusive [sic]. While the disciplines are distinct, they are usually complementary, and many people enroll in several groups in the same period . . . The ease with which people join and leave groups is characteristic of this movement, in contrast to most religious movements that claim to provide intense experience (Stone 1976, 99).

He also remarks that:

> A hallmark of the movement is the extent of multiple participation and eclectic borrowing among these organizations and disciplines. Groups that exert strong pressure for organizational loyalty or orthodoxy of belief and ritual can be considered on the fringes of the movement. Thus, Synanon and Primal Therapy are on the periphery, and growth centers such as Esalen are at the center (Stone 1976, 94).

Not only is the commitment of members to particular component parts of the movement characteristically only partial, being shared with commitment to other constituent parts, but commitment to the movement as a whole also tends to be partial, being shared with related movements within the milieu offering access to similar goals.

This results in a common pattern among members who move through the constituent elements of the movement, sampling what each has to offer, and a common pattern among therapists, group "facilitators," and other leadership cadre of synthesizing components drawn from various schools and approaches in their own practice. This could be demonstrated virtually *ad nauseam*, but one example should suffice. In her Master's thesis in Humanistic Psychology for Antioch University, presented in 1980, Helen Davis, a leading figure in the Growth movement in Britain, reports her own progress through what that movement offered, as follows:

> I am a psychotherapist and have been practising individual and group work since the early seventies. When I first launched myself into the field of humanistic psychology there was, in fact, no formal training available. I spent two years doing group work in a variety of different ideologies and techniques, with different visiting American leaders and therapists. This included open encounter, Synanon encounter, bioenergetics, psychodrama, gestalt, etc, etc.
>
> I then underwent neo-Reichian therapy for a couple of years, with David Boadella. This included workshops in bio-energy and bioenergetics with intensive training periods with David Boadella, Nadine Scott, Alexander Lowen, Karl Kirsch, Stanley Keleman, Jacob Stattman, John Pierrakos, etc. I then entered training on a formal apprenticeship with Simon Meyerson for for two years. Simon's work in experiential regression therapy was based on Freudian/Kleinian concepts. At that time I did further training in regression and rebirthing with Frank Lake, Albert and Diana Pesso and Stanislav Grof. I then did a couple of years' training in Psychosynthesis and the Transpersonal and a further intensive training programme with Frank Lake in Rebirthing. I then underwent Jungian and Transpersonal therapy and training with Barbara Somers in which I am still involved (Davis 1980, 1).

This pattern—although perhaps more extensive in the range of its undertakings than might be found in many other cases—is far from atypical. The movement contains an ever-expanding array of methods, organizations, and ideas relating to the realization of human potential. The proliferation of practices and techniques has been widely noted. From a handful of methodologies in 1950, the field has expanded almost exponentially. A recent anthology listed over 250 different methods of therapy without claiming to have by any means exhausted the field. Indeed, the compiler observes with some justice that it could reasonably be said that there are as many forms of therapy as there are therapists (Herink 1980, xv). Relatively few therapists or "facilitators," moreover, would restrict themselves to a single mode of practice, and most would draw upon several.

Thus, I would argue that a prevailing feature of the movement has been proliferation of practice. Daniel Goleman in a Foreword to Herink (1980, xvii) observes: "These times are especially congenial for therapies: their rate of proliferation is inflationary." Related to this, I would argue that the characteristic mode of relationship to the movement is one of eclectic synthesis of its components. Other central features of the movement's history have been: (1) the outstanding success of its more clearly commercial manifestations—ironic for a movement that began committed to a conception of truth as generated by each individual's experience, and in which truth is seen as a constantly unfolding and unfinished enterprise to be explored, rather than a universally applicable and completed mass-produced package; (2) the professionalism of its facilities—ironic for a movement that stresses the virtues of lay participation and the rejection of authorities; (3) a drift towards spirituality—ironic for a movement that identified itself so closely with the attainment of *human* potential and saw the barriers to that attainment in primarily naturalistic, psychological terms.

The Success of Commercial Enterprise

The typical form of practice in the Growth movement has been that of a group leader who provides leadership in a particular style of growth activity for a regular weekly, all day, or weekend session, within the context of a Growth center, a building or other accommodation through which various Growth activities are promoted. Group leaders may simply advertise their groups on an individual basis, or as part of a cooperative endeavor, with or without shared premises. In addition there are—often perhaps less centrally located within the normative order of Growth activity, yet of major significance for the introduction of new ideas within the movement as a whole—corporate mass producers of self-realization/transformation practices. Many thousands of people have been through at least some of the range of such practices made available by Scientology, Silva Mind Control, the Inner Peace movement (discussed by Scott 1980), TM, or, in a slightly older tradition, Pelmanism or Dale Carnegie. Movements of this kind organize themselves on the lines of multinational corporate businesses, promoting a product held to be uniquely efficacious, or at least far superior to anything else on the market. They often depart from conventional businesses in the extent to which their clientele is mobilized both to secure new customers and to serve as unpaid, or low paid, labor for the organization. Such movements maintain a clearly

separated identity, even though their beliefs and practices may originally have been a synthesis of ideas more generally available in the milieu.
Although such movements may face financial difficulties periodically
with declining enrollments, they have been the most enduring and
economically successful components of the Growth movement and its
milieu. TM has initiated hundreds of thousands of people in America
and Europe, some 200,000 have taken the est training, and similar
numbers had taken Arica trainings by 1978.

Professionalism

Quite early in the career of *Self and Society,* the British periodical
devoted to humanistic psychology, a correspondent commented on the
change in nomenclature which led Bob Selman to become Mr. Robert
Selman, B.A. *(Self and Society)* The movement as a whole is devoted—as
a result, no doubt, of its ideological predisposition to break through
conventional social roles to the "real" person beneath, as much as
because of its American origins—to the use of first names and
informality of style. Yet, in the course of time, there has been some
development both of formal structures and of professionalism in the
organization and practice of the movement.

Many group leaders have also developed practices as individual
therapists, seeing clients once or twice a week for an hour or two-hour
session. Many of these leaders have sought some form of certification of
their knowledge and ability. A substantial number in the United
Kingdom, for example, are, or have been, enrolled as students on the
highly individualized Master's program in Humanistic Psychology run
by Antioch University in London.

Rather than merely providing experimental groups, many of the
leading practitioners in the field have now organized formal programs
of training which issue, after two or three years, diplomas.

Another significant sign of the same phenomenon has been the
development of a concern with finding a means to validate the
competence of existing practioners in the field, establishing standards of
practice, supervision and ethical conduct. This arises, in part, because
an organization like the Association for Humanistic Psychology is
asked to recommend a practitioner from time to time, but also because
of a concern that, if this enterprise does not put its own house in order,
it will be regulated from without. The Foster Report (Foster 1971)
which followed an enquiry into Scientology, recommended the establishment of a Psychotherapy Council for just such a purpose in Britain,

although nothing in fact seems to have been done to implement this recommendation.

Efforts to create a process of evaluation and certification of practitioners are met with great problems: modes of practice vary widely between different therapists and many practitioners do not accept the authority of the body which seeks to evaluate their competence. Some reject the very principle of evaluation and certification, even by their peers, on the grounds that this conflicts with the open, exploratory spirit of humanistic psychology, and recreates the formal structure of power which exists in more traditional healing enterprises, undermining notions of mutual participation, spontaneity, taking risks, and "being real" rather than hiding behind formal rules, roles or certificates. The Association for Humanistic Psychology Practitioners' Group, which is seeking to introduce methods of peer review and supervision, and thereby monitor professional competence and standards to some extent, has not made rapid headway in its endeavors. Lacking any additional authority endowed by the state, it possesses very few resources indeed to encourage practitioners to apply for membership and undergo its scrutiny. Practitioners are able to obtain clients independently of the Association and often regard it with some contempt because of the diversity of people it contains, with some of whom, as practitioners or otherwise, they might not wish to associate; and because—as a result of the diversity of opinion contained within it and the relatively low level of commitment displayed by most members —the Association and the Practitioners' Group have not been able to achieve very much.

Spirituality, the Stark-Bainbridge Theory of Religion and Development in the Human Potential Movement

One major feature of the development of the Human Potential movement has been the increasing role of spirituality. This takes the form of more overtly spiritual character appearing among the ideas and practices available within the movement, such as Psychosynthesis and other Transpersonal psychologies; the transition of some practitioners and their organizations from largely secular to a more spiritual character: Dianology—Church of Eductivism: Abilitism—Sanatana Dharma Foundation; Dianetics—Scientology; Compulsions Analysis—the process; and the drift of secular therapists into the Rajneesh movement, "taking Orange" as Sannyasins and disciples of Bhagwan Shree Rajneesh, or of many early Esalen leaders into Arica.

In a number of recent papers, Rodney Stark and William Bainbridge have developed a theory of religion which can, they believe—among other things—account for this transition from secular to religious forms in movements of this sort. Their argument, having been developed in many papers, may suffer in the compression to which I must necessarily subject it, but I hope that I do not misrepresent its main thrust.

The argument rests upon a major distinction between *rewards* and *compensators*. A *reward* is defined as "anything humans will incur costs to obtain" (Stark and Bainbridge 1980, 115). "In the absence of a desired reward, explanations often will be accepted which posit attainment of the reward in the distant future or in some other nonverifiable context" (ibid. 121). This then leads to a definition of *compensators* as: "postulations of reward according to explanations that are not readily susceptible to unambiguous evaluation" (ibid). Thus: "When humans cannot quickly and easily obtain strongly desired rewards they persist in their efforts and often may accept explanations that provide only compensators—empirically unsubstantiated faith that the rewards will be obtained not the rewards themselves" (ibid), and: " . . . compensators are intangible substitutes for a desired reward having the character of IOUs, the value of which must be taken on faith" (ibid). Religion is defined as "a system of general compensators based on supernatural assumptions" (Stark 1981, 162). Some desired rewards are of such magnitude and scarcity that their unavailability will lead people to accept general compensators instead. Hence, the failure of rewards to be forthcoming from some group or movement of a naturalistic kind on which one's hopes were pinned may lead one to be willing to accept religious compensators instead, and thus provide a strong incentive for the leaders of such groups and movements to respond to failure by shifting what they have to offer in a supernaturalistic direction. Bainbridge and Jackson (1981) provide an account of the emergence of "Siddhi training" in Transcendental Meditation as precisely such a response to the movement's failure marked by the decline in initiations and new members. Stark (1981) advances the same argument for the transformation that occurred within Synanon, from Compulsions Analysis to The Process, and from Dianetics to Scientology.

This argument certainly seems to have some force, yet there are difficulties with it. This distinction between rewards and compensators is blurred by Stark and Bainbridge's claim (1980, 121) that "Compensators are treated by humans as if they were rewards," and further by the fact that Stark and Bainbridge talk about compensators both as

explanations of how rewards may be obtained, and as promised or
"postulated") *rewards*. Moreover, there are systematic ambiguities
connected with the ways in which compensators seem to be distinguished from rewards.

Stark, for example, offers the following example: "A shaman's
promise, that, if certain ritual procedures are observed, a person will be
cured of warts, is a specific compensator" (1981, 161). But how does
this, in fact, differ from the doctor's promise that, if certain medical
procedures are observed, a person will be cured of warts? It can only be
that Stark believes the shaman's promise to be false; for, if it were true,
it would be a tangible reward, not a substitute for it. It is not at all clear
why faith in the one promise is more "unsubstantiated" than in the
other *until* something does or does not occur to the warts; nor that one
is merely an "intangible substitute" for the other, *unless* we presume the
shaman's claim to be false. Stark and Bainbridge believe, of course, that
the doctor's method works and that his explanation is correct while the
contrary applies to the shaman. But suppose that we later discover the
doctor's explanation is also false; does his promise of cure become a
compensator and our sociological explanation of his practice and our
belief change in turn? Since all theories are potentially falsifiable and no
empirical claim is conclusively verifiable—it may always turn out to have
been a mistake—a simple verificationist theory would seem to have
substantial drawbacks for a sociological theory which depends upon a
distinction between theories (and associated promises) which are "true"
and those which are not.

The Stark and Bainbridge theory follows a major tradition of work in
the sociology of religion in which the sociologist takes sides on the
truth claims of certain (non-sociological) ideas. A thoroughgoing
evaluation of this theory must await another occasion (Wallis and Bruce
1984), but here I shall be concerned solely with the argument that the
emergence of greater spirituality in the Human Potential movement can
be explained in these terms. To recapitulate, Stark and Bainbridge claim
that the shift toward spirituality is a response to the failure of these
movements to provide the rewards desired by adherents.

The first point of doubt would relate to the method employed. Stark
and Bainbridge identify some set of events as constituting a *failure* to
provide desired tangible this-worldly rewards. They observe that this
set of events is *followed* by increased supernaturalism or mysticism. They
then argue that the former is the cause of the latter. Initiations drop off
in TM and the Siddhi training is introduced; interest in Dianetics
wanes and Scientology emerges. Yet we are not offered any evidence

that those who took up the more spiritual ideas experienced the prior set of events as a failure to provide the rewards they desired. Indeed, it is equally plausible to believe that those who did see the more secular promises and methods as a failure simply *abandoned* the movement in question and went off to try something else; and that consequently it was those who believed the earlier form *had* achieved what they sought who decided to remain involved and try what was now being offered.

I would not wish to deny that religious beliefs and practices may compensate people for present deprivations. Marx and Freud advanced just such ideas, which may be quite reasonably employed in the interpretation of certain religious interests. But religious beliefs and practices may do many *other* things as well, and we cannot merely assume that all who become committed to religious forms do so in virtue of the prior failure of this-worldly rewards to materialize. Religious goals may be sought *in addition to* this-worldly rewards. Salvation may be desired for its own sake, quite independently of the believer's mundane condition. Moreover, religious goals and methods may be pursued precisely because secular goals have been secured and their associated methods have proven successful.

LSD led many people in the 1960s in a more spiritual direction not because it failed to achieve what they sought, but because it manifestly succeeded in opening up to some of those who took it the possibility of another world, the experience of a realm beyond the mundane, which could then be explored by other—more explicitly spiritual—means.

I would argue that this is equally a possibility in TM and Dianetics. Those who abandoned these practices had either secured what they sought or they had not. But those who remained attached through the transition to more spiritual forms felt that they had gained a great deal from the practices and that there was the possibility of gaining *more*. Some had come with spiritual inclinations and welcomed the emergence of a broader range of rewards to be pursued; and, for others, the possibility that a deeper, more spiritual level of interest existed had been opened up for them by the secular practice. Synanon, too, would not seem to fall precisely into the Stark-Bainbridge case. The more religious form was introduced while the movement was still singularly successful. Being a religion certainly answered the queries of critics as to why the rehabilitated addicts did not return to conventional life, but the addicts themselves do not seem to have vigorously raised this question, their numbers were being greatly supplemented by "squares," and the movement was economically very buoyant. Similarly, in the case of the Process, it is not easy to see their greater spirituality as a response to failure. Rather, my interviews with members and former members of this movement suggest that, once again, those who made the transition were precisely the people who felt the movement had been a *success*, that it had given them substantial benefits already, and also opened up new experiences and interests which—naturally enough—required a new approach.

Thus, while failure to achieve this-worldly rewards *may* lead people and movements in a more spiritual direction as substitutes for the deprivations that persist, failure more typically works as a stimulus to an explanation of why little of a permanent kind has been achieved. But, *equally*, spirituality may be pursued as a way of providing an explanation for what *has* been achieved and out of a desire to gain *additional*, rather than substitute, values and effects.

The further virtue of the conception I am offering (I hesitate to dignify it as a theory) is that it also accounts for the fact that the shift is not all in one direction. Some movements begin as a *spiritual* enterprise and then take on more secular, psychological activities as an adjunct. Such is the history of the movement founded by Bhagwan Shree Rajneesh, which in the mid-1970s began to encourage the use of human potential activities, and the centers of which developed subsequently into veritable supermarkets of human potential activity. Another form of the same pattern is that in which a spiritual teacher, John-Roger, founder of the Church of the Movement of Spiritual Inner Awareness, could team up with Russell Bishop, a former Gestalt therapist, and encourage him to create a human potential training adapted largely from est. In both of these cases, the spiritual teacher appears to have recognized that, as with some drugs, human potential activities may encourage further exploration, may stimulate an interest in ontologically deeper, or spiritually higher, realms in the course of trying to understand the effects produced, and to enhance them further. This would seem to be the tenor of one group leader's observation in a biographical sketch prepared to advertise his services: "For me, the full acceptance of our body and feelings is both essential for our happiness, and the gateway to the realization of our spiritual nature" (Open Centre programme, London summer 1979). A similar view provides the justification for therapy groups in the Rajneesh Movement:

> Some of the (therapy) groups are designed specifically to encourage the exploration of feelings which society has forced people to repress, feelings such as anger, jealousy, fear and lust. This is the first stage of the ashram's group process: to remove emotional blocks so that an individu-

al's energy can regain its natural state as an unimpeded stream. He is then ready to enter more advanced groups which help his energy to flow freely through all the different planes of being—physical, emotional and beyond. (. . .) "Therapy is needed because people have forgotten how to be religious", explains Bhagwan. (Mimeoed unattributed sheet, Kalptaru Rajneesh Centre, London, "The role of therapy groups in the great experiment of Bhagwan Shree Rajneesh").

Indeed, this view would seem to be supported by some movements that shift in a supernaturalistic direction, since, if Stark and Bainbridge were correct, there would not be any obvious reason for continuing the more naturalistic activity, formerly the movement's mainstay. Yet TM still offers its meditation, Yogeshwar Muni still offered trainings at his ashram for "householders" who wished to succeed in the world, after having transformed himself from Charles Berner, ex-Scientology auditor and founder of Abilitism, into a yogi devotee of Sanatana Dharma Shaivism. Even Dianetics is still an offer in Scientology—albeit much changed, like everything else—and the movement still encourages people to sample its powers through tangible effects such as improvement in the ability to communicate. If these things were such evident failures, it is hard to see why they were not dropped entirely.

Explaining the Form of, and Developments in, the Human Potential Movement

My view is that these various features of the Growth movement—proliferation, eclecticism, commercialism, professionalism and spiritualization—form a syndrome arising out of the fundamental difficulties and dilemmas posed by the precariousness of the movement. This precariousness is a consequence of its diffuse belief system, and I shall argue that, underlying all these features, is the principal factor generating change, namely that authority is seen to lie with individual members of the movement. More than being merely politically democratic, the Growth movement—like some related social movements—is epistemologically individualist (Wallis 1976). I intend to show that this fundamental individualism explains the patterns and changes adumbrated above.

As we have seen, the Growth movement is possessed of a rather diffuse belief system. This can be seen too in the openness and tolerance of humanistic psychology which Shaffer (1978, 1) describes not as involving "a specific content area so much as an attitude or orientation toward psychology as a whole," and goes on to quote the "Articles of

Association" of the American Association of Humanistic Psychology, formulated at its inception in 1962, which include the following: "Humanistic psychology . . . stands for respect for the worth of persons, respect for differences of approach, open-mindedness as to acceptable methods, and interest in exploration of new aspects of human behavior." (Shaffer 1978, 2). There is in the Growth movement a commitment to whatever may enhance self-realization, but specifying little as to the constraints on how that might be achieved. Hence, members of the movement adopt an exploratory approach to what the movement makes available, sampling among the approaches and facilities offered, but usually with no extensive commitment to any single supplier.

The market metaphor seems particularly apposite. The customer is the final arbiter of whether he needs, or has benefitted from, a particular service, and there is, therefore, an incentive for suppliers to pursue a policy of product differentiation to attract customers. The ability of clients to pick and choose at will means that to survive a practitioner needs to be able to accommodate quite diverse interests and backgrounds, and needs to secure new methods and to offer an eclectic range in their practice. Will Schutz has observed: "The fact that no one method works well for everyone creates a need for a multiplicity of methods. By having a wide variety of approaches it is more likely that each person can find one or more techniques he can work with profitably" (cited in Giges and Rosenfeld 1976, 78). Moreover, there are few constraints on synthesis and innovation since each member is the ultimate repository of authority (his own "experience" being what counts most) and each possesses the right, therefore, to advance his own amalgam of techniques and new ideas as an improvement upon those which he has borrowed. Jerome Liss expresses this theme in what he says of leadership in groups: *"Everyone is leader*. The leader is leader only in so far as people let him act that way and no one supersedes his functions. Anything the leader does, anyone can do . . ." (1974, 133). There are few readily exercizable controls over suppliers or customers, since suppliers may operate quite independently of each other within the same broad market. Customers cannot effectively be controlled while they continue to view themselves as the definite authority on the virtues of the products they consume. This point is made by Liss in the following quotations:

> To respect a person means to respect the individual's point, even and especially when it is at variance with one's own . . . "What's mine is

good for me, as I claim it to be. What's theirs is good for them, just as they claim it to be. Theirs would not be good for me, nor mine for them" (1974, 85).

Ultimately, no one can speak for anyone else, only for oneself, because experience is in essence private (1974, 105).

Proliferation is thus an inevitable consequence of product differentiation promoted by the priority of the client's own experience. Equally, eclecticism is the inevitable consequence of resting decisions as to whether or not to incorporate a new idea or practice into one's corpus on the individual's judgment of fit and compatibility with his experience. Commercialism and professionalism follow from similar effects of individualism and a diffuse belief system.

Early activists in the Growth movement hoped that it would prove the basis for a way of life. Will Schutz articulates this view: "Encounter is a way of life, not just a therapeutic technique. It concerns itself with relations among people and offers an alternative to the present structure of society . . ." (1980, 179).

However, it shortly appeared evident that most people involved were not committing themselves to a total way of life. They were only partially involved in this movement, and even more partially in any particular variant of it. Although some early followers—often now leadership cadre—continued to view the Growth movement as a way of life, they found themselves very largely on their own after the initial phase of enthusiasm. The bulk of those participating in the movement wished to do so only on a part-time basis. Being only one supplier among many of a commodity or service not irreplaceably unique, groups and Growth centers had few resources to control members and could only seek to maintain commitment and enrollments by following customer demand (Clark 1956). They began to abandon the notion of the Growth center as a cooperative, mutually participatory endeavor in pursuit of a way of life, and to organize themselves on more business-likes lines or go to the wall. (This appears to embody a major transition at Esalen as I understood it from conversation with its founder, Michael Murphy, and to reflect the experience of the early London Growth centers.) Many failed to negotiate that transition successfully, became financially non-viable, and disappeared.

If the involvement of most people in the movement was only part-time and viewed as purchasing a service rather than undertaking a way of life, then it makes good sense to believe that those groups which explicitly organized themselves along commercial lines (Scientology, est, Silva Mind Control, etc.) should—while there remained a buoyant market for their particular form of the Growth commodity—prosper and meet the need of much of the available clientele. However, for those who preferred their services to be available in less glossily packaged, or mass produced form, there remained the broad range of therapists and group leaders. The latter were often drawn from among those who, in the movement's initial flourishing, had construed it as a major life interest, throwing themselves wholeheartedly into running groups, organizing centers, administering conferences and societies, only to find in a relatively short space of time that the co-participatory way of life had not developed. They were doing all the work, while a less committed body of persons consumed the services thereby provided.

The same few names are constantly the principal candidates for office in bodies like the Association for Humanistic Psychology in Britain, and more often than not the same as those who organize conferences, write for the journals, and now administer and contribute to the training courses being established.

The breakdown of the co-participatory basis of mutual exploration among people engaged in the pursuit of a way of life meant that those most actively engaged in the movement became a distinctive group of individuals accorded a separate status, rather than them merely being seen as slightly more experienced versions of the average enthusiast. Providing a service rather than engaging in a cooperative exploration, and increasingly taking on individual clients from among the groups which they led—those in need of more intensive therapeutic work than could be provided in a group context—it was a natural and obvious step for a more professional conception of the practitioner-client relationship to emerge. This was the more particularly so as, after the movement's early enthusiastic phase, its composition shifted away from the counter-cultural young, and an increasing proportion of those involved were more conventional, middle-class people often engaged in health care occupations, teaching, counseling and social work. These people often sought techniques and aids in their own work and, being used to more formalized procedures of training, were an encouragement to their emergence in the Human Potential movement.

This rapproachement with the conventional world had the further feature that the permeable boundary between the Growth movement and the traditional therapies and counseling resulted on the one hand in the introduction of ideas and practices from this more conventional area of psychology and psychiatry. This was particularly the case as some practitioners sought to make sense of experience and practice deriving from *different* modes of growth work. Eclecticism led to the need for a way of conceptualizing and making sense of experiences which could not readily be accommodated within the often rudimentary intellectual framework of any particular element of the synthesis. Some turned to the more intellectual structures of psychoanalysis and the like.

The permeability of the boundary also meant that at least some of the practices involved in the Growth movement were being carried back into conventional therapeutic and counseling practice. Group leaders were invited to provide trainings or groups in therapeutically respectable settings. The knowledge that there existed a market for human potential practices among a more respectable clientele and in more conventional institutions must also have been an incentive to practitioners to improve their collective image, regulating practice and ethics and seeking to weed out the more disreputable among their number. Developments of this kind inevitably encouraged the adoption of a professional model of the relationship between practitioners and clients.

Commercialism and professionalism emerge from a situation where a market in practices has grown from the limited and partial involvement of the bulk of participants who—reserving to themselves the right to select those components they view as true or efficacious—endow suppliers with only a limited and competing role in the provision of desired services. The emergence of commercialism and professionalism as organizational principles are a direct consequence of the movement's *epistemological individualism*.

Spirituality

Most observers agree that there has been a shift toward increased spirituality in the Human Potential movement. Don Stone (1976), who has observed this movement particularly on the West Coast of America, suggests that, beginning with groups employing T-group and sensitivity training methods in the late 1940s and 1950s, there was the development of encounter, closely followed by a growing popularity of physical methods such as massage, Rolfing and the like. By the 1970s, he notes:

There was a growing emphasis on transpersonal and spiritual experience, partly through the adaption [sic] of Eastern disciplines into Western settings . . .

This evolution during the last twenty years represents a change in emphasis from the self-transcendence of going beyond the limits of everyday life to the self-transcendence of merging with infinite cosmic energy . . . (ibid, 96).

He observes that "many growth centers . . . began with encounter and are now accommodating a more explicit search for transcendence" (ibid, 97).

I have argued that the Stark-Bainbridge theory of religion does not, as they suppose, seem adequate to explain this phenomenon. It is undoubtedly true that many people came to the movement with very high expectations which could not be fully met by naturalistic methodologies, and many of those who became early leaders continued exploring both through the various emerging forms of Growth activity, and then beyond. In other cases, the success of the methods gave rise to new questions, awakened new interests, and therefore provoked further search, again leading some into more spiritual, and therefore broader, approaches and ideas. Ma Satya Bharti captures something of this in her reflection on the movement of Bhagwan Shree Rajneesh:

All kinds of people come to Bhagwan, but the greatest single professional group is psychotherapists. It's not really surprising. Bhagwan's work incorporates what they've been doing, but goes beyond it. The ashram is filled with therapists from all over the world. *It's a natural extension to what they've been attempting on their own. They've grown themselves,* they've used all the tools the West has devised for inner growth, they've helped others to expand their consciousness and their possibilities, but unless they come to a master they remain stuck within the boundaries of what Western psychology has come to know (Bharti 1981, 82, emphasis added).

I would argue, however, that a major factor involved in the shift for many of the early enthusiasts, and undoubtedly a significant factor in the flocking of group leaders into the movement of Bhagwan Shree Rajneesh, was that they remained committed to the notion of the Growth movement as the basis for a way of life. The excitement of the early Growth centers, and the composition of the early movement overwhelmingly among the counter-cultural young, gave substance to that aspiration. As the counter-culture receded, the hippies returned to the conventional world, and the Growth movement was more clearly seen to consist of a small cadre of enthusiasts committing themselves almost full-time, and the bulk of participants involved only segmentally and transitorily. Those who could not adjust to the Growth movement as a merely commercial or professional enterprise were often strongly attracted to a movement such as that of Bhagwan, which contained an extensive round of growth activities, within the framework of a life of spiritual devotion and a community of the like-minded.

Spirituality was thus, for many, a recourse in the face of the undermining of the conception of the Growth movement as a way of life by the individualism and incipient instrumentalism that early became widely prominent. For others, it was a response to the success *or* failure of aspects of the enterprise which required explanation and remedy at some deeper (or higher) level. For others, spiritual conceptions provided a higher-order, conceptual realm under which the diversity of effects from different forms of practice could be subsumed in an integrated fashion.

The Authoritarian Margins of the Movement

Understanding the Human Potential movement in this light, as faced with a variety of dilemmas and precarious features as a result of the diffuseness of its beliefs and the individualized nature of participation within it, also provides a basis for understanding the relationship of the movement to the more authoritarian structures at its margins.

I have argued elsewhere (eg., Wallis 1976) that in such a context some of those who create synthetic packages have a powerful motivation to maintain their own priority as innovators and leaders, and to inhibit the inevitable dispersal of the distinctive features of their beliefs or practice into the common stock ebbing and flowing in the movement as a whole.

The only way in which this can be achieved is by undermining the individual's right to select and reject elements as he chooses, to undermine the epistemological individualism of participants, transforming them from clients into followers. The most readily available effective method of arrogating authority is through the proclamation of some spiritual revelation permitting the "transcendentalizing" of one's product, thereby giving it greater breadth of relevance and the promise of vastly greater efficacy, and providing the resources for demanding a higher level of involvement, commitment and loyalty than hitherto required.

There is, therefore, a tendency for mass-producers to justify their brand identity and cost by basing their claims in some unique spiritual insight possessed by the founder, otherwise their beliefs and practices will simply diffuse into the common stock of ideas and practices generally available at lower rates throughout the Growth movement and its milieu. While exclusiveness, authoritarianism and attacks upon synthesizers or *bricoleurs* who purloin some of the ideas and practices, may have some inhibitory effect, not all clients will be successfully transformed into followers—at least not permanently—and some of these will inevitably carry back such ideas and techniques into the Growth movement, often founding less authoritarian variants upon the same intellectual foundations (with additions and deletions), remaining committed to the prevailing ideal of epistemological individualism.

Notes

1. For financial assistance in the conduct of this research I am grateful to the Social Science Research Council (UK) for their most generous grant, and to The Queen's University of Belfast which provided various essential facilities and funds. I have discussed the argument of this paper often with Dr. Steve Bruce of the Department of Social Studies at The Queen's University. He deserves some of the blame even if he doesn't get to share any of the credit. I am also grateful to John Rowan, Dr. John Miller, Alix Pirani, Yogeshwar Muni, Vivian Milroy, David Boadella, and Dr. Dina Glouberman for their comments on a draft of this essay.

2. It would be quite futile to attempt an exhaustive list of connections, since one could make out little from the resulting mass of lines. I appreciate, however, that Perls acknowledges some influence from Dianetics, see Perls 1951. (I am grateful to Bill Bainbridge for reminding me of this source.) I also appreciate the role of phenomenology and existentialism through Allport and Maslow in America

153

and through R. D. Laing in Britain; but the fact of interconnected-ness and perhaps the cultic character of some of the connections are more important for my purposes here than an exhaustive representa-tion of the historical sources.

References

Bainbridge, William Sims and Daniel H. Jackson. 1981. The rise and decline of Transcendental Meditation. In *The Social Impact of New Religious Movements,* edited by Bryan Wilson. Barrytown, N.Y.: Unification Theological Seminary.

Barnett, Michael. 1973. *People Not Psychiatry.* London: Allen & Unwin.

Bharti, Ma Satya. 1981. *Death Come Dancing: Celebrating Life with Bhagwan Shree Rajneesh.* London: Routledge and Kegan Paul.

Budd, Susan. 1967. The humanistic societies: The consequences of a diffuse belief system. In *Patterns of Sectarianism,* edited by Bryan Wilson. London: Heinemann Educational Books.

Clark, Burton. 1956. Organizational adaptation and precarious values. *American Sociological Review* 21:327–36.

Davis, Helen. 1980. *Psychodynamics and the Body.* MA Thesis in Humanistic Psychology. London: Antioch University.

Foster, Sir John G. 1971. *Enquiry into the Practice and Effects of Scientology.* London: Her Majesty's Stationery Office.

Giges, Burton and Edward Rosenfeld. 1976. Personal growth, encounter, and self-awareness groups. In *The Intensive Group Experience,* edited by Max Rosenbaum and Alvin Sandowsky. New York: Free Press.

Herink, Richie, editor. 1980. *The Psychotherapy Handbook*. New York: New American Library.

Keen, Sam. 1973. Arica. *Psychology Today* (July): 2,7.

Kovel, Joel. 1978. A *Complete Guide to Therapy*. Harmondsworth: Penguin.

Liss, Jerome. 1974. *Free to Feel*. London: Wildwood House.

Misiak, Henryk and Virginia Staudt Sexton. 1973. *Phenomenological, Existential and Humanistic Psychology: A Historical Survey*. New York: Grune and Stratton.

Perls, Frederick. 1951. Introduction to J. A. Winter, *A Doctor's Report on Dianetics*. New York: Julian Press.

Rowan, John. 1976. *Ordinary Ecstasy: Humanistic Psychology in Action*. London: Routledge and Kegan Paul.

Scott, Gini. 1980. *Cult and Countercult: A Study of a Spiritual Growth Group and a Witchcraft Order*. Westport, Conn.: Greenwood Press.

Schutz, Will. 1980. Encounter therapy. In *Psychotherapy Handbook*, edited by Richie Herink. New York: New American Library. *Self and Society*. 1974. 2(11):22.

Shaffer, John. 1978. *Humanistic Psychology*. Englewood Cliffs, N. J.: Prentice-Hall.

Stark, Rodney. 1981. Must all religions be supernatural?, *The Social Impact of New Religious Movements,* edited by Bryan Wilson. Barrytown, N.Y.: Unification Theological Seminary.

Stark, Rodney and William Sims Bainbridge. 1980. Toward a theory of religion: Religious commitment. *Journal for the Scientific Study of Religion* 19(2):114–28.

Stone, Don. 1976. The Human Potential Movement, *The New Religious Consciousness,* edited by Charles Glock and Robert N. Bellah. Berkeley: University of California Press.

Wallis, Roy. 1976. *The Road to Total Freedom: A Sociological Analysis of Scientology*. London: Heinemann Educational Books. New York: Columbia University Press, 1977.

Wallis, Roy and Steve Bruce. 1984. The Stark-Bainbridge theory of religion: A critical analysis and counter proposals. In *Sociological Analysis* 45, 1:11:27.

6
Cultural Genetics

William Sims Bainbridge

CULT *is culture writ small.* When I made this point four years ago (Bainbridge 1978b), I suggested thereby that we can learn much about the generation of culture by studying religious cults. Now I would like to go further. Cults are the *drosophila melanogaster* and *escherichia coli* which will permit us to develop cultural genetics.

When biological geneticists employ fruit flies or bacteria for their studies, rather than elephants or redwoods, they exploit the brevity of these organisms' lives, the efficiency of collecting great quantities of cheap data on these modest species, and in the case of *e. coli* the ease of intervening in the processes of inheritance. Cults have all these advantages in comparison to larger and more stable social institutions. Another advantage is that cults display simple phenomena in coherent, individual organisms, which typically is not the case for the cultures of whole societies. Thus, cults also have the advantage of the viruses which contemporary geneticists have studied, in that it is possible to *sequence* the entire genetic structure, to chart the whole culture and determine the mode and source of inheritance of every part.

Certainly, it may turn out that cults operate according to a somewhat different set of principles from other aspects of culture. By employing a few examples from music in this essay, I shall show that the concepts which appear to explain cult genetics do so as well for other phenomena. I believe cults well represent a range of other human creations, and that very different phenomena can be identified and understood more easily if we already have analyzed cults. *Homo sapiens* is vastly more complex than the *phiX174* virus, yet complete sequencing of the genome of the latter was an important step toward understanding the genetics of the former.

In any case, this essay explores the possibility of a cultural genetics based on research and theory about cults. Even if this field should turn out to be limited to the sphere of novel religions, extensive research along the lines I propose would be justifiable. The great world religions, including some not yet born, emerge as cults, and religion remains one of the most important and most distinctively human objects of study for social scientists.

In order for a cultural genetics to be possible, three things are necessary: First, there must be some process of reproduction and inheritance, in which cultural structures and elements are transmitted from one "generation" to the next. Second, there must be a significant measure of stability in the transmission process, in which the replicators show sufficient copying-fidelity to transmit recognizable patterns. Third, there must be some process such as sexuality or mutation which introduces change and variety into the process of inheritance yet is sufficiently coherent itself to permit scientific analysis. In fact these conditions are met by religious cults and by at least some other phenomena such as stylistic schools in the various arts. If other parts of the wider culture fail to exhibit these features, still there will be an "inorganic chemistry" of culture if not the full richness of an organic genetics, and the rules of one can illuminate the rules of the other.

Do cults reproduce? And, if so, can we discern regularities in the processes by which parent cults give rise to novel offspring? Surely, we should not expect to find the equivalent of sexual reproduction in the cultural sphere. To say that necessity is the mother of invention is not to suggest a real counterpart to males and females among the factors which generate innovations. The idea of two deviant religious groups engaging in sexual intercourse, resulting in the birth of a third, is a bizarre image, although some rare cases might fit this metaphor.

However complex it may seem, culture reproduces through processes more analogous to those used by the most simple sexual forms of life.

Therefore, in the end we may draw more inspiration from contemporary research on viruses and bacteria than from the more classical studies of fruit flies and sweet peas. Yet, at this very early point in the development of cultural genetics, we cannot limit our search for metaphors, and should hunt widely for biological principles which might have their parallels in culture. I suggest we should read as deeply in the history of genetics as in the most recent reports of laboratory experiments (Sturtevant 1965; Whitehouse 1965; Stubbe 1972). This essay does not draw heavily upon the growing body of literature which seeks to apply sociobiology and population genetics to culture, but much future work should do so (Lumsden and Wilson 1981; Cavalli-Sforza and Feldman 1981).

In modern society, cults are born out of older cults, and most of them are known to cluster in family lineages. The very fact that Melton (1978) could organize his great encyclopedia around the family concept shows this. In an earlier paper, Stark and I delineated three compatible models of cult innovation, which represented a step toward cultural genetics. All three models could be found in the literature, although two were relatively dormant in sociology at the time we wrote. And all three have considerable empirical support. We suggested, but did not then show in detail, that the three were compatible, rather than competing, although one or another might apply particularly well in explaining a given case of cultic innovation. All three showed how people might create novel systems of compensators, but one placed the locus of innovation in an individual beset by *psychopathology,* the second in a religion-business *entrepreneur,* and the third in a small, cohesive social group undergoing *subculture evolution.*

In our discussion of the entrepreneur model, although with no presumption that the two other models fail to follow the same rules of heredity, we suggested a parallel between cult innovation and the intentional evolution currently practiced in the laboratory:

> Future research can determine the most common processes through which entrepreneurial cult founders actually invent their novel ideas. We suspect the main techniques involve the cultural equivalent of recombinant DNA genetic engineering. Essentially, the innovator takes the cultural configuration of an existing cult, removes some components, and replaces them with other components taken from other sources. Often, the innovator may simply splice pieces of two earlier cults together. In some cases, the innovator preserves the supporting skeleton of practices and basic assumptions of a cult he admires, and merely grafts on new symbolic flesh (Bainbridge and Stark 1979, 290).

De-emphasizing the distinction between "natural" and "artificial" genetics, we can expand greatly on these ideas now, first suggesting the chief modes of reproduction, which while they do not involve sexuality nonetheless can be effective means for producing new religious organisms.

Fission and Sporulation

While sects come into being through the process of schism, cults are born in what appears to be an unlimited variety of ways. However, many of the stories put out by the cults themselves to explain their origins are false, and I think most cases—and all those of interest for cultural genetics—are born through two processes I shall call *fission* and *sporulation*. Certainly, many cults may emerge through a series of events which falls between these two clear extremes, but if we define and explore these two concepts, we shall easily be able to interpolate between them and understand the range of mechanisms by which cults reproduce themselves.

Fission involves the splitting of the social group which is a cult into two or more pieces, each of which is a viable religious organization from the start, even without the recruitment of new members. Of course, fission is the common term for reproduction by splitting among micro-organisms. The sociologist of religion might immediately complain that a perfectly good term already exists: *schism*. Why should I urge a "genetics" term when we already have a good "religion" name for this process? First of all, I do not propose new terms lightly, but always have, what seems to me, a compelling reason. I am not prepared to suggest we call this process *mitosis,* for example, because I see no analogy here to that very special kind of genetic splitting.

The problem with the term schism is that it has taken on very definite connotations within the sociology of religion and might therefore mislead us by the theoretical assumptions which attach to it. For one thing, it generally describes the splitting process which gives birth to a new *sect,* a process in which there is a definite regularity which often will not be found in cult reproduction. Disputes within an existing religious organization over the proper degree of tension with the sociocultural environment prompt the emergence of *sect movements* and *church movements* (cf. Stark and Bainbridge 1979). Within a given religious body, a sect movement will want more tension, while a church movement will want less. The desire for greater tension flows from the need for more efficacious specific compensators for scarce rewards. If our conceptualization is in future accepted by the field, the term schism may thereafter imply a battle over the proper level of tension which leads to a split. Certainly it has that connotation in our own minds.

The term fission, in contrast, implies nothing about the cause of a split. Indeed, I am convinced that a number of causes—a finite number which I hope we can count—may prompt fission within cults. Certainly, the need for more efficacious specific compensators may often be the driving force, but this need not imply a dispute over the proper level of tension. Two factions in a cult may disagree over the best magical means to achieve a certain valued reward, and emphasize competing compensators even at the same level of tension. While this may happen in any religious group, I think it is more common in cults, especially in those which retain a significant degree of magic.

Geographic separation between two outposts of a cult can facilitate fission, especially when there is no peripatetic strong leader or an organizational structure capable of holding separate social cliques together. Of particular interest to cultural genetics are cases in which a cult is innovating rapidly, and in which the innovation is diffused widely throughout the membership, as described in the *subculture-evolution* model. Geographically separated branches of a cult may innovate separately, moving their cultures in different directions and thus increasing the effective social separation. Each clique will be excited by its own innovations, and perhaps ignorant of the innovations of the other clique. At some point, the growing cultural difference causes a break along the social cleavage established by the geographic separation, even if the cultural divergence was a case of pure genetic drift.

And I would not like to exclude many other possible factors which encourage fission, certainly not this early in my theorizing. Since fission is an ordinary word immediately intelligible to us, I suggest we use it as the general term for reproduction by splitting into two or more immediately viable parts, and only consider later whether to use schism instead.

The other discernable method of cult reproduction is sporulation. This term may be less familiar than fission, but it is used in biology to name the process by which organisms of certain species (the mosses, for example) reproduce by throwing off *spores*—tiny seeds. Stark and I have already described this process, but without giving it a name. Especially in the entrepreneur model of cult formation, but perhaps also in the psychopathology model as well, a single individual founds a new cult on the basis of prior apprenticeship in an existing cult. Because the entrepreneur model clearly points the way toward cultural genetics, I shall quote its outline here:

1. Cults are businesses which provide a product for their customers and receive payment in return.
2. Cults are mainly in the business of selling novel compensators, or at least freshly packaged compensators that appear new.
3. Therefore, a supply of novel compensators must be manufactured.
4. Both manufacture and sales are accomplished by entrepreneurs.
5. These entrepreneurs, like those in other businesses, are motivated by the desire for profit, which they can gain by exchanging compensators for rewards.
6. Motivation to enter the cult business is stimulated by the perception that such businesses can be profitable, an impression likely to be acquired through prior involvement with a successful cult.
7. Successful entrepreneurs require skills and experience, which are most easily gained through a prior career as the employee of an earlier successful cult.
8. The manufacture of salable new compensators (or compensator-packages) is most easily accomplished by assembling components of pre-existing compensator systems into new configurations, or by the further development of successful compensator systems.
9. Therefore, cults tend to cluster in lineages. They are linked by individual entrepreneurs who begin their careers in one cult and then leave to found their own. They bear strong "family resemblances" because they share many cultural features.
10. Ideas for completely new compensators can come from any cultural source or personal experience whatsoever, but the skillful entrepreneur experiments carefully in the development of new products and incorporates them permanently in his cult only if the market response is favorable (Bainbridge and Stark 1979, 288).

The entrepreneur who leaves one cult to found his own is the spore in sporulation. Unlike fission, sporulation does not immediately produce a viable new cult, but only the potential for a successful new religion. Before the new cult can come into full existence, the entrepreneur must find followers, and the cult goes through a process of social, institutional and even cultural germination. As we noted in presenting the entrepreneur model, some cults, like Scientology, are especially prolific in casting off such human spores who plant new successful cults, so the idea of sporulation is appropriate in describing a process in which the parent cult plays an important role in addition to the role of the entrepreneur. It is not uncommon, of course, for the spore to consist of a couple, often married, rather than a single individual. Couples were common in the family of cults which sprang from *I Am*, founded by Guy and Edna Ballard. In 1954 Thomas Printz founded a cult called The Bridge to Freedom by sporulation from I Am. Then two couples left The Bridge as spores. In 1958 Mark and Elizabeth Clare Prophet founded The Summit Lighthouse. And in the mid-1960s, Garman and Evangeline Van Polen founded The Ruby Focus of Magnificent Consummation (Melton 1978).

There may be cases which fall between fission and sporulation, but they should be intelligible in terms of the same processes which operate at the extremes. The utility of the lineage concept, and the richness of cult heredity can be illustrated by turning briefly to a single family, the one which includes Scientology at its center.

The Scientology Genus

Among the largest and most fertile cults of the past few decades is Scientology, founded by former science fiction writer L. Ron Hubbard. Figure 1 summarizes the main derivations of which I am aware, including seven descendants, three ancestors, and a cult with which Scientology exchanged some genetic material. I studied Scientology ethnographically (Bainbridge and Stark 1980) and carried out an even more extensive ethnographic study of one of its offspring, the Process (Bainbridge 1978b). Briefer research contact with Dianology, General Semantics, various Rosicrucian groups, and several cults in the Psychoanalytic tradition also contributed to figure 1. The other groups I know only through the publications of journalists and social scientists.

Scientology exemplifies the close link between magical personal-growth cults and fully religious cults. Hubbard first offered the world a supposedly scientific psychotherapy named Dianetics, announced in the May 1950 issue of *Astounding Science Fiction*. A variety of difficulties and developments caused Hubbard to establish Scientology as a new religion, two years later.

No cult founder could have been better prepared than Hubbard to create a richly eclectic pseudo-scientific cult. Science fiction literature is strewn with the bones of ancient superstitions and the half-formed embryos of deviant sciences. One of the most prolific authors in the genre, Hubbard counted the leading editor and two of the most

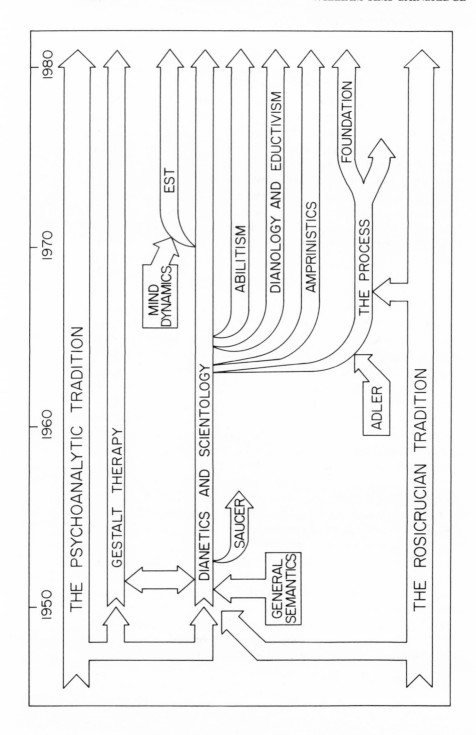

imaginative authors among his close friends. Much of Scientology's culture consists of standard science fiction ideas, such as interstellar civilizations, asserted as fact rather than as fiction.

In the earliest Dianetics publications Hubbard gives some credit to Alfred Korzybski's General Semantics cult. For a while in 1950, Hubbard lectured on General Dianetics, and one of his closest co-workers A. E. van Vogt wrote an influential novel based on General Semantics (van Vogt 1945). The General Semantics movement still exists, more than thirty years after the death of its founder, claiming to be a scholarly discipline complete with its own scientific journal. However, Korzybski's main writings combine moralism with much pseudo-scientific quackery (Korzybski 1948, 1950), and the cult for a time boasted the ability to cure alcoholism, homosexuality, kleptomania, stuttering, importence and other psychological problems (Gardner 1957).

Hubbard also admits much kinship with the psychoanalysis cult, although he disagrees with Freud on several issues (Hubbard 1956). I am sure many readers will disagree with my statement that psychoanalysis is a magical cult, but the sweeping, unproven claims of this practice certainly place it among the chief forms of modern magic (Eysenck 1965; Rachman 1971; Salter 1972; cf. Freud 1964, 86). There is some disagreement how much of Freud's cult was derived from the Jewish mystical tradition (Bakan 1965; Berkower 1969), but much of Freud's early work sprang from the tradition of Mesmerism, which gave the world Christian Science and innumerable other cults (Zweig 1962; Darnton 1970). Freud counted the founder of the Biorhythm cult among his closest friends (Bainbridge 1978a). Even if Freud's own work was indeed legitimate scientific exploration, the tendency to turn psychoanalysis into magic or religion has been irresistible for many of his followers (Fodor 1971; Rieff 1966). Psychoanalysis promised rewards of mental health and personal effectiveness which were never delivered to most patients. In the hands of various practitioners, forms of treatment multiplied, each new technique and theory constituting a novel compensator. In the case of Scientology, the therapy service evolved all the way into an incorporated church. Other derivations from Freud's cult have struggled to feign respectable scientific status, remain somewhat modest in their claims, and therefore qualify more as magic than as religion.

The thick arrow representing the psychoanalytic tradition, at the top of figure 1, is meant to include all the offshoots and immediate competitors of psychoanalysis, except for Gestalt Therapy which is diagrammed separately. One of Hubbard's closest associates in 1950, Dr. J. A. Winter, acted as a bridge between Scientology and the Gestalt cult (Winter 1951, 1962; Perls *et al.* 1951). Many psychological exercises in both Gestalt Therapy and Scientology train the patient's attention and awareness in abnormal ways. Both use techniques projecting the patient's consciousness into inanimate objects. Both use Freud's technique of getting patients to recall past traumatic experiences, but both demand extreme emotional involvement and made the patient imagine that the experience is happening *now* in present time. Through Dr. J. A. Winter and other channels, Scientology and Gestalt borrowed from each other.

The thick arrow at the bottom of figure 1, representing the Rosicrucian Tradition, is a highly simplified way of indicating influences from a whole galaxy of cults descended from European Theosophical and more-or-less "Rosicrucian" groups, including the Order of the Golden Dawn that flared briefly in England at the end of the last century. Some cultural material from these sources flows throughout science fiction, but Hubbard was also directly involved during 1945 in one Rosicrucian cult, the Ordo Templi Orientis (Melton 1978, 257).

Hubbard had such a rich cultic and pseudo-scientific background that I cannot always specify which idea came from which source. From the psychoanalytic tradition he apparently took the idea of individual treatment sessions aimed at cure through exploration of subconscious residues from past experiences. The Rosicrucian doctrine of reincarnation and the science fiction concept of time travel encouraged him to explore patients' memories of past lives. From both General Semantics and science fiction he took the idea that treatments could transform ordinary humans into godlike supermen. From Rosicrucianism he may have taken the model of many levels of initiation (little rebirths), each attained through a different technique of spiritual development. Like the various Rosicrucian groups, Scientology is divided into a hierarchical series of membership grades or ranks. Of course, Hubbard also recalled the grades in school and ranks in the United States Navy, two institutions of great significance to him. The history of Scientology's first three decades is one of constant cultural growth with proliferation of levels of membership and spiritual techniques. It has become a multi-million-dollar operation with tens of thousands of followers. No wonder it has many descendents.

The short arrow in figure 1 labeled "Saucer" represents the anonymous flying saucer cult described by social psychologist Leon Festinger and his associates in their famous study, *When Prophecy Fails* (1956).

This was a small group whose leader and some followers had been treated under Dianetics and which used early Scientology techniques to communicate with space brothers. The cult expected a natural disaster to eradicate their neighbors, but not before the saucers had come to rescue the cultists and raise them up to celestial realms.

The forking arrow in figure 1 labeled "The Process" represents the complex cult I have described at length in my book, *Satan's Power* (1978b). Two students at the London headquarters of Scientology, Robert and Mary Ann de Grimston, established their own therapy business in 1963, calling it Compulsions Analysis. Using Hubbard's techniques and the goal theory of psychoanalyst Alfred Adler (1954, 1968), they initially sought merely to improve the personal effectiveness of their clients by helping them uncover and master subconscious compulsions. But by 1966, the group of therapists and clients became a tiny isolated subculture of two dozen persons dedicated to achieving superhuman, surreal transcendence of the mundane world through a program of unlimited development called The Process.

The group left London and wound up on a beach in the Yucatan peninsula of Mexico, living out their perfervid dreams in a ruined coconut plantation. They discovered a pantheon of four gods: Lucifer, Jehovah, Christ, and Satan. They devised wild uniforms, vivid rituals, dramatic scriptures, and a scintillating lifestyle of constant change, drawing on various sources including the Rosicrucian Tradition. Economic and emotional exhaustion in 1973 caused the main group to expell Robert de Grimston from his leadership position. He set up new Process communes with a score of hyper-deviant rejects from the old cult, but failed in this second attempt over the following year, winding up in Egypt after American, Canadian, and English attempts. The main remnant of The Process renamed itself The Foundation, staggered through a series of problems and magical pseudosolutions, and on the last day of 1978 abandoned its $900,000 headquarters in New York, withdrawing to an Arizona canyon to seek a fresh start.

In the mid-1960s at least three other cults were sporulated off from Scientology: Harry Thompson's Amprinistics, Jack Horner's Dianology and Eductivism, and Charles Berner's Abilitism (Malko 1970; Cooper 1971; Wallis 1977; Melton 1978). Werner Erhard's highly successful est cult is partly derived from Scientology. Erhard had some experience with Scientology in 1969. Then he worked for a while in Mind Dynamics, itself an offshoot of Jose Silva's Mind Control (Kornbluth 1976). I assume that many other groups came out of Scientology or were greatly influenced by L. Ron Hubbard. If only we had better information, figure 1 would be a vast chart with dozens of cultic arrows.

This brief survey of the Scientology genus has given just a hint of the rich cultures of the groups named. We have little space for more than the observation that each grew out of one or more earlier cults, then acquired some further culture from others after its birth. With this background, we can begin to consider the *genes* of cultural genetics and the ways they mutate.

Cultural Genes

What shall we call the cultural units which may be inherited by one cult from another? Originally, I wanted to call them *cultural elements,* until I realized that usually they were compounds, not elements. Cavalli-Sforza and Feldman (1981, 70) prefer *cultural traits.* Lumsden and Wilson (1981, 7) suggest the neologism *culturgen,* which seems unnecessarily ornate and sounds like a nasal response to an allergen, but they list eight competing terms which have been seriously proposed. I vote for the obvious short word taken from biology: *gene.*

Some popularity has been achieved by *meme,* suggested by Richard Dawkins (1976, 203). Aside from the fact that meme is cloyingly euphonious, it carries too much theoretical baggage. As a contraction meaning *unit of imitation,* meme conjures up images of Gabriel Tarde's theories or of Symbolic Interactionism, so it is best to avoid the word and the assumptions it implies.

A compelling reason for preferring gene over the other terms is that the word is familiar and probably says well what we want to express. No one will be foolish enough to confuse the use of the word in biology and in cultural genetics. And gene has always been a very general word in biology, anyway, with continuing debates over what exactly a gene is, and still really no firm definition beyond the rather unemcumbered "unit of heredity." Is gene the same thing as *cistron?* Or is gene the same thing as *codon?* And is an *operon* a gene? Part of any such debate is the question of whether one should use gene only for the most simple units of heredity, or whether one can sometimes loosely employ the term to name anything which ever functions as a unit of heredity, however complex it might be and however it might sometimes separate into subunits.

And, while the four bases which attach to the DNA double helix define a substratum of simplicity upon which all more complex genetic structures can rest, we have no reason to assume that in culture there is a most-simple unit. Any "element" of culture is a composite of ideas. Therefore, in cultural genetics the term gene will refer to any *assemblage of ideas which functions as a unit in the cases under examination.*

In a paper about "meaning systems," Stark and I showed that the ideas of religion often do fit together into cultural units (Bainbridge and Stark 1981a). A cultural system is a set of explanations about some aspect of life connected by an overarching *general explanation* giving the system its coherence. Any organized subset of cultural elements can function as a single gene, if the general explanation which binds them together is inherited unchanged through the processess of reproduction. If a general explanation is discredited, then the gene to which it gave cohesiveness may dissolve into two or more smaller genes. Thus, cultural genetics should avoid defining gene in terms of any particular level of complexity of cultural organization, and use it for any assemblage which functions as a unit, with full awareness that a gene could become subdivided into smaller genes or combined with other cultural elements to form a larger gene.

We have seen that new cults born out of old ones replicate much of the original genetic material of the parent. This fits our ordinary notions of biological heredity. But what about the observation that cults may acquire new genes after they have been born? Surely, only latter-day Lemarckists like Lysenko could believe humans acquire new genes in mid-life, display them in their own phenotypes, and transmit them to their offspring (Medvedev 1969). Yet, we have said that cults are more similar to the simplest forms of life, and strange things happen to bacteria.

Consider the remarkable phenomenon of *transduction.* A viral infection can take genetic material out of the DNA of one bacterium and introduce it into the DNA of another bacterium. If the second bacterium survives the infection, it can then transmit the stolen genes to generation after generation of offspring.

Transduction occurs in cults, as well. An individual may join one cult, learn some useful new culture, then defect to a second cult taking this cultural material with him. If the second cult adopts some of the culture carried by the defector, then transduction has taken place. The defector plays the role of the virus. Above we mentioned the example of Dr. J. A. Winter who carried genetic material between Scientology and Gestalt. Studies of diffusion of technology often show that new ideas travel from corporation to corporation in the minds of people who migrate, rather than through disembodied media (Gruber and Marquis 1969). Consequently, we might want to define transduction this narrowly, using other terms for other means by which an existing cult can appropriate culture from external sources.

While we are all taught in school that genes are carried in the nucleus of the cell in what are called chromosomes, biologists have long suspected that *some* genes might be carried outside in the cytoplasm. Genes giving bacteria resistance to antibiotics appear often to be carried in little clumps of genetic material outside the nucleus, called *plasmids*. This is of great consequence, because plasmid genetic material can be transferred more easily than nuclear material from one species to another. This fact presents mankind with a serious medical-social problem. Wholesale, indiscriminate use of antibiotics has encouraged the evolution of resistant strains of pneumonia and gonorrhea bacteria, and through plasmid exchange this resistance may soon spread to other disease-causing bacteria.

The analogous question for cults is more benign. I suggest the nucleus of the cell is like the leadership of the cult, whether there be one leader or a formal structure of leadership. And the cytoplasm is like the mass of cult followers who cluster around the leadership. Plasmids, then, would be small competing sources of influence and innovation outside the formal leadership nucleus. While this essay, and my other essays on cult innovation stress the role of the leadership, we should be alert to processes which might take place among even peripheral cult members who might also perform important innovation and reproduction functions.

In our quotation above from the cult formation paper, we saw a strong analogy between innovation carried out consciously by the leadership and recombinant DNA genetic engineering. Stepping back for the moment from our biological metaphors and terminology, we should consider some of the processes of cultural gene splicing, then return to biological genetics for analogies to permit closer examination of the mechanisms involved.

Recombinant Cultural Genetic Engineering

Invention usually does not require the discovery of wholly new facts or concepts. Far more often, it is accomplished through assembly of existing components into new configurations. Technological invention sometimes rests on real scientific discoveries, on completely new elements of culture. Religious innovation sometimes rests on new secular cultural fads. In our times many of the most influential fads stem from scientific and technological innovation, so it is not surprising that many cults, like Scientology, pretend to be scientific technologies. Others, like Christian Science, Divine Science, and Religious Science, take at least a name from science. Innovative cults offer new configurations of familiar elements taken piecemeal from other religious organizations, from secular institutions, and from the petty details of modern daily life.

Cult invention involves finding attractive elements in the cultural environment, adding them to an existing cultic core, subtracting parts that interfere with more valuable parts, and transforming elements to make them fit their loci in the compensator package. Founders enter the cult business in search of honor and wealth, so the test they apply to evaluate new culture is: Does it sell? If one wishes to see a Darwinian principle of selection here, I have no objection. And the selection may be natural, as well as artificial, as bad choices lead to the extinction of cults, and good, if even accidental, choices produce viable new religions which can flourish in the competitive marketplace.

Addition (or *insertion*) is the simplest mechanism for creating a new culture. Throughout their working lives, cult founders cannot resist appropriating new ideas and activities from their competitors. We do not think it strange that ordinary manufacturers continually monitor their competition and adopt any innovations that seem good for business. Perhaps the otherworldly rhetoric of religion impedes our ability to see the same processes at work in sacred affairs. Religions are supposed to be God-given, and God is no tinkerer. But hardly a modern religion can be named that did not add elements from other sources as it grew. Of course, cults often want to hide their borrowings.

The E-Meter, for which Scientology is famous, is a minimal lie detector developed by Volney Mathison, an independent inventor. It was added to the Dianetic process only after the movement had become popular (Malko 1970, 57). Indeed, the Scientology movement itself says the E-Meter did not come into widespread use until after the first seven years. Dianology, est, and The Process all received the E-Meter gene from their parent, Scientology.

Another example of addition is the "Satanism" of The Process. Satan appeared in Process doctrine in 1967, four years after the beginning of the cult and just after its leaders had seen the successes of Anton La Vey's Church of Satan in San Francisco. Yet another example is the interest of Dianology and Eductivism in the concept of birth trauma, apparently stimulated by the popular successes of Janov's Primal Therapy.

Often a cult leader *prospects* for new additions, just as one might prospect for gold across a wild terrain. In June 1972, the leaders of The Process went prospecting for "the healing power." They left their home in Toronto and flew across to Vancouver, then went down to Seattle to hear the famous faith healer, Kathryn Kuhlman. Later, in Florida, they visited many local faith healers and designed new rituals to incorporate healing into the cult. The modifications required to adapt healing prayers and the laying on of hands were slight—invoking the power of four gods rather than just one.

The Process adapted many other traditional practices with only such transformations as absolutely required by existing cult doctrines. Some conventionally religious persons try to find guidance or prognostication in bibliomancy—opening the Bible at random, selecting a passage unseen, then reading personal meaning into the verses. The Process adopted bibliomancy and merely substituted its own holy book for the Bible. Later, this cult consorted with independent psychics and occult lecturers, taking from them such practices as aura reading and astrology, which seemed very popular at the time.

The extreme form of addition is *amalgamation*, in which a new cult is created in a flash by adding two previous cults or other religious bodies together. It might be an oversimplification to say that Werner Erhard's est cult is just an amalgam of Mind Dynamics and Scientology, but the 3HO cult (Healthy-Happy-Holy Organization) of Yogi Bhajan is a simplified amalgam of Yoga and Sikhism (Tobey 1976).

Addition implies *subtraction* (or *deletion*). Cults, like the more established religions, have a tendency to preserve whatever culture was every part of their repertoire, even if it may languish unused for many years. Yet when a dormant element of culture interferes with a new, vital element, it may be discarded. In general, costly unprofitable elements will be jettisoned most readily, as was polygamy by the Mormons. When L. Ron Hubbard founded Scientology on the wreck of his earlier Dianetics, he discarded much of the earlier practice. For a dozen years, however, an independent California Dianetics organization and uncounted individual Dianetics practitioners limped along. Then, as the 1960s drew to a close, Scientology reabsorbed Dianetics, a unique case of a cult re-adding culture it had previously subtracted.

When The Process expelled its founder, Robert de Grimston, it exorcised both Satan and Christ from its communes and churches, forgot Lucifer altogether, and reduced the old pantheon of four gods down to one, Jehovah. This was a case of drastic cultural subtraction. The Process already had quit using E-Meters and applying any therapy techniques to inner members. Too much deletion will leave a cult without enough beliefs and practices to function. Often, therefore, subtraction and addition go together.

Frequently, cults add and subtract culture in order to differentiate themselves from other cults which own the original elements. Sometimes, as in the case of The Process right after its fission, they drop and add to cut themselves off from their unsuccessful pasts. This is *substitution*.

When the main body of The Process expelled de Grimston at a time of organizational crisis, it felt the need to kick the dust of the past from its sandals and start anew. But many of the old concepts and practices were absolutely necessary for day-to-day functioning. To balance change and stability, the cult substituted many elements by the simple expedient of renaming them—old wine in old bottles but with new labels. Some of these substitutions are shown in figure 2. A version of this table was published in my book on the Process (Bainbridge 1978b, 235), but at that time it seemed necessary to conceal the true names of the cults. If one wants to think genetically, then each of the concepts represents a *locus* in the genetic structure, and each pair of words (*Process* and *Foundation,* for example) is a pair of alternative genes, either of which might occupy that locus.

Substitution can occur with any type of culture, although I suspect it is most likely to happen at single genes—at low levels in a hierarchical structure of culture—unless extreme crisis besets the cult (cf. Smelser 1962). Visual symbols are likely to change when there is a real or projected shift in emphasis of a cult. The style and color of Process uniforms changed frequently, yet the more general idea of having uniforms was more stable. Figure 3 shows some changes in the most central of the cult's several symbols, the P-Sign.

When the cult still thought of itself as a therapy service devoted to turning normal people into supermen, the members came to a point of strong "we-feeling" and the sense that they were a new social movement with something special to say. They sat around one evening designing possible symbols for the newly named Process. The result was a pinwheel of four straight lines, shown first in figure 3. Although it is redolent of swastika Nazism, it merely represents the letter "P" for Process, superimposed on itself with 90° rotations. People coming from the four directions of the compass (different personality types and

Figure 2 Foundation Substitutions for Process Words

Process Word	Foundation Word	Meanings
Ritual Terms:		
Alpha	Sanctum	the main ritual room
Altar	Shrine	the ritual table
Assembly	Celebration	a group ritual
Sacrifist	Celebrant	presiding priest at a ritual
Evangelist	Herald	priest that gives the sermon
Servers	Bearers	ritual assistants
Membership Ranks:		
Master	Luminary	the top leaders
Provisional Master	Minor Luminary	lieutenant leaders
Superior	Celebrant	junior "Mothers" and "Fathers"
Prophet	Mentor	senior "Sisters" and "Brothers"
IP Messenger	Covenantor	lowest rank of "ministers"
OP Messenger	Witness	student ministers
Disciple	Lay Founder	lay member who tithes
Initiate	Aspirant	new member
General:		
The Process	The Foundation	name of the cult
Chapters	Foundations	branches of the cult
IPs	Elect	core members, "ministers"
Donating	Funding	the street work of begging and recruiting
Baptize	Consecrate	to initiate to a new status
DJ (Dow-Jones)	JF (Jehovah's Finances)	financial indicator of the business done by a branch
The Cavern	The Garden	the coffee house

values) are thus represented as coming together in a common Process for a common purpose.

Later, as the group moved further in the direction of religion, Robert de Grimston redesigned the symbol, flaring out the lines to make shapes which some members saw as trumpets heralding the coming of the gods. He told me this embellishment was to give the P-Sign "an ecclesiastical and mathematical flavor." The shift from therapy to religion demanded a shift in the style of their symbol, but not in its underlying concept.

When The Foundation attempted to differentiate itself from The Process, it quickly designed a new symbol, but one which still retained this concept. Apparently, attached to the very notion of "a symbol" was a sense of the general features of a proper symbol for the group, an abstract sense of proper form more general than the particular shape of any particular symbol (cf. Boaz 1966). Their thinking shaped by the original P-Sign, the members of the cult designed a new symbol based on the capital letters "FJ" for Foundation and Jehovah. Notice that these letters are even similar to the squared capital "P" they had used, and a measure of symmetry is retained. As the background for this monogram, they chose the six-pointed star which they felt was a traditional symbol for their one remaining god, Jehovah.

For a time, the members of Jewish origin had disproportionate influence in The Foundation, since they were thought to understand Jehovah better. But when the cult continued to experience great difficulties, despite the new cultural start, Jewish elements were downplayed and a new move toward Jesus took place. The symbol was changed again to reflect this new start. Since the group was then calling itself The Foundation Faith, the monogram could be reinterpreted as the letter "F" drawn twice, but the Old Testament emphasis in the surrounding star had to be changed. As shown in figure 3, the underlying idea of six bilaterally symmetrical shapes reaching out from a center was retained, but the form became that of a flower—a lily, perhaps. For a while, formerly Jewish members started an offshoot group in Arizona, Jewish Crusade for Jesus, using the six-petal flower but with their own JCJ monogram in the center. Notice that the evolutions of the P-Sign communicate both radical changes in the cult's orientation and a sense of underlying continuity.

Rosicrucianism affords a sequence of many connected examples of addition, subtraction, and substitution. In creating the AMORC Rosicrucian order, H. Spencer Lewis took European occult principles

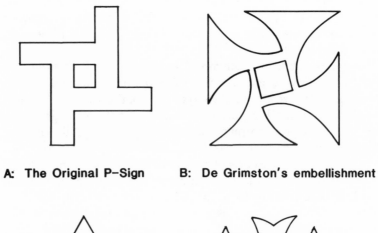

A: The Original P–Sign   B: De Grimston's embellishment

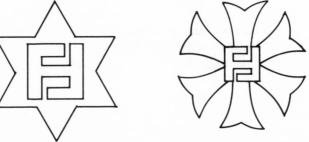

C: The first Foundation   D: The second Foundation symbol
   symbol

Figure 3 Evolution of the Process "P-Sign" Symbol

of the turn of the century, including the hierarchical social structure of an initiatory secret society, and inserted symbolism taken from ancient Egypt, thus capitalizing on public enthusiasm for Egyptian civilization that was current at the time. One may still visit the pleasant city block of gardens and simulated Egyptian buildings at his headquarters in San Jose, California. Then, I suspect, Rose Dawn imitated Lewis in creating her rival Order of the Ancient Mayans. In great measure, she merely substituted equivalent Mayan symbols for Egyptian ones. Instead of Lewis' green biweekly mail-order lessons emblazoned with Egyptian architecture and Egyptian hieroglyphics, she sold red biweekly mail-order lessons decorated with Mayan architecture and Mayan hieroglyphics.

Equivalent elements of culture which may be substituted for each other in a cultural structure may be called *alleles* or *allelomorphs,* following the terminology of biological genetics. We shall consider alleles closely in the next section. Mayan and Egyptian hieroglyphics are members of the same class of culture objects, because each is a famous, ancient form of picture-writing with sacred connotations. Another system of exotic pictographs could be substituted to create a third cult. Many elements of culture logically imply their alleles. For example, The Process took from Scientology the idea that human life is a deadly game. But where Scientology attempted to *win* the game, The Process substituted the strategy of *escaping* the game.

Another mechanism of cultic invention, *translation,* is a slightly more subtle version of addition. It refers to a category of mental transformations which includes what psychologists call *displacement, transference,* and *projection*. The term translation refers to any case in which meaning is derived from one situation and applied to another situation where it would not have emerged spontaneously. In translation a meaning is not only transported from one context to another, but also transformed in whatever way necessary to make it fit the new context.

There are two common sources of material that can be translated into a cult: They are the personal experiences of cult founders and the secular institutions of society. For an example of the first source, Robert de Grimston told me he had experienced an emotionally repressed childhood and came to feel that liberation of desires was the general cure for human problems. To translate this abstract principle generalized from his own experience into religious form, de Grimston expressed it through the image of the Great God Lucifer, deity of sensual enjoyment. An example of the second kind of source is the elite paramilitary organization within Scientology, the Sea Org. This is a branch of the cult that imitates the U. S. Navy, complete with officers, uniforms, nautical caps, and even ships.

The cult formation article explained the thrust toward cultic innovation in economic terms, but the language of Darwinian evolution might be just as appropriate. Without distinguishing the different mechanisms by which a cult can acquire new genetic material, we proposed a general principle:

> We suggest that cult entrepreneurs will imitate those features of other successful cults which seem to them most responsible for success. They will innovate either in non-essential areas or in areas where they believe they can increase the salability of the product. In establishing their own cult businesses they must innovate at least superficially. They cannot seize a significant part of the market unless they achieve product differentiation. Otherwise they will be at a great disadvantage in direct competition with the older, more prosperous cult on which theirs is patterned. The apparent novelty of a cult's compensator-package may be a sales advantage when the public has not yet discovered the limitations of the rewards that members actually will receive in the new cult and when older compensator-packages have been discredited to some extent (Bainbridge and Stark 1979, 290–291).

Instead of *product differentiation,* we can use a perfectly good genetics term for this strategy: *character displacement.* And in the sociology of religion, under whatever name this is not a new idea. Long ago, H. Richard Niebuhr noted that the churches of immigrants to the United States "were transplanted into a common social environment but at the same time they were set into the midst of a competitive system of denominationalism" (1929, 220). Initially, the linguistic and national divisions between them assured each of a laity to support its existence. But as the ethnic groups became more assimilated, the possibility that many denominations might die as their memberships were attracted to others prompted a defensive tactic of differentiation:

> Ecclesiastical and doctrinal issues replace the cultural lines of division, and the loyalty of an English-speaking, second generation is fostered by appeal to different motives than were found effective among the immigrants themselves.
>
> The need for continued differentiation and for the self-justification of an organism which is strongly desirous of continuing its existence, are responsible now for a new emphasis. Denominational separateness in a

competitive situation finds its justification under these circumstances in the accentuation of the theological or liturgical peculiarities of the group. Resistance to assimilation continues, but the immigrant church in its battle with other sects for membership and position takes up a new strategic position.

The influence of competition on doctrinal differentiation is, of course, not confined to the foreign-language churches. Whenever rivalry has arisen between culturally similar groups the doctrinal strategy has usually been adopted (Niebuhr 1929, 229–230).

Apparently unaware of Niebuhr's analysis, John A. Hostetler drew from his study of the Amish two general principles concerning differentiation:

> A sectarian movement must establish an ideology different from that of the parent group in order to break off relations with it.
>
> A sect must establish cultural separatism, involving symbolic and often material as well as ideological differences, from those of the parent group (Hostetler 1968, 35–36).

Now, I am not entirely sure how important these principles are in explaining the behavior of sects and ordinary denominations. But they are very important in explaining cult innovation. When sects emerge through schism from lower-tension denominations, the need to stress specific compensators produces an automatic cultural shift. But if the case is one of pure sectarianism, this will mean merely stressing relatively neglected parts of the existing culture of the parent group. This does not demand innovation. But in cult formation revivalism is not enough, and conscious strategies of differentiation are much more likely.

There is good reason to believe this same process is quite common between competing artistic movements, including both religious and secular examples. As the Christian church began to consolidate its ritual practices in the fourth century, it drew heavily on Jewish traditions. But, as some historians report, this produced a problem for the Jews. "They condemned the appropriation of their own heritage and even reformulated portions of their liturgy to avoid duplication of either the spirit or the occasion for the parallel Christian use" (Scholl and White 1970, 23). And in artistic painting in recent centuries, new and shocking schools of thought may simply be trying to engage in the traditional fame-business of artists, displacing the established styles through whatever combination of imitation and innovation is necessary in order to take over the market (cf. White and White 1965).

Having described mechanisms of innovation in the terms of business, it is time to reassert the genetic metaphors which played a lesser role in this section.

Allelomorphy in Cultural Genetics

It was the existence of alleles which gave Mendelian genetics its great power. Alleles are alternative genes which play the same role and have the same place in the genetic structure but give discernably different results. For example, consider eye color. A gene which produces blue eyes is the allele of a gene which produces brown eyes. In Mendelian experiments on crossbreeding, such matters as dominance and recessivity, linkage, multiple gene determination of continuous variables, and the like were explored. All depended on the existence of two or more alleles for each gene under scrutiny, and the result was a mathematics of allelomorphy.

To be sure, the larger process of biological evolution is not merely a process of substitution of alleles in fixed loci in an invariate genetic structure. Also, the structure itself changed. Species vary in their number of chromosomes, not merely in which of a closed set of alternative genes occupied a particular locus in each chromosome. Certainly, cultural genetics should be especially interested in the emergence of wholly new spheres of culture and utterly new ideas without precedent. But, interesting laws of some regularity may be discovered to describe and explain the more common innovative processes of combination and permutation of alleles. Indeed, I will suggest later that some old and unjustly discarded schools of thought in social science unwittingly went far in this direction.

For alleles to exist, and for substitutions of them to be possible, there must have developed a relatively coherent genetic structure. Stark and I have argued that secular culture seldom possesses such structure, but sacred culture easily can if promulgated by vigorous social movements or organizations (Bainbridge and Stark 1981a, 1981b). Religions are *cultural systems* composed of more-or-less hierarchically arranged *explanations*. As we said in an article which was the first step in our development of a deductive theory of religion: *"Religion* refers to systems of general compensators based on supernatural assumptions"

(Stark and Bainbridge 1980, 123). *Compensators* are postulations of reward according to explanations that are not readily susceptible to unambiguous evaluation. And *explanations* are statements about how and why rewards may be obtained and costs are incurred.

Our theory began in the observation that humans seek what they perceive to be rewards and avoid what they perceive to be costs. The human nervous system evolved to permit individuals and human groups to obtain rewards and avoid costs. Culture evolved as an adaptive way of discovering and sharing explanations. But not all human desires can find ready satisfaction in this world of toil and tears. And humans devised what seemed plausible means for achieving scarce (and non-existent) rewards, even when these explanations could not be tested easily (or even conceivably) through empirical observation. These supra-empirical explanations, which had to be accepted on faith, if at all, are compensators.

Compensators vary in terms of how general or specific are the rewards they promise to provide. Compensators which substitute for very limited, specific rewards (such as cure for a headache) are *specific compensators*. Compensators which substitute for rewards of great scope and value (such as eternal life in heaven where there are neither headaches nor stomachaches nor heartaches) are *general compensators*. Magic offers specific compensators; religion offers general compensators. And the difference is one of degree. The reason for reminding the reader of our theory of religion is to lay a basis for observing that religions tend to arrange their compensators into coherent systems with relatively fixed structures capable of supporting the regularity needed for a science of cultural genetics. Indeed, religion can get away with more structure than can many secular fields because its key general explanations cannot be discredited by empirical test, being supernatural, while secular general explanations are highly vulnerable and seldom resist long the corrosive bath of human experience.

At least some of the elements of religious culture, typically including the most important and distinctive explanations, are arranged hierarchically. Consider Christianity. The most general compensator is the notion of the *supernatural*. This is a necessary assumption for any religion. Indeed, the supra-gene of supernatural assumptions emerged very early in human history and is found in all societies (Parsons 1964). Logically under this high-level assumption, in Christianity, is the assumption that there is but *one god*. Other religious traditions postulate several gods, and any logically discernable polytheistic system constitutes an allele of monotheism. For example, dualism (as in

Zoroastrianism and Manichaenism) is a clear allele of monotheism, and substitutions between these two have occurred easily throughout history. Under the monotheism gene in Christianity, is the assumption that the Lord sent his only begotten son to redeem his people. Alleles of this assumption are the idea that the Lord always remains distant from the world and its problems (Deism) or the idea that he speaks through his prophets but never has sent a son among us (Judaism, Islam).

Religions are not the only complex cultural systems, even though most segments of secular culture are unable to find hardy general explanations to unite hierarchically the many specific explanations they possess. Schools of artistic expression may also be arranged into complex systems. But art and religion share the characteristic of being imaginative creations of human beings subject to relatively few empirical tests. Therefore, each is free to postulate general explanations without much fear of factual contradiction. To consider further the relationship of alleles to cultural genetic structure, and to show that this essay has implications outside the field of religion, I shall now consider examples taken from twentieth-century classical music.

The existence in a cultural system of a gene X creates a locus for it in the genetic structure. A cultural innovator who becomes conscious of X may create a new system by finding an alternative (allele) X' and substituting it for X. In Western classical music—*musicologists please forgive the simplifications*—there developed a general assumption that musical notes must be chosen from fixed scales. Alleles of this high-level gene, each different from the others, were developed by Indian (raga) music, Classical Greek (tetrad) music, and by American Negro (sliding tones) singing. But under the *musical scale* assumption are several alternatives. The West chose, first of all, septatonic scales, in contrast to the pentatonic scales of East Asia. And, as the Middle Ages consolidated the musical culture, a system of *model septatonic scales* emerged. Note the three genes, in order of descending generality: scales, septatonic, modal. And each of these three genes has alleles.

The years passed, and thousands of little innovations added up to great change. The most specific of the three genes, *modality,* was transformed by a gradual rationalizing process into a distinctly different allele, *tonality.* This shift necessitated an adjustment of the septatonic scales to permit modulation from one key (tonality) to another. While no single innovator can claim credit for this gene substitution, the obvious culmination of the process is Bach's *Well-Tempered Clavier.* Over the century-and-a-half which followed Bach, the tonal system was modified further through acceptance of more and more complex harmonies until the notions of *key* and predictable modulations between keys became quite ambiguous while more attention was given to highly complex musical chords. Thus appeared a third allele, *chromatic* music. The best well-known example is Wagner's *Tristan and Isolde*. Finally, before World War I, this evolution was taken to its logical extreme, *atonal* music, a fourth allele. In atonal music, the tones of the well-tempered scale became equal partners in a music which explicitly rejected the sense of a tonal home base. The tonality allele was linked (and such strong but partial linkage is well-known in biological genetics) to the original septatonic gene which was by 1910 replaced by a dodecatonic gene—twelve equally-separated tones to the octave.

By about the same year, Mendelian genetics had learned to deal with continuous variations—like the gradual historical cultural process described above—by postulating the joint contribution to single features of the phenotype by several genes, each with its own alleles. Here, too, a close examination of the history of music would reveal many tiny steps, particular minor substitutions in particular loci along with insertions and deletions, which added up to the greater genetic evolution we have but outlined. Now we shall ignore this complexity, and describe the creative reactions of two twentieth-century composers, Arnold Schoenberg and Carl Orff, who produced radically different schools of composition by making different allele substitutions in the existing structure. First we must diagram the two earlier composers we mentioned, Bach and Wagner, as can be seen in figure 4.

The vertical rectangle in each diagram of figure 4 represents a two-gene section of the genetic structure of the music. The two genes are of equal importance, rather than one being hierarchically superior to the other. The horizontal dashed rectangles represent the sets of alleles of each gene which were used in Western music. The top gene is the one we have just described, referring to the manner of using tones in the scale. It has four alleles: M = modal, T = tonal, C = chromatic, A = atonal. The other gene will be expanded upon in the following section of this essay, and represents an equally important pair of alleles: R = romanticism, L = classicism. Romanticism is a style of art which emphasizes emotional expression, while classicism emphasizes intellectual cognition. Thus the distinction is very much that between feelings and ideas.

Bach's music was tonal and classical, which we can represent by the first diagram or by the notation: [T, L]. Wagner, who wrote at the pinnacle of nineteenth-century Romanticism, can be represented by the second diagram, or notated: [C, R]. Schoenberg's early works, notably

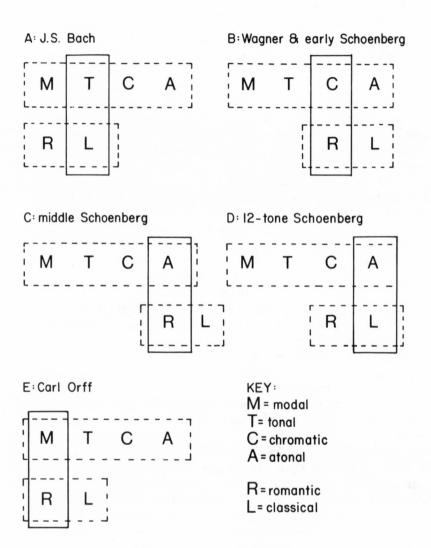

Figure 4 Allele Substitutions in Music

the Wagnerian *Gurre-Lieder,* were also chromatic and romantic: [C, R]. But in seeking to take Romanticism to its extreme, Schoenberg participated in the practically-nihilistic but highly emotional artistic movement of *Expressionism,* and substituted atonality for the related allele of chromaticism. The result, in such pieces as *Pierrot Lunaire,* is shown in the third diagram, and can be notated: [A, R]. Note that the substitution was logically available to Schoenberg, because the existence of the M/T/C gene created a locus in the genetic structure which made room for the mutation to A. But Schoenberg, at this point, made no change in the L/R gene, continuing to write highly expressive rather than intellectual music.

The result, for Schoenberg as for many listeners, was very disturbing. Perhaps the combination [A, R] has less adaptive fitness than the previous genotypes [T, L] and [C, R]. Indeed, to the sociologist [A, R] looks like an intense dose of anxiety and anomie. Many consider the greatest example of this style to be *Wozzeck,* by Schoenberg's student Alban Berg, an opera of madness, depravity, and death. In such music, the emotions are riled up without there being any satisfaction of the tensions thus produced.

Schoenberg's aesthetic response to this challenge was essentially *religious,* a quest for meaning which eventually found God's Law in this chaotic modern world of atonal music. Originally, this sense of divine order had been achieved through modality in the service of liturgical text (Gregorian chant) or tonality made especially meaningful by classic structures (Bach). But in atonality there was madness. A new set of commandments from the Lord was required to tell the composer which combinations of tones were good and which were forbidden since in atonality, all laws from previous dispensations had been lost. And thus, Schoenberg discovered the intellectual system of composition called *serial dodecaphony* or *twelve-tone.* This is a return to the values of classicism while retaining atonality, [A, L], as shown in figure 4.

The twelve-tone method of composition gained wide acceptance (if far from universal praise) in great measure because it provides coherent rules (norms) for composition, and it is attractive to composers who have rejected the older forms and who therefore may be suffering from anomie. But, seen the other way around, like the novelties of any new cult, twelve-tone achieves product differentiation. Furthermore, new composers in the [T, L] and [C, R] traditions have to compete with Bach, Beethoven and Wagner, while Schoenberg's first followers in [A, L] had no competition. It is interesting that Schoenberg's followers acted very much like those of Freud in innovating one after another in producing new "cults" of serial music. The religious nature of the twelve-tone solution for Schoenberg is shown by his biblical opera, *Moses und Aron,* where God's law is represented by a single twelve-tone row which provides the musical material for the entire long work.

Carl Orff went in a very different direction from that taken by Schoenberg. Orff's career began later than Schoenberg's, but in the same cultural place, the shadow of the late Wagnerians. At the beginning of the 1930s, when all Germany hungered for a new rebirth, Orff renounced his early [C, R] works and returned, as he saw it, to the beginnings of Western music. On this retrograde route, he orchestrated seventeenth-century operas by Monteverdi who had written at the point of historical transition between [M, R] and [T, L]. Orff's first great composition, among the most popular of twentieth-century vocal works, was *Carmina Burana,* based on an ancient text and actually incorporating hints of the music of the thirteenth century. Clearly, the style is [M, R], as shown in the last diagram of figure 4.

Orff, like Schoenberg, had found an essentially *religious* solution to the problems of modern life as reflected in the anomie of art music. But where Schoenberg had returned to the religion of the ancient Hebrews, Orff had returned to the Paganism of Greece and Rome. Throughout his career, however, Orff repeatedly admitted his pessimism, his lack of faith that the Greeks and Romans could save us, for example in the sensuous but bitter *Catulli Carmina.* Near the end of his life, Orff abandoned all hope in his last great work, *De Temporum Fine Comoedia,* and his attempt to return from [C, R] to [M, R] led him to that brave but maladaptive genotype which drove Schoenberg to his great effort at genetic engineering, [A, R].

I have considered alleles in serious Western music at length not merely to demonstrate the most basic techniques of qualitative genetic analysis, but also to show that cults are not the only phenomena capable of being studied in this way. However, I have not been able to resist using quasi-religious examples. Whenever there exist lineages of cultural systems, cultural genetics has an important role to play in achieving understanding. But I cannot hide my own assumption. All truly grand cultural systems either are explicitly religious, or tend closely toward religion. Serious music, like religion, reaches for the ultimate and offers compensators of the most general kind—to give not only pure pleasure, but also the sense that human existence is meaningful and that the limitations of everyday life can be transcended. Music has often been linked with religion explicitly, and only the non-verbal character of the music conceals the implicit link which always ties together these two areas of culture.

It is time to extend cultural genetics toward a third area of culture, one with strong links to religion if not so often to music: *social theory*. And among the brands of traditional social theory most akin to the cultural systems of religion is *structuralism* in sociology and anthropology.

Structuralism as an Analysis of Alleles

Since we have been discussing cults and music, I find the easiest transition to structural theory to be Nietzsche's first book, *The Birth of Tragedy*, a structural analysis of culture which takes its impetus from Wagner and from ancient religion. In it, Nietzsche delineated three cultural types, although people tend to forget the third: *Apollonian, Dionysian,* and *Buddhist*. In the terms of the previous section, Classicism is Apollonian, while Romanticism is Dionysian. Perhaps Nietzsche had to look outside Western culture to find a name for the Buddhist style because it was not represented in our history. But the trichotomy runs parallel to others proposed by Westerners. For example, Leonard Meyer (1967) proposed a typology of styles in contemporary serious music which correlates well with the Nietzschean types: Traditionalism (Dionysian), Formalism (Apollonian), and Transcendentalism (Buddhist). Karen Horney's three psychological styles are also similar: "moving toward people" (Dionysian), "moving against people" (Apollonian), and "moving away from people" (Buddhist).

The Apollonian/Dionysian dichotomy is very much like the tough-minded/tender-minded distinction made by William James (1963). Abraham Maslow has noted this parallelism and suggested other, related dichotomies: anal/oral, obsessional/hysterical, controlled/impulsive, dominating/receptive, suspicious/trusting, and, most controversial of all, masculine/feminine (Maslow 1969, 93). In Nietzsche's analysis, the Apollonian is intellectual and rational (Classicism); the Dionysian is emotional and intuitive (Romanticism). But in addition to this cognition/emotion distinction, Nietzsche said each type demanded a different relationship to self and other. While the Dionysian seeks to incorporate himself in the group, the Apollonian follows the *principle of individuation* (Nietzsche 1872, 25–26). The Buddhist rejects both self and other, withdrawing into mystical contemplation. We can display these three types in terms of social relationships in a simple chart of a type familiar to sociologists, in figure 5.

Nietzsche's Buddhist is not, of course, the ordinary citizen of an Asian land who follows the Buddhist faith at some distance, but the monastic Buddhist virtuoso who has left the world and abjures personal pleasure, thus someone who rejects or minimizes both self and other, symbolized in figure 5 by minus signs. The Dionysian stresses the other (+), submerging self in the social group, thus minimizing self (−). The Apollonian minimizes the other (−) and stresses self (+). This chart is not only a logical structure contrasting distinct types, but may be seen as a map of persons and worlds, a chart of approaches to existence and plans for behavior. The point at the center of the chart, where the lines cross, represents an equal mixture of types, while each of the corners marks the purest example of one style.

Figure 5 lets us see that Nietzsche's typology demands a fourth type, one in which both self and other are stressed; I often sense in Nietzsche's writings a groping for this ideal type. His famous cultic testament, *Also Sprach Zarathustra* (1885) is the story of a messiah-philosopher who achieves the greatest wisdom and enlightenment while living for ten years on a mountain accompanied only by an eagle (power) and a serpent (passion). Zarathustra descends to humanity, seeking fellows. He fails to find any worthy of his message, and he departs. Zarathustra, like Nietzsche himself, is from one perspective immature and ridiculous—like the inhibited adolescent poet who bombards a beautiful maiden with poems and demands, but remains unwilling to share her real world and its limitations. This is the obsession with purity of the Apollonian. And

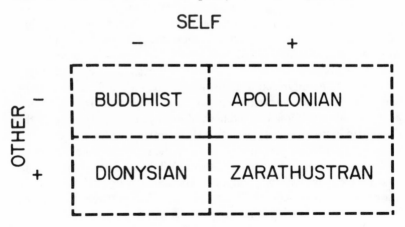

Figure 5 Structural Analysis of Nietzsche's Types

Zarathustra is an Apollonian (with a Buddhist past, perhaps), like Nietzsche, despite the dark midnight passion of his message. He speaks but does not touch. The result is failure. Apollo fails to become Dionysus. A man apart fails to become a part of the whole. The synthesis of opposing styles suggested by Figure 5 is not found.

Note that what began as an analysis of a conceptual dichotomy of social theory, quickly became an analysis of Nietzsche's fruitless quest for a new religion. And many, like the composer Delius, have tried to turn *Zarathustra* into a religion. So, we have returned to the topic of cults. And we should note that Nietzsche, a structuralist before his time, has chosen as his protagonist the cult founder Zarathustra (Zoroaster) who actually introduced a dualist religion which was based on a dichotomy like those we consider here.

Let us consider figure 5, therefore, in terms of our analytic approach to cults—in terms of cultural genetics. Superficial readers of Nietzsche, noting his famous Apollonian/Dionysian dichotomy, would say that he described a single gene, A/D, with two alleles, A and D. My analysis of what he actually wrote suggests there were at least two genes. One had to do with relationship to the *self* and had two alleles, emphasizing self ([S+]) and minimizing self ([S−]). The second gene had to do with relationship to *others* and had two alleles, emphasizing others ([O+]) and minimizing others ([O−]). The genotypes for Nietzsche's three culture types can easily be stated: Apollonian [S+,O−], Dionysian [S−,O+], and Buddhist [S−O−]. The fourth possible type [S+,O+] was never achieved by Nietzsche, but Maslow might identify it as the self-actualizing individual capable of love for others as well as personal achievement. While Nietzsche never found [S+,O+], perhaps Einstein did.

Ruth Benedict made much of the A/D distinction in her influential popular book, *Patterns of Culture* (1934). But her definitions of Apollonian and Dionysian are very different from those of Nietzsche. She agrees that the Apollonian is emotionally cool while the Dionysian is gripped by passionate frenzy. But she reverses Nietzsche's opinion of which is the group-oriented and which the individualistic type. According to her, the serene Apollonian life implies a "distrust of individualism" (Benedict 1934, 80), while the Dionysian plunges on a harried quest to break away from the normal world. And her book finds no use for the third type, Buddhist.

Neither Nietzsche nor Benedict is wrong in any objective sense. Rather, they are led in different directions by examination of different data—in great measure, data on different pagan religious traditions. I suggest the two can be made fully compatible if we merely recall the R/L gene (Romanticism/Classicism) and postulate that the A/D distinction really involves three genes, rather than just one or two. For Nietzsche, Apollonianism was [L, S+, O−] while Dionysianism was [R, S−, O+]. For Benedict, Appollonianism was [L, S−, O+] while Dionysianism was [R, S+, O−]. The history of Mendelian genetics records many cases of the discovery that what had been seen as one gene was really a composite of two or more genes which may have shown partial linkage.

Perhaps, however, there is some merit to the view that Nietzsche's real contribution was the single dichotomy A/D, as Benedict and so many others have thought. Perhaps S− is strongly (if not perfectly) linked to O+, and S+ is linked to O−. If so, it is very easy to interpret the disagreement between Nietzsche and Benedict in the terms of that arch-structuralist Talcott Parsons (1951, 67). The five "pattern-alternatives" of Parsons' system are five genes, each with two alleles. Two of the five, the two which happen to be called "dilemmas," correspond perfectly with the two genes R/L and S/O. The *gratification-discipline* dilemma is a cultural choice between affectivity [R] and affective neutrality [L]. The *private versus collective interest* dilemma is a cultural choice between self-orientation [S] and collectivity-orientation [O]. As Parsons of course recognized, two pairs of alternatives may combine in four different ways: [R, S], [L, S], [R, O], and [L, O]. Nietzsche and Benedict merely studied different sets of cultures in which a partial linkage had been made between what were in other cultures quite separate genes.

Structuralists have postulated many high-level dichotomies such as these, each of which may be interpreted as a two-allele gene, and it would take us too far afield to review more of them. But one example from anthropology will take us back to religious cults. Anthony F. C. Wallace, who uses the idiosyncratic term *mazeway* to refer to cultural systems, suggested a general principle which might explain the choice of [R] or [L] by the psychotherapeutic cults of a society (Wallace, 1959). If the society itself is highly organized [L], to offer compensation the cults should be [R], while if the society is poorly organized, the cults should provide compensatory rational organization [L]. In the case of the society Wallace used as his example, the Iroquois, invasion by the Europeans changed an ordered society into a chaotic society, thus making the therapy cults shift from [R] to [L]. This reminds us that the gene pool of a culture will be affected by environmental *selection pressures*.

A parallel example can be found in my book, *Satan's Power* (1978b). There I explained that the Process was founded by a man and a woman of very different temperaments. Indeed, one of the things which drew me to the cult as a research site was the fact that it offered competing, alternative culture systems (represented by the four gods) within a single religious organization. Thus, in the language of genetics, The Process was *heterozygous,* while most other cults appear *homozygous*. And, with two co-equal founders, the Process possessed distinctive genetic material from two sources, and thus was *diploid*. Most cults have single cultural systems created as units by single founders, and thus are *haploid*. Scientology is diploid despite having a single founder since it is the amalgam of two cults, Dianetics and Scientology, founded with conflicting principles by the same man. (If I had the space, I would further explain that Dianetics is [R], while Scientology, at least at levels below "clear," is [L].

The female founder of the Process, Mary Ann, favored *control,* while Robert favored *liberation* (Bainbridge 1978b, 25). And, as Wallace might predict, Mary Ann came from a chaotic background, while Robert struggled against the inhibitions instilled in him by a controlled upbringing. Each wanted the cult to compensate for their prior experiences, so Mary Ann wanted [L] while Robert wanted [R]. Which of these opposing genes prevailed? Dominance and recessivity are unstable in culture, depending upon the social power of the faction promoting either allele in a heterozygous cultural system. And the phenotype oscillated back and forth between [R1] and [rL] over the cult's history. On the theological level, this was conceptualized by cult members themselves as a conflict between Jehovah ([L]) and Lucifer ([R]).

In *Satan's Power* I also made use of the Lofland-Stark (1965) concept of *problem-solving perspective*. Each problem-solving perspective is a different ideal-typical way of responding to difficult human problems. Lofland and Stark identified three alleles of this high-level gene: religious, psychiatric, and political. I shall notate these as: [G] for God, [F] for Freud, and [P] for politics. I suggest that the R/L gene determines problem-solving perspective in a way quite independent of the G/F/P gene. When it was founded, The Process was a psychotherapy aimed at the liberation from subconscious compulsions, and thus had the genotype [F, R1]. Later, it became religious instead of psychotherapeutic, and control gained the upper hand, [G, rL]. When Robert and Mary Ann split, and the cult divided into two, there briefly existed two antagonistic sibling cults: Robert's Process [G, R] and Mary Ann's Foundation [G, L].

I can sympathize with any reader who feels skeptical about all this. Each writer (or cultist) who proposes a typology gives each of the types very special connotations and certainly is not thinking in terms of a pure cultural genetics. And there is no doubt that Structuralism is in disrepute within sociology—deservedly so. Stark and I have already explained the reason. Large societies are culturally diverse. They are not cultural systems logically united by over-arching shared assumptions (Bainbridge and Stark, 1981a). But this does not mean that no cultural systems exist. Within modern societies, such cultural systems as religious organizations and styles of art clearly do exist.

Structuralist analyses of cultural innovation (e.g., Merton 1968; Smelser 1962) may be very good descriptions of how innovations come into being within a cultural system. But they may have little to contribute to an understanding of change in unsystematic societies. In *Satan's Power,* I found it appropriate to use the Structuralism of Claude Lévi-Strauss to analyze parts of the Process system. But my editor objected when I wanted to say that the reason the analysis worked was that Robert de Grimston and Claude Lévi-Strauss *thought in the same way.* Apparently, one should not suggest that great anthropologists are cultists. But, perhaps they often are. To the extent that Structuralist thought produces cultural systems, Structuralist thought can help analyze them.

Much of the structural analysis in Lévi-Strauss' books concerns the pre-literate equivalent of religious cults: the poetic products of myth-spinners as refined through generations of telling and retelling. Lévi-Strauss may often be entirely wrong, but I have every reason to believe he may be right much of the time, because, like me, he is looking at the systematic products of persons who engage in genetic engineering to make culture, writ small.

Conclusion

Cultural genes are far more liable than biological genes, but I believe they do possess sufficient stability and coherence to permit a science of cultural genetics. Culture has nothing so regular as DNA to support genetic structure, for the genes are carried in the human mind rather than in a molecule. Yet, intellect creates structure, and both tradition and abstract logic produce regularities in even the most imaginative innovations.

Just as biological genetics began with studies of sweet peas and fruit flies, cultural genetics can begin with systematic research on cults and artistic schools. We need many careful empirical studies tracing the origins and patterns of transmission of cultural genes. This essay has offered hypotheses about the chief mechanisms of mutation and heredity, but only research can determine if these are the most common mechanisms which in fact play important roles. The idea that tradition often establishes a genetic locus in which different alleles substitute to produce competing viable subcultures is a true theory, combining lower-level hypotheses in an overarching explanation. Research can tell us whether it contributes significantly to an understanding of cultural differentiation.

We should not rule out the *experimental method* in research on cults and artistic schools. Lofland and Stark (1965) have already inadvertently manipulated the religious group they studied by providing it with an effective scheme for recruiting new members—although I do not mean to claim that their famous paper really gave the group its later success, such easily could have been the case. Since religion and art are human creations, there is nothing ethnically wrong or impractical about influencing or even creating such subcultures for research purposes. The growing literature on the ethics of biological genetic engineering might guide us in setting limits for similar research on culture (Wade 1977; Rogers 1977; Fletcher 1974).

Certainly we should be prepared to use quantitative techniques in cultural genetics, although I see no obvious analog of the phenotype ratios which played such an important role in the Mendelian tradition. Already, several quantitative studies have attempted to map religious groups in several dimensions. I should point out one possible source of misinterpretation, however. Two cults which in fact are closely related with several identical cultural loci, but with different alleles at each locus, may superficially seem more different than two unrelated cults with no loci in common. For example, a romantic cult [R] may give birth through allele substitution to a classical cult [L], and the two will appear at opposite ends of the R/L dimension. But two unrelated cults which both lack the R/L locus may appear similar to each other because neither is distinctively [R] or [L]. And, of course, superficial similarities are not proof of consanguinity. The knight-in-armor is no kin of the turtle, despite the fact that each has found a tough shell to be a successful adaptation to a dangerous environment. Nor is either related to the ankylosaur, glyptodon, armadillo or horseshoe crab. One must use more subtle techniques than mere quick inspection to determine relationships between cults.

This essay has been so concerned with genes and genetic mutation that it has given little attention to *population genetics* except in consideration of the principle of character displacement. Yet it should be clear that concepts from population genetics should often apply to the competitive, differentiated cultural marketplace. Many a niche may exist for specialized sects and cults, and the interplay of denominations contending for the fertile low-tension territory may be very complex. Many insights, including some embodied in subtle computer models, may come from the examination of religion as a problem in cultural population genetics.

The job of creating a cultural genetics will not be an easy one. I hope the metaphors proposed in this essay illuminate more than they obscure. I have made my oft radical proposals after failing to find adequate theory of cultural innovation within conventional sociology. In two ways this essay has been anachronistic. First, the idea that sociology can profitably use metaphors drawn from the physical sciences was abandoned decades ago. Second, in recent years sociology has tended to ignore culture as an object of study. But there are fashion cycles in social science as in everything else cultural. Therefore, I suggest there exists a great opportunity in reversing these trends and in bravely seeking a science of cultural genetics based initially on concepts borrowed from biology and on information about those exotic microorganisms, religious cults.

References

Adler, Alfred. [1927] 1954. *Understanding Human Nature.* Reprint. Greenwich, Conn.: Fawcett.

———. [1929] 1968. *Individual Psychology.* Reprint. Totowa, N.J.: Littlefield, Adams.

Bainbridge, William Sims. 1978a. Biorhythms: Evaluating a pseudoscience. *Skeptical Inquirer* 2(2):40–56.

———. 1978b. *Satan's Power: Ethnography of a Deviant Psychotherapy Cult.* Berkeley: University of California Press.

Bainbridge, William Sims and Rodney Stark. 1979. Cult Formation: Three compatible models. *Sociological Analysis* 40:283–95.

———. 1980. Scientology: To be perfectly clear. *Sociological Analysis* 41:128–36.

———. 1981a. The 'consciousness reformation' reconsidered. *Journal for the Scientific Study of Religion* 20:1–16.

———. 1981b. Friendship, religion and the occult. *Review of Religious Research* 22:313–27.

Bakan, David. 1965. *Sigmund Freud and the Jewish Mystical Tradition.* New York: Schocken.

195

Benedict, Ruth. 1934. *Patterns of Culture*. Boston: Houghton Mifflin.

Berkower, Lary. 1969. The enduring effect of the Jewish tradition upon Freud. *American Journal of Psychiatry* 125:1067–73.

Boas, Franz. [1908] 1966. Decorative designs of Alaskan needlecases. Reprint. In *Race, Language and Culture*. New York: Free Press.

Cavalli-Sforza, Luigi Luca and Marcus W. Feldman. 1981. *Cultural Transmission and Evolution*. Princeton, N.J.: Princeton University Press.

Cooper, Paulette. 1971. *The Scandal of Scientology*. New York: Tower.

Darnton, Robert. 1970. *Mesmerism and the End of the Enlightenment in France*. New York: Schocken.

Dawkins, Richard. 1976. *The Selfish Gene*. New York: Oxford University Press.

Eysenck, Hans J. 1965. The effects of psychotherapy. *International Journal of Psychiatry* 1:99–144.

Festinger, Leon, H. W. Riecken, and Stanley Schachter. 1956. *When Prophecy Fails*. New York: Harper & Row.

Fletcher, Joseph. 1974. *The Ethics of Genetic Control*. Garden City, N.Y.: Doubleday.

Fodor, Nandor. 1971. *Freud, Jung and Occultism*. New Hyde Park, N.Y.: University Books.

Freud, Sigmund. [1927] 1964. *The Future of an Illusion*. Reprint. Garden City, N.Y.: Doubleday.

Gardner, Martin. 1957. *Fads and Fallacies in the Name of Science*. New York: Dover.

Gruber, William H. and Donald G. Marquis, editors. 1969. *Factors in the Transfer of Technology*. Cambridge, Mass.: M.I.T. Press.

Hostetler, John A. 1968. *Amish Society*. Baltimore: Johns Hopkins Press.

Hubbard, L. Ron. 1956. A critique of psychoanalysis. *Professional Auditor's Bulletin* no. 92 (Scientology publication).

James, William. 1963. *Pragmatism and Other Essays*. New York: Washington Square Press.

Kornbluth, Jesse. 1976. The fuhrer over est. *New Times* 19 (March):36–52.

Korzybski, Alfred. 1948. *Science and Sanity*. Lakeville, Conn.: International Non-Aristotelian Library.

———. 1950. *Manhood of Humanity*. Lakeville, Conn.: International Non-Aristotelian Library.

Lévi-Strauss, Claude. 1962. *The Savage Mind*. Chicago: University of Chicago Press.

————. 1967. *Structural Anthropology*. Garden City, N.Y.: Doubleday.

————. 1970. *The Raw and the Cooked*. New York: Harper.

Lofland, John and Rodney Stark. 1965. Becoming a world-saver: A theory of conversion to a deviant perspective. *American Sociological Review* 39:862–75.

Lumsden, Charles J. and Edward O. Wilson. 1981. *Genes, Mind, and Culture*. Cambridge: Harvard University Press.

Malko, George. 1970. *Scientology: The Now Religion*. New York: Dell.

Maslow, Abraham. 1969. *The Psychology of Science*. Chicago: Henry Regnery.

Medvedev, Zhores A. 1969. *The Rise and Fall of T. D. Lysenko*. New York: Columbia University Press.

Melton, J. Gordon. 1978. *Encyclopedia of American Religions*. 2 vols. Wilmington, N.C.: McGrath (A Consortium Book).

Merton, Robert K. 1968. Social structure and anomie. In *Social Theory and Structure*, 185–214. New York: Free Press.

Meyer, Leonard B. 1967. *Music, the Arts, and Ideas*. Chicago: University of Chicago Press.

Niebuhr, H. Richard. 1929. *The Social Sources of Denominationalism*. New York: Holt.

Nietzsche, Friedrich. 1872. *Die Geburt der Tragödie*. Munich: Goldmann.

————. 1885. *Also Sprach Zarathustra*. Stuttgart: Kröner.

Parsons, Talcott. 1951. *The Social System*. Glencoe, Ill.: Free Press.

————. 1964. Evolutionary universals in society. *American Sociological Review* 29:339–57.

Perls, Frederick, Ralph F. Hefferline and Paul Goodman. 1951. *Gestalt Therapy*. New York: Dell.

Rachman, Stanley. 1971. *The Effects of Psychotherapy*. Oxford: Pergamon.

Rieff, Philip. 1966. *The Triumph of the Therapeutic*. New York: Harper & Row.

Rogers, Michael. 1977. *Biohazard*. New York: Knopf.

Salter, Andrew. [1952] 1972. *The Case Against Psychoanalysis*. Reprint. New York: Harper & Row.

Scholl, Sharon and Sylvia White. 1970. *Music and the Culture of Man*. New York: Holt, Rinehart and Winston.

Smelser, Neil J. 1962. *Theory of Collective Behavior*. New York: Free Press.

Stark, Rodney and William Sims Bainbridge. 1979. Of churches, sects and cults. *Journal for the Scientific Study of Religion* 18:117–31.

————. 1980. Towards a theory of religion: Religious commitment. *Journal for the Scientific Study of Religion* 19:114–128.

Stubbe, Hans. 1972. *History of Genetics*. Cambridge: M.I.T. Press.

Sturtevant, A.H. 1965. *A History of Genetics*. New York: Harper & Row.

Tobey, Alan. 1976. The summer solstice of the healthy-happy-holy organization. In *The New Religious Consciousness*, edited by Charles Y. Glock and Robert N. Bellah, 5–30. Berkeley: University of California Press.

van Vogt, A. E. 1945. *The World of Null-A*. New York: Ace.

Wade, Nicholas. 1977. *The Ultimate Experiment*. New York: Walker.

Wallace, Anthony F. C. 1959. The institutionalization of cathartic and control strategies in Iroquois religious psychotherapy. In *Culture and Mental Health,* edited by Marvin K. Opler, 63–96. New York: Macmillian.

Wallis, Roy. 1977. *The Road to Total Freedom*. New York: Columbia University Press.

White, Harrison C. and Cynthia A. White. 1965. *Canvases and Careers: Institutional Change in the French Painting World*. New York: Wiley.

Whitehouse, H. L. K. 1965. *Towards an Understanding of the Mechanism of Heredity*. New York: St. Martin's Press.

Winter, J. A. 1951. *A Doctor's Report on Dianetics*. New York: Julian Press.

————. 1962. *Origins of Illness and Anxiety*. New York: Julian Press.

Zweig, Stefan [1932] 1962. *Mental Healers*. Reprint. New York: Ungar.

7

"Dualistic and Monistic Religiosity"

R. Stephen Warner

The Argument

THERE are two general forms of religiosity in American Protestantism today, and perhaps in all Western religion. Each form is authentic, and each is distinct from the other. One recognizes a separate realm of "sacred," sets this realm off from the "secular" or "profane," and symbolizes this distinction in manifolds aspects of ritual. The other insists on organizing the whole of life around some special revelation, and it symbolizes this insistence by the infusion of traditionally religious symbols into mundane existence and by the continuity of mundane experience with worship. The former I call "dualistic" religiosity; the latter, "monistic." The former is the religion that Durkheim defined, and it tends to be found in church-like religious organizations. The latter was the special interest of Weber, and it is to be found especially among sects. Each type is currently represented in American Protestantism on both sides of the cross-cutting theologically liberal to-conservative dimension. Thus, evangelical-charismatic (theologically conservative) fellowships are often "monistic," but so also

199

are modern, social-action-oriented and theologically liberal congregations.

Typical Observations

It is a simple matter, requiring little research, to experience worship at the dualistic pole. On any Sunday morning, dress up in a conservative suit or a modest but elegant dress and go to a large mainstream Protestant church for the eleven o'clock service. Chances are, you will find much of this. Hundreds of people will be ushered to seats in an awesome space, seats fixed to the floor and all facing a raised stage. An organ will be playing suitably sober music, and conversations will be held, at best, in a whisper. You will have time to peruse the printed program that has been given you, though you will find later that few will notice if you do or do not engage in all the routines that it spells out for you. There will be, in any event, little doubt about when things begin, for those around you will respond in impressive unison as the volume of the organ changes dramatically and a corps of specially attired celebrants enters, singing vigorously. Choir and ministers will take their places, and you will know that they are to provide the leads that you will follow and indeed the entertainment and edification you might as well be prepared to enjoy. The ministers (there are likely to be several) will use a tone of voice and an inflection that you would find strange if you were not accustomed to it, and they will address the God who is the focus of all this attention in archaic language, likely referring to Him as "Thou." The congregation of which you are willy-nilly a member will respond when called upon in similarly archaic language and in a meter governed more by the group's sheer size than by the manifest sense of the words uttered. The Holy Scriptures will be read by one of the ministers from a lectern, on which is placed an enormous, ornate copy of them, and the reading will be concluded with a brief invocation of God's blessing. The scriptures will be interpreted and related to events of current cultural and political significance or to items of perennial personal concern in a long sermon which, if you are fortunate, might titillate your mind and engage your sense of humor. There will likely be another congregationally-sung hymn, and perhaps another prayer, which will have a cathartic effect. If Communion is to be celebrated that Sunday, it will be done with majestic solemnity, using specially prepared elements distributed either in the pews or at the altar, and whether or not you decide to participate will be of little moment to others. The service will then be closed with a fine sense of definitiveness, the well-trained choir adding their "amen," and you will file with others past smiling hand-shakers out onto the street. Were you to attend the next week, the elements of the experience would likely be identical. You might indeed be inclined to go again, for, despite the characterization of this dualistic experience as "dead" by partisans of religious innovation, the dualistic experience at its best has, for many, an undeniable power.

It requires rather more initiative, curiosity, and courage for an unbeliever to experience monistic religiosity. For one thing, monistic worship experiences are by no means always held on Sunday. They will be held outside of normal working hours, whether in the evening or on the weekend, and you may read an announcement in a newspaper or in some church's bulletin. More likely, though, you will receive notice, and perhaps an invitation, by word of mouth. The gathering may take place in a church fellowship hall or in someone's living room, and it will be a smaller and less formally dressed group than the one that appears at the big church on Sunday morning. If you arrive at the stated time, likely in the evening, there will be a lot of milling about and socializing, but fear not that you will be anonymous. Someone will greet you heartily, ask your name and give you a genuine welcome. If you wish to sit to gather your thoughts and your nerve, you will have trouble finding the back of the room, the onlooker's space, so to speak, for the chairs or couches will be arranged in a rough circle. You may be lucky to find a song book in which to bury your attention, but that is not likely. And it is also unlikely that there will be a printed order of service. Soon, though, someone with a guitar will begin strumming and others will take seats, and the service will begin, maybe with a song, maybe a prayer, with the attention of everyone drawn immediately to the activity. There will be a lot of singing, of songs that may or may not be written down for you to follow. If you are attending an evangelicals' meeting some of those songs may use for their texts some verses from Psalms that everyone will have in his or her Bible. If this is "contemporary worship," popular songs might be used. There will be one or more leaders, recognizable by the sheer volume of their contributions, but many members of the group will offer prayers or words of edification, to which the group will pay attention. Whole chains of prayers and comments will issue forth, each purporting to build on the last, until you may feel that you are the only one not initiating some remark. You may notice that several members are particularly adept at producing biblical citations from their well-underlined Bibles. Others may relate trivial or intimate details of their lives. Prayers will be distinguishable from testimonials, but not markedly so. The person offering a prayer may do so with eyes closed and head bowed, and he or she may choose words carefully and otherwise speak more slowly than if he or she were addressing the group. But the language and intonation will be little different. You may wonder when it will all end, and indeed you ought to be forewarned that the meeting will take close to two or two-and-a-half hours. But if there is to be a "teaching" or a "sharing of the word," you can be reasonably confident while it is going on that the end is in sight. A few more prayers and songs, and the monistic service comes to an undramatic end. However, many members (those who are for one or another reason exempt from immediate worry about children and other matters) will stay around in the worship space to visit. If you have been fortunate, you will not have been put too much "on the spot" as a visitor, but if someone has gone into the kitchen during the service to get some bread or crackers and wine or juice with which to serve a communion, your decision to partake or not cannot but have been noticed. You will likely, though, have experienced some remarkably beautiful group singing, and you will have been privileged to share in some bold and thoughtful attempts to relate the contents of the religious material to the everyday lives of those present. Unless you are moved inside by that content, however, or you are doing research, you are unlikely to attend again. It is just too demanding, too exhausting, too "living."

Elements of the Two Forms

Presenting a chronicle of typical experiences is intended to make the contrast between the two forms reasonably concrete, but it does risk the misidentification of accidental for essential elements of the forms. The Sunday service I outlined was briefer and more formally ordered, and it took place among a group of larger size than did the evening fellowship. But size is not the determinant of the form. Just as it is feasible to lecture to a group of five students and possible to engage a class of several hundred in discussion, so also dualistic religiosity can occur in small groups and monistic in large, as I have seen in massive outdoor charismatic festivals. It is indeed easier to have the monistic experience in a small group of up to fifty members, and so those desiring such an experience will tend to choose a small group setting. Nor is the spontaneous and protracted nature of the event crucial for the monistic experience. My research has led me to see that the ostensibly free-flowing liturgy of the monistics has most of the same elements of worship, in much the same order, as the dualistic experience: adoration, confession, absolution, intercession, instruction, dedication. What is essential to the contrast is the message portrayed manifestly and symbolically about the relationship of the religious experience to the world.

Dualistic religiosity conceives of the worship experience and the messages enunciated in it as special, referring to what Durkheim called the "sacred." It occurs at special times, on what is held to be a sabbath, and in specially consecrated places, distinguishable by the trappings of specially religious symbols. Within this special place, there are some places more special than others, an altar or chancel, in which the most sacred of the rituals are performed and from which leadership is directed. Those attending dress in something better than everyday clothes, and those leading are dressed in even more supramundane attire. Leadership is monopolized by those specially dressed, and they have special titles and credentials to set them off from the rest of the congregation. They speak in a language which, in vocabulary, syntax, and intonation, announces itself as different. They treat the religious symbols—the cross, the ark, the Bible, the Host—with great and solemn respect. The unity that can be experienced in the dualistic experience at its best is imposed by tradition. The entire experience is one that, by its very predictability, awesomeness, and majesty, symbolizes the persistence and extraordinary nature of a separate realm: the sacred.

Monistic religiosity refuses to recognize that the religious experience is confined to the place, time, or attitude in which the worship event takes place. It also refuses to rule out of that event matters that may have taken place outside its temporal and spatial boundaries. It takes place at any time, regularized for convenience, of course, but not special. So also it takes place in any space, a multi-purpose room, a home, or outdoors. Within that space, relevant utterances may issue from anywhere. Dress is no different than for everyday activities, though hands and faces are clean, and leaders are not distinguishable by their dress (except perhaps by their studied adherence to the everyday mode). Leadership is diffuse, there being several leaders scattered about the room and there being much opportunity for rank-and-file participants to initiate songs, prayers, and testimonials, interpretations, or opinions. Language is ordinary, though what is in ordinary use among the evangelical camp of the monists may strike the unbeliever as odd ("praise God!" and "that's a blessing!" and tongue-speech being heard as much in the kitchen and workshop as in worship). Religious symbols are seen everywhere, on car bumpers, business cards, lapels, and living room walls, as well as in worship, and, in worship, the Bible (preeminent sacred symbol of dualistic Protestants) is underlined and dog-earred like any textbook. The unity that may be experienced among monists is emergent, though unity is for them both a riskier and a more important business than for the dualists. The entire experience is one that, by its sheer ordinariness and self-styled spontaneity, symbolizes the continuity of all experience, organized around a demand for personal holiness or commitment to the realization of a public mission.

Analytic Independence of Form from Content

Although I have used observations from my research among Christian evangelicals and charismatics for my description of some elements of monistic worship (see also Neitz 1981; Harrison 1974), the monistic concept is not confined to them. Indeed, the distinction between dualistic and monistic forms has been clarified by my reading of Michael Ducey's *Sunday Morning* (1977), whose own parallel distinction between "mass ritual" (dualistic) and "interaction ritual" (monistic) was developed to account for changes in a theologically liberal and social-action-oriented congregation, the Church of the Three Crosses, in Chicago. Similarly, Hadden and Longino, in *Gideon's Gang* (1974) chronicle the fate of the politically radical Congregation of Reconciliation in Dayton, Ohio, many of whose members were secular humanists who could not abide "God talk," but who were united by their desire to present the radical challenge to unjust social institutions that they felt their values demanded. Their meetings consisted almost entirely of planning for such challenging ventures. The theologically orthodox evangelicals and charismatics that I have studied might be conceived by a dualist as demanding the invasion of the secular by the sacred; the theologically heterodox groups that Ducey and Hadden and Longino studied might be seen as inviting an invasion of the sacred by the secular. What these theologically very different groups have in common, however, is their refusal to countenance a division of experience into religious and non-religious aspects. Neither side wants its God to be kicked upstairs.

To get at the question of the meaning of religion for everyday life, Ducey begins with the worship experience, as I have also done in this paper. He develops the concepts of mass versus interaction ritual at some length and he applies them to the development of the Church of the Three Crosses in the late 1960s (1977, 6–8, 99–130). He emphasizes that church's rearrangement of the worship space, their use of secular readings in worship, their high rate of congregational participation, including "talkback" or dialogue, their frequent rearrangement of liturgical elements, and their use of non-traditional music. He interprets this "interaction ritual" as an attempt on the part of the congregation to provide new sources of meaning in a rapidly changing urban environment. He presents (101) a summary depiction of the two forms of ritual as seen in Three Crosses, on the one hand, and in three other Chicago churches that he also observed, which were more committed to the traditional "mass ritual." However, Ducey's concentration on the liberal Church of the Three Crosses leads him to identify the form of interaction ritual (monistic) with settings in which the authority of tradition is "dead," and he thus disregards the appearance of the identical form among those, such as charismatics and evangelicals, who adhere to the authority of the Bible (c.f., 40–41n). Moreover, his respect for interaction ritual leads him to denigrate the potential of mass ritual in our society. Hadden and Longino, too, and more overtly, imply their distaste for any form of religiosity other than that of their politically liberal and formally monistic case, the Congregation for Reconciliation. They maintain that religious organizations can focus either on "social change, the quality of human life, and a just social order" or "personal financial gain and comfort" (1974, 232). But this dichotomy causes the conflation the several styles of bringing religion and life to bear on each other, and entails the view that the only way for believers to meet God on the stairs is through political action. Hadden and Longino's position notwithstanding, "relevance," or what I call monism, may be found as much among the theologically orthodox as among the politically liberal (see also McGuire 1974).

Just as religious monism is to be found across the theological and political spectrums, so also dualistic religiosity is not confined to conservatives. Garry Wills, in *Bare Ruined Choirs* (1972), vividly detailed the world of the 1950s Catholic liberal, who combined his commitment to social justice with a "higher churchiness" that gloried in the archaisms of his church. "He said 'acolytes,' not 'altar boys.' And 'the Eucharist' rather than 'Holy Communion.' . . . He knew his Mass Book, the Missal, backward and forward, Latin and English—it fell open automatically to 'the prayers at the foot of the altar'" (1972, 39, 40). The liberal dualist took seriously the advice of Thomas Merton to retire periodically from the tensions of the secular world. Such a retirement refreshed the source of political energy for that secular world, but the worlds were kept distinct. Though Wills has very mixed feelings about that dualistic system (now, after Vatican II, perhaps never to return in its purity) and details the moral dread and intellectual vacuity that it often involved, he still appreciates its eternal and sacred appearance. "The ancient liturgy was a last resort, the one thing that still worked, a place where one did not hear questions, raise doubts, submit to lectures. Here all was as it had been, proof that some things do not change, that one could go home" (74). Wills then goes on to detail the changes that nonetheless did take place, as this dualistic system ceded among the highly committed to a monistic one. Formerly rustic seminaries were moved into central cities. Priests shed clerical collars, the bread of communion became "chewy stuff, or cookies, not the flat wafers of old" (208) and "the walls of division have come down" (216). So within the dimension of political liberalism, religious experience could be dualistic or monistic.

Dualists can be theological liberals, too. Just as the dualism-monism distinction is independent of politics, so also is it independent of theology. Theological conservatives have historically lived off sacred-secular dualism as a protection of their monopoly over the administration of the means of salvation, but in today's world it is not uncommon to find theological liberals among the dualists. A visitor to a mainstream Protestant church can hear a sermon calling into question some article of orthodox faith such as the Virgin Birth or the Bodily Resurrection, a sermon spoken to a receptive congregation by a richly robed clergyman speaking in churchly tones from a raised pulpit. Here, all the formal elements of dualistic religiosity are present, but the message is theologically liberal. The form of religiosity, then, is independent of its theological and political content.

The Formal Contrast and the Durkheim-Weber Question

Earlier I said that Durkheim focused on dualistic religion and Weber on monistic. It is commonly recognized that Durkheim's and Weber's sociologies of religion differ in many ways. Durkheim looked mostly at the religion of primitive cultures, and he found in it a source of social cohesion and social identity. Weber, by contrast, worked on the great world religions of literate civilizations, and he was particularly interested in, though he did not always find, religion as a source of social change. To some extent, these perspectives complement one another; they can sensitize us to different aspects of the same thing. Religion may be based on an oral as well as a written tradition, and it may provide social stability as well as become a source of upheaval. But an emphasis on theoretical synthesis ought not obscure the possibility that Durkheim and Weber were attuned to two different things.

For the purposes of his cross-cultural analysis, Durkheim defined religion as a system of beliefs and practices that divide the world into the two realms of the sacred and profane (1915, 62), but Weber, though he characteristically neglected a definition of religion, wrote his first major essays on the topic about enthusiastic forms of Christianity that had as their theological essence the sanctification of mundane activities and the systematic organization of life as a religious calling (1930, 80, 83, 117). Weber saw in pre-Reformation Catholicism the human cycle of sacred and profane that Durkheim also saw in the Australian tribes, but Weber was more attuned to the monistic experiences of the Reformation Lutherans, Pietists, Baptists, and, especially, Calvinists. The Reformation surely recognized states of sin as well as salvation, but the sin/salvation dichotomy is not identical to the profane/sacred one. Indeed, a contemporary fundamentalist congregation is likely to be addressed by its pastor as either "sinners" or "saints." And Durkheim insisted that his "sacred" category was not to be confused with the "good," for the realm of demons was sacred, too. The moral rigorism of the Reformation was not sacred/profane dualism (Bellah 1964; Parsons 1978, 335–6). But Durkheim held that it is of the essence of religion to recognize religiously relevant (the spiritual and extraordinary) and irrelevant (sensual and mundane) aspects of existence, and if his definition is not simply to be scrapped we must see that he has grasped one form of religiosity.

In Durkheim's dualistic religiosity, the unity of the community is celebrated at special times and places through the use of special and "forbidden" artifacts. The effervescence of emotion that accompanies these celebrations becomes the social-psychological cement on which the continuity of the community depends. Both in *The Elementary Forms* and in *Suicide*, Durkheim concerns himself little with the content of the doctrine that the religion enunciates. He does not so much dismiss doctrine—he was not that radical a secularist—as insist that the truth in doctrine is to be found in its latent recognition of the power and continuity of the society that produces it. "Durkheim was, after all, a spoilt rabbi, and constructed from his experience the relation of religion to social identity and unity" (Martin 1978, 15). That there is a consensus within the community on doctrine, Durkheim takes for granted, and he extracts from it the basic organizing conceptions of abstract thought that Kant had imputed to the individual mind. But the details of theology were of no moment for Durkheim. As a guide to the orientations of many, if not most, lay churchgoers, Durkheim is not far from the truth. He knows the soul of religious dualism.

Weber is known to have admitted that he was "religiously unmusical," and his vast sociology of religion says very little about worship or, indeed, about emotions other than anxiety. He has a great deal to say about the formal organization of religious hierarchies, and volumes about the implications for practical life of the content of doctrinal systems. Weber did not suppose that the world of the religious participant was divided into two realms, but instead he analyzed that world in terms of his categories of ideas and spiritual and temporal interests (Warner 1970). Rather than accepting the dualism between material and ideal principles in his analyses of the effect of religion on economic life, Weber transcended it by conceiving of religious needs as theoretically parallel to interests and religious ideas as parallel to beliefs about the empirical world (Warner 1978).

What the divine order proclaimed impinged as much on the believer's work as upon his or her salvation, and the desire for salvation was as much an interest as the desire for a good meal. But through all of Weber's investigations of the practical ethic of the world religions runs the assumption that the nominal adherent to a religious system takes its cognitive formulae seriously, that Calvinists believed in predestination, pre-exilic Hebrews in the covenant with Yahweh, and Hindus in transmigration of souls. If Weber's sociology of religion is limited and vulnerable, it is precisely on this score, that so much of the dynamic he portrayed depended heavily on doctrinal commitment. That is why Weber's sociology of religion is so appropriate for the analysis of sects, for there are to be found the religious monists who do attempt to organize life around the religious revelation. They do not always succeed in organizing it just as their ethical compendia demand, for Weber held that only conduct upon which premiums are placed will come to be regularized. Nonetheless, for Weber the details of their belief system are part of the determination of their conduct.

Talcott Parsons's attempt at fusion of the Durkheimian and Weberian perspectives brings together the former's emphasis on the affective realm with the latter's emphasis on the content of doctrine, and unites them under the assumption of value consensus across the whole of a modern society. To do that, however, he had to propose that the value system (the cognitive content of which is consensually affirmed by way of the affective process of socialization) has become as secularized and generalized as a technological and pluralistic society requires (1969, 463–469; 1978, Part III). That proposal, in turn, has influenced the development of the concept of "civil religion" (Bellah 1967; cf. Marty 1976, ch. 8), and meanwhile it seems to prevent its adherents from having much to say about anything other than liberal Protestantism in contemporary America (Warner 1979, 1981; cf. Bellah 1964). If there is a single value system, and if it is upon it that social cohesion and continuity depend, then it must be de-mythologized and vague to accommodate a pluralistic society. Given these presuppositions, however, adherence to a different value system, one that challenges or transcends the culture from either the side of orthodox Christian doctrine or the side of radical Social Gospel doctrine, must be characterized as merely one of the growing pains of society. It would be better to recognize that the two forms of religiosity and their several doctrinal expressions are robust.

Peter Berger has provided another creative synthesis of the Durkheimian and Weberian traditions in *The Sacred Canopy* (1969) and *A Rumor of Angels* (1970). To define religion, he employs, with some reservations and amendents (1969, 175–177), the Durkheimian idea of the sacred as a "totally other" realm. This realm is experienced by the ordinary believer only intermittently, and rituals function to remind the believer of its reality. Indeed, religion, in its essence, is the "alienated" phenomenon *par excellence,* a human creation that appears to us as if it were a part of an utterly different world (1969, 25–6, 40–1, 87, 124). This sacred world is by definition a non-empirical world, and beliefs about it are of a different order than beliefs about the everyday world (1970, 2–3, 34–37). Those beliefs are reaffirmed in the mythological formulae of ritual.

To this basically Durkheimian, or dualistic, frame, Berger grafts on a Weberian concern for the content of doctrine. Indeed, he goes Weber one better by paying greater attention to the vagaries of Christology, or doctrines pertaining to the understanding of the person of Jesus (1969, 74–77, 196). He shows how the orthodox interpretation of Jesus as both man and God served to answer the perennial problem of theodicy, or the justification of the divine order in the face of human suffering. Yet his synthesis, in the end, gives us little help in the understanding of vital religion today. Berger is convinced that the secularization and especially the pluralism of our society renders genuine belief in the doctrines of orthodox Christianity impossible for all but those in the backwaters. Meanwhile, he is skeptical at best and contemptuous at worst of efforts to develop a monistic Christianity in a radical direction. He would prefer the neo-orthodox withdrawal of ultimate commitment from any human institution, a withdrawal that simply leaves most local congregations cold, but he sees little possibility for "relevant" or monistic religiosity in modern society (1969, 98–99; 1970, 20–23, 83–84). *A Rumor of Angels*, then, is whispered not about any actual contemporary religious beliefs, but only their potentiality, a potentiality about which Berger is hardly sanguine.

On Evangelical Monists

Meanwhile, other rumors about the death of religion are greatly exaggerated. Despite the debacle of monistic attempts to make the church live in social action, theologically and politically conservative churches are strong (Kelley 1977; Hoge 1976), and self-proclaimed evangelicals, adherents to orthodox Christianity, are popping up in the most unlikely places. How are we to regard these signs of vitality? Are they merely aspects of a retreat from social concern, representing exasperation and fatigue or even outright reaction (Fry 1975)? To some extent they are, but to concentrate too much on such a view is to explain only the decline of liberal monism. It is also to reduce religiosity to politics, as if most churchgoers were primarily interested simply in getting their liberal or conservative opinions sanctified.

Such a view is not to explain the vitality of the monistic and dualistic evangelical bodies. Evangelical dualists do find in their intermittent religious experience the affirmation of traditional moral values on which many of them were raised, the humble values of honesty and charity. They may have little involvement with the niceties of theology that their churches adhere to, but they are emotionally refreshed by their weekly confrontation with the sacred. Both the poor-but-honest Fundamentalist and the privileged Evangelical are comforted in their recognition of benign powers outside of their grasp. Their religion does contribute to one of Talcott Parson's four functions, that of "pattern maintenance." Their faith may be, in the old Roman formula, mostly "implicit," but then they share that kind of faith with most of those who have been counted as adherents by the world's religions. It is a faith of mostly normative and affective content, which reanimates its life through the awe in which its dimly understood symbols are approached.

Evangelical monists, on the other hand, are not maintaining patterns. Their models are likely to be the struggling young congregations founded by the Apostles in the First Century (Edwards 1974; Snyder 1975), and many think of themselves as set in opposition to the sinful (not simply "profane") culture about them. Theirs is a religiosity of challenge and commitment, though their challenge is likely to be unheard by the wider society. Their groups are small, and their communication channels—religious radio and television stations and mail-order lending libraries of tapes and tracts—are specialized out of the mainstream (cf. Proctor 1979). In some ways, their groups must be small, for the mutual-aid ethics they proclaim (and, to a remarkable extent, practice), the participatory worship they desire, and the deviant cognitive system (Berger 1970, esp. ch. 1) they articulate can best be maintained in small, and very parochial, settings. Whether or not they live communally (Harris 1973; Jackson and Jackson 1974), they form little *Gemeinschaften,* visiting and bearing each other up in normal times and coming to each other's aid in times of crisis. They find much to be done at home, in the community. Their worship must not be thought of as solely a time of ecstasy, and there is probably a higher ratio of sheer emotive force to cognitive content per hour in the best-run dualistic service than there is in their house gatherings. They share thoughts that they have had about the implications of some scripture passage for dealing with their children's pains in school or their own dealings at work. They compare different translations of scripture. They sing songs of praise and deliverance. And they pray, endlessly pray. They pray for the healing of spirits, bodies, and machines, and they thank God for his answers—whether "yes" or "no"—to these and other unarticulated prayers. They speak to and about God, in one or another of his three persons, in terms of astounding familiarity. "I spoke with the Lord last night, and He said to me—with this little smirk on his face . . . ," an evangelical monist once began a testimony. These normative, affective, and cognitive commitments are such as to demand a facing inward to self, family, and parish (to use an old-fashioned word). Consequently, evangelical monists are inclined to care little for the wider world. Those I spent time with during the campaign year of 1976 showed remarkably little enthusiasm one way or another for Jimmy Carter. They sent their children to a private Christian school. They trusted as much in the ministrations of those few of their number "blessed" with the gift of healings as in those of the medical profession.

But there is no aspect of their lives that is innocent of religious meaning. They are not "otherworldly."

Tensions Within and Between the Forms

This is surely an "ideal type" of evangelical religious monism that I have drawn, and I have drawn it heavily on the basis of my own intensive field observations. It is easier to find purely monistic worship events and participating individuals than it is to find purely monistic organizations or congregations. For reasons to be developed shortly, religious organizations derive some of their vitality from a coexistence of dualistic and monistic tendencies. But evangelical monism is not as unusual as a secularized academic reader of this account might assume, as indeed I assumed when I began the research. Theologically orthodox monistic groups are now to be found all over the country and all across the spectrum of social strata, and tendencies in this direction have appeared within even the staid mainstream churches (Connelly 1977). Some sort of monism is always an immanent tendency within tradition-al dualistic religion.

Like Weber, Troeltsch focused on the content of doctrine, specifically Christian doctrine, and he held that the sectarian impulse of resistance to worldly compromise was an inherent opportunity within that doctrine. But even within the Durkheimian tradition, dualistic religiosi-ty can be seen to have its inner tensions, as it is seen by Erickson (1966) in his study of the Massachusetts Puritans. Whatever the doctrine, there are those who will attempt to adhere to it without regard for the necessities of institutionalization, and, Erickson implies, there will always be an Anne Hutchinson to test the boundaries of that institu-tionalization by challenging its leaders on their own professed doctrinal grounds (1966, 97–8, 122, 129–30). But the challenge to institutional "hardening of the arteries" need not come only from those who are concerned with questions of spiritual salvation. It may come from those who are entrusted to be the carriers to the often neglected doctrinal formulae of the dualistic institution. Thus Wills (1972, 68–70) shows that it was the clerics, not the laity, who demanded the change toward the vernacular in the Catholic Mass. They were tired of the rigidity, the "museum-exhibit semilanguage" that stultified growth. Thus, also, numerous studies of Protestant clergy (Hadden 1969; Hoge 1976; Quinley 1974; Schroeder, et al. 1974) have shown that it was they, not their charges, who carried the impulse toward the worldly relevance of political action in their churches. The great Universal church, when not in thrall to Inquisitions, was able to handle these strains with the institutions of monasticism, in which monists' enthusiasms could be channeled, but that intricate system has long ago broken down.

Monistic Christianity, too, is a tension-filled business. Its demands for holiness or for social commitment and its insistent stance of judgment against a sinful or craven world are very hard to live up to. Though it conceives of the religious and the everyday life as one, it divides the world into categories of good and evil, of the regenerate versus the unregenerate or the challengers versus the comforters. These demands and these divisions are such as to threaten the unity of many a religious organization. This is true not only for the now notorious case of the politically-oriented monism of the 1960s; not only demands to do something about social injustice can divide a religious body. Moral rigorism can be similarly divisive. The greatest internal trauma and the greatest loss of members of the charismatic group I studied in 1976 had been occasioned two years before by the decision of the elders of that body to excommunicate a female member who was persistently living "in sin" with a "non-Christian" man. The scars from that expulsion never did heal, and many members of the group asked themselves and each other whether the attempt at purity can be borne by a collectivity of mere humans. Not only liberal monists can feel chastened by their attempts to put their faith into practice.

Monism can also succumb to faddishness. Without the anchor of the sacred symbols entrusted to special roles, the trends of the day can overtake the monistic community and can threaten, in the long run, the message that was the source of its appeal. A few years ago, a group of Catholic charismatics was admonished by William Cardinal Baum to beware of such tendencies. "Cardinal Baum told the charismatics that without the firm ground that the church can offer, 'the Jesus of my experience could be the projection of my psychological needs, whose worship could be idolatrous'" (*Washington Post* 10 March 1978, A28). The more "modern" camp of the monists were admonished in similar terms by Peter Berger: "A secularized Christianity (and, for that matter, a secularized Judaism) has to go to considerable exertion to demonstrate that the religious label, as modified in conformity with the spirit of the age, has anything special to offer. Why should one buy psychotherapy or racial liberalism in a 'Christian' package, when the same commodities are available under purely secular and for that very reason even more modernistic labels?" (1969, 20–21). That these warnings issue from dualists who have a stake in the maintenance of the traditional system does not gainsay their pertinence to the monists' situation. Monists themselves are aware of these risks and will warn each other about the dangers of identifying God by his gift of a spiritual "high" or by his carrying of a political banner (cf. Wills 1972, 95).

In the face of tendencies toward division and entropy and of the inevitable question of finding successors for the founders, monists may seek refuge in the orderliness and stability of institutionalization. It is the fate of every charismatic movement (and here I am using "charismatic" in its Weberian sense) to become routinized, and dualism is one of the most convenient forms of routinization. The sect of Methodism becomes the denomination of Methodists (Neibuhr 1929, 70–72). The impulse to transform life becomes a grace note upon it. That note of grace, however, contains within it a key to something more, and the most staid religious organizations are still nurturing local monistic fellowships, from social action corps to charismatic encounter groups.

Conclusion

In this paper I have used the device of presenting ideal types of two forms of worship to argue that there are two distinct practical conceptions of the relationship between the worldly and the sacred, or the human and the divine. The outline of these two forms was then used to address some outstanding problems in the literature. First, by way of contrast to oversimplified notions of a dilemma between comforting and challenging religion, I argued that the form of religion is independent of its particular theological or political content, with the corollary that culture-transcending religion is to be found on both sides of the right-to-left ideological spectrum. Second, I argued that Durkheim and Weber differ about religion in part because they were talking about two different things; attempts to synthesize their contributions—and this paper is one such attempt—can founder if they disregard the profundity of their differences. Third, and most important from the perspective of contemporary topical concerns, I suggested that the distinction between religious monism and dualism facilitates the doing of emperical justice to the current evangelical resurgence. Evangelical dualists may indeed be seekers of comfort from an otherworldly realm, but evangelical monists—including so-called neo-evangelicals, Jesus People, and many charismatics—have a religious life of challenge and active cognitive involvement (traits easy enough to portray with sympathy to a secular, academic audience) as well as of piety and parochialism (which are stereotypically less admirable traits which, however, are deeply bound up with the other two, bound up in the round of monistic life). Fourth, I briefly outlined some of the tensions endemic to both forms and indicated that these tensions provide the key to the understanding of the relationship between them. Monism will always tend toward becoming dualism, as all charismatic movements tend to become routinized. But dualism, too, has the seeds of monism within, and purists and extremists will challenge their complacent institutional environments. In this sense, monism and dualism are symbiotically united even as they are symbolically distinct.

Notes

1. The first draft of this paper was written in May 1978 and delivered at the Annual Meetings of the Association for the Sociology of Religion in Boston in August 1979. I became aware that a serious confusion might be entailed by my use of "dualism" and "monism" to refer to formal properties of religion shortly after writing that first draft when I read the very informative survey article by Robbins, Anthony, and Richardson (1978; hereafter called RAR). RAR, among other scholars (e.g., Martin 1978), use the terms dualism and monism to refer to a contrast in the content of religious ideologies. For RAR, a religion is dualistic when it presupposes a metaphysical distinction between God and man. For RAR, dualism obtains when religious persons distinguish, for example, between sin and salvation or between good and evil as principles of existence. Christianity, in nearly any version, is thus inherently dualistic. RAR's monism, therefore, tends to be an attribute of pre-modern or Eastern religions, which presuppose an immanent cosmic unity. I have no quarrel with RAR's use of dualism and monism to refer to this contrast of ideological content, but it will become clear that my own conceptual distinction is orthogonal to theirs. In my scheme,

216

dualism and monism are attributes of the form of religious experience. As we shall see, Christianity can be both dualistic and monistic depending on the organization of adherents' lives.

For some time I sought to find a substitute terminology to avoid this possible confusion. I considered calling dualism "transcendence" and monism "immanence," but decided that this usage would invite the reader to think that evangelical monists are proponents of theological immanence. So far as I understand evangelical theology, this would be a grievous distortion. I also considered "totalism" for monism and "pluralism" for dualism but discarded this idea because of the evaluative loadings of both those possible substitutes. For similar reasons, I decided not to use segmented/holistic, structured/liminal, institutional/movement, or churchly/sectarian. At length I decided to ask the reader to set aside any connotations of dualism and monism that have to do with theological content. Used in a formal sense, the terms communicate better than any alternative a significant contrast in styles of religiosity.

2. This paper was developed in the context of extensive conversations with Anne Heider, to whom I am deeply obligated. I am fortunate to have read the work of Michael Ducey and Martin Marty early in my resocialization as a sociologist of religion, and I am grateful to Joy Charlton for pointing me in their direction and for discussing their theories and other sociological matters with me. The late David Street gave me early, quick, pointed, and supportive feedback on my first draft. I miss him greatly. Mary Jo Neitz shared her observations on Catholic charismatics with me, to my edification; her suggestions have improved this paper. Other persons who gave useful and perceptive comments on the earlier drafts were Lewis Coser, Kai Erikson, Arthur W. Frank, Arthur Hillman, and Barry Seltser. I thank them all.

References

Bellah, Robert N. 1964. Religious evolution. *American Sociological Review* 29 (June): 358–74.

———. 1967. Civil religion in America." *Daedalus* 96 (Winter):1–21.

Berger, Peter L. 1969. *The Sacred Canopy.* Garden City, N.Y.: Double-day Anchor.

———. 1970. *A Rumor of Angels.* Garden City, N.Y.: Doubleday Anchor.

Connelly, James T. 1977. *Neo-Pentecostalism: The Charismatic Revival in the Mainline Protestant and Roman Catholic Churches in the United States, 1960–1971.* Unpublished dissertation; University of Chicago, School of Divinity.

Ducey, Michael H. 1977. *Sunday Morning: Aspects of Urban Ritual.* New York: Free Press.

Durkheim, Emile. 1915. *The Elementary Forms of the Religious Life.* London: Allen & Unwin.

Edwards, Gene. 1974. *The Early Church.* Goleta, Calif.: Christian Books.

Erikson, Kai T. 1966. *Wayward Puritans.* New York: John Wiley.

218

Fry, John R. 1975. *The Trivialization of the United Presbyterian Church.* New York: Harper & Row.

Hadden, Jeffrey K. 1969. *The Gathering Storm in the Churches.* Garden City, N.Y.: Doubleday.

Hadden, Jeffrey K., and Charles F. Longino, Jr. 1974. *Gideon's Gang: A Case Study of the Church in Social Action.* Philadelphia: Pilgrim Press.

Harris, W. Russell, III. 1973. *Urban Place Fellowship: An Example of a Communitarian Social Structure.* Unpublished dissertation; Michigan State University, College of Education.

Harrison, Michael I. 1974. Preparation for life in the spirit: The process of initial commitment to a religious movement. *Urban-Life and Culture* 2 (January): 387–414.

Hoge, Dean R. 1976. *Division in the Protestant House.* Philadelphia: Westminster Press.

Jackson, David, and Neta Jackson. 1974. *Living Together in a World Falling Apart.* Carol Stream, Ill.: Creation House.

Kelley, Dean M. 1977. *Why Conservative Churches Are Growing.* Revised edition. San Francisco: Harper & Row.

Martin, David. 1978. *The Dilemmas of Contemporary Religion.* New York: St. Martin's Press.

Marty, Martin E. 1976. *A Nation of Behavers.* Chicago: University of Chicago Press.

McGuire, Meredith B. 1974. An interpretive comparison of elements of the pentecostal and underground church movements in American Catholicism. *Sociological Analysis* 35 (Spring): 57–65.

Neitz, Mary Jo. 1981. *Slain in the Spirit: Creating and Maintaining a Religious Reality.* Unpublished dissertation; University of Chicago, Department of Sociology.

Niebuhr, H. Richard. (1929) 1957. *The Social Sources of Denomination-alism.* Reprint. Cleveland and New York: World Meridian.

Parsons, Talcott. 1969. On the concept of value-commitments. In *Politics and Social Structure.* 439–72. New York: Free Press.

———. 1978. *Action Theory and the Human Condition.* New York: The Free Press.

Proctor, William. 1979. *The Born-Again Christian Catalog: A Complete Sourcebook for Evangelicals.* New York: M. Evans and Co.

Quinley, Harold E. 1974. The dilemma of an activist church: Protestant religion in the sixties and seventies. *Journal for the Scientific Study of Religion* 13 (March): 5–21.

Robbins, Thomas, Dick Anthony, and James Richardson. 1978.

Theory and research on today's 'new religions.' *Sociological Analysis* 39 (Summer): 95–122.

Schroeder, W. Widick, Victor Obenhaus, Larry A. Jones, and Thomas Sweetser, S. J. 1974. *Suburban Religion: Churches and Synagogues in the American Experience*. Chicago: Center for the Scientific Study of Religion.

Synder, Howard. 1975. *The Problem of Wineskins: Church Structure in a Technological Age*. Downers Grove, Ill.: Inter-Varsity Press.

Warner, R. Stephen. 1970. The role of religious ideas and the use of models in Max Weber's comparative studies of non-capitalist societies. *Journal of Economic History* 30 (March): 74–99.

———. 1978. Toward a redefinition of action theory: Paying the cognitive element its due. *American Journal of Sociology* 83 (May): 1319–49.

———. 1979. Theoretical barriers to the understanding of evangelical Christianity. *Sociological Analysis* 40 (Spring): 1–9.

———. 1981. Parsons's last testament. *American Journal of Sociology* 87 (November): 715–21.

———. 1978. Baum cautions Catholic charismatics. *Washington Post* (March 10): A28.

Weber, Max. 1930. *The Protestant Ethic and the Spirit of Capitalism*. New York: Scribner's.

Willis, Garry. 1972. *Bare Ruined Choirs: Doubt, Prophecy, and Radical Religion*. New York: Delta.

8
The Politics of Morality in Canada

John H. Simpson and Henry G. MacLeod

F OR the first time since the rise and fall of Prohibition a number of social issues that are intertwined with personal morality have considerable salience in the national political arena of the United States. Such issues as abortion, homosexuality, prayer in the schools, and matters pertaining to the role of women in the family have been vigorously promoted as public issues of ultimate concern to the society by a variety of groups identified with the New Christian Right. While it is unclear whether the Moral Majority, Inc., and similar organizations have had an impact on voters' decisions, it is the case that religiously inspired, well-funded, organizationally sophisticated efforts continue to be made in pursuit of a politics of morality at the national level.

Given the geographical proximity of Canada to the United States, as well as the cultural and economic interpenetration of the two nations, the resurgence of fundamentalism in the American political arena raises the question of whether a movement of similar type and magnitude could occur in Canada. Will religiously based interest groups supported by the conservative/fundamentalist spectrum of Protestantism become a recognized and important factor in electoral politics and government in contemporary Canada?

Our response to this question is based on a distinction which is frequently taken for granted but seldom explicated in either popular or academic comparisons of the two nations. We refer here to the characteristics and behaviors of individuals versus the features of the larger milieu of social organization in the two societies within which action takes place. Our argument will be that despite some similarities at the individual and church levels, Canada is not ripe for a Moral Majority-type movement. We assume that imitators always stand ready to exploit fashions, trends, and movements which arise in one country and gain exposure in the other through the mass media. However, there are certain organizational and institutional differences between the two countries which, in the case of Canada, operate as barriers inhibiting the transfer of the politics of morality from the south to the north side of the forty-ninth parallel. At the same time these barriers serve to dampen the progress of indigenous movements attempting to politicize matters of personal morality.

Some Similarities

Canada and the United States house a similar range of religious traditions and denominations. This is not surprising given the overlap in sources of colonial settlement and immigration in the nineteenth and early twentieth centuries. Moreover, many of the smaller religious bodies found in Canada are the offshoots of indigenous American denominations and sects such as the Mormon Church, Jehovah's Witnesses, and the Seventh Day Adventists. Roman Catholicism, liberal or mainstream Protestantism, the varied forms of conservative or evangelical Protestantism, Judaism, the Greek Orthodox, and numerous sects, cults and new religions all have some representation in both countries. Also, church membership, as a percentage of total population, and the percentage of the population attending services weekly are roughly the same.[1]

This homogeneity of religious types and expressions in Canada and the United States has, no doubt, been greatly aided by the undefended border which has allowed not only the free flow of people (more or less) but also the uninhibited transit of religious ideas, forces, and expressions. Americans have stimulated the religiosity of Canadians and Canadians have returned the favor. For example, early nineteenth-century American preachers kindled the flames of revival in Upper Canada and filled the mourner's bench with repentent sinners (Clark

1948, 93–102). Today, the American electronic churches (in addition to our own versions), feed the souls of the anxious and troubled in the comfort of Canadian living rooms *A Mari Usque Ad Mare*. And in 1979 the Canadian audience responded by donating almost $10 million to the American electronic churches (roughly 3% of their total contributions).[2]

The Canadian connection in the United States is well established: The Reverend A. B. Simpson, the renegade Canadian Presbyterian, founded the Christian and Missionary Alliance in New York in 1887. Another example is Aimee Semple McPherson, the guiding light of the International Church of the Foursquare Gospel in Los Angeles, and, arguably, the most colorful gospel huckster of the 1920s and 1930s. Before his conversion in 1958 to the role of secular Toronto media guru, Charles Templeton was, perhaps, Billy Graham's most successful competitor in the race to save North American souls in the large and ripe market of the post-war era. The contemporary scene includes David Mainse's 100 Huntley Street and Newfoundland's Larry Howard of Future Church, both pastors of Canadian electronic churches available on cable TV stations in the United States.

The above examples by no means exhaust the range or even provide a fair indication of the volume of religious traffic crossing the border in both directions. Furthermore, many anxious seekers in Canada and the United States resonate on the same moral and religious frequency, particulary those drawn from the ranks of conservative or evangelical Protestantism. At the individual level the moral pronouncements of a Jerry Falwell undoubtedly receive a sympathetic hearing from a not insignificant number of Canadians. In this regard it is worth noting that the orientations of Canadians and Americans to a number of socio-moral issues that have been politicized in the United States by the Moral Majority and its sister organizations are remarkably similar.

Table 1 contains comparative figures for the attitudes of Canadians and Americans toward abortion, pornography laws, and homosexual relations between consenting adults. The figures were obtained from recent nationally representative sample surveys of the two countries (Davis 1980; Bibby 1982). The distribution of attitudes in the two countries toward legal abortion in a variety of circumstances is virtually the same. Canadians and Americans also share a similar perspective on pornography laws. Canadians appear to be slightly more liberal than Americans in their attitudes toward homosexuality but the difference is not significant.

Finally, recent membership trends in Protestant denominations in the United States and Canada show that mainstream Protestant denominations in both countries have been declining in membership since the mid-1960s while the conservative churches (Evangelical/Pentecostal/Fundamentalist) have continued to enjoy growth.[3] There is evidence that variation in mainstream Protestant and Roman Catholic strength over comparable civil divisions has a similar association in each country with sect and cult membership (Stark and Bainbridge, 1985). Thus, the forces of secularization which tend to corrode the holding power of the mainstream Protestant denominations and the Roman Catholic church appear to have similar consequences in the two countries at least as far as recruitment to cults and sects is concerned.[4]

Patterns of Religious Pluralism

Although the range of traditions and denominations in Canada and the United States is similar, we find that the variety and the distribution of the populations within denominational categories are not. While the United States is characterized by a very high degree of denominational differentiation, Canada is less pluralistic and is dominated by Roman Catholicism and mainstream Protestantism. Jacquet (1982) lists membership statistics for 82 distinct religious bodies in Canada compared with 218 in the United States. In Canada the Roman Catholic, United, and Anglican churches, together, account for 86% of the total religious membership and three-quarters of the entire population while in the United States it takes the 19 largest denominations to account for the same percentage of total reported membership in religious bodies (Westhues 1979). Furthermore, as Fallding (1978) has pointed out: "(i)n Canada (the Roman Catholics) make between 40 and 50 percent of the (total population), in the United States between 30 and 40 percent" (146).

More striking is the proportion of mainstream Protestants in each country. In Canada 36% of the population, based on the 1971 census, identified itself with either the United Church of Canada, the Anglican, Presbyterian, or Lutheran traditions. In the United States, on the other hand, only about 18% of the church population is Methodist, Presbyterian, Lutheran, or Episcopalian. In Canada 3% of the total population is Baptist (of which 60% is mainstream or Convention Baptists) while 20% of church members in the United States are affiliated with some Baptist denomination (Westhues 1979; Fallding 1978). Hiller

Table 1 Attitudes of Canadians and Americans
Toward Selected Social Issues*

	CANADA	UNITED STATES
Abortion		
Should it be possible for a pregnant woman to obtain a legal abortion if	% "NO"	
there is a serious defect in the baby?	12%	17%
the woman is married and doesn't want anymore children?	53%	53%
the woman's health is endangered by pregnancy?	5%	10%
the family has low income and can't afford any more children?	44%	48%
the woman is not married and doesn't want to marry the man?	49%	52%
	% "Always wrong" or "Almost Always wrong"	
Homosexual Relations Between Consenting Adults	69%	79%
Laws Restricting Pornography Distribution		
there should be no laws	8%	6%
there should be laws forbidding distribution to those under 18	57%	53%
there should be laws forbidding distribution to everyone	35%	41%

*The data for Canada are from Bibby 1982. The data for the United States are from the 1980 General Social Survey (Davis 1980).

(1978) calculates that for every Baptist church member in Canada there are 136 in the United States while the ratio of the American population, as a whole to the Canadian population is only 10 to 1.

In Canada, then, roughly 84% of the total population identify with churchly Christian traditions (Roman Catholic and mainstream Protestants excluding Baptists). Baptist, Pentecostal, and sectarian Protestants account for only 9% of the remaining population (the rest being Jewish, Greek Orthodox, or unaffiliated). At the same time, the presence of the United Church Renewal Fellowship and the charismatic renewal movement in the Roman Catholic church suggest that a small proportion of the members of the mainstream denominations are oriented towards an evangelical tradition. Bibby (1982) has found that 22% of Canadians are committed to a traditional version of Christianity. Hence, between 9 and 22% of the Canadian population can be classified as evangelical/conservative/fundamentalist Christians.

In the United States roughly 50 to 60% of church members are either mainstream Protestant (excluding Baptists) or Roman Catholic. Clearly, not all of the remaining church members are sectarian Protestants, but if they were, 40 to 50% of church members would fall into that category. Assuming the Protestant sectarianism is an indicator of the tendency to generate a politics of morality, the proportion of the population in Canada and the United States that forms a base for such a movement is not the same. A significantly higher proportion of the American population is potentially oriented in the direction of Moral Majority-type politics. Fewer people in Canada have that affinity. Thus, the demographic pattern of religious affiliation in Canada in comparison with the United States limits the appeal that a politics of morality could have here.

Religion and Politics Under the Maple Leaf and the Stars and Stripes

Even if Canada had a much larger proportion of Protestant sectarians than it does have, the likelihood of a successful Moral Majority-type political movement occurring here is small because it would be difficult, if not impossible, to forge a link between the individualistic, puritanical morality of sectarian Protestantism and the imputed welfare of the nation as has been done in the United States. There is no tradition in Canada of touting the nation as the New Israel of God whose national strength and fortunes depend upon the morality of its citizenry, with morality being defined in terms of puritanical ethics and practices.

"The scream of the great American eagle has become the twitter of a frightened sparrow. America must be born again or join the graveyard of the nations." So spoke the Reverend Adrian Rodgers, the head of the Southern Baptist Convention, to a gathering of 200,000 Evangelical Christians at the Washington for Jesus Rally in April 1980 *(The Globe and Mail* 30, April 1980, 18). Such rhetoric linking the fate of the nation with conservative/fundamentalist piety and morality would make little sense in Canada. This is so because Canada exists as a nation by virtue of an historical accommodation between Roman Catholic and Protestant English Canada which vitiates the logic of one nation standing under the aegis of a Protestant Evangelical God.

When the British gained military and political control over France's territory in North America in the middle of the eighteenth century, they allowed the French in Quebec to maintain their religion and language as a matter of practical colonial policy. This pattern of accommodation between ethno-religious groups and communities, each encouraged not to forget its language, religion, customs, and mores was set for British North America from the beginning and persists to this day. This contrasts sharply with the American model of assimilation to a mythic American way of life and American identity (Simpson 1977).

In Canada religiosity and concomitant moral practices may celebrate the peoplehood of one's ethnic group and its place in the Canadian mosaic, but they do not underwrite a singular notion of Canadian nationhood. There is no way to participate through religious practice in a symbolic unity called Canada. As a result the rustle of the Canadian Maple Leaf cannot be reduced to silence by the immorality of Canadians since Protestant sectarian morality only celebrates the boundaries of its carrier groups and does not weave its practitioners into the symbolic fabric of a unitary Canada and identification with it.

The notion of Canada as a mosaic has been underscored by the fading of the nineteenth-century Protestant vision of Canada as "His Dominion." Born in league with the effort to win the developing frontier for the Kingdom of God, the Protestant attempt to make Canada "His Dominion" ultimately failed because liberal Protestantism was unable to express an ideology of Canadianism which was acceptable to all within the pluralistic domain of Canadian society (Clifford 1973, 323). The notion of "His Dominion" has been revived recently by conservative Protestant bodies in Canada, but it is endorsed now by only a small number of Canadian Christians.[5]

The consequences for Canada of being a nation of "two solitudes" at its inception form one set of institutional constraints retarding the development of a politics of morality. Other constraints not unrelated to the small proportion of Protestant sectarians in the population arise from the historical insipidity of Fundamentalism as a cultural force in Canada. Canada's Fundamentalists have never had a William Jennings Bryan to champion their cause. Furthermore, Fundamentalism in Canada has always been confronted by a sizeable and powerful tradition of Protestant moderation in the Anglican church and the United Church of Canada and its predecessors. This seems to have had the effect of making Canadian fundamentalists less strident and adventurous than their American counterparts. Thus, when the German discipline of higher criticism began to spread through the Canadian churches at the end of the nineteenth century, it had less impact here than in the United States. About one-fifth of the Baptist churches broke away from the Baptist Convention of Ontario and Quebec and formed a fundamentalist communion, but there was nothing comparable to the American fundamentalist movement or to the Scopes ("Monkey") trial in Tennessee.

It is not surprising then that the Reverend Ken Campbell has described the constituency for his Renaissance International, which is based in southern Ontario, as Canada's *moderate* moral majority *(The Globe and Mail,* 8 August 1981, F3). Indeed, the platform of "the voice of the Moral Majority in Canada" distinguishes it from its American counterpart. It is opposed to capital punishment and has a more tolerant attitude toward homosexuals. Renaissance has sponsored visits to Canada by Jerry Falwell and Anita Bryant and has polled political candidates on their attitudes towards family, freedom, and faith and published the results in newspapers. However, there is no indication that these activities have influenced the outcome of elections or had a visible effect upon any political party.

Like the early fundamentalist movement in Canada and today's creationist groups, Renaissance's impact is at the local level. A few school boards have been pressured to remove certain books and to teach creation science, but otherwise it has had no great influence. Usually groups such as Renaissance have ties with American organizations, and sympathetic Canadians are more likely to support the southern bodies directly, further weakening the possibility for a successful political movement here.

To the differences between Canada and the United States outlined above may be added differences in the understanding of church-state relations and the church's role in politics. Although there is no established church in Canada as found in England and some European countries, there is also no strict separation as in the United States. The churches accept the form of separation but, at the same time "(b)oth Roman Catholics and Anglicans, while making no claim to be 'the national ecclesiastical institution' tend to identify with the state administration" (Peake 1967, 85). The United Church of Canada in rejection of strict separation has identified with the position that "the Church is to be the conscience of the state" (Mutchmor 1965, 142). In fact, the major denominations have been able to act as the conscience of the state in such matters as liquor control, social welfare, and sabbath observance through the exercise of influence in a way that has effectively preempted a sectarian politics of morality.

Within Canada's parliamentary system of government (federal and provincial) there is no strong tradition of interest group politics as there is in the United States. Governments in Canada are not brokerages for dealing with a multitude of extremely well-organized and publically visible pressure groups. Rather there is a tradition of interests and issues being dealt with through formal and informal channels of representation and communication: briefs to leaders, Royal Commissions, and a quasi-diplomatic network of relations between governments and recognized, well-established groups and organizations. The major denominations in Canada feel that they have the right to influence the decisions of government using these means and they have always been heard through them.

It is probably the case that not all representations and appeals made through such channels are equally likely to succeed. The size of an appellant's constituency and its position in the social order affect the probability that government action will follow a representation. So it is that the United church is more likely to be successful than the Presbyterians, and what the Anglicans lack in size as a determinant of impact they make up in social position. The proportionately small number of Protestant sectarians in the population noted above places very severe limitations on the likelihood that Renaissance International or similar organizations could attract a sufficiently large following to be taken seriously by governments. In this regard Renaissance's loss of its tax-free status as a religious-chartered organization may be related to its attempts to gain the attention of governments through newspaper advertisements and public rallies. It tried to be a political lobby.

Renaissance's unsuccessful attempts to penetrate the chambers of government may be contrasted with the well-known activities of the Reverend James Mutchmor, one of the most powerful spokesmen for the United church in the 1950s and 1960s. His briefs, press releases, and night letters were not attempts to muster public support for the church's views in order to catch the attention of a government. They were the church's advice to governments which, it was assumed, would be taken seriously without causing a stir in the public arena.

Finally, we note that there have been close ties between religion and certain political parties in Canada. The Social Credit Party was founded by William Aberhart who broke with the Baptists and established the Prophetic Bible Institute at Calgary, built a large radio following, and won the Alberta provincial election of 1935. His government retained some aspects of a conservative, religious movement, and the party was not defeated until 1971. As a socio-political movement the Social Credit has had very little success as a fourth party at the national level, but it was more successful, and secular, in British Columbia (where it is the party in office) and Quebec.

The socialist Cooperative Commonwealth Federation Party (now the New Democratic Party) was founded in 1933 by, among others, Tommy Douglas, a Baptist minister who later became Premier of Saskatchewan and national leader of the party. Unlike the small socialist parties that operate on the edge of the political arena in the United States, the NDP is an established national party (the third major party) and is also strong in certain provinces. At its inception the CCF incorporated principles of Christian socialism and the CCF/NDP has maintained a notable following among the religiously committed ever since (Allen 1971). Thus, a moderator of the United Church of Canada (the largest Protestant denomination in the country) has publically described himself as a "Christian socialist and basic evangelical liberal" *(The Globe and Mail* 2 October 1982, E18).

Although Social Credit and the NDP are at opposite ends of the political spectrum, they do share a feature expressing an important theme in the relationship between religion and politics in Canada. At some point in their development both parties linked religious principles with economic policies and based their appeal, in part, upon this union. Where religion has successfully mixed with politics in Canada it has done so in terms of underwriting economic policies of either a rightist (Social Credit) or leftist (NDP) variety. In this regard Canada stands in sharp contrast to the United States where religion and politics have tended to become intertwined in the area of social and moral issues. A religiously motivated concern for economic matters has never been successfully institutionalized in the political party system of the United States.

A More General View

Clearly, there are historical, institutional, and demographic differences between Canada and the United States. Furthermore, these differences are associated with the current flurry of political activity among American fundamentalists and the considerably more subdued and less successful efforts in the political arena of Canadian right-wing Protestants. We now want to suggest that there may be a more fundamental difference between Canada and the United States than any of those advanced so far and that this difference may be sufficient to explain variation in the politics of morality between the two countries.

In a perceptive essay on religion and politics, Bourg (1981) refers to what he calls the phenomenon of "pluralization." By this he means not only the tendency in advanced democratic societies for the number and diversity of legitimated acting units to increase over time but also the tendency for individual and collective actors to cast what were previously private concerns into the public arena as focal points in the struggle for power. Perhaps, the best recent example of pluralization in the United States was the movement for civil rights in the 1960s. The goal was not only to remove existing legal discrimination e.g., voting laws in certain states, but also to attack the bastion of customary and private discriminatory practices through law. The current effort of the Moral Majority to legalize their views on so-called social issues e.g., homosexuality, the woman's role, etc. is another example of pluralization.

While there has been an increase in the number of collective actors in Canadian society since World War II (Clark 1968) the public arena in Canada has not been filled with a host of interest groups each operating on the principle that its existence is entitled and that its claims underwrite the common good. Pluralization exists in Canada but it is not as virulent as it is in the United States. Even when a movement occurs in Canada which appears to be similar to a movement in the United States, there are, usually, crucial differences between the two. Student protests are a prime example.

From about the middle of the 1960s until the early 1970s, college and university campuses throughout North America were swept by organized student protest and collective disturbances. There is convincing evidence that students who protested in Canada and the United

States during this period were remarkably similar in certain ways. In both countries the activists, in comparison with the more quiescent students, tended to be less attached to the family of origin, subscribed to beliefs that differed considerably from parental views, had less of a stake in conformity (getting an education, finding a job, pursuing a career), and were less involved in conventional activities such as attending church (Meier and Orzen 1971; Hagan and Simpson 1977).

While student activists in Canada and the United States were similar with regard to their relationship to the primary mechanisms and agents of social control, there were differences in the issues that were the focus of protest in the two countries. The civil rights movement and the war in Vietnam were major sources of campus unrest in America. Canadian campuses were not affected in any sustained or serious way by these issues. The great issue in Canada was parity. The movement for parity was an attempt by students to have a presence in the governance of a university's affairs equal to that of administrators and faculty members. The intensity of the students' demand for parity was aptly summarized by the biblical emendation of a senior university administrator in the midst of the fray at the time: "And now abideth faith, hope, parity, these three; but the greatest of these is parity" (Bissell 1974, 156).

It has been argued (Simpson and Phillips 1976) that the disparity in the issues over which students were prepared to do battle in the United States and Canada during the 1960s and early 1970s reflects a fundamental difference in how the constituent units of collectivities (including individuals) in the two countries relate to the collectivities of which they are a part. In the United States the majority of students who protested were angry at specific decisions which they felt were adversely affecting their lives or were morally wrong. The majority of protesting American students were not attempting to change the balance or structure of power in the collective units which made the decisions they were protesting. In Canada, on the other hand, students were interested in acquiring a substantial role in the structure of governance itself. They were not protesting the perceived negative consequences of authoritative decisions for their individual lives. Rather, they were attempting to restructure the distribution of power in the universities in their favor.

Clearly, student protest and the politics of morality have nothing in common in terms of the substantive issues that are at stake in each case. However, at another level of analysis student protest in Canada and the expression of views on moral issues by Canadian churches are formally similar. And they can be distinguished from that which student protest and the politics of morality have in common in the United States. As we have pointed out, Canadian students in the 1960s and early 1970s sought a voice in the governance of universities. They wanted to become part of the system. By the same token, the major denominations in Canada have always made their views known on issues, including moral issues, assuming that they were part of the system. Both students and churches, then, act on the premise that the legitimate expression of views, purposes, and claims is done from *within*. Only units that are part of some whole—the governing body of a university in the case of students or, in the case of churches, the quasi-diplomatic web of relationships between governments and recognized organizations—have full legitimacy as acting units in the system.

In the United States, on the other hand, there is a cultural logic which underwrites expression from *without*. Both student protest and the current politics of morality there proceed on the assumption that interest groups can legitimately lay claims on a system of which they are elements but which grants them an identity on the basis of their specific interests and accords them legitimacy as acting units because they are vigorously pursuing those interests.

More generally, the difference between student protest and the politics of morality in the United States and Canada can be attributed to an analytical distinction between the two societies which sheds further light on the likelihood that a politics of morality will develop in contemporary Canada. We refer to what Swanson (1971) calls "constitutional" differences. In Swanson's usage, a constitution does not refer to a differentiated aspect of government nor, necessarily, to formalized documents or understandings. A constitution, according to Swanson, is the legitimated procedures and rules (written or unwritten) which any collectivity e.g., a friendship, family, primitive society, complex nation-state, employs and which participants use to undertake collective action in a sphere of jurisdiction or legitimated area of action to which such procedures may be applied. Swanson classifies constitutional systems in terms of variation along two dimensions which distinguish the fundamental ways in which the participants or units in a collectivity can act:

> The participants in a collectivity have a dual status. All of them try to use the collective relationship for their private—their special—interests. But, at the same time, they find that to use the collectivity they must maintain it and hence must serve as its agents: they must be sensitive to its requirements and must support its interests. In the first capacity, these participants are *constitutent bodies*. In the second, they are *agents*. Constitutional systems vary in the . . . recognition they provide for this distinction (Swanson 1971, 611–612, emphasis added).

To the extent that a collectivity emphasizes the action of agents it has a social system focus that is analyzed by considering the functions which agents perform in order to maintain and support the system (cf. Parsons 1966). To the extent that a collectivity emphasizes the action of constituent bodies it has an associational focus. Its analysis deals with interactions between constituent bodies and the outcomes of exchanges between them (cf. Homans 1961). According to Swanson all collectivities can be classified in terms of the extent to which the maintenance and service of the collectivity itself is emphasized.

Clearly, modern nation states are very complex collectivities and, in this regard, Canada and the United States are no exception. But despite their complexity and similarity, we are convinced that a simple analytical distinction can be drawn between the two societies. The United States tends in the direction of being an associational collectivity emphasizing the rights and actions of constituent bodies, while Canada tends in the direction of a social system with an emphasis upon the support and maintenance of the system itself.[6] A number of illustrations support this distinction. Its essence seems to be captured by the well-known phrases which sum up the ideals and values of the two societies. For the United States there is "life, liberty, and the pursuit of happiness." Canada subscribes to "peace, order, and good government."

The Canadian author Margaret Atwood has argued that in Canadian literature there is a persistent theme stressing the struggle for survival in an inhospitable environment (Atwood 1972). She contrasts this emphasis with its attendant need for action in the service of collectivities with the American glorification of the frontier and its natural setting as an opportunity for exploitation and achievement.

The American expatriate sociologist Edgar Z. Friedenberg, now resident in Canada, has written a volume devoted to what he considers the great theme of Canadian life—deference to authority (1980). But what is deference to authority if it is not the curbing of special interests at the individual level in favor of action that maintains and supports the collective wholes of which one is a part? This theme is obliquely refracted in the motto of *The Globe and Mail*—"Canada's National Newspaper": "The subject who is truly loyal to the Chief Magistrate will neither advise nor submit to arbitrary measures."

Finally, unlike the United States, the Canadian political system has a viable socialist alternative in the New Democratic Party at both the national level and in many of the provinces. One could argue that the emphasis in socialism, as a mode of organizing the collective life of a

society, is almost exclusively focused upon collective interests. Socialism, in principle, makes little provision for the private interests of
constituent members, and it can only become institutionalized as a
political force in societies emphasizing agency.

Conclusion

Granted that Canadian society has more of a social system "flavor"
while the United States is more associational in "favor," the most
fundamental reason why the prospect for a politics of morality in
Canada is dim is the society's emphasis upon agency. Rather than using
the system to pursue its own special interests as in a politics of morality,
organized religion in Canada has tended to be a participant as an agent
in the governance and maintenance of the society (cf. Fallding 1978). It
is the "deep structure," then, of Canadian society that imposes limits
upon the possibility that a successful Moral Majority-type interest
group politics will occur here. That the Moral Majority in tune with the
"deep structure" of American society is engaged in interest group
politics there has been argued elsewhere by Simpson (1983).

Notes

1. In 1980 church membership as a percent of the U.S. population was 60.5, compared with 63.8 in Canada (Jacquet 1982). The 1980 weekly church attendance in Canada and the United States was 35% and 40% of the population, respectively.
2. In addition to Rev. Jerry Falwell's *Old-Time Gospel Hour,* Rev. Pat Robertson's *The 700 Club,* Jim Bakker's *The PTL Club,* and Rev. Robert Schuller's *Crystal Cathedral* have a significant Canadian audience.
3. For the United States see Hoge and Roozen 1979, and Kelley 1977. For Canada see Hiller 1978, and MacLeod 1982.
4. Simpson and Hagan (1981) following Winter (1974) argue that evangelical Protestantism has an affinity with entrepreneurial capitalism and that managerial capitalism has an affinity with liberal Protestantism. To the extent that theological liberalism finds its home in the mainstream Protestant denominations, they are vulnerable to the forces of secularization according to Stark and Bainbridge (1985). Hence, it may be the case that Canada is more susceptible than the United States to secularization since it has a higher proportion of mainstream Protestants. However, this may be

236

offset by the fact that Canada's resource-based economy is, arguably, more entrepreneurial than managerial in organization and style.

5. For examples of the continued use of this image see Clifford 1973, 326, n. 38. In 1977 the bulletin *Church Growth: Canada* published by the Christian and Missionary Alliance, was renamed *His Dominion*.

6. Conflict between the federal and provincial governments in Canada which seems to be endemic may be due to the powerful position of the provinces in a situation in which authority is exercised only "when commonalities have been mobilized to defeat diverse identities" (Baum 1980; 83). According to Baum, such mobilization provides the grounds for authority in a collectivity which has a social system focus. In a collectivity with an associational focus authority is warranted when "diverse social identities have constructed a common purpose (Baum 1980, 83). The more power is decentralized in a collectivity with a social system focus, the more conflict there will be because it becomes more difficult for the center to mobilize commonalities to defeat diverse identities.

References

Allen, Richard. 1971. *The Social Passion: Religion and Social Reform in Canada 1914–28.* Toronto: University of Toronto Press.

Atwood, Margaret. 1972. *Survival: A Thematic Guide to Canadian Literature.* Toronto: Anansi.

Baum, Rainer C. 1980. Authority and identity: The case for evolutionary invariance. In *Identity and Authority: Explorations in the Theory of Society,* edited by Roland Robertson and Burkart Holzner, 61–118. Oxford: Basil Blackwell.

Bibby, Reginald. 1982a. Religionless Christianity. Xerox. Lethbridge, Alberta: The University of Lethbridge, Department of Sociology.

———. 1982b. *The Moral Mosaic: Sexuality in the Canadian 80s— PROJECT CAN80 Release No. 1.* Lethbridge, Alberta: The University of Lethbridge.

Bissell, Claude T. 1974. *Halfway Up Parnassus.* Toronto: University of Toronto Press.

Bourg, Carroll J. 1981. Politics and Religion. *Sociological Analysis* 41(4): 297–316.

Clark. S.D. 1948. *Church and Sect in Canada.* Toronto: University of Toronto Press.

238

————. 1968. *The Developing Canadian Community*. 2d. Toronto: University of Toronto Press.

Clifford, N.K. 1973. His dominion: A vision in crisis. *Studies in Religion* 2(4): 315–26.

Davis, James A. 1980. *General Social Surveys, 1972–1980: Cumulative Codebook*. Chicago: National Opinion Research Center.

Fallding, Harold. 1978. Mainline Protestantism in Canada and the United States of America: An overview. *The Canadian Journal of Sociology* 3(2): 141–60.

Friedenberg, Edgar Z. 1980. *Deference to Authority: The Case of Canada*. White Plains, N.Y.: M.E. Sharpe.

The Globe and Mail. 30 April 1980. Repentance rally draws 175,000 in Washington." 18.

————8 August 1981. F3.

————2 October 1982. Church moderator sees irony in rescue of Dome Petroleum. E18.

Hagan, John and John H. Simpson. 1977. Ties that bind: Conformity and the social control of student discontent. *Sociology and Social Research 61(4): 520–38.*

Hiller, Harry H. 1978. Continentalism and the third force in religion. *The Canadian Journal of Sociology 3(2): 183–207.*

Hoge, Dean R. and David A. Roozen, editors. 1979. *Understanding Church Growth and Decline: 1950–1978*. New York: The Pilgrim Press.

Homans, George C. 1961. *Social Behavior, Its Elementary Forms*. New York: Harcourt, Brace and World.

Jacquet, Constant H., Jr., editor. 1981. *Yearbook of American and Canadian Churches*. Nashville: Abingdon.

Kelley, Dean M. 1977. *Why Conservative Churches Are Growing*. New York: Harper & Row.

MacLeod, Henry G. 1982. A comparison of trends in Protestant church membership in Canada, 1946–1979. In *Yearbook of American and Canadian Churches 1982,* edited by Constant H. Jacquet, Jr. Nashville: Abingdon.

Meier, Harold C. and William Orzen. 1971. Student legitimation of student activism: Some survey findings. *Social Problems*. 19(2): 181–192.

Mutchmor, James Ralph. 1965. *Mutchmor*. Toronto: The Ryerson Press.

Parsons, Talcott. 1966. *Societies: Evolutionary and Comparative Perspectives*. Englewood Cliffs, N.J.: Prentice-Hall.

Peake, F.A. 1967. Movements towards Christian unity in the post-confederation period. *Journal of the Canadian Historical Society*. 9(4).

Simpson, John H. 1977. Ethnic groups and church attendance in the United States and Canada." In *Ethnicity,* edited by Andrew M. Greeley and Gregory Baum, New York: The Seabury Press.

———. 1983. Moral issues and status politics. In *The New Christian Right,* edited by Robert Liebman and Robert Wuthnow. Hawthorne, N.Y.: Aldine.

Simpson, John H. and John Hagan. 1981. Conventional religiosity, attitudes toward conflict crime, and income stratification in the United States." *Review of Religious Research* 23(2): 167–79.

Simpson, John H. and Walter Phillips. 1976. Understanding student protest in Canada: The University of Toronto student strike vote. *The Canadian Journal of Higher Education*. 6(1): 59–67.

Stark, Rodney and William Sims Bainbridge. 1985. *The Future of Religion: Secularization, Revival and Cult Formation*. Berkeley: University of California Press.

Swanson, Guy E. 1971. An organizational analysis of collectivities. *American Sociological Review* 36(4): 607–24.

Westhues, Kenneth. 1979. Religious organization in Canada and the United States. In *Yearbook of American and Canadian Churches 1979,* edited by Constant H. Jacquet, Jr. Nashville: Abingdon.

Winter, J. Alan. 1974. Elective affinities between religious beliefs and ideologies of management in two eras. *American Journal of Sociology* 79:1073–1119.

9
The Lord's Battle: Paisleyism in Northern Ireland

David Taylor

I N Northern Ireland there exists a close relationship between fundamentalist religion and conservative protestant politics. As one of its most prominent leaders, the Reverend Ian Paisley has successfully combined religion and politics into a formidable social movement with two equally important organizational pillars: The Free Presbyterian Church of Ulster and the Democratic Unionist Party (DUP). In this regard this paper addresses itself to two related themes.[1]

First it examines the nature of Paisley's appeal among Protestants as an evangelist, a politician, and an expositor of anti-Catholic sentiments. Three questions are addressed which help to explain Paisleyism's success: (1) What are the historical and ideological bases of anti-Catholicism in Northern Ireland? (2) How did sectarian conflict (The Troubles) between Catholics and Protestants in that country during the late 1960s augment the growth of Paisley's church and political party? (3) How do religion and politics converge in an important and powerful way within the sectarian milieu of Northern Ireland, with Paisleyism being a prominent example of this phenomenon?

Second, this paper explores the relationships and commonalities between the Paisley movement and those militant fundamentalists in America who share a similar involvement in the politics of the radical right.

In conclusion we will suggest some of the more important cultural, historical, and religious reasons why fundamentalists in America and Northern Ireland tend to participate in socially conservative causes and organize right wing political movements.

In 1979 Paisley, moderator of the Free Presbyterian Church of Ulster, announced that the Pope would not be allowed to visit Northern Ireland in conjunction with his September 1979 visit to the Irish Republic. Paisley claimed to speak for Protestants of Northern Ireland based on an overwhelming mandate received in his election to the European Economic Community Parliament (he received 170,000 votes to his nearest protestant opponents 60,000). While many Protestant church leaders and laymen publicly denied that Paisley spoke for them, a significant segment of the Protestant population considered that a Papal visit was not in the best interests of Protestantism. It may appear incredible that a statesman representing any modern nation would attempt to prohibit the presence of any religious leader, yet it is not so astonishing in the context of a deeply divided community like Northern Ireland. Rev. Paisley is most representative of those who contend that Protestant religious and political beliefs must be defended against Catholics and Catholicism. They are generally those who see the Roman Catholic Church as a monolithic and authoritarian structure unrelentingly hostile to Protestants and Protestantism. Paisley's support is found among those Protestants who view Catholicism in this manner. This perspective is known as "ultra" Protestant, and it believes that the constitutional connection with Great Britain must be maintained in order to preserve the distinctively Protestant features of Northern Ireland.

Over the past fifteen years the Reverend Dr. Paisley has emerged as a symbol of Protestant opposition to Catholic participation in political power. His passionate anti-Catholicism is grounded in his fundamentalist beliefs which he construes as entirely incompatible with Roman Catholicism. Paisley and his religious following conceive the central theme of modern history to be a constant struggle between Bible Protestantism and the religious tyranny of Romanism. Paisley's resolute purpose in Northern Ireland's political and religious affairs is to continue the heritage of Luther, Calvin, Knox, and other Protestant heroes: To fight for the "True Faith" against the Catholic church and efforts of its co-conspirators to usurp Reformation Protestantism.

Paisley's rise to prominence occurs within a historical context of 200 years of sectarian conflict. He matured into the Ulster tradition of Evangelical Fundamentalism and loyalty to the British Crown, and he credits his father, a Baptist minister, with teaching him the principles of true patriotism and civil and religious liberty. Paisley has often said that he will remain British only as long as the Queen remains Protestant. This position is consistent with his Calvinist faith that subordinates the exercise of political liberty to the defence of a certain conception of religion.[2] Religious liberty became an especially important issue when the campaign for Ireland's separation from British sovereignty was initiated. Ulster, the northeastern province, being predominantly Protestant, was generally opposed to inclusion in an independent Irish state. With the introduction of the Home Rule Bill in 1912, Paisley's father and 218,205 other Protestants signed Ulster's Solemn League and Covenant because they believed that Home Rule would be ". . . subversive of our civil and religious freedom, destructive of our citizenship and perilous to the unity of the British Empire."

The Government of Ireland Act (1920) provided for the establishment of two Parliaments in the country, permitting the Irish Free State to become a self-governing domain and creating a provincial government for the six north-eastern counties at Stormont, the Northern Ireland Parliament. Sir Edward Carson, Ulster's leading opponent of Home Rule, declared that the six counties would always be governed by a "Protestant Parliament for a Protestant people." For evangelical Protestants this pledge was significant because a Protestant state with a constitutional connection with Great Britain was believed essential to preserve their religious liberty. The existence of a large nationalistic Catholic minority in Ulster reinforced the link between union with Great Britain and Protestantism. Political issues over the past fifty years have been dominated by these constitutional and religious loyalties. Concurrently, the Unionist party emerged as the dominant political force in Northern Ireland. Unionism was a defensive response to the external threat of Irish Republicanism. For Protestants the continuation of two separate states was essential because Ireland continued to claim sovereignty over Northern Ireland and responsibility for its Catholic minority.

The Ulster Protestant community lacked a genuine nationalism of its own to counter Catholic nationalism in Ulster and the Irish Republic. They thus found themselves in need of some alternative ideological basis of integration, which led to an exaggerated version of traditional Protestant views of Catholicism. David Miller suggests that according to this myth, liberty is the defining characteristic of Protestantism.[3] Protestant liberty thus came to be juxtaposed against the "tyranny" of Roman Catholicism by evangelical preachers in Ulster both before and since partition from Ireland. Paisley maintains this tradition by preaching that the doctrine of salvation by faith alone is the only means of access to heaven, while Catholicism is a system of spiritual enslavement. In part he has acquired a broad base of support among ultra Protestants because his condemnation of the Catholic church appeals to their prejudice against, and distrust of, Catholicism.

The rational basis of the integrative myth is the moral superiority of Bible Protestantism over Catholicism. The core of the Protestant fundamentalist faith is the saving truth of the Bible which specifies that Christ is the only mediator between God and man. The soul is free to commune with his Maker if one is a Protestant believer, but not if one is a Catholic. A priest is considered a false intermediary between God and man, thus the Catholic is essentially unfree; his relationship with God, by whose grace he must be saved, is mediated by a human agency. Attitudes about "priestcraft" pervade the anti-Catholic folklore of Ulster Protestantism. For instance, Catholics are depicted as having to beg a mortal priest to forgive their sins with the priest characterized as being of dubious moral integrity.

As a preacher Paisley is most widely known for his condemnation of the Papacy. He cites the Westminister Confession of Faith declaration that the Pope is the ". . . anti-Christ, that Man of sin and Son of perdition." Paisley also quotes from the pulpit biblical evidence that "exposes" the Pope as a manifestation of evil. The reference to the scarlet whore of Babylon in the Book of Revelation is believed to mean the Pope residing in Rome as the anti-Christ. Other central themes are also drawn from the Book of Revelation. The "Last Things" in Revelation are interpreted to be taking place at the present time. The beast with ten heads, is believed to symbolize the ten European nations which form the Common Market (founded by the Treaty of Rome, an ominous sign in itself). Inevitably all the European nations, except Great Britain, will be ruled by the Catholic church. Paisley points out that the E.E.C. is comprised mostly of Catholic countries, a certain sign that biblical prophecy is being fulfilled. He and his followers assume that the Catholic church controls the political and social institutions in all these nations and seeks to achieve control of the world. Catholic dominance of the E.E.C. is the final phase before Armageddon. Great Britain will be the nation which inherits the promises God originally gave to Israel because it had remained a Protestant nation.

The millennial aspects of Paisley's version of fundamentalist eschatology take on political implications: Ulster is accorded a special place in God's intentions because it is the only part of Great Britain that has remained true to the principles of the Reformation. Paisley often informs his congregation that "God has chosen Ulster." This "nation of ours" is the last country where Protestant liberty is revered and defended. (England and other countries are dominated by "apostasy.") Ulster's role in God's revelation provided all the more reason why reformed Protestantism must continue its vigilance against internal enemies, especially Roman Catholicism.

Paisley's "exposure" of Roman Catholicism receives widespread approval in those Protestant working-class communities most involved in the protracted conflict with Catholics, even though only a small proportion are religious, in the formal sense. They believe the Catholic community is tightly organized and dominated by the political and religious influence of the Catholic church. Both priest and parishioners are considered highly partisan to nationalistic movements, including the Irish Republican Army. The certainty among many Protestants that Catholics hold an opposing nationalistic aspiration to theirs, provides them with a powerful incentive to share political power with the Catholic community. Frank Wright notes that this "extreme perspective holds that concession to any such demands, merely gives strength to their determination to seek for more power."[4]

To summarize briefly, fundamentalist beliefs about the Catholic church's control of its communities generates a comprehensive ideological perspective. Catholicism is viewed as inherently political and irreconcilably hostile to the political and religious liberties of Protestants. Given the existence of this condition, Protestantism *must* also be political, but for defensive reasons. This integrative myth, based on the preservation of religious liberty in Ulster, was sustained by Presbyterian street preachers, most notably Hugh Hanna and Thomas Drew. They sought to maintain the connection between religion and politics, sometimes stimulating sectarian violence.

The Growth of Free Presbyterianism

Paisley has patterned his preaching career after these early Protestant ministers. His "contending for the Faith" has included leading souls to Christ through aggressive evangelism, exposure of the evils of Popery, and militant opposition to modernistic trends in Protestant churches, generally labelled as religious apostasy. In 1951 after establishing a reputation in the Belfast area as a "soul winning" preacher, he was invited to lead a gospel campaign sponsored by the local Presbyterian congregation at Crossgar, a small town near Belfast. A schism developed within the church, and Paisley was invited to minister to the more conservative faction. They called themselves "Free" Presbyterians to distinguish themselves from their former brethren. During the 1950s, doctrinal modernism was becoming predominant among Ulster's Protestant churches. Many Christian believers were opposed to liberal trends, including the de-emphasis of the Bible as the literal word of God, and denial that salvation by grace through faith in Christ was the only means of reaching heaven. Regarding these issues Paisley cultivated notoriety as an uncompromising reformed Protestant preacher. His church gradually grew, mostly attracting believers who desired to separate themselves from the modernist apostasy of most Protestant denominations. Paisley established ten other churches in Ulster during the 1950s. In 1951 Paisley amalgamated his Belfast following into the Free Presbyterian Church. Once the Crossgar congregation was firmly established, he resumed his leadership of the Belfast congregation. Paisley turned his attention towards expanding the church and founded a new congregation within the Belfast area, and eventually county Antrim - in and around his hometown of Ballymena. He managed to set up ten new churches between the years 1951 and 1959: three churches in 1951, one in 1952, one in 1954, two between 1956 and 1957, and three during the following two years.

After returning from Crossgar to his Belfast congregation, Paisley was dissatisfied with the church's lack of progress and evangelical zeal. The membership hovered around thirty until Paisley called for a marathon prayer meeting to revive the congregation from its doldrums. He recalls that it was "as dead as Julius Caesar." But the repercussions from the prayer meeting brought "revival blessing" to the church. It has not since experienced a period of torpor or lack of enthusiasm. The meeting lasted three days. Joining Paisley were two followers, Messrs. Scott and Welsh, who prayed nonstop, day and night, while eating nothing but toast and tea. Welsh recalls that their prayers were initially mocked by some members of the congregation and those who passed by peered through the windows at the three men on their knees, beckoning God for a response. Yet, Paisley managed to inspire his immediate following and to attract others after this famous prayer meeting. The following Sunday he proclaimed from the pulpit that he and the other two men had been filled with the Holy Ghost. Also,

Paisley boasted that God had told him that another "Great Revival," on the order of Ulster's great 1859 Revival, was imminent. It would begin in the Free Presbyterian church.

The expansion of the Free Presbyterian Church is neither due to people freely gravitating to Ian Paisley's political views nor merely to his reputation as a great gospel preacher and dynamic leader. Since the early years of his church, Paisley has prodded and prompted Free Presbyterians to emulate his efforts to increase their numbers through well organized and diligent evangelism. At present, the forty Free Presbyterian churches established in various parts of Ulster are nearly all the result of highly coordinated "old-fashioned" gospel campaigns which serve as foundations for new churches. Locations for the gospel "crusades," which last about three weeks, are not chosen at random. Usually people express an interest to a Free Presbyterian minister or lay member from a nearby town that they would like a crusade in their area. Those who request the crusade are people likely to support a new church through regular attendance and contributions to the building of a church. Although Paisley's church grew at a steady rate from 1951, it did not begin its most rapid growth until 1966, after Paisley and his followers became involved in politics and sectarian protests.

The Emergence of Protestant Unionism

Paisley's religious protests had political consequences when he began anti-ecumenical demonstrations during the early 1960s. For Paisley and other Reformed Protestants, ecumenism was a betrayal of the Reformation because its ultimate aim is reunification of all Christian churches. This issue clearly demonstrated Protestant fears of the Catholic church. Wright adds that Paisley means that ". . . even if ecumenism does not achieve Protestant union with Rome, it has compromised the Protestant churches in that they no longer preach the gospel and they have forgotten the principle doctrine."[5] Ecumenism then, along with the Catholic church, becomes an enemy. With the gospel being preached in fewer and fewer churches, Protestant liberty is further jeopardized.

To convince Ulster Protestants that Protestantism was endangered, Paisley organized a large number of "Reformation rallies" during the mid-1960s. The rallies were contrived mass media events, designed to draw attention to his stand against ecumenism. Paisley insisted that Ulster's church leaders were selling their Protestant heritage "lock, stock, and barrel . . . This is not the time for a velvet tongue. It is a day of war and war to the death. The enemy we fear is the enemy within. . . . These are the men we have in Ulster. If they want to go to Rome, then let them go, but they are not taking Ulster with them."[6]

Ecumenism was a central issue of Paisley's political assault on Prime Minister Terence O'Neill and his Unionist government between 1963 and 1969. During this period Paisley toured the country denouncing both "O'Neillism" and ecumenism. He endeavored to convince Ulster Protestants that ecumenism represented the theological side and ideological side of O'Neill's controversial reform program. Simultaneously Paisley continued to attack leaders of the moderate churches, asserting that they were arm-in-arm with O'Neill and his administration; both were proponents of ecumenism and were thus "selling out" to Rome. In the minds of many Ulster Protestants, ecumenism signalled the encroachment of Catholic political power, especially after Paisley attacked O'Neill's cooperation with Catholic politicians on both sides of the border. Paisley contended that a conspiracy existed between O'Neill's Unionists and the Irish Republic to eventually unite Ulster with Ireland. As events transpired Paisley established a reputation as a prophetic voice, offering predictions about O'Neillism that seemed to be coming true.

O'Neill was challenged by Paisley on a third issue: his plans to offer social, economic and political concessions to the Catholic community. On all these issues, the Reverend Dr. Paisley represented himself as a defender of Protestant rights and heritage against an administration which appeared to be undermining the vested interests of Northern Ireland's Protestant majority. His stand against O'Neill was instrumental in the Prime Minister's eventual resignation. As a beneficiary of his demise, Paisley was elected to both the Northern Ireland Parliament and the United Kingdom Parliament at Westminister in 1970.

John Harbinson offers this comment on O'Neill's reaction to the Paisley movement: "To many in the Unionist Party (an almost all Protestant party, and at the time the only Protestant party) this was too much. They did not see the parallel. What they saw was an attack on the traditional Unionism of Carson and Craig, who had themselves shown contempt for established authority on occasions, organized monster procession rallies and appealed to patriotism."[7] O'Neill's condemnation of Paisley alienated many Unionists, particularly among those ultra-Protestants inclined to agree with Paisley's religious beliefs, or his intransigent loyalism. Paisley's support increased after he was sentenced to three months imprisonment for his part in the General Assembly protest.

In order to quell further such outbreaks, the government banned meetings of three or more people in 1966. McBride reports in her study of the geographical diffusion of the Free Presbyterian Church, that the ban stimulated growth of the church outside Belfast.[8] Due to the ban Free church ministers concentrated on holding frequent rallies outside Belfast to evangelize and express their opinion on the situation initiating an increasingly intense phase of the battle to save the reformed faith from an array of enemies: Republicanism, Catholicism, Ecumenism, and O'Neill's Unionism.

The Sunday before his imprisonment, Paisley warned that it might be their last religious service. He announced that the government had declared war against Protestants: "We will take up the battle. We are going to fight to maintain our glorious heritage." He made it clear that he was prepared for martyrdom like other Christian martyrs: "If the battle against apostasy and betrayal means this life has to go, it will go in that cause. There are others with me willing to sacrifice. There will be 1,000 and 10,000 who will rise up against this evil."[9] Paisley was able (and still is able) to simplify complex issues and problems, then present them to his following as adversities threatening their Protestant way of life; but *he* was willing to stand, and possibly die, for the cause.

In the same year, Paisley organized the Protestant Unionist Party (renamed the Democratic Unionist Party in 1972). First and foremost, the party existed to safeguard the Protestant faith, and second to preserve Ulster's union with the Crown. Protestant Unionism was the first pro-union alternative to the Unionist party's domination of Ulster politics since 1921. The party immediately attracted people from outside Free Presbyterianism, including members of loyalist societies and former Unionist party members.

The formation of a political party was an important transition point in Paisley's career as a Protestant leader. Before then he had relied entirely on the strength of his personality to secure grass-roots support during the anti-ecumenical and anti-O'Neill movements. In the countryside, he had mobilized farmers and tenant workers, while his Belfast constituency was found among the middle-class members of the Free Presbyterian Church; but now distinct and burgeoning support emerged in working-class communities. The development of an official political following, endowed Paisley with a more respectable type of leadership and opened channels of support from a more diverse area of the population.

Even though Paisley generated wide support for his stand against ecumenism and the Unionist administration, his church experienced rapid growth only after he launched his opposition to the Civil Rights movement, which many Protestants regarded as a form of Catholic nationalism. The Unionist administration, so it seemed, had suddenly switched to favor Catholics, in the face of pressure from the Civil Rights movement. These Protestants saw the government committing itself to extending to Catholics allegedly equalizing privileges, which they felt, they had yet to experience themselves.[10] Paisley provided a natural and instinctive direction in which to turn for leadership. With his exceptionally powerful personality, he became the center around which most opposition to Civil Rights, Republicanism and Official Unionism formed. By projecting a clear image as the "defender of the common man," a non-compromising Protestant, Paisley effectively transformed a religious protest movement into a political movement, with broad support from fundamentalist and non-fundamentalist Protestants.

The politicalization of Paisley's religious movement was also the key factor initiating the further growth of Free Presbyterian fundamentalism. In a study of the geographical diffusion of the Free Presbyterian church, McBride reports that between 1951 and 1961 the church increased from only ninety-two to 991 members. But by 1971 there were over 7,000 members. Most of this growth was in the latter half of the 1960s when Protestant opposition to the Civil Rights movement and fear of a United Ireland was strongest. The establishment of Free Presbyterian churches appears most frequently during years when conflict between the two communities was most intense. In 1965 there were only twelve Free Presbyterian churches, an average of fewer than one founded each year. But in 1966 and 1967 eight new churches were founded. According to McBride, the political events from 1966 onwards ". . . acted as a catalyst, causing many to become Free Presbyterians."[11] Paisley's brief imprisonment for his role in "The Troubles," was one of many events which alienated Protestants from the Unionist regime and stimulated popular interest in the Free Presbyterian Church. A government ban in 1966 on open air rallies in Belfast stimulated growth of the church in rural Ulster. Free Presbyterians held frequent countryside meetings to evangelize and express their views on the enemies of the Reformed Faith.

The church continued to grow as an opposition to the Civil Rights movement and the Unionist government increased. Between 1968 and 1969 six new churches were established, bringing the total number to 26. The church had more than doubled in four years (1966–1969) the number of congregations founded in the previous fourteen years. But the rate of growth of Free Presbyterian churches decreased as the intensity of social and cultural crisis diminished. Five more churches were founded in 1970 and 1971 while the conflict was still acute, four in 1972 and 1973, three in 1974 and 1975, and two more in 1976 and 1977 and only five new churches have been founded since then; between one and two additional churches each year.[12]

Doing the Lord's Battle: Religio-Political Convergence

As we have noted earlier, Ulster politics has always had a strong religious orientation, with particular emphasis on loyalty to the Queen, as the Protestant head of the British Church and State. This religious orientation in Loyalist politics has meant that ministers have always played an active role in politics. Since the Irish Home Rule movement began in 1886, many Protestant preachers have actively opposed the inclusion of Ulster in an autonomous Irish State. Fear of domination by the political and religious influence of the Catholic church has formed the basis of conservative Protestant politics, from the Reverend Henry Cooke's ascension to leadership of the Irish Presbyterian Church in the 1830s to Paisley's present version of fundamentalist Protestantism. Their political outlook has always been defined by the link with Great Britain on the one hand, and the necessity for a Protestant political hegemony on the other.

This form of Protestant loyalism, since Cooke's period, has been shaped and extended by the evangelical zeal of the preachers who held these views. Especially during periods of conflict between the two communities, evangelical meetings have taken on the dual function of soul-saving and raising sectarian animosities. Open-air rallies, asserting the principles of Protestant ascendency and religious liberty, have often stimulated violence between Catholics and Protestants.[13] Paisley's preaching career is only the most recent in a long line of those who have used such rallies to motivate Protestants towards sectarian demonstrations. Paisley's modern version of "contending for the Faith" also includes extension of his ministry into the political affairs of Ulster. Power is sought in the name of God and through his guidance. Paisley rationalizes his political involvement by reminding his followers that prophets like Moses and Daniel were not only men of God, but also, politicians. Free Presbyterians accept, without reservation, their preacher's political motives. Many church members are active members of Paisley's Democratic Unionist Party, while virtually all Free Presbyterians support the party's goals and principles: To safeguard the Protestant faith and preserve Ulster's union with the Crown. The former receives primacy. A late elder in the church and leader of one of the DUP's largest branches explained to me: "I have been with Dr. Paisley for over thirty years. The church has always come first and I belong to the party for the sake of the Faith." Free Presbyterianism remains the dominant force behind the party and an indispensable part of Paisley's political organization.

Free Presbyterians served as Paisley's organizing cadre for his political and religious protests during the late 1960s and early 1970s. When the Paisleyite movement evolved into a political party during the late 1960s, church leaders and ministers continued as the key workers for the election campaigns, party-sponsored protest demonstrations, fund raising, and spokesmen for the party. At present, leaders of nearly all party branches are either Free Presbyterians or members of another evangelical Protestant church. Paisley views the "true" Protestant's political involvement as a Christian responsibility. In an address to the World Congress of Fundamentalists in 1976, he said:

> Fundamentalists dare not shirk their responsibility in the nation. I pray that more and more fundamentalists will enter the political arena, raise the standard of Christ's righteousness, and use their influence and position to see that the law of God becomes the law of the nation. Instead of God's law being derided and scorned and rejected, let us have in our city councils, on our education boards, and in all places of government, God's men fighting God's battle.[14]

Paisley and other Free Presbyterian ministers announce DUP activities, including fund-raising dinners, and solicit help in local and Parliamentary election campaigns from their pulpits. The party depends heavily on the church as a clearing-house for political information. In turn, church members view the pulpit as a source of explanation for current events and issues, especially with regard to any sectarian crisis.

Paisley's sermons often dwell on political issues. It is my impression that his Sunday evening services draw large numbers of non-Free Presbyterians to hear him expound political themes. Church attendance always increases during periods of political crisis and conflict. As a preacher, Paisley has a strategic advantage over other Northern Ireland politicians. The church is a weekly forum where he politically educates a loyal following and attempts to persuade newcomers and curiosity-seekers of the viability of his views. For his following the sermons also serve as a sort of consciousness-raising session. Paisley's pronouncements often narrow down alternative ways of looking at issues, and help his audience crystallize their opinions.

Paisley's success both as a minister and politician is best understood in terms of his ability to influence the action and thinking of Protestants towards a spirit of militant action. His sermons and speeches over the past fifteen years nearly always portray Protestants as engaged in battle against enemies of God and Ulster. The term "battle" is not merely metaphorical, but an actual fact of confrontation politics. The battle is depicted as taking place on two fronts, religious and political. The parameters of the battle have now widened beyond anti-Catholicism and anti-Republicanism. Ultimately, every group and institution outside the realm of traditional Protestantism becomes a negative factor. Modernist ecumenical churches become enemies because they are moving towards accommodation with the Catholic church; the population of Southern Ireland is feared because they are anti-Protestant and favor a United Ireland; and the British Government is distrusted for consistently turning its back on Ulster, and for favoring any political solution except a return of a devolved government with Protestant majority rule.

Paisley instills in his Protestant following a strong sense of identity. They take pride in their battle to preserve Protestantism's "glorious heritage and culture." At a DUP Annual Christmas Dinner in 1979, he told his audience: "For God and Ulster is our motto and always will be our motto. Your forefathers consecrated Ulster as holy ground. Let's pass it on to the next generation as holy ground." Paisley later announced his candidacy for the EEC Parliament: "We are in a battle and we are going to get into it and enjoy it. I like a good fight and it is one we can win, so dedicate yourself to the cause." The power of Paisley's oratory is augmented by his ability to interweave controversial and serious statements with anecdotes and humour. "I'm going to get all I can for Ulster (at the EEC Parliament) . . . every grant we can possibly get our hands on. Then, when we have milked the cow dry, we are going to shoot the cow!"

Paisley has the facility of knowing thoroughly the needs and predispositions of his audiences. This enhances his ability to articulate their fears and feelings coherently, in such a way that they come to believe that Paisley has been chosen by God to stand for Ulster. To each of his audiences (e.g., party meetings, political rallies, or the church) he applies an appropriate rhetoric that allows them to experience certainty and exclusiveness, in a dichotomized world, apart from all others who do not share their particular version of Protestantism. To Free Presby-

terians he says, "Thank God you are a free people, a separated people
[from apostasy] and a saved people. Thank God we are all going to
heaven."

The promise of vindication and "revival blessing" is an instrumental
part of Paisley's ability to reconcile his following in advance to possible
adversity and failure. He transforms the history of Christian persecution into a myth of triumph and deliverance for Protestants. Although
they have been accused of bigotry and extremism, "God shall vindicate
his own people." Christian metaphors of power are evoked to reassure
his followers that the "tide will turn and their numbers will increase."
"Power in the blood of the Lamb" can draw masses of lost souls to
Christ as in the days of Ulster's Great Revival in 1859. The "power of
prayer" can stimulate God's intervention, if collectively they are sincere
and fervent. Paisley's articulation of this vindication theme encourages
Protestants to remain faithful in the face of persecution and the devil's
temptations.

Paisley provides a similar version of the same theme to explain success
expressed in terms of the "forward movement" of "True Protestantism."
Paisley attributed his election to the EEC Parliament to the power of
God in overcoming the deceit of his opponents. At a subsequent church
service he said:

> Everything was done to confuse and confound and break up the power
> of a dedicated people who were determined to register their convictions
> . . . but we saw triumph of the spiritual over the temporal. The
> bamboozling of the establishment was in vain. This was no victory
> because the DUP had a better candidate than the other parties, not a
> victory because there was cunning and craft in our electioneering that
> outpointed the others. This was the Lord's doing . . . You can explain it
> by the understanding of God's over-ruling power . . . I want to tell you
> friends, you can't explain it by human terms, but I can explain it, for the
> Lord opened people's eyes!

Hence, God's power can bring spiritual blessings in answer to their
prayers, and simultaneous temporal blessing through intervention in
the democratic process.

Paisley also resorts to the vindication theme to account for his own
political setbacks. After his opposition to the Pope's visit to Ulster
received wide public disapproval, Paisley categorized himself as a
persecuted prophet. By drawing parallels between his experience and
the persecution of Joseph and the condemnation of Jesus, he provided

his own justifications. He often declares that condemnation is an inevitable outcome of his public stand for God.

> Show me a man of whom is said every evil and wicked slander. Show me a man who becomes the recipient of wave after wave of condemnation: who is condemned out of hand, who is accused of the most outrageous of crimes and I will show you a man whom God has commissioned, whom God has called, whom God has sent to be a prophet to his generation.[15]

This theme permits Paisley to reinterpret any situation to prove he and his followers are right. Every success, from election victories to the conversion of sinners, is proof of God's blessing. On the other hand, persecution and adversity are explained as the devil's domination of an evil world. True Protestants doing God's work are perennially subject to opposition, even martyrdom. Consequently, the effective use of such language drawing upon scriptural authority, enables Paisley to establish symbolic boundaries around himself and his followers.

Popular Attraction of Bible Protestantism

Paisley's religio-political appeal includes an ideological perspective which views Catholicism as a monolithic power. Because the Catholic church is a force bent on political control of Europe, including the whole of Ireland, Protestantism must rally to the defense of religious liberties against the tyranny of Rome. This type of appeal makes it fairly clear why many conservative Protestants, both working class and lower middle class are drawn to Paisley's leadership. But why should any leader of a relatively small fundamentalist sect, even Paisley, attract the political support of significantly large numbers who have no formal religious convictions? Working class Protestants are the largest segment within the Protestant community and also happen to be the least religious in terms of weekly religious attendance. And the sheer fact of this group's size and voting strength entails the necessity of their consent for any possible change in Northern Ireland's political structure. For this reason, Paisley's political strength is dependent on their sustained support.

Though only nominally religious, they have perhaps been as much exposed to evangelical Protestantism as any other single group in Europe. In Belfast's Sandy Row and Shankill Road areas, gospel halls, missions, and churches have been predominant since the early nineteenth century. For instance, in the shipyards of Belfast where these Protestants have traditionally worked, evangelists have for decades witnessed, preached, and distributed tracts to them. Paisley himself evangelized this "labor aristocracy" in the late 1940s while trying to cultivate a congregation, and simultaneously spoke at Unionist campaign rallies. Also, since the last century, contact with sectarian preaching contrasting Protestant "light" with Catholic "darkness," has been part of the universal experience of growing up in working-class Belfast. The Reverend Martin Smyth, Grand Master of the Orange Lodge in Northern Ireland, suggests why working class Protestants from the Shankill Road and similar neighborhoods have immense respect for this type of Bible Protestantism when he says: "They are Bible lovers even if not Bible readers." Consistent with this reverence for the Bible, working class parents currently send their children to a Free Presbyterian Sunday School or to the children's mission hall in Ackram Street in Sandy Row (or to similar evangelical gatherings) even if they never attend church. My observations support Wright's observation: ". . . the feeling was that children should be taught about God. It should not be *denied* to them to learn about religion."[16] Working class Protestants are receptive to evangelicals witnessing to their children and are not adverse to their children becoming saved as a consequence, even if they are unbelievers and religiously inactive themselves. Also, Paisley's political popularity among these people is certainly bolstered when his buses diligently ferry their children to Sunday Schools and Friday night meetings. Even marginal believers and non-believers feel that: "Belief was a good thing and something to be valued."[17] And these same people speak approvingly of Dr. Paisley in terms we have cited earlier: "He is a man of God."

Wright further suggests that there are many unsaved Protestants who experience anxiety about their unbelief: "They recognize that in some sense, the things they value depend upon some people believing: that is probably why they are so concerned about their children's attendance at Sunday Schools. It might be argued that this was a calculative concern for religion based upon political motive: but to say this seems to me to run rather easily over the often very real reverence for the "open Bible."[18]

We have outlined the various ideological and theological reasons why Paisley's sect maintains organizational separation from other religious groups, which do not share its fundamentalist beliefs. Furthermore, to sustain the doctrinal purity of the church, Free Presbytrians often find it necessary to extend this form of boundary maintenance into hostile behavior (e.g., protests), directed towards the Catholic church and ecumenically inclined Protestant churches. Paisley's "militant separatism" is also characteristic of his political party's posture in relation to other Unionist parties, which share the same broad goals, yet are constantly subject to harassment from him and his followers for their alleged political apostasies. This sectarian, intransigant Loyalist politics has earned Paisley's movement the label of "right wing." Paisleyism's militant style and ideology are quite similar to other right wing oriented social movements, especially in America. The focus of this section is to examine some of the historical, ideological, and moral relationships between fundamentalism and radical right politics, particularly taking Paisleyism as a prominent example.

Historically, fundamentalism and earlier forms of conservative Protestantism have been linked in various ways to radical right politics. There have been occasions when Protestants have been inspired by the principle that the Bible was entirely true and divinely inspired, and hence, engaged in a socially concerned Christianity, rather than gravitate to the political right.[19] They found in the Bible a radical social message which motivated them to attempt social reform. For instance, eighteenth century-English evangelicals were actively involved in the abolition of slavery. Other believers have interpreted the Bible in support of a view that the state exists to devote itself to the maintenance of Christian principles; and thus, the state does not deserve their loyalty or approval if it does not live up to those principles. As a consequence, groups like the Brethren and Reformed Presbyterians which hold this view are generally apolitical and try to remain as independent of the state as possible.[20] Many within such sects do not accept social benefits nor vote in elections, but they do continue to pay their taxes and rates. Yet despite the fact that some conservative evangelicals and even fundamentalists are either activists for social reform or politically apathetic, the overwhelming preponderance of attitude among them is in the direction of the political right and the extreme right.

Aspects of Paisley's version of separatist fundamentalism are patterned after those who espouse a similar militant stance in America. As we know from our analysis of the growth and development of Free Presbyterianism, Paisley is much indebted to the Reverend Bob Jones and other fundamentalist leaders who are steeped in the tradition of American radical right politics. One organizational feature which Paisley shares with Jones and other fundamentalists is separatism, a theme which is emphasized as we briefly trace the origin and development of American fundamentalism, and then compare this to the historically schismatic tendencies in Ulster Presbyterianism. We will discover that in both America and Ulster, the process of schism of more conservative minded Protestants into sects and separatist groups often allowed these groups to undertake a radical activism that they might not otherwise have managed had they remained within their original churches. Paisley and his Free Presbyterians would not have had such a dynamic impact on politics in Northern Ireland if they had remained within the denominational confines of Irish Presbyterianism and other Protestant denominations.

After discussing how schisms have historically led to the emergence of fundamentalist oriented movements, we examine the Paisley movement's rationale for militant opposition towards its adversaries. It is particularly important to identify how features of their beliefs about salvation, the millennium, good and evil, shape their political perspectives and provide them with a moral mandate for zealous political involvement. Paisley's fundamentalist politics are then compared and contrasted with the revival of neo-fundamentalist politics in America— the Christian New Right. We provide some examples of how each attempts to impose its values and ideals on society. Both of these movements have historical precursors: The Christian New Right is a form of what Linton has called nativistic movements: "Any conscious and organized attempt on the part of society's members to revive and perpetuate selected aspects of its culture."[21] Thus, Paisley's movement attempts to preserve aspects of the culture which have long been held dear by Protestants in Ulster. Before tracing the historical background of right wing fundamentalism in America and Northern Ireland, we begin with a brief discussion of Paisleyism in the context of right wing "preservationist" movements.

Nativism

Right wing movements both contemporary and historical, share common features in their origin, development, ideology and structure. Generally movements associated with the radical right are so labelled because of their anti-pluralistic character, or because in Kornhauser's terms, they are "monistic."[22] Monistic movements have a static system of values that are often in contrast and conflict with the more pluralistic, flexible, and fluctuating values of the larger society. Monistic movements are intolerant of difference and dissent expressed by other groups, especially if these groups are attempting to bring about some form of social change. In Ireland the most immediate example is the

Ultra-Loyalist response to the Civil Rights movement in the late 1960s. A counter-movement led by the Reverend Ian Paisley and other loyalist groups objected, in a militant fashion, to the Civil Rights movement's expression of dissent and demand for reform.

Paisley's movement was similar in various respects to right wing groups in America which have often engaged in undemocratic or even illegal action to maintain features of the existing culture and social hierarchy. For example, the Ku Klux Klan was part of a broader collection of movements that opposed the efforts of the Civil Rights movement in the 1960s to achieve social integration. The Klan employed vigilante action and various forms of violence to prevent integration of schools and neighborhoods. During the same decade Paisley's Ulster Protestant Volunteers declared that they would resist, by force if necessary, any change in the constitutional arrangements between Great Britain and Northern Ireland. Paisleyism and the Orange Order, its historical precursor, shared a common *raison d'etre*. They were both exclusively Protestant movements, opposed to Irish Nationalism, and seeking to protect Protestant liberties and heritage against any perceived threat which might imperil the Protestant Ulster connection with Great Britain. These various forms of resistance echo a long history of preservationism in both America and Ireland. These movements have been typified as "preservationist" because for 150 years they sought to preserve their economic, political, and cultural status during periods of social change which threatened to displace them from positions of dominance. Nearly all these groups are underpinned by a moralistic ethos drawn from an Anglo-Saxon Protestant culture. There were very similar patterns in the development of preservationist movements in Ireland and America. As we have seen in America, the continual nineteenth-century immigration of ethnic groups which introduced "un-Protestant" and "un-American" values and styles of behavior were often blamed by nativistic groups as the main source of threat to their values and position. In Ireland the Orange Order was founded to maintain the Protestant ascendancy against the collective action of agrarian Catholic secret societies (banded together for their own mutual protection against landlords and debt collectors). The Orange Order has been the most consistent and formidable movement seeking to preserve the traditional features of Protestant culture, as well as the economic and political dominance of Protestant groups and parties within the province of Ulster, and more recently, the state of Northern Ireland.

One characteristic feature of these right wing movements in both

America and Ireland is anti-Catholicism. These preservationist groups
were also called nativistic movements in America because they were
composed of native born, white Protestants in opposition to ethnic
groups. The Ku Klux Klan, the most infamous nativistic movement,
was not originally an anti-black movement, but had its roots in a series
of anti-Catholic political movements that emerged during the nineteenth century. Each of these movements was preservationist in
character, attempting to arrest the declining cultural dominance and
public influence of the American Protestant establishment.[23] They had
colorful names which reveal their patriotic orientation: the anti-Masons
of the 1830s, the Star Spangled Banner Party in the 1840s, which
evolved into the Know Nothing Party in the 1850s and 1860s, and the
American Protective Association of the 1880s. These nativistic preservationist movements were precursors of the modern right wing movements in America. Their rivals are no longer Catholics because the
issues and historical circumstances have changed. Their antagonism has
shifted towards Communists, Jews, and Blacks. Besides the modern
Klan, these movements have included George Wallace's populist American Party, the John Birch Society, and militant fundamentalism. All
these movements had, or have, a narrow moralism based on nativistic
Protestant values and anti-pluralistic intolerance towards more innovative or liberal groups. We will return to this "new" nativism when we
examine the Christian New Right.

The moralism and monistic intolerance traditionally finds its source
in a common ethos: An ethos which primarily asserts that those
Anglo-Saxon and white people who identify with these movements are
ethnically and racially superior to other groups. That forms of fundamentalism have frequently converged with or have been in unofficial
alliance with preservationist movements, in the late nineteenth and
twentieth centuries, is hardly coincidental. Fundamentalism often
served as an ideological basis for right wing preservationist movements
in America, Northern Ireland, and elsewhere.

Fundamentalism and Radical Right Politics

Fundamentalism is a term used in many different ways. Here we are
referring to a twentieth-century movement that aggressively opposed
modernist theology and the cultural change associated with it. It is a
phenomenon that is now unique to Northern Ireland and America in
the sense that elsewhere, this type of Protestant response to social

change did not occur, but its conspicuous role in the churches and national culture is not as extensive elsewhere.[24]

One of the troublesome aspects of identifying and describing fundamentalism is how to differentiate it from evangelism. Both movements evolved from the revivalist tradition within mainstream evangelical Protestantism. But since their progressive division at the turn of this century, they have engaged in acts of self definition in order to draw boundaries between themselves. Absolute distinctions are difficult because they share a commitment to the same beliefs: The deity and virgin birth of Jesus Christ, his vicarious atonement for sin, his bodily resurrection, his second coming, and the divine inspiration and authority of the Bible. Yet, fundamentalists feel it necessary to separate completely from every manifestation of liberalism and modernism (as they define them) while evangelicals have made a concerted effort to restrain this separatist impulse and have displayed a concern for social problems which fundamentalists lack.

In the last quarter of the nineteenth century, evangelical Protestantism dominated the mainstream of American religion, controlling most of the major denominations and theological seminaries. Also, evangelicalism was closely tied to revivalism, the leading motif of religious life throughout America prior to the Civil War.[25] Revivalism exerted considerable cultural influence, especially over American education at every level. On this basis, many evangelical leaders declared that America was, in nearly all respects, a Christian nation.

By the turn of the century however, the evangelical tradition was rapidly approaching a crisis. Part of the crisis was internal: The findings of biblical criticism and Darwin's evolutionary theories gained acceptance, at first in universities and subsequently within Protestant denominations. Evangelicals were faced with a choice between "modernistic" liberal theology that explained life in terms of natural development, or the old religious ways that stressed supernatural explanations based on biblical authority. The other part of the crisis was external. Evangelicals found themselves in an increasingly secular culture where their mores, values, and intellectual assumptions were no longer dominant. A progressive loss of evangelical strength in the nation resulted from broad demographic and ecological changes occurring between 1829 and 1920. The changes were due primarily to the expansion of large scale industry, rapid urban growth, and the immigration of millions of Jewish and Catholic immigrants. Finally, the problems of industrialism and urban poverty gave rise to a widespread movement for the social gospel, another modernist tendency. Faced with the inevitable choice between fundamentalist Christianity and theological liberalism, evangelicalism fragmented in three distinct directions. Liberally inclined evangelicals tried to merge their orthodoxy with biblical criticism and evolutionism. Others were less concerned about orthodoxy and gravitated towards liberal Protestantism; still others moved in the direction of conservative evangelicalism which usually emphasized a premillennial eschatology and the infallibility of the Bible.

By the 1920s the latter group, now identified as fundamentalists, engaged in furious public battles to control and maintain the purity of Protestant denominations, as well as to preserve the "Christian" character of the wider culture. Fundamentalists became bitter and resentful as large portions of the evangelical movement adopted modernist views and thereby betrayed orthodox faith. Failing to dominate these denominations, fundamentalists progressively separated from both the theological error of their brethren and from secular forms of evil within society to establish their own subculture. It was an inclusive institutional network including new denominations and Bible institutes to train their own theologians.

Fundamentalists became known for their zealous denunciation of all aspects of modern life. As a movement acting upon strong religious convictions, fundamentalists tolerated no ambiguities, no equivocations, no reservations, and no criticisms. They were no longer able to reconcile those convictions with new currents in thinking and rapid social change. Hence, the struggle to maintain cultural influence evolved into a social movement; a synthesis of fundamentalist religion and fundamentalist Americanism, very often with a heavy overlay of morality. Worldly pleasures were labelled "unGodly." Fundamentalists organized and supported crusades against drinking and gambling, and condemned dancing and sexual deviation. The masculine temperament of this movement was epitomized by the preaching of Billy Sunday: "moral welfare makes a man hard. Superficial peace makes a man mushy . . . I have no interest in a God who does not smite."[26]

After a successful legislative effort to prohibit the manufacture and sale of alcohol, fundamentalist politics became more wide ranging and controversial. Close cooperation with the Ku Klux Klan was based on a shared belief that white Anglo-Saxon Protestants represented true Americanism. Fundamentalists, the Klan, and other right wing groups were part of a diversified nativistic movement which encouraged prejudicial treatment of ethnic groups and advocated legal restrictions on their immigration. Fundamentalists also led the opposition to public funding of Catholic schools and campaigned against the nomination in 1924 of Al Smith, a Catholic, for President.[27]

Fundamentalist preachers periodically supplied more radical right organizations, like the Klan, with biblical justification for the view that the Anglo-Saxon race was superior to Blacks, Catholics, and other immigrant groups. Klansmen saw themselves as "real white men" with a racial pride based on ". . . the unrevoked decree of Almighty God and deserved . . . the everlasting gratitude of all lovers of pure American principle throughout the nation."[28] The Klan and other preservationists shared with fundamentalists a fear of the Catholic church for many of the same reasons that Paisley attacks Catholicism. The church was seeking deliberately to "Romanize" the United States. Moreover, Catholics were encouraged to marry outside the church and to bring up any children they might have as Catholics in accordance with "Romanist" doctrines. Also, the Catholic church was too egalitarian and guilty of exploiting the gullibility of Negroes by raising their hopes of equality.

Al Smith's defeat, legislation outlawing the teaching of evolution in various southern states, and the rigid defense of prohibition indicated the tenacious strength of fundamentalism, yet these were only temporary victories and vain attempts to reassert influence. Smith's nomination four years later and the repeal of Prohibition were preludes to the movement's loss of influence and respectability. The famous 1925 Scopes trial in Dayton, Tennessee symbolized the near total debacle of fundamentalism as a social movement.

The Scopes trial dramatized the confrontation between fundamentalism and modernism. To fundamentalists the trial represented an effort to save the religion of their children by stopping the teaching of "Godless" Darwinism. But the trial was elevated to a national media event with fundamentalism depicted as the final desperate outcry of an outdated and intellectually repressive religious establishment. William Jennings Bryan, America's most distinguished and eloquent fundamentalist, appeared as counsel for the prosecution, an appropriate role, since he had been responsible for the enactment of several anti-evolution laws. Although the fundamentalists won a legal victory, they lost the wider battle to modern science and morality. Bryan was humiliated by the press and he was personally embarrassed by the arguments of his opponent, Clarence Darrow. Henry Commager provides an insightful summary of the trial's significance: "For all his eloquence he [Bryan] was unable to demonstrate the connectedness between fundamentalism and morality, or explain the relevance of fundamentalism to the complex problems of the twentieth century or infuse the fundamentalist cause with vitality or dignity."[29]

The repudiation of Bryan was not the demise of fundamentalism but stimulated further isolation from the new and more liberal mainstream of Protestantism and the general culture.

Fundamentalists progressively separated from their former brethren, the evangelicals. Evangelicals as well were determined to distance themselves from the image and reputation of fundamentalism. They showed renewed interest in social reform and embraced Roosevelt's New Deal policies, while fundamentalism continued to be a significant component of right wing politics.[30]

Carl McIntyre's formation of the American Council of Christian Churches in 1941 initiated a dogmatic "pro-gospel and anti-modernist" reorganization of fundamentalism. The movement was so sectarian that the doctrine of separation was often a test of fidelity. All those joining were expected to withdraw from the liberal Federal Council of Churches and all its affiliated denominations. This stance is characteristic of the "double separation" of contemporary fundamentalism: A separation from evil and a separation from those not separated from evil.

Current fundamentalism's self-depiction as "militantly separatist" accurately characterizes its opposition to all forms of apostasy and threat to Christian culture. Bob Jones, Carl McIntyre, and other fundamentalist leaders devote enormous resources to public criticism of mainstream Protestantism, both evangelical and liberal alike. For instance, liberals are condemned for no longer preaching a soul-saving gospel, while Billy Graham and other evangelicals are attacked for associating with the Catholic church and Protestant liberals. Simultaneously, fundamentalists project to the nation their self-perception as the new elect of God.

The embattled spirit of American fundamentalism is also found in Northern Ireland. There, efforts to preserve the Christian character of the culture began in the mid-nineteenth century, but not with full-fledged militance until 100 years later. Ian Paisley's stand against the "betrayal" of Protestant denominations to modernism evolved into a flourishing fundamentalist movement which has had considerable socio-political impact. Two features of American Fundamentalism also figured prominently in the development of fundamentalism in Northern Ireland: First, the separation of conservatives from established denominations over doctrinal issues; second, the separated churches' hostility towards apostasy often expanded into organized opposition to

Catholicism, and the nationalism associated with, and forms of change perceived as threats to their version of Protestantism.

The roots of fundamentalism in Northern Ireland are found primarily in Calvinist Presbyterianism brought from Scotland to Ulster in the seventeenth century. Irish Presbyterianism inherited from the parent church a strong tendency to schism. Like their American counterparts, Ulster evangelicals inherited some denominational loyalty, but they have generally lacked clear principles of such group authority. The primary unit of authority among evangelicals is the individual conscience informed by the Bible. The importance attached to individual conscience is derived from the Calvinistic tradition that sought the individual's voluntary decision to accept Christ. Churches and congregations were, therefore, viewed as voluntary associations wherein individuals were free to join and from which they were free to leave.

Not surprisingly, a tendency for schism and separation in Ulster Presbyterianism began in the eighteenth century when the Church was first divided over a doctrinal issue. The synod's more conservative majority attempted to force the less orthodox members to subscribe to the Westminister Confession of Faith. Rather than submit to the demand, the "New Light" groups of non-subscribers established a separate synod. Strangely, the original synod permitted non-subscription to continue for eighty years, until the occurrence of another non-subscription dispute in the nineteenth century. Throughout that period the liberalism of New Light and Unitarianism held the most influence within the denomination, but supporters of these two schools of thought withdrew from the synod in 1830 after a nine year struggle with the evangelical "Old Light," led by Dr. Henry Cooke.

The non-subscription controversies illustrate the inherent tension in Presbyterianism, between traditional ecclesiasticism and the right to act according to conscience. A.T.Q. Stewart noted the tension within Presbyterianism in each region: ". . . an almost Manichean duality of outlook, Old Light and New Light, fundamentalist and intellectual, extreme and moderate."[31]

The balance shifted towards conservatism, in part by the renewal of conflict between Catholics and Protestants during the Old Light/New Light controversy. Henry Cooke exacerbated Protestant fears that Catholic priests were part of a Rome-directed conspiracy against Protestant culture everywhere. The withdrawal of the New Light supporters allowed Cooke to reunify the synod with the original Seceders. Since then, Presbyterianism has represented a cultural unity that saw itself as the defender of Protestant and British culture, intent

on turning the whole province into the patrimony of the Reformation.[32] Defense of the Reformed Faith meant vigilance against all
internal threats: apostasy in Protestantism, and Catholicism and its
connection with Irish nationalism (a posture that most Presbyterians
have abandoned, but which was revived by Ian Paisley).

We previously explained how Paisley instills in his congregation a
sense of continuity between their beliefs and the historic Protestantism
of Calvin and Knox. Paisley has stressed the importance of vigilance
against both religious heresies and opposition to secular trends which
seemed to undermine their religious heritage. He consistently warns
that if Free Presbyterianism is to remain true to God, it must maintain
its purity within the tradition of reformed Protestantism. The church's
self-perceived roots in that tradition have become an ideological
legitimation for its opposition to various aberrations of conservative
Protestant politics and culture. Furthermore, Paisley's leadership is
grounded in this historical legitimation. His accomplishments, as an
ideological leader, stem from his ability (1) to identify specific opponents (or "enemies") who threaten the Free Presbyterian religious
heritage; (2) to instill in his followers a strong identity and *raison d'etre*
for a militant posture towards these adversaries; and (3) to establish a
framework within which beliefs and values can be translated into social
and political activism.

The Free Presbyterian ideological perspective is both coherent and
cogent among its followers. Nearly identical beliefs and political
outlooks are shared by those who have listened to Paisley's pronouncements over the past thirty years. This ideological consistency has
formed the basis of a cohesive, sectarian community. Strict consensus
and cooperation, not often found in more pluralistic groups, has
proven to be the key to successful, concerted action against their
adversaries. Paisleyism's militant stance is possible, and to a large extent
effective, because Free Presbyterians hold an absolute assurance that
their fundamentalist cause is virtuous and all other forms of faith and
political persuasion are erroneous to the extent of their departure from
fundamentalism—a position very similar to militant fundamentalism in
America.

The fundamentalist worldview provides the believer with a totalistic
set of values and beliefs through which he can interpret the world. He
can confidently assume that his responses to issues and events in his
daily life are in accordance with the will of God. Since his relationship
to God is clearly revealed through his own, and his minister's, literal
interpretation of the Bible, he feels secure that his response is proper

and righteous even when contrary to prevailing public opinion. Since the Bible is the locus of authority among Free Presbyterians and other fundamentalists, they resort to absolute and infallible scriptures for answers that have a symbolic or allegorical relationship to controversial questions they face. The believer locates Bible verses and events that are metaphorically similar to his own. Passages that describe how the "people of God" defended their beliefs against infidels and heretics are accepted as analogous to their own situation and a concrete justification for their fight against forms of apostasy and political opposition.

Paisley's biblical rationale for the separatist position of his church is readily embraced by his followers because there is little choice, other than to risk contamination of their own faith. As he frames their options, fundamentalists are obliged to perceive apostasy as an aggressive force which must be countered by militant means, or else they are not true to the defense of their own faith. Not all Free Presbyterians actively contend with those they conceive to be only nominal Christians, but there is a widely accepted notion that it is one's Christian duty to disassociate himself not only from apostate organizations but also to challenge any person (or group) who espouses beliefs that are incompatible or inconsistent with his fundamentalism. One Free Presbyterian said to me:

> I believe it is the responsibility of every believer to attack apostasy in any environment that he is in. In no way do I believe a believer can have fellowship with an apostate. But there are other environments where he might be called upon to speak out. It is very easy to support what Dr. Paisley says in an environment like this [Martyr's Memorial Church]; but outside of it, it is the believer's responsibility to attack the enemy.

His reference to the "enemy" means that any religious or secular position which the fundamentalist conceives as "ungodly" is subject to attack. Also, the view that the fundamentalist's Christian stand for God involves a "battle," is apparently not a metaphor exclusively used by the Reverend Dr. Paisley. And when doing battle, the believer should "know the enemy." The same person said:

> I think the believer should know both sides. Both the enemy's [version] and the truth. I admit that that can be a very dangerous thing because if the believer is weak, he might get drawn to the other side. It is our duty to attack apostasy. You know war is not a very nice thing. It is the worst of all things. But one minister I heard said that, "We, the Lord's people, are not called to a Chesterfield [a couch], we are called to a Battlefield!" I

know we do not want to go to war, but that is what the Lord has called us to do.

This passage reveals a unique aspect of the fundamentalist world view which allows, and even requires, the adherent to adopt a sectarian posture towards groups and individuals who have different attitudes and beliefs. Nearly all religious communities can develop acrimonious relationships with other sects and denominations, but their differences are most often ephemeral or kept within certain limits. But fundamentalist's differences with "non-believers" are often rigid and non-negotiable. Fundamentalists tend to categorize non-believers into mental pigeonholes. Perceived as standing outside the providence of God, they are thought of as potentially threatening. Fundamentalists assume a simple rule of thumb, adapted from Matthew 10, the King James version: "If they are not for us, then they must be against us." This type of sterile thinking is extended to diverse sections of the Northern Ireland community, merely because these groups are antithetical to their conservative Christian ethos.

Entrenched as they are in these assumptions that separatist fundamentalists are privileged with an absolute truth, no one who advocates any other form of Protestantism is thought of as equal before God. Also, they find it impossible and repugnant to cooperate with anyone who does not conform to the same pure and rigid beliefs as themselves. In terms of this uncompromising position, we can understand why it is imperative for Paisley to advocate organizational separatism from apostate denominations. Without clear-cut lines of demarcation, he could not have an adequate basis for attacks designed to win Protestants away from establishment churches to his own.

Separatism has been a relatively simple task for Free Presbyterians, and, in addition, has been extended into antagonism towards religious and political "enemies" over many years; a feat that must not be underestimated. Few, if any, fundamentalist groups in or outside Northern Ireland have managed such a sustained opposition towards adversaries. To hold tenaciously to the view that it is one's Christian duty earnestly to "contend for the faith" is also intrinsic to the survival of fundamentalism in Ulster. As the world about them becomes increasingly secularized, with the historical differences between various faiths (Catholic and Protestant, Presbyterian and Anglican) becoming less and less distinct due to the endeavors of ecumenists, it is more and more essential that Paisley and other fundamentalists differentiate themselves from apostasy within the religious sphere. Within the broader context of culture and politics, the same reasoning applies. In the fundamentalist mind, society is becoming progressively more "worldly," and hence immoral: Thus traditional Protestantism must be defended. Outside observers usually understand Paisleyite grounds for separatism but are often left in a quandary over why it manifests itself with such ferocity.

We have discussed Paisley's adroitness in persuading his followers that their cause *is* the Lord's battle and righteous beyond any doubt. As long as their struggle is carried out under the auspices of Protestantism and God's will, they can exude a sense of intemperate self-assurance that usually exceeds that of other parties or groups, both Protestant and Catholic particularly during public confrontations. For instance, at a protest rally against homosexuality in 1979, the Free Presbyterians shouted towards their opposition, "the victory will be ours . . . God *is* on our side!" This kind of bravado further indicates how Paisley's rhetoric supplies his followers with confidence that God is indeed protecting them in all their endeavors. Paisley further assures them that they have no reason to fear: ". . . did not Christ say to his followers, 'Fear not, for I am with you . . .'? The Lord is fighting for his people!'" It is this relationship to God which provides their rationale for sectarian combativeness. That Paisley firmly believes he is favored above all other politicians and clerics because he is chosen by God to defend Ulster, explains why he is often radical, despite the generally unpopular reactions provoked by his vehement speeches and paramilitary flourishes. If Paisley and his followers believe absolutely that God is their benefactor, then he will most certainly intervene whenever they strive to further the cause of Ulster Protestantism. Hence, why should Paisleyites not conduct themselves as if God were part of their personal armor?

Millenarianism

After twelve years of violence in Northern Ireland, the Troubles are readily accepted among Free Presbyterians as paramount evidence that the millennium is near. Even in Ulster, which is considered a God-fearing, pious country, unprecedented conflict and social disorder has occurred. What over arching explanation for this debacle is available other than that the sins of mankind have provoked God's wrath? Free Presbyterian eschatology view the Troubles as a warning, a sign that this is only the beginning of more terrible times to come if the nation does not turn itself "back to God." One of the Reverend David

McIlvern's favorite sermon themes on Wednesday nights is that those
who drink initiate a vicious circle of dire consequences. It begins with
men drinking more and more, then loosing their wages in betting
shops. They are then forced to give up, or are fired from their jobs
because they are too incapacitated to work. The decline caused by sinful
behavior continues; under the influence of the "devil's buttermilk,"
some men, particularly Catholics, have the false courage to engage in
paramilitary murders, robberies, and other crimes. The Free Presbyterians' simplified way of explaining complex social problems is to blame
the devil and the institutions and groups that he controls. His power
over man spreads like a cancer. Sin begets more sin in a downward
spiral of debauchery and attraction to the "things of the world." Thus
what other fate could possibly befall an increasingly corrupt and secular
world than a sudden final judgment from a benevolent, but just God?
He will intervene after all corners of the world have been evangelized,
when life on earth has become so intolerable that He must invoke the
millennium to relieve the unnecessary suffering of his people and also
punish the wicked.

Such millennial conclusions are reached by Free Presbyterians who
assume that there is indeed a hell for the punishment of unforgiven
sinners. As one Free Presbyterian woman put it: "How can those
people who do not come to Christ ever be welcome to live in God's
heaven? Could God accept them if they denied his Son while living on
this earth?" She and her fellows believe that everyone will be offered a
clear opportunity for salvation before the apocalypse arrives.

Dichotomization

When dividing the world into such strict dichotomies (i.e., good,
manifested as God's realm and evil as Satan's sphere of influence), there
is very little room for ambiguity. The primary type of dichotomy on
which Free Presbyterians base their judgments regarding any social
situation, relates to their main source of identity, as "born again"
Protestants and Ulster Loyalists. Thus, the question they pose for
themselves in any form of personal relationship is whether that
individual is also saved. Groups, organizations, and institutions are also
separated into those that represent and defend Protestant principles,
and those that do not. For instance, the Orange Order is largely viewed
as essential to the defense of their heritage because it has traditionally
stood for Bible Protestantism, even though not all Orangemen are

saved. Yet, the Irish Presbyterian Church is an enemy because many of its members are not saved and the church is apostate. The division of individuals into saved and unsaved categories is subtle and not often an immediate cause of the severance of social relationships. A relationship is hardly possible, however, for someone who believes himself bound for a heavenly afterlife, while his neighbor, acquaintances, friends, or even relatives are doomed to hell. The center of the believer's ultimate concern is the question of absolute truth—which he believes is to be found in the literally interpreted Bible—and the nature of salvation—which the Bible specifies to be the acceptance of Christ. There is, then, inevitably a division existing in the mind of the fundamentalist between himself and those who do not share his status. Life is conceived as ephemeral, and only a transitory stage between birth and eternity which follows death. The fundamentalist cannot ignore the fact that he and other believers are destined for life after death that corresponds to all the traditional imagery of what heaven is supposed to be like—celestial music, an ageless body, and angels—all facets Paisley insists to be the reality of heaven. As for those non-believers who "die without Christ," the "true Christian" must assume that they are to be punished for the remainder of time, otherwise the fundamentalist's vision of his own future is not viable or even possible.

In the fundamentalist cosmology there can be no heaven without a hell. Yet the indisputable fact that relatives and friends who are "unsaved" suffer the consequence of hell is a continual source of worry and sorrow for Free Presbyterians. They dread the possibility of them dying unconverted; nonetheless, that is the harsh justice of God's plan. Furthermore, although there may not always be a conscious perception of these differences in salvational status, Free Presbyterians cannot help but feel themselves to be in a special position in relation to non-believers not destined to share their celestial eternity. No matter how difficult life becomes, there is solace in the fact of an eventual "glorious reward" for themselves while those whom they regard as adversaries are excluded, including Catholics and those Protestants who are immersed in apostasy instead of "born again" Protestantism. A Free Presbyterian may socialize or cooperate on a political level with another Protestant, yet that person is still stereotyped in terms of his relationship to Christ. Members often comment to one another on a particular individual's salvational status: "He's not saved, you know." This kind of remark may follow immediately after amiable relations, when working or conversing with an unsaved person. This rigid, dualistic thinking has a persuasive influence on the way in which a Free Presbyterian constructs his entire social reality.

Since most Democratic Unionist politicians are either Free Presbyterian or members of another conservative evangelical church, they take to heart Paisley's insistence that Christians in politics must see that God's law becomes the law of the nation. The enforcement of such a restriction is inspired by fundamentalist Protestantism. Therefore, the ultimate source of moral authority on which they rationalize their political decisions is a literally interpreted Bible. When this form of authority is applied in the course of political decisions, there is little room for compromise. Obedience to the stipulations of the scriptures is theoretically the first and foremost guideline for political action.

The aim of their fundamentalist-oriented politics is to see society ordered along the lines of social ethics as derived from biblical interpretations. The Bible, as God's will for all mankind, would serve as the ideological "guarantor" of a social order governed along the lines of biblical principles. One might expect that the fundamentalist would see the state and society in a mutual light, as secular quantities, since by their definition neither is governed by "true Christians"; but under conditions where religion and politics are so closely connected, this is reversed towards a desire for a more medieval Christendom, a Christian country dominated by Christian values, using its power to vanquish enemies in heroic style, and enforcing God's will through law and politics. Paisley has said, "God's law should become the law of the nation," and he rationalizes his own involvement on the precedent of Old Testament prophets:

> . . . there were breaches in God's law in the government and in the land . . . the prophets of God entered into confrontation with evil at the highest possible level. How ridiculous it is to say that I should fight evil at the lowest possible level, but when that evil climbs onto the Throne, I have no responsibility to pull it from that Throne. Let us get our priorities right in this matter. As a Christian I have the responsibility in every walk of life to exercise my Christian stand and to exalt the righteousness of the Lord.[33]

If Paisley and his followers are to act in true conformity with this conception of the Old Testament prophets, they must accept their Christian "responsibility" and reform Ulster in line with their vision of a Godly nation. Confrontation with God's enemies in the name of the Lord is thus a necessity and their destiny as righteous, militant fundamentalists. Through this reasoning, Paisley has convinced many "born again" Protestants that their beliefs are a spiritual mandate for political involvement and activism.

Conclusion

An important part of the fundamentalist's religious commitment is unconditional support of political groups and moral crusades that represent the defense of Protestant culture and religious practice. In his *History of Fundamentalism,* Steward Cole speaks of fundamentalism in a way that applies both to the American and the Ulster context: ". . . the organised determination of conservative churchmen to continue the imperialistic culture of historic Protestantism within an inhospitable civilisation dominated by secular interests and a progressive Christian idealism."[34] In the foregoing discussion we found that social and political activism among fundamentalists was most militant and influential when their Protestant heritage was perceived to be imperilled. Fundamentalists in America and Ulster have made a significant impact on socio-political events, especially during times of cultural upheaval. Fundamentalism became part of various movements for cultural preservation and provided, at least in part, an ideological rationale for right wing extremism. Organizational separatism is an essential feature of this involvement on the political right. In America the establishment of their own subculture provided the organizational autonomy necessary to mobilize fundamentalists for effective campaigns against evolutionism and advancement of ethnic groups. In Ulster, the separation of Paisley's Free Presbyterians allowed him to utilize them as an organizational cadre for his loyalist political party.

It is not mere opportunism that causes politically-minded fundamentalists to gravitate towards the far right. The fundamentalist begins with a definition of that which is absolutely right, and looks upon politics as an arena in which that right might be realized. Fundamentalists have a comprehensive world-view, and they are only satisfied when religious and political antipathies can be linked together. They have a propensity to combine seemingly unrelated animosities, so as to make them mutually reinforcing. For example, contemporary American fundamentalists link their religious sentiments to the support by liberal politicians for measures that are for all practical purposes socialistic—and socialism is nothing more than a variant of communism, which of course is atheism. In Ulster fundamentalists view liberal Unionism's general support for the Ecumenical Movement as an endorsement of eventual unity with the Church of Rome, which inevitably means Catholic domination of Protestantism and the spiritual enslavement of "God's people."

The fundamentalist response to these antipathies is shaped by strong religious convictions. Their interpretation of crucial issues differ from that of non-fundamentalists in respect of the eternal implications at stake. Fundamentalists insist there is an enduring conflict between Satan and God, in which Satan is engaged with ecumenism and Romanism to destroy the true faith and the Protestant character of Ulster. For Paisleyites in this case, only the most militant measures of defense are in order. Of course such beliefs and responses to crisis were also influenced by a more general cultural experience, but distinct religious motives are central. The fundamentalist Christian life has always emphasized the personal and collective battle against worldliness and apostasy. Militance is a result of those convictions.

This attitude is a historical outcome of the revivalist tradition that determined the character of twentieth-century fundamentalism. As mentioned before, in America and Ulster revivalism flourished in cultures considerably influenced by Puritan Calvinism. The basic assumption of Calvinistic thought was a radical distinction between the saved and the unsaved. Furthermore, revivalism disposed individuals to think in such simple dichotomies. The world is divided into the realms of Satan and God. In such a dichotomized view of reality, few ambiguities exist between the saved and the unsaved, the spiritual and the worldly, or absolute truth and error. Fundamentalists apply this dichotomized view and its eternal implications in the interpretation of rapid social change. The issues of the actual world are transformed into a spiritual Armageddon—an ultimate reality that looks upon the world as an arena for conflict between absolute good and absolute evil. Accordingly they scorn compromise and can tolerate no ambiguities.

William Jennings Bryan and his fundamentalist colleagues of the American 1920s, suffered a devastating setback because they were not able to demonstrate the relevance of their world view to the problems of a rapidly changing secular world. Yet, in Northern Ireland fundamentalism continues to prosper because its "no compromise" religious interpretation of the present conflict is congruous with the sectarian views of large numbers of Protestants. Furthermore, the current re-emergence of the Christian Right has proven the salience of fundamentalist politics in America; a perspective which offers "a new beginning" for America as a "nation under God," once again dominated by conservative Protestant values.

This is not to say that the influence of a Calvinist world view is the sole explanation for participation in right wing movements. However, we do argue that theological and moral intolerance is activated by these traditional Calvinistic thought patterns among fundamentalists. We have also stipulated that fundamentalist's long history of separatism from liberalizing denominations is an outcome of their dichotomized view of reality. They have not been willing to accommodate or tolerate views and beliefs contrary to their own. Furthermore, we find that these forms of militant fundamentalism emerge out from the Calvinist-Revivalist roots as part of an attempt to maintain traditional Protestantism in situations of socio-cultural change.

Notes

1. The data for this paper was collected in the course of a three-year ethnographic study of the Free Presbyterian Church of Ulster and the DUP; and the relationships between the church and protestant politics in Northern Ireland.
   All quotations without footnotes are drawn from direct observation and field notes.
2. From Calvin, *The Institutes of Christian Religion,* in selected passages of writing on *God and Political Duty,* ed. John T. McNeill.
3. David W. Miller, *Queen's Rebels: Ulster Loyalism in Historical Perspective* (Dublin: Gill and MacMillan, 1978), 85.
4. Frank Wright, "Protestant Ideology and Politics in Ulster." *European Journal of Sociology* 14, (2): 226 (1973).
5. Ibid., 226.
6. *Belfast Telegraph,* (Belfast, Northern Ireland, 1966).
7. John Harbinson, *The Ulster Unionist Party 1882–1973* (Belfast: Blackstaff Press, 1973), 217.
8. Paula J. McBride, *A Geographical Analysis of the Free Presbyterian Church 1951–1978* (B.A. Honors diss., dept. of geography, The Queen's University of Belfast, 1978), 11.

9. Ian Paisley, *This Is My Life,* taped message no. 4, (Belfast: Free Presbyterian Church of Ulster, 1979).
10. McBride, 67.
11. McBride, 13.
12. Private notes.
13. Andrew Boyd, *Holy War in Belfast* (Republic of Ireland: Anvil Books, 1970), 34–44.
14. Ian Paisley, "The Fundamentalist and his State," (Address to the W.C.F. Edinburgh, Greenville, S.C., 1976), 4.
15. Ian Paisley, *The Revivalist,* "When a Prophet ceases to be stoned, he ceases to be a Prophet" (Sermon delivered in Belfast, August 1979), 3.
16. Wright, 245.
17. Wright, 245.
18. Wright, 246.
19. James Barr, *Fundamentalism* (London: SCM Press, 1977), 108–109.
20. Steve Bruce, *Firm in the Faith: The Survival of Conservative Protestantism* (Brookfield, Vt.: Gower Publishing Company, 1984).
21. Robert Linton, "Nativistic Movements in America," *Anthropology* 45 (1945): 230.
22. William Kornhauser, *The Politics of Mass Society* (New York: The Free Press, 1965).
23. Sydney Ahlstrom, *A Religious History of the American People* (New Haven: Yale University Press, 1972), 556.
24. George Marsden, "Fundamentalism as an American phenonemon a comparison with English Evangelicalism" *Church History* 46 (1977): 215.
25. Perry Miller, *The Life of the Mind in America from the Revolution to the Civil War* (New York: Harcourt, Brace & World, 1965), 7.
26. William G. McLoughlin, *Billy Sunday Was His Real Name* (Chicago: University of Chicago Press, 1955), 158.
27. Richard Hofstadter, *Anti-Intellectualism in American Life* (London: Johnathan Cape, 1957), 123.
28. William Pierce Randel, *The Ku Klux Klan* (London: Hamish Hamilton, 1965), 655.
29. Henry Steele Commager, *The American Mind: An Interpretation of American Thought and Character since 1880* (New Haven: Yale University Press, 1950).
30. George H. Williams and Rodney L. Peterson, "Evangelicals: Society, the State, the Nation (1925–1975)" in *The Evangelicals,*

ed. David F. Wells and John D. Woodbridge (Nashville: Abingdon, 1975), 220.

31. A.T.Q. Stewart, *The Narrow Ground: Aspects of Ulster 1609–1969* (London: Faber and Faber, 1975), 99.

32. Desmond Bowen, *The Protestant Crusade in Ireland, 1780–1870* (Dublin: Gill and MacMillan, 1976), 32.

33. Ian Paisley, *The Fundamentalist and His State* (Address to the World Congress of Fundamentalists, Edinburgh, 15 June 1976), 3.

34. Steward Coles, *History of Fundamentalism* quoted in "Politics of Right-Wing Fundamentalism," David Danzig, *American Political Radicalism,* ed. Gilbert Abcarian (New York: Ginn and Company, 1971), 172.

10
The Revival of Astrology in the United States

J. Gordon Melton

OCCULT religions form the most important, and yet the most neglected, segment of modern alternative religion in America (i.e., the so-called "New Religions"). While focusing attention on the new Eastern organizations or a few new Christian groups such as the Children of God or the Way International, researchers have missed the alternative to which the greatest following has been attracted. No alternative religion can claim so many adherents among both older adults (Theosophy, Spiritualism) or younger believers (Wicca, Church Universal and Triumphant).

Even the new Eastern groups owe much of their success to the occult community which for the last century has been the major channel of Eastern religious ideas to the West. The first Hindu and Buddhist groups which broke out of their ethnic ghettos found their following among people already open to alternative perspectives from their prior participation in occult activities.

When the new generation of Eastern adepts swept across America, they found fertile ground previously prepared by the large occult community. Occult magazines announced the coming of each new guru or swami. Occult organizations invited them to address their audiences, and occult bookstores marketed their publications.

The neglect of occult history resulted from the long-standing scholarly disdain for the occult. Libraries did not save occult materials, and while a vast occult literature exists, it is almost invisible. Because it was rarely seen, many assumed that the occult had had little effect on modern alternative religion.

Of course, quite the opposite is true. It shall be the task of this paper to continue the recovery of occult history by focusing upon one of its major aspects, astrology. Individuals' participation levels varied enormously from the mere reading of the astrology sun-sign columns in magazines and newspapers to joining an astrological religion like the Church of Light. The revival of astrology in the nineteenth century produced a community of believers who not only adhered to an alternative world view, but who passed that alternative to each generation to this very day.

The Rebirth in England

The modern rise of occultism can be said to date from the eighteenth century and the popularity accorded such teachers as Emmanuel Swedenborg and Franz Anton Mesmer. Their writings set occultism on a new foundation and gave it a new impetus. Mesmer, who is best known for his work on magnetic healing and hypnotism, was a particularly important figure in the revival of astrology. He began his exploration of psychic healing from some astrological hypotheses elucidated in his doctoral dissertation.[1]

In the English-speaking world, astrology can be said to date from the 1816 publication of James Wilson's *A Complete Dictionary of Astrology*.[2] Though earlier astrologically-oriented works by Francis Barret and Nicolas Culpepper had stirred some interest, Wilson's popularly reprinted volume gave a new public the basic astrological information they needed to construct astrological charts and interpret them. A decade later Robert C. Smith (1795–1832), writing under the pen name Raphael, launched a publishing venture still in existence today. His first book, a *Manual of Astrology*[3] was an immediate success. He also produced an ephemeris, a book of charts showing the position of the planets in the sky day-by-day. *Raphael's Ephemeris*[4] remains a standard astrological textbook. After Smith's death, a succession of men carried on his work using his pen name and producing a wide range of books about astrology as well as the materials needed for charting.

The various Raphaels and the two men who wrote under the pseudonym of Zadkiel (Richard James Morrison and Alfred J. Pearce) produced the library of books that circulated in America and through which Americans rediscovered astrology.

In the 1890s the work of the Raphaels and the Zadkiels found an unexpected ally in the Theosophical Society. Founded in New York City in 1875, the Society quickly gained a British membership. At the turn of the century, it was the main instrument through which Eastern thought, both Hindu and Buddhist, filtered into the West. The Society's founder, H. P. Blavatsky remarked that had she the time to pursue astrological reflections on the Cabala, she could "show that astrology deserves the name of science as well as any other."[5] Her later occult explorations convinced her: "We must admit the truth of the latter (the Science of Horoscopy) whether we will or not."[6]

Given Blavatsky's support, it is not surprising to find practitioners of astrology among members of the society. The first important Theosophical astrologer, Walter Gorn Old, became famous under his pen name Sapherial. As popular as Sapherial became (and his books are still in print), his work was eclipsed by that of a man he introduced into the Society and to astrology, William Frederick Allen (1860–1917), better known by his pen name Alan Leo. After Old introduced Allen to Blavatsky, he became a dedicated Theosophist. Allen launched the very successful *The Astrologer's Magazine* (later renamed *Modern Astrology*), and in 1896, with Old, he organized the first modern astrological society which still exists today as the Astrological Lodge of the Theosophical Society. Among its outstanding members were Allen's wife, known under her pen name, Bessie Leo, and one of the first British astrologers not to use a pen name, Charles C. O. Carter.

Astrology in Nineteenth-Century America

The study of Astrology came to America's shores with the early colonists and persisted throughout the eighteenth century. Under the leadership of Johannes Kelpius (1673–1708), the first American astrologers, the Rosicrucians, established an astrological laboratory and observatory on Wissahickon Creek in what is now Germantown, Pennsylvania. Among other activities, they helped upgrade the almanac published by Daniel Leeds. And in 1698 Johann Seelig, one of their better astrologers, was commissioned to cast the horoscope for the Swedish Lutheran Church at Wisaco, Pennsylvania, in order to determine the best date to commence building a new church. After the demise of the Chapter of Perfection, as Kelpius' group was known, surviving members became the first hexmeisters, the well-known folk magicians of eastern Pennsylvania.

The popularity of astrology went through a decline for many decades, but starting in 1840 several new publications renewed America's interest in the subject. Thomas Hayes began the *Hayes United States Horoscope and Scientific and Literary Messenger* which lasted for eight years. It was followed by Mark Broughton's *Monthly Horoscope*. In 1844 possibly the first professional astrologer since the days of the Chapter of Perfection arrived from Sweden: C. W. Roback worked in Baltimore, Philadelphia, New York, and Boston, and during his first nine years in the United States he claimed to have cast 38,000 horoscopes. He was not just an astrologer, but an occultist in general, combining astrology with palmistry, clairvoyance, and magic. Roback also wrote the first modern book advocating astrology (as well as magic), *The Mysteries of Astrology and the Wonders of Magic* which he published in 1854.[7]

In spite of the vast clientele he claimed, Roback's impact was minimal: The revival of astrology in America was the responsibility of Roback's contemporary Luke Dennis Broughton. Broughton came from a family of astrologers. His grandfather, a physician, had become an enthusiastic student of astrology after reading Culpepper's *Herbal*[8] which gave astrological information about each herbal plant. His interest was passed on to his grandsons. Mark Broughton began publishing an almanac and an ephemeris while living in England, and, as mentioned before, after immigrating to the United States, he began publishing *Monthly Horoscope*.

In 1860 Luke Broughton published *Broughton's Monthly Planet Reader and Astrological Journal* from his Philadelphia home. His move to New York City three years later spurred the birth of that city's astrological establishment. He soon became the major American distributor of British astrological books and the teacher of the next generation of American astrologers.

Broughton authored several astrology books himself. His *The Elements of Astrology*[9] issued the year of his death summed up astrological knowledge to that point including a history of astrology, a survey of astrological theory, information on horoscope interpretation, and a lengthy defense of astrology in response to criticism.

The four decades of Broughton's career saw the movement of astrology from an almost non-existent state to the point where practitioners could be found in all the major cities. Broughton claimed that in 1860 he knew "nearly every man in the United States who had any knowledge of the subject, and probably at that time there were not twenty persons who knew enough of astrology to be able to erect a horoscope, and they were all either French, English, or German. There was not an American, either man or woman, in the whole United States who could even erect a horoscope at that time." But forty years later, Broughton could say: "At the present day [1898] there are many thousand American people who are studying astrology, and some have become quite proficient in the science."[10]

The growth of astrology in the 1880s and 1890s did not go unnoticed, and attacks upon it were frequent. Broughton assigned himself the role of "defender of the faith" and at every opportunity made the case for the fledgling science. He vigorously opposed laws that prevented astrologers from freely doing their work, and in 1886 Broughton came to the defense of a Mr. Romaine who had been sentenced to eighteen months imprisonment for practicing astrology. He accused Romaine's attackers of ignorance. Why, he asks, is "astrology the only science or art in existence concerning which expert testimony is entirely discarded, and in regard to which only the opinions of men who are the most ignorant of the subject are entertained."[11] Broughton would go on to do battle with other opponents of the heavenly art such as Charles A. Dana, editor of the *New York Sun,* astronomer Richard A. Proctor, and popular encyclopedists Thomas Dick, and William and Robert Chambers.

Broughton took it upon himself to police his own field, and turned his pen upon practitioners whom he felt were unqualified. He denounced Roback as a fraud who merely pretended to follow astrology while knowing nothing about it. Roback, he said, even stole his book from the seventeenth-century astrologer John Gadbury. He attacked Hiram Butler and Eleanor Kirk as authors of pseudo-astrological books to be strictly avoided by the serious student.

Obviously Broughton was neither the only astrologer nor the only astrology teacher practicing in the late nineteenth century. Boston had developed its own astrological establishment which included astronomer Joseph G. Dalton, who in 1898 published an American ephemeris.[12] And, at least three astrological religions had emerged. The first dates back to 1876 when Emma Harding Britten published her book *Art Magic,*[13] within which she included the teachings of an occult order, the Brotherhood of Light, which she claimed dated from ancient Egypt. The nineteenth-century head of this Brotherhood was a European, M. Theon. Thomas H. Burgoyne (d.1894), a Scotsman, made contact with Theon, and when he subsequently came to America, he pulled a group of Brotherhood members around him. He wrote a series of lessons for the modern Brotherhood which were eventually published as *The Light of Egypt*.[14]

The Brotherhood had a unique organization: It was headed by a scribe, an astrologer, and a seer. Burgoyne was the original scribe. Minnie Higgens was the original astrologer, and Mrs. Anderson the seer. When Higgens died in 1909, her post was taken by Elbert Benjamine, destined to become one of the outstanding astrologers of the twentieth century.

At roughly the same time as the Brotherhood of Light was forming, a young lumberjack, Hiram Butler, forced out of work by an accident that cost him several fingers, retired to a hermit's life in rural California. He began to have visions which he shared with others. A group of twelve formed around him, and pooling their resources, they moved to Applegate, California where they formed the Esoteric Fraternity. There Butler taught them what he called Esoteric Christianity, a form of Christian occultism.

Astrology was integral to Butler's religion, although he called it "Solar Biology," the title he gave to his massive volume published in 1887.[15] Butler's system differed only slightly from the more orthodox astrology. He made a change to adjust for the Copernican revolution. The practical effect of Butler's adjustment was to reverse the signs, so that a Libryan in solar biology would have all the characteristics of a person born under Aries in the more traditional system. As with most attempts to revise the horoscope, Butler's Solar Biology found little acceptance outside of the Fraternity.

The Order of the Magi (magi being equated with astrologer) was founded in 1889 in Chicago. Its founder, Olney H. Richmond had begun his occult career as a soldier during the Civil War. According to his own account, in the spring of 1864, while stationed in Nashville, Tennessee, he was accosted by a stranger who identified himself as a member of the Order of the Magi, an ancient order that flourished in Egypt thousands of years ago. The stranger designated Richmond as his successor as head of the Order and initiated him with a series of signs and passwords. In the 1870s Richmond settled in Chicago and met another member of the Order who became his teacher. Eventually Richmond became a teacher to a group of thirty men and women and in 1889 opened a Temple in Chicago on South Division Street. The following year a second Temple opened in Lansing, Michigan.

The emergence of the Order of the Magi and other astrological religions merely underscores the genuine revival of astrology and the occult in general which was occurring in America during the last half of the nineteenth century.[16]

The Astrological Universe

In trying to revive astrology in a culture which had banished it centuries before and to a public largely ignorant of it, adherents attempted to align astrology to the increasingly influential world of science. The single affirmation common to all nineteenth-century astrologers was that "astrology is a science." As F. M. Lupton asserted: "Astrology is an exact science, and . . . as a science, is pure mathematics, and there is no guesswork about it."[17] This affirmation was made in the opening paragraph of almost every book published on astrology during the nineteenth century and was repeated frequently throughout the texts.

Like other sciences astrology had a specific realm of knowledge assigned to it. Astrology described the nature of planetary influences on human life, and thus the astrologer's task was to know and describe the zodiacal forces and the laws that govern them.

Astrologers claimed that the science of astrology was thousands of years old, dating back to ancient Chaldes and Egypt. Its influence in biblical times was obvious from the many Old Testament references,[18] and more than one astrologer reminded readers that the New Testament opened with the account of Chaldean astrologers following the star to the Christ child. Astrology, as it was practiced in the nineteenth century and as we in the 1980s have come to know it, is ancient. It derived from Ptolemy, the second-century Greek author of the *Tetrabiblos*. Rather than developing a new body of knowledge, nineteenth-century astrologers copied Ptolemy's system and took their information on the significance of the signs and planets from the *Tetrabiblos*.[19]

While affirming astrology as a science, astrologers were certainly aware that it was science with a slight difference. They called it an occult science, by which they meant that it described the hidden (and some would say "spiritual") forces of the universe. Astrologers claimed that centuries of observations had demonstrated the truth of their assertions that the planetary movements through the zodiac effected human life. Since they were at a loss to pinpoint the exact nature of the force of connection between the stars and the earth, they had to fall back on an esoteric or occult connection.

Most astrologers postulated a universe of heavenly correspondences to earthly conditions. Burgoyne described it thus:

Astrology, per se, is a combination of two sciences, viz.: astronomy and correspondences. These two are related to each other as hand and glove; the former deals with suns, moons, planets and stars, and their motion, while the latter deals with the spiritual and physical influences of the same bodies; first upon each other, then upon earth, and lastly upon the organism of man.[20]

This law of correspondences had been a major building block of Emmanuel Swedenborg's thought in the previous century and ultimately derived from the hermetic principle: "As above, so below." Hermetics assume the individual to be a microcosm of the universe, the macrocosm. For astrology, the movement of the planets through the zodiac activated the correspondences. Only in the twentieth century have some astrologers moved away from the hermetic approach, though, a majority still rely upon it.

As an occult science, astrology tried to have the best of both worlds. As a science, it was as new and modern as the latest scientific journal and aligned to the wave of the future. As an occult body of thought, it was allowed to make religious affirmations about the place of individuals in a universe of meaning, purpose, and morals. Minimally, these affirmations might be little more than reflections about the nature of life, but astrology, taken to its natural conclusion, led directly to the religion of the stars.

Astrologers, even the most secular, knew that they were offering a religious alternative to Christianity. Olney Richmond decried as unscientific the traditional creator deity whom he saw as a mere convenience for those who pretended to give people the directives of the Almighty.[21] "A far off God and a remote heaven," said Eleanor Kirk, "are no longer attractive. The quickening spirit has breathed a thought to those who have ears to hear and hearts to feel, of the Eternal Now, and a God and a heaven in every human soul."[22] The astrologer's God was an impersonal but immanent force or a principle of order and causation. Butler described God as the Cause World.[23]

The astrological universe which replaced the traditional Christian one pictured God and nature and humanity as intimately connected in a matrix of correlates. God was not someone or something apart from human beings. Each individual, affirmed F. M. Lupton, was a soul which comes from God "and is a part of It—a part of the Great One."[24] This monist approach so central to nineteenth-century astrological metaphysics was passed down through the occult community and became a central affirmation of what has come to be called the "New Religious Consciousness."

The Twentieth Century, 1900–1920

The nineteenth century ended as the bright lights of nineteenth-century astrology slowly burned out. Astrology felt the loss of leaders such as Burgoyne and Broughton, but they were soon replaced by astrologers who have far outstripped them in accomplishments.

The twentieth century for astrology actually began in 1899 as a new astrological light appeared in the person of Evangeline Adams. Evangeline, a descendant of the Massachusetts Adams, was reared in the conservative atmosphere of Andover, Massachusetts. Though not in Boston, she was close enough to the city to be a part of the large psychic community developing there. This community included former president of the Society for Psychical Research, Williams, and a number of his academic colleagues including Dr. J. Heber Smith, a professor of medicine at Boston University who introduced Evangeline to the practice of astrology and to Eastern religion.

In 1899, having already chosen astrology as her life's work, Adams moved to New York City and took up residence in the Windsor Hotel. The proprietor, Mr. Leland, was her first client. Since the following day, Friday, 17 March, 1899 would be in his opinion, a bad luck day, Leland came to her for advice. Adams cast his chart only to find him under the "worst possible combination of planets." Danger and disaster were imminent. Friday, following an equally ominous reading Leland walked out of Adams's hotel room to find his fashionable hotel on fire.

Saturday morning New Yorkers awoke to read of the fire and of the new celebrity in their midst. In bold type on the front page of newspapers was Leland's statement that Adams had predicted the fire. Adams became an instant astrological superstar, America's first. Thus began her career as an astrologer to the rich, famous, and powerful. Adams gave astrology a respectability it had not previously enjoyed. By 1914 she had gained enough leverage to challenge and have overturned New York's statue against "fortune telling," at least as it applied to astrologers.

While Adams took over the leadership of the New York astrological establishment, one of Broughton's students, Catherine H. Thompson, became the leading light of the Bostonians. In 1901 she published the very successful periodical, *The Sphinx*, which appeared for many years.

While Boston continued as a center of astrology, Chicago, the major occult center of the era, developed its astrological community. At its hub was Professor Alfred F. Seward who for many years published astrology books, taught astrology by mail, and claimed to be America's largest agent for astrological giants on the West Coast—Elbert Benjamine, Max Heindel, and George Llewellyn.

Elbert Benjamine (1882–1951) had been a member of the Brotherhood of Light for nine years when in 1909 he was summoned to the home of Mrs. Anderson, one of the governing three. He was informed that Minnie Higgens, the Brotherhood's astrologer had died, and they wanted him to take her place. They also wanted him to undertake the task of authoring a complete set of lessons on the twenty-one branches of occult science. The next year he agreed to take the position and assume the task and he spent the next five years preparing himself. In 1915 he began conducting classes to Brotherhood members and in 1918 to the public at large. Work on the twenty-one volumes began in 1914 and took the next two decades. For this task Benjamine wrote under the pen name C. C. Zain, a name he assumed to separate his official Brotherhood of Light lessons from his other writings, which were numerous. He wrote a series of twelve reference books in astrology, a number of booklets and pamphlets, and many articles in astrological and occult periodicals.

Under Benjamine's leadership the Brotherhood of Light developed into a large occult body with centers across the United States and international centers in England, Mexico, Canada, and Chile. As a whole the Brotherhood was one of the major centers for learning for astrologers of the century.[26]

Max Heindel migrated to the United States from his native Germany in 1903. He had been a Theosophist, serving as head of the Los Angeles Lodge in 1904–05. On a trip to Germany in 1907, he claimed that a being, described as an elder brother of the Rosicrucian Order, appeared to him. The Rosicrucian led Heindel to a secret temple near the border between Germany and Bohemia and there taught him the material later published in *The Rosicrucian Cosmo-Conception,* Heindel's major book.[27]

In 1908 Heindel formed the Rosicrucian Fellowship with its first chapter in Columbus, Ohio. Within two years chapters appeared in Los Angeles, Seattle, Portland, Oregon, and North Yakima, Washington. In 1911 headquarters were moved to Oceanside, California where they remain to this day.

The Fellowship teaches the whole range of occultism including astrology. It remains a regular feature in the monthly *Rays of the Rosy*

Cross. Heindel wrote several popular astrological texts, all still in print and used far beyond the Fellowship's borders. The Fellowship began the publication of an annual *Ephemeris* and a *Table of Houses,* the two books of tables used by astrologers. Like the Brotherhood of Light, the Fellowship became a national and international organization during its first decades of existence.[28]

As outstanding as Benjamine and Heindel were, neither approached the accomplishments of Llewellyn George. Welsh by birth (b.1876), George grew up in Chicago. At the turn of the century he moved to Portland, Oregon and in 1901 established the Llewellyn Publishing Company and the Portland School of Astrology. In 1906 he published the annual *Moon Sign Book* and two years later the *Astrological Bulletina.*

A main thrust of George's career was his lifelong attempt to separate astrology from occultism. Such an attempt was a natural outcome of the articulation of astrology as a science and the growing status that science was gaining in society in general.

To that end his publishing house, school, and magazine dealt solely with astrology to the exclusion of such occult topics as card reading, tarot, palmistry, and numerology. He was able to drop much of the traditional language of astrology. He ultimately failed, in that astrology is an occult science which must rely upon occult forces to explain its operation.

George did try to move away from the magical, i.e., hermetic, explanation of astrology. Instead of talking about correspondences between individual and universal phenomena, he spoke of planetary vibrations. Some of these cosmic vibrations were plainly physical, such as gravity and radiation. "A radio broadcasting station," asserts George, "vibrates all those receiving sets within range which are attuned to it . . . Each station sends out its own particular program . . . In astrology every planet is a broadcasting station; the nervous system of every person is a 'receiving set.'"[29]

George also tried to associate astrology with the findings in the natural sciences rather than the ongoing development of occult thought. He lauded experiments in astrology which demonstrated the truth of particular astrological propositions, while denouncing the misuse of astrology for fortune telling. But, as stated above, George's success could only be relative.

Astrology was, and still is, intimately linked to the occult, and physical "vibrations" or influences were never located to account for all the astrological effects. Also, most people attracted to astrology were also attracted to the occult in general. Both offered a religious world

view to those attracted to science, but not to various secular philoso-
phies such as rational humanism. In the end we find Llewellyn
Publications circulating their catalogue offering "hundreds of books on
progressive subjects, including psychism, hypnotism, prophecy, spiritualism, character reading, magic, personality, prayer, yogi, personal-
development, careers, diet and health, employment, business success,
etc."[30]

Along with the emergence of the new astrological giants, these first
two decades of the twentieth century became the time when Eastern
thought, especially Hinduism, found astrology as one avenue for its
assault upon America. Hinduism had a new surge in the United States
after Swami Vivekananda's appearance at the World's Parliament of
Religion in Chicago in 1893 and the subsequent founding of the
Vedanta Society. Within a decade other Hindu (and some would say
pseudo-Hindu) teachers would appear. Possibly the most famous, next
to Vivekananda was W. W. Atkinson who authored a set of books
under the pen name of Swami Ramacharaka.

Chicago became a center for the spread of Hinduism and astrology.
Professor Seward offered in his catalogue, not only a wide range of
astrology texts, but the writings of Swami Ramacharaka, Swami
Panchadasi, and Swami Bhakta Vishita. Across town L. W. de Laurence
established himself as a teacher of Hindu magic and India's occult
knowledge, including astrology. In New York Bhakti Seva, the Blissful
Prophet, contributed a regular column to *The New York Magazine of
Mysteries,* which in turn promoted his work, *The Hindu Book of
Astrology,* possibly the first volume on the subject published in the West.

Along with the rest of the occult world, astrologers absorbed Hindu
thought which became an integral part of the occult body of knowledge. Within a few years, Americans such as Llewellyn George's
student Robert DeLuce would attempt to expound a popularized form
of Hindu astrology, and articles on the subject regularly appeared in
astrological magazines. With the added impetus of the Theosophical
Society, which was becoming closely aligned with Hindu thought,
Hindu mysticism began to permeate the occult world.

Expansion Between the Wars, 1920–1940

Astrology moved into the 1920s formally established and with a
growing clientele across the United States. However, it had yet to break
into the mass market. The two decades between World Wars I and II
were the years of that accomplishment.

Prior to the 1920s only one astrology book had been published by a major American publisher, Katherine Taylor Craig's *Stars of Destiny*, published by E. P. Dutton in 1916. Most books were printed by their authors or by an occult specialty house. That changed in 1924 when Dodd, Mead and Company published the first of four major volumes by Evangeline Adams, *The Bowl of Heaven*. Within a decade, J. P. Lippencott, David McKay, and Doubleday published volumes on astrology and opened a whole new audience to the wonders of astrological speculations.

Astrology grew in popularity during the 1920s with the public reading a number of successful periodicals on the subject. Prior to World War I a number of periodicals had been started and had attained some degree of success within the astrological community, but as a whole they had been unable to break into the mass market or the newsstands. That situation changed in 1923 when Paul G. Clancy began publishing *American Astrology*, the single longest-running astrological periodical. His effort was followed the next year by that of Sidney K. Bennett, better known by his pen name Wynn. *Wynn's Magazine* quickly joined *American Astrology* on the newsstands, and Wynn's books flooded the popular astrology market.

A third magazine, *Astrology Guide*, arrived on the streets in 1937. It brought Dal Lee to the attention of the astrological public. Lee remains one of the outstanding literary lights of the community. Within a few years he initiated *Your Personal Astrology Magazine* and the annual *Astrology Yearbook* for the *Guide's* publishers, Astro Distributing Corporation. *Stars and Planets, World Astrology Magazine* and *Today's Astrology* also began in the 1930s.

Though several astrological societies had been formed before 1920, the first organizations to claim widespread membership were formed after World War I. A group of New Englanders had formed the National Astrological Society around 1909 and began to publish a bi-monthly magazine, *Prophecy*. This group was limited by its alignment to the Universal Church of Aquarius and that church's occult religion. In 1916 the American Academy of Astrologians was founded in New York. This academy included some of the most outstanding astrologers such as its president John Hazelrigg, but the Academy was limited to 30 members and lasted only a few years.[32]

Then in 1923 Llewellyn George and A. Z. Stevenson founded the American Astrological Society, and George helped found the National Astrological Society four years later. That same year a group of New York astrologers founded the Astrologers' Guild which grew into the

Astrologers' Guild of America. The various national and regional organizations spurred the formation of many local groups such as the Oakland Astrological Society founded in 1925 and the Friends of Astrology founded in Chicago in 1938. They also led to the formation of the American Federation of astrologers in 1938. The A.F.A., the most prestigious of the several astrological organizations, has tried to bring professionalism to the field and create a favorable public image for members of the Federation.

Occult groups which included astrology as a central or key item in their teachings continued and new groups appeared during the 1920s and 1930s. Max Heindel of the Rosicrucian Fellowship issued his major astrological texts,[33] and Elbert Benjamine's productiveness reached its peak with both the Church of Light lessons and other astrology books. A third occult group, the Universal Church of Aquaria, which had appeared shortly before World War I, expanded from its New England base to include congregations in Detroit, Chicago, Toledo, Spokane, Los Angeles, Milwaukee, and several locations overseas. Possibly the single most successful affiliate was the First Temple and College of Astrology. The Temple emerged as an astrological establishment in southern California in its own right and published its own magazine, the *National Astrological Bulletin*.

First making their impact in the 1920s were two important astrology and occult teachers—Manly Palmer Hall and Marc Edmund Jones. Hall emerged as a young occult scholar and in the 1920s became head of the Church of the People in Los Angeles. As a total occultist, Hall's interests ranged from Eastern mysticism to magic and astrology, and he made significant contributions to the occult world in each area. A strong advocate of the occult, Hall wrote at a level unusual for occult writers; his educational background placed his material far above most of his contemporaries. He also collected a large occult library, currently housed at the Philosophical Research Society in Los Angeles, which had succeeded the Church of the People in 1934. Over the years Hall frequently contributed astrology articles to periodicals, and he authored several classics in the field.[34]

Marc Edmund Jones was an early associate of Hall, and like Hall was well educated, having received his Ph.D. from Columbia University. Jones founded the Sabian Assembly in 1922 from an astrology class he was teaching in New York City. Like Hall, Jones drew from the total field of occultism, but focused on the Cabala and astrology. The society was structured as a working group, and members joined Jones in his occult researches. The Assembly was a small, but potent group. Their influence was felt through Jones's books which they helped to research. And, outside of the Assembly, Jones taught many astrologers.

A third occult organization to participate in the growth of astrology was the Rosicrucian Anthrosophic League founded in 1933 in San Francisco by S. R. Parchment. Parchment's occultism drew heavily on Western occult traditions—Masonry and alchemy—but also picked up such Eastern ideas as vegetarianism. His massive volume *Astrology/ Mundane and Spiritual*[35] found immediate acceptance in the astrological community at-large and has been kept in print by the American Federation of Astrologers.

The enormous growth of astrology in the 1920s and 1930s set the stage for another spurt after World War II. Only one step, the spread of the sun-sign columns now carried in most daily newspapers and many monthly magazines remained to create the popularity level so evident today. Since the turn of the century, astrologers had tried to break into the popular press. Sapherial had a column briefly, but in the end his forecasting ended in disaster for both him and the cause of astrology. Not until 1930 did a successful column appear in England. P. I. H. Naylor wrote it, but it was suppressed in 1942 as England began to use astrology in its intelligence efforts against Hitler. After the war newspapers on both sides of the Atlantic began to publish astrology columns and quickly recognized their popularity with the public.

Conclusions

The story of the revival of astrology provides much food for thought about alternative religions in America. In particular it offers some reflections upon the idea of the new religious consciousness which some have hypothesized developed in the last two decades. This hypothesis suggests that during the 1960s a new phenomenon occurred as the youth of the nation began a radical exploration of alternative lifestyles. They began to look at Eastern religion and various means to alter consciousness. Turning from traditional religion, they found a new spiritual impetus from mystical faiths and cults that offered an exploration of self-awareness. A major element of this new religious consciousness was supplied by the massive immigration of religious teachers from India, Japan, and Tibet.

This account of the rise of astrology, and of the occult community in general, calls into question the idea of a new religious consciousness. Studies on which the idea is based neglected occult groups (with one minor exception), and did not include in its historical section the consideration of the metaphysical and physical traditions developed in the nineteenth century by such people as Emmanuel Swedenborg, Phineas P. Quimby, Mary Baker Eddy, and Andrew Jackson Davis. Primarily, the exponents of the new religious consciousness idea did not consider the possibility that a large community that already adhered to the new religious consciousness existed and that the burst of Eastern and mystical spirituality was a continuation of that community's life.

In fact the examination of the occult community demonstrates that all the elements which have been put forth as characteristic of the new religious consciousness are in fact constituent elements of the occult perspective. These elements have had a vital life in America since the days of Transcendentalism and the rebirth of occultism in the nineteenth century. At least since the late nineteenth century, a large occult community had passed this alternative consciousness to an ever-growing following generation-after-generation.

It is suggested that the new religious consciousness perceived in the 1970s is primarily caused by the passing along to a new generation of the old alternative occult mysticism of previous generations and the burst of new movements is best seen as a continuation of the growth of the occult community during the last century. The new religious consciousness did not emerge out of a cultural discontinuity or a massive importation of new ideas from Asia, but it signalled a sudden spurt in the growth rate of a movement that has been gaining momentum for many decades.

Much attention has been given to the Eastern element in the new religious consciousness, and in fact the specifically Eastern component of alternative religion in America is quite important. However, the growth of that Eastern component cannot be easily ascribed to a sudden cultural shift in which traditional Christian ideas and piety have been abandoned for a more up-to-date spirituality. The history of alternative religion, specifically of occult religion, suggests a different perspective.

Throughout the twentieth century, Westerners have shown an increasing enthusiasm for the East. Beginning with the formation of the Vedanta Society, Eastern religion has become more-and-more influential as a viable alternative to traditional religions in the United States. Gurus found ready acceptance and have been able to organize movements and train disciples. More importantly, occult leaders absorbed Eastern ideas and practices. Frequently, these Eastern teachings were disguised with occult jargon and merged with Western perspectives.

Thus, the sudden burst of Eastern religion in the late 1960s is deceptive in several ways. First, a number of new Eastern religious organizations were formed after 1965. It cannot be assumed that these new religions sprang up merely in response to an overt need in America. Set in historical perspective, 1965 marked the lifting of the Asian exclusion law, so for the first time in many decades, large scale immigration from India and Japan was possible. Many teachers of Eastern religion came to the United States at that time.

Second, the success of these organizations has been somewhat limited. While as many as 200 new Eastern religious organizations have been founded, they have not attracted large followings; the most successful numbering several thousand with the majority of them numbering in the hundreds. Transcendental Meditation is the one exception, but even so, only a small number of the many who took the TM course became either permanent meditators or members of the TM organization.

Third, the burst of Eastern religious organizations has not meant a significant growth of Eastern religion in Western society as a whole. There is little evidence that Eastern religion claims a larger percentage of the population today than in decades past.

Finally, there is little evidence that the new gurus have had a major impact on mystical thought manifest in such broader cultural movements as humanistic psychology and holistic health. To the contrary, there is every reason to suggest that the permeation of American society by elements of the new religious consciousness can best be accounted for by the continued growth and maturation of the occult community. That Eastern religious organizations could find adherents after their formation in the late 1960s is due to the preparation given the American public in the occult community (and also in the growth of the history of religious discipline in colleges and universities). The permeation of the culture with the alternative religious tradition centered in occultism enabled the new gurus to find a receptive audience.

Astrology is a science and leads to the religion of the stars. Yoga is a science, but one that leads individuals into union with the ultimate. No understanding of the alternative religions will be possible apart from their self perceived role in relation to science.

As a whole the new religions have seen themselves as totally aligned with science: Eastern religions in particular have welcomed psychologists and parapsychologists into their orb. The latest findings of both have been used to substantiate the value of yoga and meditation. The

Unification Church has hosted an annual Conference on the Unity of Science. Occult groups pay close attention to any tidbit thrown by them by psychical research.

While many of their detractors see occult religions as a rebirth of superstition and the irrational, their adherents see them as the most modern and scientific of religions. The occult provides rational and scientific people with a religious, and a spiritual perspective more comprehensive than scientific rationalism which, they would claim, provides little in the way of a meaningful explanation of life or moral guide. Occultism, Eastern religion, astrology: The alternative perspective provides not only a scientific outlook, but gives to the individual a purposeful, optimistic, and spiritual world within which to live.

Notes

1. The text of the diss. can be found in George Block, comp., *Mesmerism* (Los Altos, Calif.: William Kaufmann, 1980), 4–20.
2. (London: W. Hughs, 1819) repr. (Boston: A. H. Rolfe, 1885).
3. (London: C. S. Arnold, 1828).
4. Current editions are being published by W. Foulsham & Co., a major occult publisher in London.
5. *Isis Unveiled* (Wheaton, Ill.: Theosophical Publishing House, 1972), 2: 465.
6. *The Secret Doctrine* (Pasadena, Calif.: Theosophical University Press, 1963), 1: 105.
7. (Boston: the Author, 1854; Mokelumne Hill, Calif.: Health Research, 1970).
8. Nicolas Culpepper, *Complete Herbal* (1652; reprint, London: W. Foulsham, n.d.).
9. (New York: the Author, 1893).
10. The Author, xiii.
11. The Author, 383.
12. *The Sixteen Principle Stars, 1824–1948* (Boston: Occult Publishing, 1898).

13. (New York: the Author, 1876).

14. Thomas H. Burgoyne, *The Light of Egypt* (San Francisco: Religio-Philosophical Publishing House, 1884; Albuquerque, N. Mex.: Sun Publishing Co., 1963), 2 vols.

15. Hiram E. Butler, *Solar Biology*, 25th edition (Applegate, Calif.: Esoteric Publishing Co., 1922).

16. Olney H. Richmond, *Temple Lectures* (Chicago, 1891); repr. as *Religion of the Stars* (Chicago: B. C. Peterson, 1905); and *Evolutionism* (Chicago: Temple Publishing Co., 1896). Cf. Arline L. Richmond, comp., *Yenlo and the Mystic Brotherhood* (Chicago: Arline L. Richmond, 1945).

17. F. M. Lupton, *Astrology Made Easy* (Baltimore: I. & M. Ottenheimer, 1897), 5.

18. Cf. Karl Anderson, *The Astrology of the Old Testament* (Boston: Karl Anderson Publisher, 1892).

19. Editions of the *Tetrabiblos* in English were numerous. Broughton cited at least five translations he had read.

20. Burgoyne, 1:199.

21. Richmond, *Evolutionism*, 5–6.

22. Eleanor Kirk, *The Influence of the Zodiac Upon Human Life* (New York: the Author, 1894), 10–11.

23. Butler, 20.

24. Lupton, 6.

25. (Baltimore: Eureka Publishing Co., 1902).

26. *The Church of Light Quarterly* 50 (2 and 3): i–vi (Spring-Summer 1975).

27. (Oceanside, Calif.: The Rosicrucian Fellowship, 1909).

28. Augusta Foss Heindel, *The Birth of the Rosicrucian Fellowship* (Oceanside, Calif.: The Rosicrucian Fellowship, n.d.).

29. Llewellyn George, *Astrology/ What It Is/ What It Is Not* (Los Angeles, Calif.: Llewellyn Publishing Co., 1931), 27.

30. Llewellyn George, *Astrological Chats* (Los Angeles: Llewellyn Publications, 1941), 124.

31. Evangeline Adams, *The Bowl of Heaven* (New York: Dodd, Mead and Company, 1924).

32. John Hazelrigg, *Metaphysical Astrology*. (New York: The Philosophic Co., 1900); *Yearbook of the American Academy of Astrologians* (New York: Hermetic Publishing Company, 1917).

33. Max Heindel, *Simplified Scientific Astrology* (Oceanside, Calif.: The Rosicrucian Fellowship, 1928); Max Heindel and Agusta Foss

Heindel, *The Message of the Stars* (Oceanside, Calif.: The Rosicrucian Fellowship, 1927).

34. Manly Palmer Hall, *Astrological Keywords* (Los Angeles: Philosophical Research Society, 1958); *The Story of Astrology* (Los Angeles: Phoenix Press, 1933).

35. (San Francisco: Rosicrucian Anthrosophic League, 1933).

11
Europe's Receptivity to Religious Movements

Rodney Stark

N recent work my colleague William Sims Bainbridge and I have proposed a controversial new theory of secularization (Stark and Bainbridge 1980; 1981; 1985). We have expanded the dynamic aspect of conventional church-sect theory to religious economies as whole systems. That is, we have identified secularization as a process affecting not only societies, but individual religious organizations. If secularization means a decline in otherworldliness—a decline in supernaturalism—then at the level of individual religious organizations, it is identical with the long-recognized process by which sects are transformed into churches. To say, for example, that the Methodists are no longer a sect is to say this body has been greatly secularized.

Secularization as an aspect of whole religious economies is the sum of many such secularizations at the organizational level. Over time, repeated failures by successful sect movements to retain their high level of tension with this-world, and the repeated conflicts and controversies as new sects have errupted from the older, more secularized bodies, cause the fundamental credibility of a religious tradition itself to wane. That is, as the record of sect movements that have failed to withstand secularization builds up, it becomes less plausible to suppose that new organizational efforts to create sects will suffice. Rather, as a drunkard loses credibility when he has taken the pledge too often, so too a great religious tradition may become suspect when it has produced too many episodes of secularization.

Viewed this way, secularization is not something new under the sun. It did not begin with the rise of science. Instead, we postulate secularization as a universal feature of religious economies, as something that goes on all the time. Always the most popular and conventional religious organizations are in the process of being secularized and thus in adding an increment to the secularization of the whole cultural tradition they sustain. Sometimes the process is quite rapid, as it seems to have been in the West since the Enlightenment. Sometimes it is relatively slower.

But, fast or slow, the most important implication of our theory is that secularization *does not bring the end of religion*. Rather, secularization is self-limiting in that it stimulates significant processes of reaction in other sectors of any religious economy. The first of these is the familiar feature of conventional church-sect theory: As secularization weakens particular religious organizations, schisms result and new organizations appear. We call this process *revival*—sects break away to revive the original vigor of the conventional religious tradition. But secularization prompts more than revival, it also stimulates *innovation*— rather than being only new organizations of an old faith, groups also appear that constitute *new faiths*. We identify these as cult movements. The greater the degree of secularization experienced by a conventional religious tradition, the more cult movements that will appear, and the greater the probability that one or more of them will successfully supplant the old tradition of faith. For example, it was the excessive secularization of the pagan faiths of the Roman world that gave Christianity its opening to triumph in that religious economy. In effect, we argue that secularization causes shifts in the *sources* of religion within a society, while the *amount* of religion remains relatively constant.

These views are contrary to the conventional wisdom, especially that expressed by social scientists. It is widely believed that this is the end of the "illusion" of faith and that we live at the dawn of an age of science and reason, wherein mysticism and supernaturalism will have lost their plausibility. For more than a century, now, social scientists have expected the death of religion and the most sophisticated writers on the subject—even those who do not relish the thought—still think it is just a matter of time (cf. Martin 1978; Fenn 1978; Wilson 1975b, 1979). I disagree.

In a series of recent studies, my colleagues and I have found strong empirical support for the proposition that secularization stimulates revival and religious innovation. Cult movements are more numerous and stronger in places where the conventional churches are weaker, while sect movements cluster where the conventional churches are stronger. These patterns exist in the United States today and were as strong and consistent in America of fifty years ago (Stark and Bainbridge 1980, 1981). We find the same patterns in Canada and even within the Province of Quebec (Bainbridge and Stark 1983).

As sociological propositions go, this adds up to a good deal of empirical testing. Even so, it is troublesome that our research has been so restricted in time and space. While chemists need not worry that an element might have a different atomic structure in China than in Canada, or in the sixteenth century as compared with now, sociologists must have such worries because much of what we study does vary by time and place. These concerns have particular force vis-à-vis the proposition concerning secularization. For that proposition seems to fail when confronted with perhaps its most pertinent test—modern Europe.

From the beginning, I have been fully aware (and colleagues often have pointed out) that the theory appears to fail when applied to Europe. Since many nations in Western Europe would appear to be considerably more affected by secularization than is the United States, other things being equal, they ought to have developed or attracted more cult movements. Of course, "other things" are *not* equal. Later in this essay I note the impediments to religious movements imposed by established churches, repressive states, and by influential left-wing parties. However, to invoke mitigating circumstances in defense of theories inevitably seems like special pleading. The theory must be subject to considerable doubt if America is the center of cult and sect movements, while Europe shows little receptivity to them.

I was not prepared to give up so easily.[1] So, rather than assume that Europe constitutes a devastatingly negative case, I decided to proceed on the assumption that the theory is correct and that it is the widespread perception of religion in Europe that is faulty.

I began this study, mindful of the weight of intellectual authority in opposition. A series of distinguished European visitors has marvelled at the grass roots vitality of American religion and the immense variety it sustains. And each, like Max Weber (1946), has assured us that nothing like this does, or could, go on back in Europe. Moreover, it is European scholars, from Sigmund Freud (1927) to David Martin (1978), who have dominated scholarly work on how religions die, while it is Americans, from H. Richard Niebuhr (1929) to Charles Y. Glock (1964), who have given the greater attention to how religions are born. This transatlantic division of labor has been thought to reflect differences in local conditions.

Yet, there are contradictory signs. Perhaps the most important of these is that all the while reports flow from Europe of empty cathedrals and widespread religious indifference, scores of American-based religious movements annually report great success in their European missions. If the Mormons, the Jehovah's Witnesses, Seventh-Day Adventists, Assemblies of God, and varieties of Baptists, to say nothing of the Scientologists, Moonies, and Hare Krishnas, all are making headway in Europe, why do we hear of it almost exclusively from them? Or is it that there is a whole lot of religion going on in Europe, but that European scholars fail to see it, or deem it of no importance?

I think this is the case. Consider David Martin's (1978) recent study of secularization. By all odds it is the best current attempt to characterize religious trends and conditions in Europe nation by nation. It does not escape his notice that the Netherlands and Switzerland, for example, abound in varieties of deviant religious movements, from Tibetan Buddhism to counterculture Jesus Freaks, or indeed that the Jehovah's Witnesses are active everywhere in Europe. To him, however, these are but ephemeral symptoms of the crumbling of faith, not to be taken seriously. Moreover, Martin is so particularly interested in how major Christian bodies interplay with the politics of European nations (a theme he pursues with great insight), that he is not inclined to attend to any movements that seem not (or not yet) deeply involved in the political process, or whose effects are unimportant. One supposes that Roman scholars might have dealt in much the same fashion with a weird messianic cult movement having a small following in Palestine early in the first century.

All observers will note new religions once they have waxed powerful. But the theory tells us to look for the beginnings of such movements in the form of early stirrings, when a host of "trivial" movements will be clustered in places of potential opportunity. That means, of course, that we must attend to all manner of religious novelty, some of it seemingly silly, much of it fated to amount to little.

Elsewhere I have noted the particular inclination of European intellectuals, as well as social scientists, to dismiss most newer cults and sects as mere pseudoreligions. To a far greater extent than David Martin, most scholars treat them as unworthy of note (Stark and Bainbridge 1980). Moreover, for many European scholars *all* religions are unworthy of note. Hence their judgment about the state of religion often seems but gossip about their immediate social circle (a tendency frequent among American intellectuals as well). In any event, one must be wary of the reliability of reports of the decline of religion from sources who seem only too eager for the "post-religious era" to begin. Indeed, comparisons of "secularized" Europe with "still-pious" America too often seem intended primarily to reaffirm European claims to greater cultural maturity and enlightenment. Surely, this raises the possibility that reports on religion in Europe ought not be taken at face value.

Indeed, if it is true that Americans have tended to pay more attention to the formation of new cults and sects because they are close at hand, one must wonder why the center of such scholarship is not at one of the California universities, but is instead at All Souls College, Oxford. Clearly, the most important recent contributions to cult and sect literature, particularly case studies of specific groups, have been made by Bryan Wilson (1961, 1970, 1975a, 1981, 1982) and his circle of students (cf. Wallis 1975). This is true even for groups that originated in the United States. Thus it was Wilson's student Roy Wallis (1976) who wrote the first major scholarly study of Scientology. And, while Americans did the first important work on the Moonies (Lofland and Stark 1965; Lofland 1966), the more sustained study has been by Eileen Barker (1979, 1981a, 1981b) of the London School of Economics. These scholars did not need to fly to America to do their work. They found these groups well developed and close at hand.

In this essay I will attempt to show that expert opinion is wrong. It is true that in much of Europe the long dominant and established denominations have fallen on bad times—as have the highest status and most liberal Protestant bodies in America. However, fully in accord with our theory, secularization produces religious revival and innovation in Europe as well as in North America. That is, I intend to demonstrate, that the United States is not especially prolific of cult and sect movements; that many European nations are even more receptive to such movements than is America. Indeed, I shall show that many distinctively American cult and sect movements are doing better across the Atlantic (and the South Pacific as well) than they have ever done back home.

Lacking the resources to undertake a major research project, an effort to assess the prevalence of cults and sects in Europe is necessarily somewhat crude. One cannot simply go to the library and find material on cults and sects in Europe even slightly comparable with such works as J. Gordon Melton's *Encyclopedia of American Religions* (1978), with its more than 1,200 entries. Indeed, not even the telephone books for most of Europe offer the resources to be found in the Yellow Pages in America. Therefore, I have used a hodgepodge of sources, many of indifferent quality, and none of which attempted to be complete. Indeed many were compiled by believers who listed groups they liked, and did not list those they did not like. These biases will be discussed as each source is utilized.

Taken together, however, the inadequacies of the sources work *against* the conclusions. For the result surely is an undercount of deviant religious movements in Europe. If, despite this problem, I still can demonstrate that parts of Europe are more receptive to cults and sects than is the United States, I will take this to be very strong support of the theory.

A second bias against the theory is that often, because of the greater availability of good data, I shall be examining American-born religious movements in Europe. These groups usually have had much longer to build a following in America than abroad, and it also seems reasonable to suppose that movements tend to thrive more in their native habitats than in overseas missions. However, these data will be very useful to make comparisons *among* European nations—to draw conclusions about their relative receptivity to sects and cults.

A third possible bias is that persons leading novel religious movements may accept expert opinion and thus believe that the United States is more fertile soil than is Europe. Therefore, they may direct more effort into building a movement in America. For example, the Unification Church and the Hare Krishnas seem to have placed initial emphasis on their American operations.

In what follows, I first discuss a cult movement rate for England and Wales and compare this with the rate for the United States. I then consider data on the prevalence of Indian and Eastern cult centers and communities in most European nations. Next I examine data on several specific cult movements. I then give attention to the relative success of a number of American-based sects in Europe. Finally, I attempt to show that the cults and sects are concentrated in accord with the theory—that the cults thrive in the more secularized nations, while the sects make their greatest gains in the least secularized nations.

Before turning to the data, I must acknowledge the perils of cross-national studies. It is impossible to be an expert on each case utilized in studies based on a number of societies. Hence, to undertake such research is always to risk error. Moreover, comparative studies always place sociologists in conflict with specialists. The latter are rewarded for particularizing, for stressing how different their case (society) is from others. The sociologist is required to stress similarity and comparability. Thus, while a specialist might, for example, stress the ways in which the Haugian movement has made Norway's Lutheranism very different from that of Sweden, my task as a sociologist will be to note the deterioration of Lutheran State Churches all across Scandinavia. This is in no way to suggest that details such as Haugism are trivial, merely that they are not pertinent to the larger generalizations I seek here.

Cult Movements: England and Wales

Cult movements are religious organizations in a deviant religious *tradition* (Stark and Bainbridge 1979). This sets them apart from sects. The latter are deviant as organizations, but remain within a conventional religious tradition. For example, when a dissident faction breaks away from the Church of England in order to restore the traditional otherworldliness which the church has abandoned, this group is deviant. But it remains within a respectable religious tradition in England—Christianity. This leaves open the possibility that over time the group can cease to be deviant as it modifies its rejection of the surrounding society. But, when a group adheres to a deviant religious tradition—Hinduism in England, for example—it will remain deviant even if it becomes quite worldly. Not until or unless it grows large will it become a conventional faith. Sect movements, then, are new organizations of an old faith. Cults are new religions (at least new to the society in question). In terms of long range historical trends, cult movements are of greater interest than are sects. While sects are efforts to renew an old faith—to keep it going—cult movements are efforts to found new faiths.

All religions, including all of today's great world faiths, begin as tiny, deviant cults. In the beginning each seems trivial, and indeed most cult movements *are* fated for oblivion. But a few—Christianity, Islam, Buddhism—change the world. If we live in a time of advanced secularization of Christianity in the industrialized West, then our religious future may exist today much as Christianity did in A.D. 31—as a tiny and obscure group following a self-proclaimed messiah.

Given the importance of cult movements for the theory I would like to have a cult movements rate for every nation in Europe. For the United States I calculated such a rate by counting all the known cult movements and dividing the total by the population. Such a calculation is appropriate for comparing different areas. For a cult to form, a founding nucleus must be obtained. Clearly, the larger the population, the easier it will be to find enough such persons, and therefore, the greater the number of groups that can form. To compare areas without taking population into account is simply misleading. Thus, for example, California has long enjoyed a reputation as the cult center of the United States because so many cult groups are active there. But California also is the most populous of the United States. With population taken into account, California is only in third place in terms of cult movements, being surpassed by Nevada and New Mexico. Other West Coast states have nearly as much cult activity as California. I labor this point because I think much of the misperception of the United States as the center of cult and sect movements is due to a failure to take into account the great size of its population. Thus, for example, the United States undoubtedly has many more cult movements than does Denmark, just as California has 28 times as many cult movements as does Nevada. But California has more than 40 times the population of Nevada, as the United States has more than 40 times the population of Denmark. California's 167 cult movements therefore are proportionately less than Nevada's 6, but this will not be obvious *unless* rates are calculated. By the same token, a relatively small number of cults would indicate that Denmark was more receptive to cults than is the United States.

For the United States, as of the late 1970s, I computed that there were 2.3 independent cult movements in existence for every million Americans (Stark, Bainbridge, and Doyle 1979). It was only possible to compute this rate because of the immense previous work done by others, especially by Melton (1978), to compile the necessary data. For lack of adequate source material I was unable to compute a cult movement rate for nations on the European continent. But I was able to compute such a rate for England and Wales.

The most valuable source was a compilation of cult movements prepared by Stephen Annett (1976).[2] While an admirable work, Annett's sympathies lie with "New Age" and Eastern religions and he failed to include a substantial number of groups in other cult families, especially the magick[3] and witchcraft groups. I built upon Annett's work from a number of additional sources. One of these is a mimeographed *Occult Directory* compiled by Ken Ward, the North American corresponding secretary of the Ordo Templi Orientis Antiqua (in the Crowley tradition of magick), who lives in Saskatoon, Saskatchewan, Canada. The first edition of this directory came out in 1973 and supplements have appeared through 1976. Ward's directory understandably concentrates on American and Canadian groups, but includes a number of English groups as well. An additional source was *The Aquarian Guide to Occult, Mystical, Religious, Magical London and Around* (Strachan 1970). I also made much use of *A Pilgrim's Guide to the Planet Earth* (1981), which is described fully in the next section. I compiled the list of cult movements in England and Wales by cross-checking these sources to eliminate the transitory and trivial. I also drew on Melton's immense resources to determine where American-based groups had significant overseas branches.

Admittedly, a count of cult movements is not a count of cult members. While some of these groups are large and well established (Spiritualists, Theosophists, Mormons), having branches in many locations, others are very small, consisting of but one group meeting in one place. Furthermore, some of the groups are led by sincere believers, while others are led by cynical entrepreneurs. Most of these groups will never amount to much, but some already do.

Despite these great variations, close examination of all such groups reveals considerable commitment among their adherents. And it is for this reason I disagree with scholars who would dismiss cult movements as mere pseudoreligions—as superficial and insignificant. Indeed, one would reach rather an opposite impression from comparing the salience of their faith among, for example, Anglicans and Hare Krishnas. In any event, I have used the same criteria in selecting cult movements in England and Wales as we did for the United States. The two sets of data contain a reasonably similar mix of types and sizes. Indeed, the data for England and Wales underscore our conclusion, based on American and Canadian data, that where the bigger and older cults are one finds a host of smaller and newer ones.

The final list consisted of 153 cult movements operating in England and Wales. I am certain that this is a serious undercount. For one thing, I have no Black movements on the list such as the many forms of Vudon (we have very few of these in our American data either). I failed to find any UFO-based cult movements, but I am certain some exist. And I am equally sure that I have missed the greater proportion of the magick and witchcraft groups. These groups are extremely secretive, and it took Melton years to win sufficient trust among them in the United States so that he could secure good data.

Nevertheless, even with all these deficiencies, the rate for England and Wales is 3.2 cult movements per million population, which is substantially higher than the American rate of 2.3. *There is almost one additional cult per million in England and Wales than in the United States.*

It was this result that encouraged me to push on and to try to assess other parts of Europe to the extent data could be obtained. For, rather than presenting the theory with a problem, the state of religious deviance in England and Wales is as the theory would predict. The well-publicized weakness of conventional faith in Britain is producing many efforts to create or adapt new faiths.

Of course, this is not to say that cult movements have taken up all the slack left by the secularization of conventional faiths. The theory does not predict just when a new religion well suited to the market will arise and attract a mass following. It merely tells us where to look for such a new movement and why. And, when we look at England and Wales we see many current efforts to found and build such movements. Is the same true across the channel?

Indian and Eastern Cult Movements

I have already mentioned the potential bias of comparing Europe and America on the basis of religious movements that originated in the latter. But the reverse could also be biasing. That is, the United States would appear more receptive to deviant religion if Scientology membership were examined, while Europe could appear much more receptive if Anthroposophist membership were used. The most unbiased comparisons would be based on novel religious movements native neither to Europe nor to the United States. The recent influx of new religious movements from India and the East presents such a standard of comparison. Fortunately, I was able to obtain the most comprehensive international data on these particular groups.

For the past ten years a group calling itself Spiritual Publications, located in San Rafael, California, has been producing guides to "New Age" groups, centers, communities, bookstores, and restaurants. In 1979 the fourth edition of the *Spiritual Community Guide,* covering the United States and Canada, appeared. In other work we have made considerable use of rates based on these data (Bainbridge and Stark 1980; Stark and Bainbridge 1980). The very high correlations between these rates and many others lend confidence to the worth of the data. In 1981 this same group produced *A Pilgrim's Guide to Planet Earth,* attempting to provide the same kinds of lists for Europe.

The publishers of these guides are devotees of a variety of Hindu religious movements. In constructing their listings they gave primary emphasis to such groups. They also paid considerable attention to other Eastern faiths: Buddhism in its many forms, Jainism, and the like. In contrast, they seldom list groups in the Moslem tradition, and have been hit-or-miss in their coverage of new religions based on Western culture. Thus, for example, they list Theosophy, noting its links to the East, but seldom list the Unification Church despite its Korean origins, perhaps because of its strongly Christian emphasis.

Since it is clear that listings outside the Eastern and Indian traditions were inconsistent and incomplete (more so for Europe than for the United States), it was appropriate to edit all the listings to count only groups within the Indian and Eastern traditions. I also chose to ignore occult bookstores, health food restaurants, and the like, and to count only religious organizations—centers where cult members regularly gather and communities (primarily communes) organized on the basis of common religious practice.

Some of the centers listed are branches of a single cult organization such as 3HO. But many have no actual ties to a larger organization and are independent, local, cult organizations. However, whether independent groups, or branches of a larger organization, the simple density of these centers and communities is clear indication of the receptivity of an area to cult movements imported from India and the East.[4]

Having edited the listings for each nation, I then computed rates, dividing the number of listings by the population to produce the number of these centers and communities per million. I was forced to omit Norway and Portugal from these computations because it was obvious that the Spiritual Community people had failed to cover them adequately.[5]

Many interesting comparisons appear in table 1. But, of most significance, is the American-European comparison: Europe's rate is significantly higher! Given that the Spiritual Community editors had been working on their American data for at least a decade, while the European data are their initial effort, the undercount of Europe ought to be greater and the true difference even larger.

Moreover, the European rate is depressed by inclusion of Spain and Italy, very populous nations which we would expect to be much lower in cults than the United States. And, in fact, the truly revealing

comparisons are nation to nation. Only three nations of Western
Europe (Italy, Spain, and Belgium) have rates lower than the United
States. Most of the others have considerably higher rates—and the rates
tend to rise the further north the nation. Switzerland has the highest
rate (later in this paper I devote a section to Switzerland as a deviant
case), followed by Scotland and Denmark. I expected England and
Wales to surpass the United States rate, as they do, but I was surprised
to see France also well above America. This reminds us of the waves of
occultism in French history (Darnton 1970; McIntosh 1972) and the
intimate connections between the occult and revolutionary traditions in
France, and, indeed, in Europe more generally (cf. Billington 1980).

At the bottom of the table we show the other "English-speaking
democracies." The Canadian rate is close to that of the United States,
but Australia and New Zealand far surpass all other nations for which I
have rates. While this surprised me, it did not surprise the editors of the
Guide. Of Melbourne, they wrote: "Generally accepted to be the 'yoga
capital of the world,' Melbourne houses more yoga schools per capita
than any other city on the planet" (1981, 258).

But it is not simply yoga-mania that gives Australia its high rate. All
manner of Indian and Eastern faiths abound there—a pattern confirmed in the other data to be examined. New Zealand is much the
same.

Looking within Europe we see that the three nations with the lowest
rates are overwhelmingly Catholic countries in which the church
remains very vigorous (unlike Catholic France, where the church is
much weaker). Impressionistically, at least, the data pattern is in accord
with what are believed to be greater and lesser degrees of secularization.
Great Britain and Scandinavia are higher, southern Europe is low
(Martin 1978). That Spain has the lowest rate prompts mention of the
fact that until 1967 it was illegal for any non-Catholic religion to
operate openly in Spain, and it was not until 1970 that the 1967 act of
religious tolerance was actually implimented. Prior to this time only the
most militant non-Catholic groups attempted to operate in Spain,
primarily the Jehovah's Witnesses and the Pentecostals. Yet, in only a
decade Spain has caught up with Italy in terms of Indian and Eastern
cult centers—a "catch-up" that will be seen in other tables as well. In
the conclusion I shall discuss more fully the impact of state repression
on deviant religious movements as well as the impact of strong state
churches.

Overall, these data do much to dispell the notion of America as the

**Table 1: Indian and Eastern Cult Centers and Communities
Per Million Population**

	Number	Rate per million
Denmark	16	3.1
Sweden	21	2.5
Finland	13	2.8
England and Wales	146	3.0
Scotland	18	3.2
West Germany	85	1.4
Netherlands	28	2.0
Austria	16	2.1
Switzerland	23	3.8
France	133	2.5
Belgium	10	1.0
Italy	38	.7
Spain	23	.6
Europe*	573	1.8
United States	290	1.3
Canada	35	1.5
Australia	77	5.3
New Zealand	16	5.2

*Total population based only on nations listed above

land of novel religious movements, while Europe leads the way into an enlightened future. Imported faiths from Asia seem to be doing even better in much of Western Europe than in the United States. I think these data justify my unwillingness to accept learned opinion. Rather than a lack of cults in Europe calling our theory into question, it appears that our theory accurately has called into question the notion that there are but few cult movements in Europe. But many other data remain to be assessed. These too challenge the image of America as the land of cults.

Scientology

Scientology is an American-born movement, the creation of L. Ron Hubbard, an American science fiction author with a background in the occult. Scientology began as a secular psychological therapy movement, but soon evolved into a full-fledged religious movement (Wallis 1976; Bainbridge and Stark 1980). Scientology operates out of a large number of small centers. But these are subordinated to Scientology churches, rather as parish churches are subordinated to a cathedral. As of 1979 there were 51 Scientology churches worldwide. Of these 23 were in the United States, 14 in European nations, and 14 in Canada, South Africa, New Zealand, and Australia.

Table 2 reports the distribution of Scientology churches in terms of rates per million population. Also shown are the number of Scientology staff members in each nation, also computed as rates per million (Church of Scientology 1978). Of course, the data on churches are based on very small numbers of cases and thus are potentially subject to considerable random fluctuation. But the staff data represent a very large number of cases, 1,527 staff members in Europe alone, and thus will be very reliable statistically. As it turned out, the rates based on churches are reliable, too, for both sets of data tell precisely the same story (r » .95). Denmark, Sweden and the United Kingdom are high, as they were on Indian and Eastern cults, while France, Belgium, the Netherlands, and Austria are low.

The American origins of Scientology do show up in the higher overall rates for the United States as compared with Europe. However, Denmark and Sweden surpass the United States in receptivity to Scientology, while Canada, Australia, and New Zealand also equal or surpass America. Once again we see that the popular image of the United States as the land of cults is inaccurate. Other nations, including some in Europe, are even more fertile ground for religious novelty.

Hare Krishna

Appearances to the contrary, Hare Krishna is essentially an American-born cult movement, founded in 1965 by A.C. Bhaktivedanta Swami

Table 2: Scientology and Hare Krishna

		Scientology Churches	Scientology Staff		Hare Krishna Temples
	N	Churches per Million Population	Staff Members per Million Population	N	Temples per Million Population
Denmark	3	.59	50.0	1	.20
Sweden	3	.36	16.4	3	.36
United Kingdom	5	.09	10.5	3	.05
West Germany	1	.02	4.5	3	.05
Netherlands	1	.07	2.5	1	.07
Austria			2.7	1	.13
Switzerland			14.3	1	.16
France	1	.02	2.7		
Belgium			2.0	2	.10
Italy				2	.04
Europe	14	.07*	6.9**	17	.08***
United States	23	.10	17.9	33	.15
Canada	4	.17	18.3	7	.29
Australia	4	.27	13.9	6	.41
New Zealand	1	.32	17.7	2	.65

*Population of Europe includes only nations with a Scientology church
**Population of Europe includes only nations having a staff member
***Population of Europe includes only nations having a temple

Prabhupda. Although Bhaktivedanta developed his religious ideas in India, it was only after coming to the States that he recruited a following and launched his now-familiar cult movement. Still, the movement presents itself as of ancient Hindu lineage and indeed has diverted substantial resources to establishing the movement in India. Despite the irony of American converts teaching Hinduism to Hindus, the movement has in fact been rather successful in attracting an Indian following. Moreover, the movement has made strides in becoming a worldwide phenomenon, now having temples on every inhabited continent (Shinn 1982).

As with Scientology churches, rates based on Hare Krishna temples suffer from the small number of cases involved. That the Scientology church rates correlated almost perfectly with the rates based on staff lends credibility to the Hare Krishna data as well. It is possible, of course, that rates based on organizations and staffs might not reflect true differences in membership. It seems likely, however, that religious movements will tend to build temples and station staff where they are strong and spurn places where they are weaker. For some other groups examined later in this essay, data were available on actual membership as well as on congregations, and the two kinds of rates give the same result. Finally, the many quite different cult movement rates discussed in this paper correlate very highly, thus lending credibility to one another. Indeed, that is why I examine so many different sources of data. Each can be criticized. Taken together, however, they become credible.

Once again, in table 2, the same nations stand out for being high and low. While the overall United States rate for the American-based Hare Krishna movement is significantly higher than the rate for Europe, Denmark and Sweden noticeably exceed the American rate. Switzerland and Austria are about the same as the United States, and Italy and Spain are low. New Zealand has the highest rate of all, and Australia is also very high.

Christian Science

Elsewhere I have made considerable use of data on Christian Science to assess cult receptivity (Stark, Bainbridge, and Kent 1981; Stark and Bainbridge 1981), and I had anticipated doing so in this study of Europe as well. But, when I examined current data on Christian Science, I discovered it was too late. Everywhere, Christian Science is a movement in rapid decline. I shall give extended attention to the rise and decline of Christian Science in a forthcoming essay. Here it is sufficient to point out that social "ruins" can reveal very important facts, but only about the past and only after careful reconstruction. This is not the place for such an undertaking, and Europe's residual Christian

Science congregations do not reflect current religious conditions with any clarity.

Mormons

The Mormons are the most successful and significant of all the novel religious movements initiated in America. They have maintained a substantial rate of growth for 150 years. Their high fertility offsets both mortality and defection, while they continue to attract many new converts. Mormon data are not useful for assessment of local receptivity to cult movements within the United States, because the Mormons are highly concentrated in the West through massive migration, not through local recruitment (Stark and Bainbridge, and Kent 1981). A reverse problem mars the comparison of Mormonism in Europe and America. Until after World War I converts to Mormonism were assisted in immigrating to the United States. Thus, despite high rates of recruitment by Mormon missionaries in Europe (especially in Scandinavia), no local Mormon congregations sprang up. Instead, European Mormonism remained a scattering of missionaries as the waves of converts boarded ships headed West. Following World War I, Mormons ceased urging immigration on European converts and in recent decades have discouraged it. Still, European congregations are of deceptively recent vintage.

Nevertheless, by 1977 there was more than 150,000 Mormons in Europe. Table 4 converts these statistics into national rates per million population. The findings are very like those for Indian and Eastern cult centers and movements. Indeed, the two sets of rates are highly correlated ($r = .77$, based only on the European nations and excluding Switzerland, for reasons I take up later). The United Kingdom and Scandinavia are quite high in their Mormon rates, and the rates fall the further south the nation in Europe. Canada and Australia also have quite high rates, and New Zealand actually surpasses the United States. Much of the Mormon success in New Zealand is among the Maori population. Indeed, the Mormons are doing extremely well in the whole South Pacific, especially in Samoa.

I did not expect to find Mormonism more successful in Europe than in America, and, in fact, the European rate is much lower. But I think the Mormon data are a valid guage of the relative receptivity of various nations of Europe to novel religious movements. Indeed, where the exotic religious movements of India and the East abound, where

Scientology and Hare Krishna also cluster, there one finds the higher rates of Mormon membership.

Seventh Day Adventists and Jehovah's Witnesses

At least thirty-three American religious bodies can be traced back to the "Great Disappointment" of 22 October 1844 when the millennium failed to occur. It was the second time that year that thousands of followers of William Miller had gathered, many garbed in white ascension robes, to greet the Second Advent. When nothing happened the Millerites splintered into many groups, most of them intent on converting the faithless (Festinger *et al.* 1956).

The first major group to emerge in the aftermath of the failed prophesy were the Seventh-Day Adventists. They were led by Mother Ellen G. White who claimed divine inspiration for reforming Christianity in order to usher in the Second Coming. Today this group has 3.4 million members worldwide in 21,327 congregations. Only 17% of members and of congregations are in the United States.

In 1879 Charles Taze Russell, who had reworked Miller's original calculations, launched a new movement to prepare for the Second Coming in 1914. Adopting the name Jehovah's Witnesses, the group aimed to convert a band of "elect" Christians who would ascend in glory. In 1914 the world did not end, but World War I was interpreted as the onset of the Apocalypse. By the war's end, Russell was dead. His followers evolved a new doctrine concerning the start of an invisible rule of Christ in 1914 and began extremely intense missionary work under the slogan, "Many now living will never die." Today the Jehovah's Witnesses have 2.2 million members, 25% of them in the United States.

These groups pose a problem of classification: Are they sects or cult movements? Each claims full membership in the Christian family—indeed, each tends to claim to be *the* Christian church. Yet, many cults also claim direct Christian descent. The Mormons, Moonies, and Christian Scientists do not reject the Old and New Testaments. They are cults, however, because they add a significant amount of deviant culture to the Christian tradition—in effect each has added a third testament and recent revelations. The Seventh Day Adventists and the Jehovah's Witnesses do not possess third testaments. Yet, each has added a good deal of novel, modern prophesy to traditional Christian doctrine, and each remains ardently pre-millennial (although now each

Table 3: Mormons per Million Population

	Rate per million
Denmark	786
Sweden	700
Finland	775
Norway	845
England and Wales	1353
Scotland	1678
West Germany	423
Netherlands	531
Austria	361
Switzerland	770
France	204
Belgium	356
Italy	105
Spain	67
Portugal	108
Europe	481
United States	11,001
Canada	3036
Australia	2327
New Zealand	11,725

prohibits "date setting"). Moreover, both groups are markedly and very visibly deviant. Seventh-Day Adventists observe extremely strict norms of Sabbath-keeping and indeed have moved the Sabbath back to Saturday. They also stress vegetarianism. The Jehovah's Witnesses refuse military service, will not swear oaths or salute flags, reject blood transfusions, and are highly visible as door-to-door and street corner missionaries.

Thus, each of these groups is near the borderline between sect and

TABLE 4: Seventh-Day Adventist and Jehovah's
Witnesses Congregations Per Million

	Seventh-Day Adventists Congregations per million	Jehovah's Witnesses Congregations per million
Denmark	10.78	44.90
Sweden	6.59	37.11
Finland	11.49	53.40
Norway	18.25	45.50
United Kingdom	2.68	20.84
West Germany	6.37	23.43
Netherlands	3.33	20.21
Austria	5.47	28.80
Switzerland	9.37	36.19
France	)	22.28
	) 2.14	
Belgium	)	28.67
Italy	1.26	23.02
Spain	1.19	20.03
Portugal	5.05	40.10
Europe	3.67	25.28
United States	16.46	34.16
Canada	10.71	43.74
Australia	)	36.83
	) 24.43	
New Zealand	)	38.39

1979 more than 650 American and Canadian mission organizations spent well over $1 billion to support more than 40,000 missionaries abroad. The primary emphasis is on missions to Africa, Latin America, and Asia (there are more than 10,000 mission congregations in

Korea alone). But there has also been a remarkable shift from earlier mission days: Today a substantial missionary effort is devoted to Europe.

Even in the nineteenth century some of the more radical American sects gave high priority to European mission work (Wilson 1970), thus reversing the historic flow of religious novelty from Europe to America. But in recent times Europe has become a major mission field even for conventional and well-established evangelical Protestant bodies such as the Southern Baptist Convention, the largest Protestant denomination in the United States.

Data from all American and Canadian Protestant overseas missions are collected by World Vision of Monrovia, California, and published every several years in the *Mission Handbook*. I consulted the most recent (12th) edition. I found not only annual budgets and the number of personnel assigned to each nation by a given group, but also the number of mission-supported congregations in each nation. These provide a firm basis for assessing the full impact of North American Protestant sects overseas. After careful editing to remove groups that merely provide services (such as tracts and audio-visual materials) to local congregations, and to remove several inappropriate groups,[6] I was able to compute rates that ought to be very accurate—the number of American and Canadian evangelical Protestant mission congregations per million population. These are shown in table 5.

Here we can see a quite dramatic shift in the data. America's Protestant sects are not making their greatest inroads in the same places as are the cult movements. They are virtually absent from Scandinavia. Since the data are based on such a large number of evangelical missions, who have established a huge number of churches in some European nations, the zero rates for Finland and Norway are extremely meaningful, as are the near zero rates for Denmark and Sweden. North American sects are also obtaining some success in the United Kingdom, West Germany, the Netherlands, and Austria. And, once again Switzerland exhibits a huge rate—forty-three mission congregations for every million Swiss. As we move south the reverse trend is obvious. France has a high rate of mission congregations. But overall, North American evangelical missions are doing the best in the solidly Catholic Latin nations—Portugal and Italy are numbers two and three in terms of mission congregations per million. Even Spain, long virtually impossible for foreign faiths to penetrate because of government restrictions, shows a substantial number of mission congregations and exceeds seven of the fourteen European nations included in the table. Similarly, while

New Zealand and Australia have consistently displayed high cult rates, they show only medium-level mission rates.

Another way to look at these data is that Denmark, Sweden, and Finland have many more Indian and Eastern centers and communities than they have mission congregations (I could not compute this cult rate for Norway, but since Norway is known to have some of these cults the same generalization holds). For other nations of Europe the reverse is true.

I must caution against over-interpreting these data. They certainly do not show that there are no sect movements active in Scandinavia, for many vigorous sects are to be found there (cf. Mol 1972). What the data do show is that, while American evangelical groups continue to

Table 5: North American Evangelical Protestant Mission Congregations Per Million

	N	Rate per million
Denmark	3	.59
Sweden	1	.12
Finland	0	.00
Norway	0	.00
United Kingdom	213	3.89
West Germany	266	4.34
Netherlands	68	4.82
Austria	57	7.60
Switzerland	272	43.17
France	1143	21.31
Belgium	64	6.53
Italy	1624	28.49
Spain	225	6.00
Portugal	400	41.24
Australia	128	8.76
New Zealand	21	6.77

send missionaries to Scandinavia (55 to Sweden and 43 to Finland, for example), they have failed to have significant results in terms of founding congregations. Even the Assemblies of God, who have thousands of congregations in Western Europe, and who even have large numbers in Eastern Europe, have none in Scandinavia. But where the sects have failed, the cults have thrived.

Measures of Cult Strength

We have examined a variety of measures of cult activity in Europe. Some seem better measures than others. The Indian and Eastern centers rate overcomes the bias of American-origins. The Mormon data are better than those for Scientology and Hare Krishna simply by being based on large numbers of cases thus lending statistical reliability. The Jehovah's Witnesses rates, and especially those for Seventh-Day Adventists, suffer from ambiguity over the status of these groups as cults or sects.

Table 6 permits examination of the correlations among these six sets of rates. That data are limited to European nations (Switzerland is excluded as will be discussed later). The correlations reveal the relative worth of various rates as measures of cult activity. The Indian and Eastern cult rates are very highly correlated with the Mormon rates. The Indian and Eastern rates also are highly correlated with those for Scientology and Jehovah's Witnesses, but fall short of significance with the Hare Krishna rates. The Seventh-Day Adventist rates are negatively correlated with *all* others. Clearly, this group does not measure cult strength, and we shall drop it from further analysis. Given the small number of cases, these are powerful results indeed.

Churches, Sects, and Cults

The theory suggests that cults will thrive where conventional religions are weaker while sects will be more active where conventional religion is stronger. In previous research we have found that a variety of cult rates for the United States and Canada are very strongly negatively correlated with rates of membership in conventional churches. But we have found the correlation reverses for sects.

Does the same hold in Europe? Initially, on the surface, it would appear so. It is widely believed that the Scandinavian churches suffer from advanced secularization, while those of Southern Europe retain

Table 6: Correlations (r) Among Cult Measures (Europe Only)

	Indian and Eastern Centers	Mormons	Scientology Churches	Scientology Staff	Hare Krishna	Jehovah's Witnesses	Seventh-Day Adventists
Indian & Eastern	X	.77**	.55**	.54**	.33	.53**	−.13
Mormons		X	.37*	.37*	.24	.30	−.22
Scientology Churches			X	.95**	.75**	.32	−.39*
Scientology Staff				X	.60**	.30	−.29
Hare Krishna					X	.15	−.22
Jehovah's Witnesses						X	−.27
Seventh-Day Adventists							X

** p .05
* p .10
N varies from 11 to 13 depending upon missing data. Units of analysis are: Denmark, Sweden, Finland, Norway, United Kingdom, West Germany, Netherlands, Austria, France, Belgium, Italy, Spain, and Portugal.

considerable vigor. But first impressions can be wrong. Indeed, one purpose of this paper is to show that the impression of America as unusually prone to sects and cults is wrong.

In 1968 the Gallup Poll published the results of surveys taken in a number of nations (Sigelman 1977). One item asked: "Do you attend church in a typical week?" Eight of the nations included in our present study were among those polled by Gallup. Comparable data could be located for four others (Mol 1972). These confirm the impressions of differential secularization. Church attendance is very low in Scandinavia (Norway's 14% reporting weekly attendance is by far the highest), substantially higher in the Germanic nations, and higher again in the Catholic South.

Table 7 reveals stunning support for the major hypotheses. Each of the cult measures is strongly negatively correlated with rates of church attendance. Indeed, despite the small number of cases, five of the six are highly statistically significant. Moreover, since this represents six

Table 7: Correlations (r) of Cult and Sect Rates with Rate of Weekly Church Attendance

	Population Attending Church Weekly	
	(%)	
	r	significance
Cult Measures		
Indian and Eastern Cult Centers	−.82	.002
Mormon Membership	−.69	.009
Scientology Churches	−.55	.04
Scientology Staff	−.53	.05
Hare Krishna	−.27	NS
Jehovah's Witnesses	−.71	.006

Sect Measure		
Rate of North American Protestant Mission Congregations	.69	.009

N varies from 10 to 11 depending on missing data. Units of analysis are the same as in table 6, except Spain and Portugal are not included.

independent tests of the hypotheses, the multiplication rule is applicable, which means that the odds that these are chance results are extremely small. Clearly, in Europe as in the United States and Canada, the cults cluster where the churches are weakest. Keep in mind that we are measuring the weakness of the conventional religious *organizations*, not widespread rejection of religious ideas and beliefs. Gallup also asked about belief in God. In all of these nations a very large majority expressed belief in God, and international variations were minor, especially in contrast with differences in church attendance. Thus in Scandinavia the bulk of the population is effectively unchurched, but continues to credit the existence of the supernatural. What better potential converts to a new religion?

Below the broken line in the table we see data bearing on the second major hypothesis: Sects will cluster where the churches remain stronger. This, too, is strongly supported by a large, significant positive correlation between rates of Protestant mission congregations and church attendance.

In addition to weekly church attendance, there is available an inferential measure of the strength of conventional religion: Of all new books published in a year, the proportion that are on religious topics. The use of these figures (which are published annually in the United Nations' *Statistical Yearbook*) as a cross-national indicator of religious commitment was first suggested by Robert Wuthnow (1977). By basing the rate on all new books published per year, rather than on population, it is possible to overcome extreme variations across nations in the number of books they publish (smaller nations tend to have much higher per capital publication rates). However, it is clear that this measure leaves much to be desired. It does not tell us how many people read these books or the relative sales of religion books vis-à-vis others. Nor do we know anything of the contents of these books beyond their designation as dealing with "religion." Thus many could in fact be cult movement books. If so, this would work against our hypothesis.

I chose to examine this measure because it permits the inclusion of several nations for whom I do not have church attendance statistics, and because it lets me assess the potential use of the measure in other research. Thus table 8 re-examines the findings shown in table 7 with religious books substituted for church attendance. The findings are weaker, but sustain the same conclusions. Cults cluster in nations with proportionately low rates of religious book publishing, while the reverse is true for sects. Had this been the only measure of secularization available, it would have confirmed the hypotheses, albeit with less statistical power. This is particularly interesting because the correlation between the church attendance rates and the religious publication rates is not especially strong (.26) and, on so few cases, falls well short of statistical significance. I cautiously conclude that this inferential measure of national religious commitment can be used in cross-national research, but, being a somewhat weaker measure than church attendance, care must be taken about rejecting hypotheses that might well be supported by more adequate data.

The theory also suggests that cult and sect rates will be negatively correlated. Table 9 strongly supports this prediction. All correlations are in the right direction, most individually achieve significance, and once again the multiplication rule is applicable producing a high level of overall significance. Thus data for Europe support my fundamental view that church and sect coexist, while cults challenge where both church and sect are weakening.

Table 8: Correlations (r) of Cult and Sect Rates with Religious Book Publication Rate (Europe Only)

	Proportion of all books published that are on religious topics	
	r	significance
Cult Measures		
Indian and Eastern		
Cult Centers	−.58	.03
Mormon Membership	−.26	NS
Scientology Churches	−.40	.10
Scientology Staff	−.38	.13
Hare Krishna	−.51	.05
Jehovah's Witnesses	−.03	NS

Sect Measure		
Rate of North American		
Protestant Mission		
Congregations	.21	NS

N varies from 11 to 13 depending on missing data. Units of analysis are the same as in table 6.

Switzerland: Exploring a Deviant Case

Nations are not ideal units for analysis, for they are often so heteroge-neous. For example, the rates presented here for the United States and Canada obscure the vast internal variations that have been the subject of a number of our recent studies. Had it been possible, I would have preferred to use European cities, or at least provinces, as our units of analysis in this paper—thus working with units of relatively equal area and population and having some degree of cultural unity. But I could only create rates for nations. I therefore am comparing some tiny and relatively homogeneous societies (e.g., Denmark and Finland) with some that are very large and often quite diverse. Diversity can produce misleading averages. Thus, for example, in our study of the United States, New Mexico turned up as a highly deviant case having both a very high cult rate and a very high church-membership rate. Looking inside New Mexico, county by county, revealed that the hypothesized correlation existed: Counties high in church membership lacked cults; the few counties with very low church-membership rates had the cults. Summed up, however, New Mexico distorted the correlations across states.

A similar problem arose in this study because of Switzerland. Switzerland excels on all measures. It is number one in its rate of publishing religious books, has a high level of church attendance, has the highest rate of sect congregations, stands first on Indian and East-ern Centers, and stands high on Jehovah's Witnesses, Seventh-Day Adventists, Mormons, and Hare Krishna temples. With Switzerland included, the correlations shown in tables 6 through 9 are changed substantially, for Switzerland always sits far from the slope of the correlation badly distorting it. Given large numbers of cases, some such anomalies could be ignored, for they would have less impact. With no more than fourteen cases available, one extremely deviant case has ruinous effects. Therefore I have excluded Switzerland from these analyses.

This decision would be justified even if I lacked all insight into why Switzerland is so deviant. But, in fact, there are indications that Switzerland is the New Mexico of Europe—that its extraordinary heterogeneity produces strange averages.

Switzerland is, in many vital ways, several nations. It is about equal-ly divided between Catholics and Protestants, and into four distinctive language groups: German, French, Italian, and a form of Latin. Moreover, language and religion combine to form geographical

Table 9: Correlations (r) of Cult Rates with the Sect Rate (Europe Only)

	Rate of North America Protestant Mission Congregations	
	r	significance
Cult Measures		
Indian and Eastern Cult Centers	−.45	.08
Mormon Membership	−.62	.01
Scientology Churches	−.34	.12
Scientology Staff	−.32	.14
Hare Krishna	−.37	.10
Jehovah's Witnesses	−.17	NS

N varies from 11 to 13 depending on missing data. Units of analysis are the same as in table 6.

units of considerable solidarity. Indeed, if any nation is likely to be too heterogeneous to serve as a useful unit of analysis, it is Switzerland.

Overall, however, Switzerland seems a nation in which the conventional Protestant and Catholic churches are still relatively vigorous. Campiche (1972) reports levels of church attendance that are substantially higher than those reported for most of Northern Europe and Scandinavia (cf. Mol 1972; Sigelman 1977). But why, then, does Switzerland score so high on all of the cult measures?

To answer that question I sought means to examine internal variations in Switzerland's cult rates. Few adequate data could be obtained. Those I have, however, tell a clear and convincing story.

Returning to the data on Indian and Eastern cult centers, I determined the city in which each of Switzerland's twenty-three cult centers is located. Ten of them were in Geneva! This is an extraordinary number given that Geneva is a rather small city having only about 175,000 people in the 1970 census (and it since has become less populous). Translated into a rate this produces the astonishing figure of 57.5 cult centers per million. I know of no other city with anything like this level of cult receptivity. For the sake of comparison, San Francisco, America's cult capital, has a rate of 19.8 Indian and Eastern centers per million, while Los Angeles has a rate of only five per million. Indeed, London only has a rate of 6.9, Copenhagen's rate is 16 per million, and Stockholm's is 19.9.

Geneva is truly off the scale in terms of cult centers. If we simply excluded Geneva from the Swiss data, the nation's Indian and Eastern cult center rate drops to 2.1 per million. This is not a remarkable rate, indeed it is the same as that of Austria. Thus, one city raises Switzerland's rank among European nations from the lower half to the top of the list. It might be argued that Geneva's rate is mere artifact, that for some reason the Spiritual Community people simply were much more thorough in discovering Geneva's cult centers than they were elsewhere. This seems unlikely, however, because the same finding turns up when Mormon data are examined.

Because the boundaries of Mormon congregations do not always conform to Swiss political boundaries, I could not compute membership rates for each canton or for each major city. Fortunately, I could do so for Geneva and for several other major Swiss cities. The Mormon data are gathered and reported with great care (and are subject to audits), and thus can be taken as very reliable. Once again, the national rate is greatly inflated by Geneva. While Geneva has little more than 2% of the population of Switzerland, it accounts for *12% of the nation's Mormons*. Geneva has 2,406 Mormons per million, while Zurich, the largest city in Switzerland, has only 1,573 Mormons per million. Keep in mind that Zurich is *not* a bastion of Swiss resistance to religious innovation. In terms of Indian and Eastern cult centers, Zurich ranks number two among major Swiss cities with a rate of 11.8 per million. Thus, it is not that Zurich is so low in cult centers or in Mormons, but that Geneva is so extraordinarily high.

Since two independent measures reveal that it is Geneva that is greatly inflating Switzerland's apparent receptivity to new religious movements, it seems appropriate to examine more closely John Calvin's old stronghold. What makes Geneva so receptive to cult movements? Table 10 offers some very suggestive answers. There we see data for the nine major cities of Switzerland, all having populations of 50,000 or more.

Of particular interest is the column reporting the percent with "no religion." Overall, 1.1% of the Swiss reported their religion as "none" in the 1970 census. Another 0.4% gave no answer, which also is taken to indicate no religious affiliation. And, 0.1% gave their religion as "other." Published data for individual cities lump these three categories together. Examination of these data for each canton, however, suggests

Table 10: Comparing Swiss Cities (50,000 and Larger)

	Indian and Eastern cult centers per million	No Religion %	Protestant %	German Speaking %	Jews per million
Geneva	57.5	8.0	37.8	11.3	79,551
Zurich	11.8	3.6	55.0	82.7	12,947
Basel	9.4	5.1	51.3	81.8	9,723
Lausanne	7.2	4.1	54.8	8.7	10,175
Bern	0.0	2.5	71.3	82.3	3,463
Biel	0.0	1.7	62.2	56.5	2,781
Lucerne	0.0	1.7	20.8	87.8	5,866
St. Gall	0.0	2.0	42.2	86.3	3,346
Winterthur	0.0	2.8	62.8	83.4	892

that the mix in each is about the same—that is, about one "other" for every ten "nones" and five "no answers." Thus, what is being measured here is almost wholly a lack of religious affiliation. According to our theory, cults should be clustered where the defection from conventional religion is highest. And, indeed, in our study of Canada we found that the proportion reporting no religious affiliation to the census was an excellent measure of secularization. The same relationship can be seen in table 10. Geneva greatly excels, not just in cult centers, but in the proportion without religious affiliations. And, in fact, the correlation between these two rates is .92, significant beyond the .001 level.

The table also shows that Calvin's Geneva is no longer a Protestant city, being predominantly Roman Catholic. Catholicism, however, has no overall connection with cult activity when all nine cities are examined. Geneva also is a French-speaking city (64%) and two of the top four Swiss cities in terms of cult centers are French-speaking. But, like Catholicism, French seems unrelated to cults, overall.

However, the proportion of Jews is extraordinarily related to cult activity (.99). The four cities with cult centers greatly exceed the other five in terms of their Jewish populations, and Geneva has more than six times the proportion of Jews as the next highest city. What do Jews have to do with receptivity to cults? Elsewhere I have discussed at length studies showing that Jews are unusually likely to join cult movements, especially those which include little or no Christian culture (Stark 1981; Stark and Bainbridge 1985). Larry Shinn (1982) has found that more than 30% of Hare Krishna converts in the United States are from Jewish backgrounds, and the proportion of Jews probably exceeds 50% in the upper levels of this group. J. Gordon Melton (1980) has found very substantial Jewish over-representation in pagan, magick, and witchcraft groups. Of further interest, not one of those with Jewish backgrounds in Melton's data had come from an Orthodox home. For a variety of historical reasons, persons raised in Jewish homes, especially persons who today are young adults, were quite likely to have been raised in secularity. That is, their parents were only cultural, not religious, Jews. People raised in irreligious homes are highly prone to convert to a religion as adults (Stark and Bainbridge 1985). Since this has been more common for people with Jewish than Christian backgrounds, Jews are unusually vulnerable to new religions. However, the long conflict between Christians and Jews makes even cultural Jews reluctant to embrace Christianity—or even cults that extend the Christian tradition such as the Moonies. Hence Jews have been extremely receptive to Indian and Eastern cult movements. Since these are the groups measured in table 10, I think the very high correlation with Jewish population rates is as substantively, as it is statistically, significant.

To sum up: Geneva is a highly secularized city, quite out of step with the levels of religious commitment prevailing in other parts of Switzerland. It has such high cult rates it inflates the national rate greatly. In effect, then, Switzerland is the New Mexico of Western Europe. However, an internal analysis of Swiss data serves to replicate our other findings. Secularization of the conventional faiths does prompt a good deal of religious experimentation.

Conclusion

I believe I have adequately accomplished the primary aims in this paper. I have found considerable evidence that cults do abound in the most secularized parts of Europe as our theory would predict. Moreover, sect activity seems clustered where the conventional churches remain strongest. But, I hardly suggest that secularization is the only factor affecting the amount of religious variety or novelty in societies. Other factors also bear on religious economies.

The case of Spain shows that state repression can strongly limit at least the public activities of deviant religious movements. Moreover, to the extent that religious dissent is forced underground, recruitment will be impeded. If it is risky to admit to others that one is committed to an illicit faith, it will thereby be more difficult to recruit others. Of course, no amount of state repression will eliminate all religious deviance. The medieval state could not, nor could Franco Spain. While the jails of Spain housed many Jehovah's Witnesses, they still gathered a significant following which burst forth into public view in 1970 when it became legal to establish Kingdom Halls. Nor have the secret police in the Soviet bloc stamped out religious dissent. The Jehovah's Witnesses do not publish nation-by-nation figures on congregations and members behind the Iron Curtain, but they admit having 3,896 illegal congregations. The Assemblies of God report truly substantial numbers of congregations in Poland (5.7 per million), Czechosolvakia (6.0), Bulgaria (24.1) and Romania (37.4). In contrast they report only 2.4 for West Germany and 13.3 for Italy. This logically leads to a discussion of the influence of left-wing politics.

It is widely recognized that left-wing politics often serve as a functional alternative to sect and cult movements (cf. Martin 1978; Stark 1964). To the extent that nations have serious left-wing political movements, some of the energy that might otherwise have been channelled into religion will be diverted. To the extent, then, that the left is far stronger in many European nations than in Canada and the United States, comparisons of sect and cult rates will be influenced— without as much radicalism, the more secularized European nations ought to be even higher than they are on cults, and Southern Europe ought to be even more receptive to sects.

But, as I suggest elsewhere, this pattern changes dramatically if radical regimes come to power (Stark and Bainbridge 1982). The facts of relative deprivation persist. The zeal and sense of purpose that once found outlet in efforts to make the revolution now find no effective secular expression. Thus, while left *politics* divert potential religious impulses, left *regimes* reanimate them. And, it is this I think can be read in the data on Jehovah's Witnesses in Eastern Europe and the high rates of Assemblies of God congregations. Note also that the rates are lowest in the two East European nations that are most restive under their Communist regimes (Poland and Czechoslovakia), and where it would appear that the Catholic church retains greater integrity and independence. The Assemblies of God rates are very high indeed in Romania and Bulgaria, in comparison. There, perhaps, it could be argued that religion is substituting for political resistance—or indeed that religion is the form taken by political resistance.

Established state-supported churches also influence the variety within religious economies even if they do not invoke the repressive powers of the state to limit competition. For one thing they can continue to appear dominant despite serious defection, for their funding is not via voluntary contributions. Thus in Germany, for example, the Lutheran and Catholic clergy are civil servants. This easily can encourage widespread notions that religion is "free," a sort of welfare mentality of faith. Indeed, this is precisely what Weber noted when he expressed his amazement upon learning that a group of German immigrant lumberjacks in America were contributing $80 a year to their church out of an annual salary of $1,000.[7] "Everyone knows," Weber wrote, "that even a small fraction of this financial burden in Germany would lead to a mass exodus from the church" (1946, 302). To the extent that Weber was correct, competition with state-supported faiths is made more difficult. For competitors will have to be financed by voluntary contributions. Off-setting this may be a tendency for people to value religion in terms of what it costs. Cheap state churches would not fare well in this comparison. But, money aside, established churches will dominate the public forum. To get the religious implications of various issues, for example, the press will turn to the state church. Moreover, the existence of an established church or churches, helps to define the legitimate sphere of religious options very narrowly. That is, where it is somewhat exotic to be a Protestant, or even a different major brand of Protestantism, it will be extremely deviant to belong to a Christian sect, let alone to a cult movement. Put another way, the more faiths that are seen as legitimate, the more easily a new faith can escape being seriously stigmatized.

Indeed, quite aside from the matter of established churches, is the matter of religious homogeneity. In and of itself homogeneity depresses religious variety. Not only in the obvious statistical way, that if nearly everyone belongs to the same faith there will be few left over to sustain other faiths. Rather, to the degree that people pursue one faith it will be increasingly costly and deviant to pursue *any* other faith—at the extreme, people will not believe that there are any other faiths. This tendency for homogeneity to limit variety will be especially marked when people live in relatively stable, small communities with high individual visibility. As Claude Fischer (1975) has argued, the larger and denser a population, the greater the tendency for deviant subcultures to form and the easier they are to maintain, simply because individuals are protected (and more weakly tied to the normative culture) by their anonymity.

Great novelty can appear in a religious economy because of crises that overtax the conventional religions. Collisions between groups having quite different levels of technology typically prompt great religious innovation in the less advanced groups—these are the well-documented culture-shock religions (cf. Wallace 1956). Plague, war, famine, flood, economic collapse, all may reveal serious weaknesses in the conventional faiths and encourage innovation (cf. Cohn 1961; Wilson 1975a; Stark and Bainbridge 1985).

Many pressures bear upon religious economies. But, in the final analysis, I argue that only by examining the operation of *whole religious economies,* not simply the behavior of a few "firms" in these economies, can religious change be understood. The rate at which new firms enter an economy and their relative success is determined by the extent the established firms are permitting market opportunities to exist. When the conventional faiths are young, vigorous, and not yet greatly secularized, competition is difficult. When these firms have lost vigor and no longer provide a product satisfactory to many, new faiths will move into the gap. Those that offer the superior product will grow. And this, of course, shown of historical detail and theological rhetoric, is the fundamental story of the rise of Christianity, of Buddhism, of Islam, and of all today's great world faiths. They came at the right time, when the conventional faiths no longer satisfied demand, and they offered the better product. More recently, this also is the story of Mormonism—although we are still in the first chapters. Are the Mormons on the way to being a great world faith? Or does the more dramatic future success lie with one of the obscure groups included in our cult rates?

As with the theories of physics, so with those of sociology. It takes a great deal of engineering and empirical trial and error to bridge the gap between general theories and specific empirical applications. Our theory cannot pick winners out of a pool of new religious movements. It cannot even say when a really effective new movement will begin. But it can tell us when and where to look for such a movement and why that movement will gain momentum. And, once again, when we look closely where the theory tells us to look we see a great deal of innovative religious activity taking place.

Notes

1. Here I observed that first law of theorists which is taken from the first law of wing-walking: "Never let go of what you have hold of, until you get hold of something else." In this case I had hold of a theory that parsimoniously integrated many disparate elements of the sociology of religion—that combined secularization theory with church-sect theory—and which seemed to work very well not just in the Western Hemisphere, but historically in accounting for the shifts in dominant religions.
2. I am indebted to my colleague Eileen Barker for obtaining this out-of-print and extremely hard to find volume.
3. Groups in this tradition use this archaic spelling of magick in order to differentiate themselves from stage magic—for they purport to perform the real thing.
4. I must stress that these are *not* simply ethnic, immigrant churches and hence, simply a function of the relative size of immigrant populations. While the leader often is from the East, for the groups we have counted the followers are not. For example, I am not counting ashrams frequented by Hindu immigrants, but ashrams frequented by persons of European stock. Undoubtedly, large

immigrant populations have some indirect effect on the prevalence of these faiths—perhaps simply by making this culture less alien. But surely the great prevalence of Tibetan Buddhist groups in North America and Europe has nothing to do with any substantial immigrant Tibetan population.

5. In the United States, Jehovah's Witnesses are perceived as a cult (Bainbridge and Stark 1980).

6. I removed the Seventh-Day Adventists because their rates already have been examined individually. Jehovah's Witnesses data are not collected by World Vision, nor are those for Christian Science and Mormonism collected. I also dropped one group because their data obviously were not believable. (They reported exactly 100 churches in each of three nations, exactly 50 in four others, 30 in two, 10 in two, and 5 in two—never a deviation from perfect units of five. The world is not that neat.)

7. Note that these lumberjacks were not tithing, however.

References

Annett, Stephen. 1976. *The Many Ways of Being*. London: Sphere Books.

Bainbridge, William Sims. 1978c. *Satan's Power: Ethnography of a Deviant Psychotherapy Cult*. Berkeley: University of California Press.

Bainbridge, Williams Sims and Rodney Stark. 1980. Client and audience cults in America. *Sociological Analysis* 41:199–214.

Bainbridge, Williams Sims and Rodney Stark. 1983. Church and cult in Canada. *Canadian Journal of Sociology*.

Barker, Eileen. 1979. Whose service is perfect freedom. In *Spiritual Well-Being,* edited by David O. Moberg. Washington: University Press of America.

———1981a. Who'd be a Moonie? In *The Social Impact of New Religious Movements,* edited by Bryan Wilson. New York: The Unification Theological Seminary.

———1981b. The one's who got away. Paper presented at the Conference on Alternative Religions, Chicago.

Billington, James H. 1980. *Fire in the Minds of Men*. New York: Basic Books.

Campiche, Roland J. 1972. Switzerland. In *Western Religion,* edited by Hans Mol. The Hague: Mouton.

Church of Scientology. 1978. *What is Scientology?* Los Angeles: Church of Scientology.

Cohn, Norman. 1961. *The Pursuit of the Millennium.* New York: Harper.

Darnton, Robert. 1970. *Mesmerism and the End of the Enlightenment in France.* New York: Schocken.

Fenn, Richard K. 1978. *Toward a Theory of Secularization.* Ellington, Conn. Society for the Scientific Study of Religion.

Festinger, Leon, H.W. Riecken, and S. Schachter. 1956. *When Prophecy Fails.* New York: Harper.

Fischer, Claude S. 1975. Toward a subcultural theory of urbanism. *American Journal of Sociology* 80:1319–41.

Freud, Sigmund. [1927] 1961. *The Future of an Illusion.* Reprint. Garden City, N.Y.: Doubleday.

Glock, Charles Y. 1964. The role of deprivation in the origin and evolution of religious groups. In *Religion and Social Conflict,* edited by Robert Lee and Martin E. Marty. New York: Oxford University Press.

Khalsa, Parmatma Singh. 1981. *A Pilgrim's Guide to Planet Earth.* San Rafael, Calif.: Spiritual Community Publications.

Lofland, John and Rodney Stark. 1965. Becoming a world-saver: A theory of conversion to a deviant perspective. *American Sociological Review* 30:862–75.

Lofland, John. 1966. *Doomsday Cult.* Englewood Cliffs, N.J.: Prentice-Hall.

Martin, David. 1978. *A General Theory of Secularization.* New York: Harper & Row.

McIntosh, Christopher. 1972. *Eliphas Lévi and the French Occult Revival.* New York: Weiser.

Melton, J. Gordon. 1980. The neo-pagans of America: An alternative religion. Paper presented at the American Academy of Religion in Dallas, Texas.

————1978. *Encyclopedia of American Religions.* 2 vols. Wilmington, N.C.: McGrath (A Consortium Book).

Mol, Hans, editor. 1972. *Western Religion.* The Hague: Mouton.

Niebuhr, H. Richard. 1929. *The Social Sources of Denominationalism.* New York: Henry Holt.

Shinn, Larry D. 1983. The many faces of Krishna. In *Alternatives to American Mainline Churches,* edited by Joseph H. Fichter. Barrytown, N.Y.: Unification Theological Seminary.

Sigelman, Lee. 1977. Multi-nation surveys of religious beliefs. *Journal for the Scientific Study of Religion* 16:289–94.

Strachan, Francoise. 1970. *The Aquarian Guide to Occult, Mystical, Religious, Magical London, and Around.* London: The Aquarian Press.

Stark, Rodney. 1964. Class, radicalism and religious involvement in Great Britain. *American Sociological Review* 29:698–706.

———Forthcoming The rise and decline of Christian Science.

Stark, Rodney and William Sims Bainbridge. 1980. Secularization, revival, and cult formation. *The Annual Review of the Social Sciences of Religion* 4:85–119.

———1981. Secularization and cult formation in the jazz age. *Journal for the Scientific Study of Religion* 20:360–73.

———1985. *The Future of Religion.* Berkeley: University of California Press.

Stark, Rodney, William Sims Bainbridge, and Daniel P. Doyle. 1979. Cults of America: A reconnaissance in space and time. *Sociological Analysis* 40:347–59.

Stark, Rodney, William Sims Bainbridge, and Lori Kent. 1981. Cult membership in the roaring twenties. *Sociological Analysis* 42:137–62.

Wallis, Roy. 1975. *Sectarianism.* New York: John Wiley & Sons.

———1976. *The Road to Total Freedom.* New York: Columbia University Press.

Weber, Max. 1946. *From Max Weber: Essays in Sociology.* New York: Oxford University Press.

Wilson, Bryan. 1961. *Sects and Society.* Berkeley: University of California Press.

———1970. *Religious Sects.* New York: McGraw-Hill.

———1975a. *Magic and the Millennium.* Frogmore: Paladin.

———1975b. The secularization debate. *Encounter* 45:77–83.

———1979. The return of the sacred. *Journal for the Scientific Study of Religion* 18:268–80.

———1981. *The Social Impact of New Religious Movements.* Barrytown, N.Y.: Unification Theological Seminary.

———1982. *Religion in Sociological Perspective.* New York: Oxford University Press.

World Vision. 1979. *Mission Handbook*. Monrovia, Calif.: World Vision.

Wuthnow, Robert. 1977. A longitudinal cross-national indicator of societal religious commitment. *Journal for the Scientific Study of Religion* 16:87–99.

Contributors

William Sims Bainbridge Associate Professor, Department of Sociology, Harvard University, Cambridge, Massachusetts

Robert W. Balch Professor, Department of Sociology, University of Montana, Missoula, Montana

Eileen Barker Dean of Undergraduate Studies, London School of Economics and Political Science, University of London, United Kingdom

Henry MacLeod Member, Department of Research and Evaluation, Catholic Children's Aid Society of Metropolitan Toronto, Ontario, Canada

J. Gordon Melton Founder, Institute for the Study of American Religion, Evanston, Illinois

Arvind Sharma Lecturer, Department of Religious Studies, University of Sydney, Australia

Larry D. Shinn Dean, College of Arts and Sciences, Bucknell University, Lewisburg, Pennsylvania

John H. Simpson Director of the Graduate Centre for Religious Studies, University of Toronto, Ontario, Canada

Rodney Stark Professor of Sociology, University of Washington, Seattle, Washington

David F. Taylor Lecturer, Sociology, Oregon Institute of Technology, Klamath Falls, Oregon

Roy Wallis Professor of Sociology, The Queen's University, Belfast, Northern Ireland

R. Stephen Warner Associate Professor, Department of Sociology, University of Illinois at Chicago, Illinois

345

INDEX